Praise for *Ministers at War*

'It is certainly true that the prime minister dominated his nation's affairs more than Roosevelt did those of the United States. But Jonathan Schneer's book, *Ministers at War*, provides a corrective, emphasizing the important parts played by the War Cabinet... to whom Churchill had the good sense to delegate many matters in which he was uninterested, and which he knew himself unqualified to arbitrate.' **New York Review of Books**

'Insightful... Schneer has done a wonderful job.' **Good Book Guide**

'A smoothly written and insightful examination of the men who aided Churchill during the years fraught with danger from the Nazi war machine. For most readers, this will be a book that cannot be put down until the last page is reached. An exceptional history on an extremely important topic.' **Library Journal, starred review**

'A striking look inside the British government during a time when some of the most interesting characters of a challenging era were fighting for both the nation's salvation and their own ambitions. Churchill's role as a wartime leader is well-known from a myriad of histories, but this is one of the best recent treatments of his role as a head of government. Clear, thoroughly entertaining and full of lively detail.'
Kirkus Reviews, starred review

'Very timely... gripping and a pleasure to read.' **Press Association**

'A lively and readable book... Schneer's telling makes the tale fresh, owing to his compelling portraits of Churchill's cabinet members and his emphasis on the importance of postwar planning.' **Foreign Affairs**

'Jonathan Schneer's *Ministers at War* provides a fascinating and lively account of the "team of rivals" that led Britain to victory during the Second World War. His insightful research and vivid writing bring to life an intriguing array of personalities whose role in Winston Churchill's coalition government was crucial to th~ ~~~'
War skillfully draws back the curtain
most eventful years in Britain's history
Lee Pollock, Executive

A Oneworld book

First published in Great Britain and the Commonwealth by
Oneworld Publications, 2015

This paperback edition published 2016

ISBN 978-1-78074-832-0
eISBN 978-1-78074-614-2

Printed and bound in Great Britain by Clays Ltd, St Ives plc

Oneworld Publications
10 Bloomsbury Street
London WC1B 3SR

Stay up to date with the latest books,
special offers, and exclusive content from
Oneworld with our monthly newsletter

Sign up on our website
www.oneworld-publications.com

MINISTERS AT WAR

Winston Churchill
and his War Cabinet

Jonathan Schneer

ONEWORLD

A Oneworld book

First published in Great Britain and the Commonwealth by
Oneworld Publications, 2015

This paperback edition published 2016

Copyright © 2015 by Jonathan Schneer

ISBN 978-1-78074-832-0
eISBN 978-1-78074-614-2

Printed and bound in Great Britain by Clays Ltd, St Ives plc

Oneworld Publications
10 Bloomsbury Street
London WC1B 3SR

To Margaret, Ben and Seth

CONTENTS

GLOSSARY OF NAMES

These brief notes are provided as an aid to the identification of the people discussed in this book.

AITKEN, WILLIAM MAXWELL, FIRST BARON BEAVERBROOK (1879–1964): A Canadian who moved to Britain before World War I, Beaverbrook made a fortune and became proprietor of the *Daily Express*, the *Sunday Express* and the *London Evening Standard* as well as two newspapers in Scotland. He was also an enthusiastic supporter of imperial economic cooperation and strongly supported Neville Chamberlain's policy of appeasement. Nevertheless, Churchill put him in charge first of the Ministry of Aircraft Production and then the Ministry of Supply. Beaverbrook suffered from ill health, and eventually Churchill let him resign. But then Beaverbrook took up a new crusade, "All Help to Russia," and supported the idea of opening a Second Front in the war.

ALEXANDER, ALBERT VICTOR (1885–1965): Alexander was a Labour politician who began his career as parliamentary secretary to the British co-operative movement. He served in the second Labour government (1929–1931) as First Lord of the Admiralty, and Churchill returned him to that position in 1940.

AMERY, LEOPOLD (LEO) CHARLES MAURICE STENNETT (1873–1955): A Conservative politician who advocated economic protectionism and cooperation within the British Empire, Amery served as colonial secretary under Prime Minister Stanley Baldwin from 1924 to 1929, but remained on the backbenches throughout the 1930s, partly because he did not enthusiastically support Chamberlain's policy of appeasement. On May 7, 1940, he delivered a great speech against Chamberlain that helped lead to the latter's downfall. A few days later, Churchill appointed him secretary of state for India.

ANDERSON, SIR JOHN, FIRST VISCOUNT WAVERLEY (1882–1958): Anderson, a remarkably effective and efficient civil servant who entered Parliament in 1938 independent of any party, was appointed home secretary and minister of home security by Chamberlain at the outbreak of war. When Churchill took over in May 1940, Churchill asked Anderson to remain in these posts, but he later made him Lord President, with a seat in the War Cabinet, to replace the dying Chamberlain.

ATTLEE, CLEMENT RICHARD, FIRST EARL ATTLEE (1883–1967): A Labour Party politician first elected to Parliament in 1922, Attlee served briefly in the Labour government of 1929–1931 and ascended to the party leadership in 1935. Churchill brought him into his first War Cabinet in May 1940 as Lord Privy Seal and then promoted him in 1942 to become secretary of state for the dominions and deputy prime minister. Many underestimated Attlee, mistaking his diffidence for weakness.

BEAVERBROOK: *See Aitken, William Maxwell, First Baron Beaverbrook (1879–1964).*

BEVERIDGE, WILLIAM HENRY, BARON BEVERIDGE (1879–1963): A prickly, ambitious and able academic and civil servant, Beveridge was appointed during the war to head a committee studying the coordination of social services. He turned this small task into a broad investigation of their deficiencies, and in the Beveridge Report made sweeping recommendations for their improvement in postwar Britain. His report caused a sensation.

BEVIN, ERNEST (1881–1951): Bevin, a former carter on the Bristol docks, built the Transport and General Workers' Union into the largest workers' organization in Europe during the interwar period. Churchill knew he needed Bevin's support to make his national coalition government work and so appointed him minister of labor and then promoted him to the

War Cabinet. Churchill judged Bevin and Beaverbrook to be his most dynamic and able colleagues, among an outstanding group.

BRACKEN, BRENDAN RENDALL, VISCOUNT BRACKEN (1901–1958): Bracken was a Conservative politician with a background in journalism and was devoted to Churchill. When the latter became First Lord of the Admiralty in 1939, he made Bracken his parliamentary private secretary. In 1941 Churchill appointed Bracken to be minister of information.

BROOKE, ALAN FRANCIS, FIRST VISCOUNT ALANBROOKE (1883–1963): A highly respected career soldier with much experience both of war and preparing for war, Brooke was appointed by Churchill as commander in chief of home forces during the summer of 1940, and then, in December 1941, as commander of the Imperial General Staff. Soon thereafter Brooke became chairman of the Chiefs of Staff Committee and thus the principal strategic adviser to the War Cabinet. When necessary he stood up to the prime minister.

BUTLER, RICHARD AUSTEN (RAB), BARON BUTLER OF SAFFRON WALDEN (1902–1982): Butler was a Conservative politician who was closely associated with the appeasement policies of Neville Chamberlain. In May and June 1940, he supported Halifax, who desired a negotiated peace with Germany. Churchill nevertheless appreciated his parliamentary skills, and far from sacking him, eventually made him minister of education. At this post Butler carried through important reforms.

CADOGAN, SIR ALEXANDER GEORGE MONTAGU (1884–1968): Climbing to the top position in the Foreign Office, permanent undersecretary, Cadogan advised first Halifax and then his successor as foreign minister, Anthony Eden. He sat in on War Cabinet meetings. And he kept a diary.

CECIL, JAMES EDWARD HUBERT GASCOYNE-, FOURTH MARQUESS OF SALISBURY (1861–1947): Belonging to the famous Salisbury political dynasty (his father had been Conservative prime minister), Cecil himself became a Conservative Party grandee and one of Britain's most influential peers. He opposed Chamberlain's appeasement policy. During the war, he led a "watching committee" that played a major role in forcing Chamberlain's resignation.

CHAMBERLAIN, NEVILLE (1869–1940): Chamberlain was the Conservative prime minister and architect of the appeasement policies that failed to prevent World War II. He was replaced by Churchill as prime minister on May 10, 1940.

CRIPPS, SIR (RICHARD) STAFFORD (1889–1952): Cripps, a wealthy and successful lawyer who served in the Labour government of 1929–1931, veered far to the political left during the 1930s, alienating the leadership of his party, who expelled him. Churchill appointed him ambassador to Russia in 1940 and brought him into the government in 1942.

DALTON, (EDWARD) HUGH NEALE, BARON DALTON (1887–1962): A strong opponent of appeasement and of Chamberlain, Dalton took part in the most important discussions among the Labour Party leadership about what to do in May 1940. Churchill did not appoint him to the War Cabinet, but rather to the larger cabinet as minister of economic warfare.

DAVIES, CLEMENT EDWARD (1884–1962): Davies was a member of Parliament (MP) first of the Liberal Party, then of the National Liberals, but in 1940 he served in the House of Commons as an Independent. He became head of "The Vigilantes," an anti-Chamberlain parliamentary group that played an important role in bringing down the prime minister. But Churchill did not appoint him to a government post.

EDEN, (ROBERT) ANTHONY, FIRST EARL OF AVON (1897–1977): A Conservative MP, Eden resigned as Chamberlain's foreign secretary in February 1938 over policy disagreements regarding Italy. Tory rebels who opposed appeasement looked to him for leadership, but he did not provide it. With the outbreak of war, Chamberlain brought him back into the government as dominions secretary. Churchill moved him to the War Office. At the end of 1940, Churchill sent Halifax to Washington, DC, as ambassador and made Eden foreign secretary again.

GREENWOOD, ARTHUR (1880–1954): In 1940 Greenwood was deputy leader of the Labour Party. Churchill brought him into the original War Cabinet, where Greenwood played a crucial role opposing Halifax's proposal that Britain approach Mussolini to find out what Hitler's terms would be for a negotiated peace. But Greenwood's addiction to alcohol destroyed his usefulness, and Churchill sacked him in February 1942.

HALIFAX: *See Wood, Edward Frederick Lindley, First Earl of Halifax (1881–1959).*

HANKEY, MAURICE PASCAL ALERS, FIRST BARON HANKEY (1877–1963): A career civil servant and adviser to prime ministers from World War I until 1938, Hankey accepted a position in Chamberlain's government at the outbreak of World War II. He was a strong supporter of appeasement and a Chamberlain loyalist, and not surprisingly, Churchill sacked him in March 1942. He vented in his diary.

HOARE, SAMUEL JOHN GURNEY, VISCOUNT TEMPLEWOOD (1880–1959): One of the "Men of Munich," Hoare was a Conservative politician and Cabinet minister who enthusiastically supported Chamberlain's appeasement policy. He paid the price. When Churchill took power, he sent Hoare to Spain as British ambassador.

HORE-BELISHA, (ISAAC) LESLIE, BARON HORE-BELISHA (1893–1957): Hore-Belisha was a National Liberal who served in Chamberlain's government as minister of war and who began to believe, after Munich, that conflict with Germany was inevitable. He quarreled with leading generals, and Chamberlain tried to move him to the presidency of the Board of Trade. Hore-Belisha declined this post. He hoped Churchill would bring him into his Grand Coalition, but it did not happen. He kept a revealing diary.

JOWITT, WILLIAM ALLEN, EARL JOWITT (1885–1957): Jowitt, originally a Liberal, switched to the Labour Party in order to serve in the government of 1929–1931. Churchill brought him into the Grand Coalition as solicitor general in May 1940, and in March 1942 appointed him paymaster general. In that capacity he chaired the Reconstruction Problems Committee, which helped to lay the groundwork for the Beveridge Report.

KEYES, ROGER JOHN BROWNLOW, FIRST BARON KEYES (1872–1945): A former admiral of the fleet and a staunch opponent of appeasement, Keyes wore his old uniform when, on May 8, 1940, as a Conservative MP, he made a House of Commons speech condemning British military tactics in Norway and praising Churchill.

LYTTELTON, OLIVER, FIRST VISCOUNT CHANDOS (1893–1972): Lyttelton was a businessman with extensive knowledge of and interests in the metals industry. He was also a friend of Winston Churchill, who brought him into the government in October 1940 as president of the Board of Trade. In February 1942 Lyttelton would succeed Beaverbrook as minister of production.

MARGESSON, (HENRY) DAVID REGINALD, FIRST VISCOUNT MARGESSON (1890–1965): Margesson was a Conservative MP who served as government chief whip throughout the 1930s. He was much feared by Conservative backbenchers. He supported Chamberlain's policy of appeasement, yet Churchill kept him as chief whip and then made him minister of war, only to let him go in the reshuffle of February 1942.

MARQUIS, FREDERICK JAMES, FIRST EARL OF WOOLTON (1883–1964): A successful businessman with a background in settlement work, Woolton became director and chairman of the Lewis Department Store chain. With the outbreak of World War II, Chamberlain appointed him minister of food, although Woolton belonged to no political party. Churchill kept him in that post until 1943, when he appointed him minister of reconstruction.

MONCKTON, WALTER TURNER, FIRST VISCOUNT MONCKTON OF BRENCHLEY (1891–1965): A friend of Stafford Cripps, and, like Cripps, an extraordinarily successful lawyer, Monckton became the confidant of King Edward VIII and yet maintained good relations with the man who succeeded him, King George VI. He served in a number of government posts during the war, but refused to make a parliamentary career.

MORRISON, HERBERT STANLEY, BARON MORRISON OF LAMBETH (1888–1965): Morrison, a Labour politician who had served in the 1929–1931 Labour government, had ambitions to lead the party and the country, which made him a rival of Clement Attlee and the bête noir of Ernest Bevin. He took part in important Labour Party strategy sessions before and during the Phony War; he also played an important role in bringing down Neville Chamberlain, although he appears to have thought that Halifax, not Churchill, would succeed him. Churchill appointed him first as minister of supply and later as home secretary, with a seat in the War Cabinet.

Simon, John Allsebrook, First Viscount Simon (1873–1954): Beginning as a Liberal and gaining Cabinet rank in Asquith's pre–World War I government, Simon moved to the National Liberals in 1931. He served in various Cabinet posts throughout the following decade, rising to become Chamberlain's chancellor of the exchequer. He strongly backed Chamberlain's appeasement policy and paid the price when Churchill took over. The new prime minister excluded him from his Cabinet and made him Lord Chancellor, with a seat in the House of Lords.

Sinclair, Archibald Henry Macdonald, First Viscount Thurso (1890–1970): Sinclair was a Liberal MP who had become leader of the party in 1935. He favored rearmament, opposed appeasement, and turned down Chamberlain's offer of a government post when World War II began. His old friend Churchill offered him the Air Ministry when he became prime minister, and this post Sinclair accepted.

Wood, Edward Frederick Lindley, First Earl of Halifax (1881–1959): Halifax was a Conservative politician who served Chamberlain as foreign secretary after Anthony Eden was forced out. He was considered a "Man of Munich," but developed hesitations about the appeasement policy after Hitler invaded Czechoslovakia. When Chamberlain stepped down, he hoped that Halifax, rather than Churchill, would replace him. Later, Halifax suggested asking the Italians to find out Hitler's peace terms. Churchill would have none of it and eventually sent him to Washington, DC, as ambassador.

Wood, Sir (Howard) Kingsley (1881–1943): Wood was a Conservative politician who served in various Cabinet-rank posts during the 1930s, most relevantly as minister of air from 1938 to 1940, and then for a short period as Lord Privy Seal. Although he supported appeasement, under his direction British production of aircraft increased dramatically. His role in Chamberlain's downfall is ambiguous. Churchill made him chancellor of the exchequer, at first without a seat in the War Cabinet. Wood gained his place there in October 1940, but then lost it in the reshuffle of February 1942, although he retained his position as chancellor until his unexpected death in 1943.

ALL BEHIND YOU, WINSTON

INTRODUCTION

On May 10, 1940, King George VI of great britain reluctantly accepted the resignation of his prime minister, Neville Chamberlain, and following Chamberlain's advice asked First Lord of the Admiralty Winston Churchill to form a new government. The king would have preferred to ask someone else—even though, like most people, he recognized that the First Lord possessed extraordinary qualities and talents. But he did not trust Churchill to control them. He judged him to be unbridled, a loose cannon.

The disgraced Chamberlain did not trust Churchill either. He would have preferred to steer Britain's highest political post to Lord Halifax, the foreign secretary, whom he considered a much steadier personality. But Halifax would not take it, for complicated reasons, while Churchill wanted it badly. During the previous decade Churchill had occupied the political wilderness, shunned by most Conservatives largely because he would not toe the party line of appeasement. Finally, with the outbreak of war, when Churchill's counsels had proved prescient, Chamberlain grudgingly appointed him First Lord of the Admiralty in charge of the great British Navy. Now came this further elevation. It marked the climax of Churchill's political rehabilitation and capped his lifetime ambition.

Britain stood in deadly peril at this moment—how deadly, no one, not even the prime-minister-to-be, recognized. Germany, which had taken Round One of the war, by defeating Poland in a matter of weeks, and then Round Two, with lightning attacks that established German control over Scandinavia, had just opened Round Three. Adolf Hitler had just unleashed a Blitzkrieg upon Luxembourg, Holland, Belgium and France. Panzer divisions were racing through Western Europe and the Luftwaffe roaring above it, and no countervailing force could stop them or even delay them much. Britain and her French ally were taken by surprise; Germany had pushed them back onto their heels. Indeed, France was nearly on her back. Churchill confronted emergency from his first day in office.

This is a book about Winston Churchill and the small group of extraordinary men he selected to help him guide Britain through this great crisis, and about how he and they continued to cope for the next five years, until Germany had been defeated. It is a book about Churchill the politician, and Churchill the manager of men, for he had to inspire and direct and chivy and soothe and manipulate the shifting cast of remarkable individuals who formed his unbeatable team. In these roles he usually succeeded, but not always.

It is a book, too, about relations between and among War Cabinet ministers. Churchill stood at the helm, but then right behind him stood the elegant Anthony Eden, whom he would designate his political heir; and his longtime friend the piratical Canadian-born press baron, Lord Beaverbrook; and the human bulldozer who was head of Britain's largest trade union, Ernest Bevin; also the unassuming leader of the Labour Party, Clement Attlee; and Attlee's rival, the ambitious Herbert Morrison; and the puritanical, high-minded socialist Stafford Cripps, among others. Taken together, these men constituted as tough and as capable a group as has ever governed Britain.

It is a staple of the memoirs of such figures that for five years they formed a matchless band of brothers, and there is more than a grain of truth to this. Had they failed to cooperate, Britain never could have survived the war. In fact, however, even at the most desperate moments—for example, in June 1940, with France on its knees and the British Expeditionary Force cut off at Dunkirk, facing likely extinction, and Britain itself bracing for invasion—the War Cabinet ministers were continually poking and prodding at one another and questioning each other's judgment. During the wearying years that followed, some of them began to entertain fantasies about claiming the premiership themselves. Two took tentative steps to translate this thought into action. The national emergency did not eclipse personal ambition. For all that they were sometimes a band of brothers, certain of Churchill's men warred against each other and their leader, even while they were running the war against the Axis Powers.

Meanwhile, in the country as a whole, Britons increasingly thought as the war ground on that the government should level the playing field of life by providing social security in the broad sense of the term to all citizens. They did not want to return to prewar conditions. They wanted a new Britain. Why else fight, and risk death to save it? They wanted the government to guarantee health insurance, old-age insurance, family allowances, free education, decent housing and full employment. But Winston Churchill had little sympathy with this outlook. Because he had limited interest in domestic policy, he failed to understand the power of the building wave of leftist sentiment in his country. He sought only half-heartedly to satisfy it, and therefore he failed to do so. As for the War Cabinet, it split over the desirability of such measures and over how generous the government should be if it adopted them.

Thus ideology divided the band of brothers as much as jealousy, personal distrust and conflicting ambitions did. The ensuing arguments presaged and helped provoke the fractious general election of 1945. Moreover, the growing confidence of the Labour men, and the corresponding decline among Conservatives, provided a forecast of the election's results, although few grasped this at the time. This book, then, traces not only personal struggles among Churchill's War Cabinet colleagues, but also an ideological struggle that never ceased—one in which the prime minister played a role and that adumbrated the great Conservative electoral defeat of 1945.

Practically everybody knows that Churchill was a giant to whom we all owe an unpayable debt. This book will not contradict that judgment. Nevertheless, I hope to have twisted the historical kaleidoscope to reveal familiar pieces in unfamiliar patterns. The internal workings of the War Cabinet, with its complex interactions of conflicting personalities and ideologies, and Churchill's attempts to manage them, and the drama to which the conflicts gave rise, have been too often overlooked. They constitute the main focus of this book. I hope readers will discover in it novel aspects of a story they thought they knew well already. And I hope those who are entirely fresh to the subject will learn much about the remarkable "team of rivals" who steered Britain to victory in World War II, and about the even more remarkable figure who led them.

PROLOGUE

On Monday morning, May 6, 1940, the British light cruiser HMS *Aurora* cut across the icy waters of Ofotfjord, just offshore from Narvik, a far-northern Norwegian port. Winston Churchill, Britain's First Lord of the Admiralty, had sent her there nearly a month earlier. Gray and grim she cruised the firth, a menacing portent of the terrible struggle soon to be fought by Great Britain and Germany in the unforgiving waters of the North Atlantic Ocean. On that Monday morning, however, she represented more than a portent to knowledgeable men. All Britain's hopes for any kind of success in the present early phase of World War II focused upon her, for everywhere else in Norway the British campaign had been disastrous.

Aurora served as the flagship of a small fleet of destroyers under the command of Admiral William Boyle, the twelfth Earl of Cork and Orrery. A tough, pugnacious seadog from an ancient Irish aristocratic family, Lord Cork that morning stood upon *Aurora*'s bridge gazing at the shoreline and at the bombed-out skeleton buildings of the little port. He knew well what his primary objective was and how it should be attained. He must launch a frontal amphibious assault upon the ruined settlement whatever the odds; he must kill, capture or disperse the 5,000 German soldiers and sailors who held it. He must do it now before they received reinforcements.

But there were difficulties. The port of Narvik sits on a relatively flat peninsula of land near the end of a long fjord of spectacular beauty. Jagged cliffs and mountains rise up from the water on every side. On May 6, 1940, drifts of snow five feet deep in places covered the high ground; they lay as much as four feet deep on the flat peninsula below. British forecasters had predicted that the spring thaw would come two weeks later than usual this year, even as daylight hours grew ever longer. This meant the British could never surprise the Germans holding the port; the darkness did not last long enough. Moreover, conditions on land would be difficult once they fought their way ashore.

The Germans had descended upon Narvik nearly four weeks previously, part of a much larger invasion force that took Norway completely by surprise, and simultaneously Denmark (which surrendered practically without firing a shot). They swooped down upon Norway from the sea and from the sky. They captured Trondheim, Bergen, Stavanger, Oslo—and Narvik. Almost wherever they went in Norway they succeeded, sometimes after bitter fighting, sometimes after no fighting at all. Desperately, belatedly, the Norwegian government appealed to the Allies for help. And Britain, which itself had been planning to take Narvik for her own purposes, and whose plan the Germans unwittingly had forestalled by a single day, hastily sent troops without proper ammunition or guns, or camouflage, or training, or even skis and snowshoes. They sent their main force to relieve Trondheim, where a debacle ensued: the Tommies floundered, hip deep in snow, perfect targets, black outlined on white, unable even to dodge as Luftwaffe gunners shot them down. In fact, nearly everywhere that Britons met Germans in battle, their enemy defeated them. Shocked, dismayed, furious with the politicians and strategists who had sent them off to war so unprepared and ill-equipped, those British troops who survived fell back all the way to the ships that had brought them there, and that now would bring them home.

Only in the far north, at the Ofotfjord, after a first Battle of Narvik produced inconclusive results, did British forces in a second encounter score unambiguous victory. There the Royal Navy bottled up the German battle group, denying them access to the open sea. Then the battleship *Warspite* and nine destroyers sank or disabled every German ship in the fjord and side fjords. German troops, who had arrived in Narvik by land already, and German sailors who had survived the pounding inflicted by British guns and had found their way to shore, or who had scuttled their ships and rowed ashore in lifeboats, now holed up in the little port, supplied mainly by seaplanes.

Lord Cork believed he could have taken the village in a frontal assault one day after the decisive naval battle finished, but at that time he shared command with Major General Pierse J. Macksey, who preferred a more cautious approach. Macksey proposed a land campaign, which he said could not begin until the snow melted. Reluctantly, Lord Cork stayed his hand. He directed his fleet to shell the Germans instead. Now his targets crouched amid the ruins of the village, cold, hungry, weary, even frightened perhaps—but not hopeless. Their comrades held most of the rest of the country. In time they would come to the rescue. Lord Cork understood, as General Macksey apparently did not, that for Britain time in Norway was running out.

Originally the British had wanted Narvik because from that port they could have stopped shipments of iron ore, an important resource for the enemy war machine that the Germans transported from Sweden down the long Norwegian coast into the Baltic Sea. Had they taken Narvik, Britain would have commanded all northern Europe's coastal trade. She might have been in a position to stop the German invasion of Norway. Britain's First Lord of the Admiralty, Winston Churchill, had pushed hard for the occupation of Narvik, but his colleagues had resisted. Some thought the campaign would be a diversion. Some may simply have lacked the stomach for aggressive action. Eventually they approved Churchill's plan, but too late. Now the British needed to capture Narvik for an un-anticipated reason: to show the world that Germany was not successful everywhere. The government in London waited with increasing impa-tience for the telegram from Lord Cork saying he had redeemed Britain's reputation, and their own, by accomplishing this mission at least.

That morning Lord Cork did indeed send a telegram to the Admiralty and War Office. It arrived at 4:21 A.M. In it he confessed that he was writ-ing "with great reluctance," at the behest of his military colleagues with whom he disagreed. He served now as commander in chief, above General Macksey, but he must take his subordinates' opinions into account. The message said, in part: "There are insufficient assault landing craft. . . . Men in open boats will be subject to air attack for at least 4 hours. . . . Troops will be unable to dig [in] on account of rocks and frost. . . . There will be no adequate defense [for them]." Lord Cork reported that he would like to launch the assault anyway, and that he believed there was a fair chance of success, but that all his "military officers experienced in war" opposed him. They insisted with General Macksey upon the approach from the ground.

When Winston Churchill and his colleagues at the Admiralty Office read this telegram several hours later in London, they must have ground their teeth.

PART I

MAKING A
WAR CABINET

CHAPTER 1

Challenging the Prime Minister

LONDON SEEMED FAR REMOVED FROM EMBATTLED SOLDIERS AND SAILORS that Monday morning, May 6, 1940. The week that would end with Winston Churchill realizing his lifelong ambition to become prime minister of Great Britain dawned cloudless and sparkling, another perfect morning in a series of such mornings. True, Britain had been at war with Germany for nine months, but London's peace was not yet much disturbed. There were blackouts at night, which were a nuisance. Unsightly sandbags protected buildings from bombs, and men had dug trenches in the parks to provide shelter should the bombs fall. But none did. It was a period of "phony war," "the bore war" Londoners called it, and the longer it continued the better. They thought that Germany's economy could not sustain a long conflict, but Britain's could. They believed what Prime Minister Neville Chamberlain had told them a month earlier, on April 4: the fact that the enemy had not attacked them yet, nor France, meant that Germany's moment had passed, time was on the Allies' side, and Hitler "had missed the bus." On the weekend preceding a crisis that would shake the earth, they appear to have felt few misgivings or forebodings. They filled London's restaurants, which had plenty of food; they attended the theaters and cinemas as always. The green grass in the parks was fresh, the chestnut trees were in blossom, the bluebells and primroses were out, and the residents of Britain's greatest metropolis took advantage of it all, enjoying their city and the wonderful spring weather.

It could not continue like this. The man or woman in the street did not know it, or rather, as news about Norway began to penetrate, may have sensed it but ignored growing doubts, and walked in the park and dined out anyway. Others who were better informed understood: the German juggernaut had rolled up Poland in a matter of weeks; it had just taken Denmark by surprise and had conquered that country and most of Norway over a similar period. The disparity between German preparation and Allied procrastination, between German decisiveness and Allied muddle, between German success and Allied failure, was too great. Britain and France, if they continued as they were, stood in grave danger of losing the war. The current British government was not fit to prosecute let alone win it. The fiasco in Norway further demonstrated this.

So on that Monday morning all along the corridors of power in Whitehall men met in little groups, in their clubs, in committee rooms, in each other's flats and homes, to consider their political options. A two-day adjournment debate in the House of Commons before it rose for the annual Whitsuntide recess would begin the next afternoon, Tuesday. The subject for discussion would be Norway, and the prime minister would explain what had happened there. This would provide his critics not merely with an opportunity to condemn the government (which some of them had done many times already), but finally with a chance to remove him from office once and for all—if the opposition Labour Party dared end the debate with a vote of censure.

But the Conservative prime minister had an unassailable majority in the House, more than twice as many votes as Labour. His party whips enforced iron discipline. Few backbenchers in the parliamentary party dared cross them: it would mean an end to all hopes of promotion. From where, then, would come the votes to bring down the government? Equally important: If Labour demanded the vote, and against all odds assembled a majority with Liberal members of Parliament (MPs) and members of splinter groups and dissident Tories, and so finally did dislodge the prime minister, who would be the best man to replace him?

AT 11:30 THAT MORNING CHURCHILL READ ALOUD LORD CORK'S telegram to Chamberlain's eight-man War Cabinet, a subset of the much larger Cabinet that governed the country. It contained six Conservatives, one National Liberal (an offshoot of the Liberal Party dating from 1931), and one non-party man. All its members except Churchill had supported appeasement of Germany more or less warmly before the war, although the foreign secretary, Lord Halifax, developed reservations after Hitler invaded Czechoslovakia in 1938. Now Halifax suggested that opening negotiations with Germany might buy Britain time to prepare Lord Cork's invasion of Narvik. To Churchill it sounded reminiscent of the earlier approach. He exploded, and the foreign secretary backed down. Chastened, he passed Churchill a note: "You are really very unjust to my irresponsible ideas. They may be silly, are certainly dangerous, but are not high treason." The First Lord wrote in reply: "It was a very deadly thought in the present atmosphere of frustration. You could not foresee this. Forgive me."

At 5:00 in the afternoon the First Lord chaired a meeting attended by the two other service chiefs, Oliver Stanley, secretary of state for war, and Kingsley Wood, secretary of state for air. To this "Military Coordination Committee" he argued that "the texture of the French Army required strengthening" by British imperial units. He reminded his colleagues of previously agreed strategies should Germany invade Holland, or should a great land battle develop elsewhere on the continent. He drew attention to many significant deficiencies in British war production. The record shows that on Monday, May 6, he displayed comprehension of Britain's tenuous position, and also fortitude.

That was what might have been expected from Winston Churchill, for he knew a lot about war, not only from study—although he had studied it much—but also from personal experience and predilection. His father, the brilliant, erratic, ultimately tragic Conservative politician Randolph Churchill, had recognized early his son's penchant for all things military (toy soldiers, to begin with). Eventually he sent him to the Royal Military College at Sandhurst, where young Winston joined the Fourth Queen's Own Hussars. After graduating, Churchill saw combat at the siege of Malakand on the Northwest Frontier in India in 1897. The experience moved him to write that "nothing in life is so exhilarating as to be shot at without result." He took part as a horseman in the last great British cavalry charge at the Battle of Omdurman in Sudan in 1898. He fought against the Boers in South Africa in 1899—first while serving as a correspondent for the English newspaper the *Morning Post*, when Boers attacked the train on which he was traveling, and later as a commissioned officer in General Redvers Buller's army. Captured by the Boers after the attack upon the train, he had escaped and made a difficult journey of three hundred miles to rejoin the British. This exploit made him famous.

When Winston Churchill went to war he always sought the most dangerous place and always demonstrated bravery, dash, determination, originality and intelligence. Moreover, he wrote about it brilliantly and beautifully.

In 1900 Churchill resigned from the army and stood successfully for Parliament as a Conservative. Four years later he rebelled against the party's anti-free-trade policies and joined the Liberals. In 1908 Prime Minister H. H. Asquith invited him to join the Cabinet as president of the Board of Trade, and in 1911 promoted him to First Lord of the Admiralty. Churchill became expert on the navy as well as the army. When World War I began, he advocated the ill-fated landing at Gallipoli as a way to avoid the charnel house in the West, knock the Ottomans out of the war, and take the Central Powers from the rear. Knowledgeable people understood the complexities of the situation, but Churchill shouldered all the blame and resigned when the campaign failed. He volunteered for service on the Western Front. There again he sought the front lines, as a major with the 2nd Battalion, Grenadier Guards, and as a lieutenant colonel commanding the 6th Battalion, Royal Scots Fusiliers. Unlike so many others, he survived this killing field, too, and returned to politics and to Cabinet rank. By 1924 he had borne ministerial responsibility for the War Office and the Royal Air Force (RAF) as well as the Admiralty. Then, as the postwar Liberal Party tore itself apart, he reverted to the Conservatives and rose further, becoming chancellor of the exchequer under Stanley Baldwin.

Everyone knew that Churchill possessed extraordinary qualities and capacities—but he also had a restless bellicosity and taste for combat. In 1919, when he was at the War Office and Iraqis were rebelling against British rule, he produced a minute that said, in part: "I am strongly in favor of using poisoned gas against uncivilized tribes." At about the same time he helped create the infamous "Black and Tans," a group of former soldiers whom he sent to Ireland to suppress the nationalist movement. Churchill would not condemn or disown their brutal and bloody methods. During the British General Strike of 1926, his enthusiasm for a showdown with the unions led the prime minister to sidetrack him by putting him in charge of the government newspaper, the *British Gazette*. On top of all this Churchill still differed fiercely with Conservative policy over free trade and over policies regarding India (he opposed any move toward self-government), and later over appeasing Hitler. Not surprisingly, the party leaders began to distance themselves; after 1929 they kept him from the front bench altogether.

Of course, the very qualities they distrusted were the ones most needed when Britain went to war again. Then, albeit with misgivings, Baldwin's successor as prime minister, Neville Chamberlain, returned Churchill to the Admiralty. "Winston is back," the permanent officials at Admiralty House said, rubbing their hands. "Now the fur will fly." And it did. He wanted to bring the war to the Germans, not to lie back waiting. He meddled in other departments, arguing, dispensing advice, determined to have his way. He thought he knew better than his colleagues how to fight and win wars. To their consternation he never hesitated to say so. The campaign he advocated in Norway is an example.

Yet Churchill, too, had dithered when Germany launched its invasion the day before Britain had scheduled hers. He allowed his military advisers to persuade him first that Trondheim should replace Narvik as Britain's initial objective, and then that he should call off the well-planned frontal naval assault on that town in favor of a pincer movement. Allied troops would converge on Trondheim from Namsos to the north and Andalsnes to the south unsupported by the navy. But the pincers never came together, the Germans destroyed them both, and now some people were whispering that Churchill remembered Gallipoli and foolishly had sought to make up for it by invading Norway. He should have left it alone. Others whispered the opposite: that Churchill should have overruled his military counselors. He should have insisted upon the seaborne frontal assault to accompany the pincers, but had remembered the disaster at Gallipoli and did not dare.

The men beginning to plan Chamberlain's fall probably did not think Churchill had lost his nerve; they thought him expert and brilliant but unbridled. Many of them preferred Halifax, whom they considered a steadier personality.

HAD WINSTON CHURCHILL NOT BELONGED TO THE GOVERNMENT, THEN surely on May 6 he would have been leading one of the cabals aiming to bring it down. Before the war he had been its most formidable critic. But in the wake of the calamity in Norway the First Lord uttered no word of reproach. He could not, since he shared responsibility for it; indeed, he had been its primary advocate. Moreover, he felt loyalty to the government to which finally he belonged, although most of his present colleagues in the Cabinet had derided and shunned him before the war. Churchill's loyalty extended even to the prime minister, who privately said that Winston talked too much, that he was bumptious and impetuous and took unseemly enjoyment in the war, and that his inflated reputation needed bursting, but that he himself could not do it. Yet Chamberlain felt no compunction about asking Churchill to wind up for the government at the end of the coming two-day debate—and the First Lord, who was the Conservative Party's most accomplished speaker, agreed to do it. On that Monday, both men knew that the debate would be sharp, but neither suspected it would end with Labour calling for a vote of censure.

The two main Opposition parties, Labour and Liberal, wanted more than sharp debate on May 6. They wanted to depose Neville Chamberlain if they could. Their leaders had refused at the beginning of the war, and then several times subsequently, to broaden his administration when he unenthusiastically invited them to join. They hated him. They could not forget how Chamberlain had treated them before he needed them: "like dirt," one Labour man would recall. More importantly, they did not trust him to run the war effectively or aggressively. They would remain outside the government to act as constructive critics. "The time will come," prophesied Clement Attlee, the head of the Labour Party, "when the nation will demand a change, and when that time comes we are ready." On Sunday, May 5, Herbert Morrison, another Labour Party leader, went further: "I am going to reserve the right to get rid of Chamberlain as soon as I jolly well can." The next day, as news trickled in about the debacle in Norway and as the parliamentary debate loomed, the realization began to dawn among Labour Party leaders that this was the week it might be done. For the first time, they seriously began to consider demanding the vote of no confidence.

The majority of backbench Conservative MPs staunchly supported Neville Chamberlain and his government, but a minority of rebels within the party—"troublesome young men," they have been called—likewise began seriously to ponder a vote of censure that weekend. Some of them belonged to a "watching committee" led by the seventy-nine-year-old fourth Marquess of Salisbury, James Cecil. This group contained "men of influence and experience," as Salisbury termed them (not all of them young, either, by any means), from both Houses. More, belonging to the "Eden Group," were young and wealthy Conservative allies of the also young and elegantly handsome foreign secretary, Anthony Eden, who had resigned from the government in 1938 to protest Chamberlain's appeasement of Mussolini when Italy invaded Ethiopia. Chamberlain referred sneeringly to them as "glamor boys." Now that Eden was in the government again, as dominions secretary, a former Conservative colonial secretary, Leo Amery, led his group. Finally, Clement Davies, an independent MP who previously had belonged to the Liberal Party and then to the National Liberal Party, led a third parliamentary combination, called the "Vigilantes." They were members of Parliament from the three main parties, although Conservatives dominated numerically. Cross membership among the three dissident groups was common, at least for Conservatives. And, significantly, Davies had close relations with the leader of the Labour Party, Attlee, and the deputy leader, Arthur Greenwood, dining regularly at the Reform Club with both of them.

ON MAY 6, THE FIRST DAY OF THAT FATEFUL WEEK, UNDER THE headline "A New Ministry?" the *Daily Mail* printed on its front page a letter written by "a leading member of the House of Commons whose name is known throughout the world but who wishes, for the moment, to be anonymous." The author of the mysterious letter was Stafford Cripps, a leading figure on the British left and an independent MP since the Labour Party had expelled him in January 1939 for advocating cooperation with Communists and Liberals in a united front against fascism. Cripps did not belong to any of the rebel parliamentary groups. Although he was a formidable if unorthodox and momentarily relatively isolated figure, at this critical moment his choice for replacing Chamberlain was not Winston Churchill, but Lord Halifax. He called, in addition, for the "New Ministry" to be streamlined, as David Lloyd George's War Cabinet had been during World War I: four ministers only (Churchill being one of them), with no departmental duties, so they could focus all their energies on the war, would help the new prime minister to lead it.

The heads of British Liberalism agreed with him. Before publishing his "Open Letter," Cripps had approached Lloyd George himself, who was now seventy-seven years old but still the MP for Carnarvon Boroughs. Lloyd George had replaced Asquith in the middle of World War I as Britain's Liberal prime minister, and then against heavy odds had steered his country to victory with the aid of that small War Cabinet. In 1918 many called him "the man who won the war," but most Conservatives hated and feared him. During the 1930s they excluded him from the Conservative-led National Governments; he had been "a giant without a job." Now he agreed with Cripps that Chamberlain must step down and that "Winston could not be P.M., and that it would [have] to be Halifax." On May 3, the morning after he consulted with Lloyd George, Cripps breakfasted with Archie Sinclair, leader of the Liberal Party (sadly diminished since Lloyd George's heyday). Sinclair, a close friend of Churchill's for many years (they had served together in France during World War I), "was impressed and favorable and very complimentary at the ingenuity of the list" of four ministers.

Cripps did not approach the Labour Party leaders, who had had nothing to do with him since his expulsion, but they, too, believed not merely that Chamberlain must go, but that Halifax, rather than Churchill, should replace him. On Monday afternoon, May 6, the day after promising to "get rid of Chamberlain as soon as I jolly well can," Herbert Morrison met with Halifax himself. There is no record of their discussion, but Morrison's biographers wrote that he left the meeting believing Chamberlain would soon fall, that Halifax would replace him, and that he would offer Morrison high office in a new administration. Perhaps Morrison reported to Attlee, for the next day Labour's leader warned Churchill's parliamentary private secretary (PPS) that if a new government did indeed take power, "his people . . . would expect it to be under Halifax." And the day after that, a close aide to Halifax reported to him that another prominent Labour man, Hugh Dalton, had told him that "his party would come into the govt under you but not under the PM," and that "this was the view which he & his friends hoped I would pass on to you."

So men from all parties plotted the government's downfall. Chamberlain did not need to read Cripps's article to know this. On Saturday, May 4, he wrote to his sister: "I don't think my enemies will get me down this time." By Monday, however, one of his private secretaries was observing that "the P.M. is very depressed," and at the War Cabinet that morning the permanent undersecretary at the Foreign Office, Alexander Cadogan, judged the atmosphere over which Chamberlain presided to be "very bad and gloomy." "He is worried about things," reported another knowledgeable observer, "but both he and his friends think that they will weather the storm." This was the meeting at which Churchill and Halifax passed each other notes. Note passing appears to have been common practice. While everyone else at the Cabinet meeting was discussing the

Norwegian situation, Conservative Party chief whip David Margesson passed one to the prime minister. He was thinking about how the government might spin tomorrow's debate. Labour would not demand a vote of confidence, he predicted, since probably they would lose it. Therefore, "we can represent it here and abroad that [they] and our own malcontents . . . did not wish to challenge us or offer themselves as alternatives"—in other words, they were scared to. They were cowards.

Margesson nearly got it right. Perhaps at the very moment when he passed the note to Chamberlain, Labour Party leaders Attlee and Greenwood were discussing the vote of confidence with Clem Davies of the Vigilantes. Attlee had developed cold feet. Making the announcement before the debate took place, he argued, would give Conservative whips more time to prepare; it might force wavering Conservatives back into line, and if the government survived the vote, it would only be strengthened. It might even call a snap general election, which it would win in a landslide. The Labour Party, Attlee now informed Davies, must reserve judgment on this crucial matter.

TUESDAY, MAY 7, WAS ANOTHER FINE SPRING DAY. CHURCHILL ATTENDED a War Cabinet meeting at 11:30. He reported that Lord Cork had sent yet another telegram, this one proposing an assault upon Narvik after all, to begin in forty-eight hours: "I do not believe success is certain, but there is a good chance . . ." The Cabinet ordered Lord Cork not to wait, but rather to proceed at once. Unknown to all except a select few, since the government could not talk about ongoing military operations, hard fighting would follow in snowbound Norway. Britain would occupy the port—and then evacuate precipitously when the focus of the war shifted to Holland, Belgium and France.

Meanwhile, the crowds that had begun to gather that morning in front of the Houses of Parliament were a sign that the popular mood indeed was turning. They knew Norway would be discussed; perhaps they sensed the prime minister's peril. A privileged few filed inside. But the dissident Tories, aware already that Attlee had waffled, were in despair. A member of the "watching committee" wrote to his son: "I am much afraid that the weakness of the Opposition . . . will leave Chamberlain at the head of affairs." Another rebel, one of the most active and determined, who belonged to both the Eden Group and the Vigilantes, predicted to two friends with whom he was taking refreshment in the House of Commons tearoom that the government would survive the debate. Perhaps it should, he added bitterly: "Let those who have sown the wind reap the whirlwind."

Margesson had directed all members of the Parliamentary Conservative Party who could possibly attend to do so. About twenty Conservative members arrived in uniform. They had left their regiments for the debate. Some of them had only just returned from Norway. The "glamor boys" and Vigilantes fell upon them individually and in groups, urging them to disown their leaders in the government. Who knew better than these returning soldiers how poorly prepared and ill-equipped the British troops in Norway had been, and how maladroit and uninspired were most of the men who sent them there? In the House of Commons tearoom, in the smoking room, in the corridors, in the committee rooms, in the bars, even outside on the terrace overlooking the Thames where members and their guests took lunch, men and women tried to convince each other to support or to oppose the government. Tory rebels tried to persuade the Labour leaders to demand the vote of confidence. Hugh Dalton told Harold Macmillan, the future Conservative prime minister who was a member of the "watching committee," that his party would make that decision the next morning. Macmillan immediately reported the news to Lord Salisbury. Meanwhile two Vigilantes tempted fate by hopefully discussing alternative Cabinets.

THE LUNCH HOUR PASSED, AND THE DEBATING CHAMBER BEGAN TO FILL. By about 3:30, members had packed it. Churchill took up his position on the Conservative side of the table that divides government from Opposition in the great room. He carried no notes. He would not be speaking that day. Behind him rose tiers of seats occupied to overflowing with backbench Conservatives; Labour MPs, across the table, sat facing him in ascending rows. When Chamberlain appeared they jeered: "Missed the bus, missed the bus," an appropriate jibe, given what the prime minister had said about Hitler on April 4. At 3:48 PM, as Chamberlain rose to speak—pale, determined, cold, scornful—they continued to heckle.

Prime Minister Neville Chamberlain, former successful businessman, former minister of health, former chancellor of the exchequer, son of the great imperialist and renegade radical Joseph: he held most of the Conservative Party in thrall. Those who did not love him feared him, for he set the tone followed by those party whips. Yet the vast majority of backbenchers did love and respect him, although few knew him well, for he did not invite friendship or confidences. They were content to entrust the fate of the country to his hands. They judged him incisive, supremely competent, a man who did not suffer fools. They believed in his cool judgment, his unemotional self-confidence. Wrote one admirer: "[He] has a clear and logical mind, and in controversy expresses very forcibly the reasons why it is evident that the Opposition is talking nonsense."

Chamberlain almost always thought his opponents talked nonsense. On that day, at that hour, in that great debating chamber, he felt for his hecklers only chilly contempt. He believed that he had taken their measure during the 1920s, when Labour had opposed his schemes to weaken the power of Labour-dominated local governments, and during the early 1930s, when as chancellor of the exchequer he had advocated austerity measures they had bitterly resented. He judged his Labour opponents windy and sentimental. He believed that today Labour would exaggerate the consequences of the setback in Norway for party-political reasons. He would correct them. "There were no large forces involved," he reminded them condescendingly when he rose to speak. "The fact was, it was not much more than a single division and our losses, therefore, were not really great in number, nor was there any considerable or valuable amount of stores left behind." So loud was the hooting from Labour benches that the Speaker of the House had to intervene to quiet them.

Chamberlain blamed the Norwegian government, not Britain's military advisers, for the decision to try to succor Trondheim before Narvik. He blamed Norwegians, too, for the ensuing debacle. He resisted calls for a more streamlined and efficient War Cabinet. Those who called for one did not know what they were talking about. As Labour continued to taunt him, he made "a little rather feminine gesture of irritation." But he gave no ground, refusing even to attempt to conciliate his critics. When he finished he had ceded nothing.

At first the ensuing debate ran along predictable lines. Attlee rose to rebut at 4:45 P.M. He was never windy or sentimental, whatever Chamberlain might think; nor was he a great public speaker. Still, characteristically, he made the crucial point: "It is not Norway alone. . . . Norway follows Czechoslovakia and Poland. Everywhere the story is 'Too late.' . . . [We] see everywhere a failure of grip, a failure of drive." Then Sinclair, speaking for the Liberals, reeled off the series of government failures of omission, commission and judgment that had led to the present disaster, an awful catalog. The prime minister's defenders counterattacked with

simple exhortations for unity, then with ridicule, and finally with poison-
ous insinuation: "The speech of the right hon. Gentleman will certainly
give great satisfaction in Berlin," said one. Chamberlain's principal private
secretary wrote that, at about this point, "it was generally agreed that the
government was going to 'get away with it.'"

Two speeches delivered later that afternoon and evening, however,
would sweep aside the government defenders and overshadow the orations
of earlier government critics.

THE CONSERVATIVE MEMBER OF PARLIAMENT FOR NORTH PORTSMOUTH,
Admiral of the Fleet Sir Roger Keyes, a hero of the previous war for leading a daring and successful raid on German submarine pens in Zeebrugge,
Belgium, appeared before the House at ten minutes past seven o'clock
wearing his full dress uniform and rows of medals. For the past week he
had been pleading with the Admiralty to let him attack Trondheim, with
a fleet of old ships if necessary, so as not to risk the new ones. He had
unsuccessfully lobbied Churchill, his friend of many years, to back this
assault. He knew he did not speak well in public, so he wrote out his address beforehand to read aloud. That breached House protocol, but when
he did speak no one objected; his words fell like hammer blows, and the
rowdy audience hushed.

"The capture of Trondheim was essential, imperative and vital," Keyes
insisted, contradicting the prime minister. It would take a brave man to
heckle a war hero in full regalia who spoke with such obvious feeling and
authority, but no one did: the House remained silent. "I need not go into
the details, but I would suggest that if a few ships had entered Trondheim Fiord, immediately the Army was ready to co-operate, the capture of
Trondheim Fiord with its vital aerodrome for our fighters, and quays for
landing heavy artillery, tanks and our mechanized transport, could have
been speedily effected." But the government had refused the naval action
at the last moment while fecklessly pushing forward the two-pronged land
attack, thus dooming it. The entire business had been "a shocking story of
ineptitude, which I assure the House, ought never to have been allowed
to happen."

Keyes turned from describing the inept British campaign in Norway
to explaining it: during wartime, inefficiency and incompetence at the top
led inevitably to disaster. Like Stafford Cripps, he wanted a streamlined
War Cabinet with new leadership. Unlike Cripps, he did not think the

leader should be Lord Halifax. From his perch above the front bench he gazed down at his old friend, the First Lord of the Admiralty. Did Churchill meet his eye? Keyes said—to him, as much as to the House at large: "I have great admiration and affection for my right hon. Friend. . . . I am longing to see proper use made of his great abilities. I cannot believe it will be done under the existing system. The war cannot be won by committees, and those responsible for its prosecution must have full power to act, without the delays of conferences."

"The House listens in breathless silence," wrote one who was there. "When Keyes sits down there is thunderous applause." Indeed, the mood had shifted, even from the previous week. The defeat in Norway had changed everything. Men the government was accustomed to count upon had just cheered the man who had condemned it. Clem Attlee, sitting at the center of the Opposition front bench, took note. But now, with Keyes finished, members began to stir. They wanted dinner. The chamber slowly emptied. And still the most dramatic moment of the evening was to come.

LEO AMERY, TEMPORARY LEADER OF EDEN'S GROUP OF "GLAMOR BOYS," wished to speak—albeit not to a vacant House. This formidable politician, administrator and intriguer had been inspired to enter politics by Neville's charismatic father, Joseph Chamberlain, the champion of imperial federation. He had climbed high, serving as a Cabinet minister under Baldwin. After Hitler had taken all of Czechoslovakia in 1939, having promised to be content with merely the Sudetenland, Amery had concluded that war with Germany was inevitable, but that Britain was unprepared to fight it, and he said so. As a result, he faced the same brick wall as Churchill. It did not come down for him when the war began, however. Now he played a leading role in two of the three anti-Chamberlain parliamentary groups. That was why the Speaker of the House, who was a Chamberlain supporter, although supposedly impartial, did not call on him until the chamber was nearly empty. "The whole effect of what I had to say depended on the response of a live House," Amery was to write. But "the Speaker knew I meant trouble."

Amery nearly sat down again; his listeners were so few. But Clem Davies whispered in his ear. He would round up an audience if his colleague could only stall for a few moments. Then, with the leader of the Vigilantes racing round the building calling in chits and debts, appealing to members to return to the chamber, Amery cleared his throat, straightened his tie, looked at the ceiling, made a few inconsequential introductory remarks, and checked his watch. He looked around the room again, saw he "had at any rate the makings of a House," and launched in. His intention was "to bring down the government if I could."

He delivered a blistering indictment: of the government's approach to the Norwegian campaign; of its failure to anticipate the German assault; of its strategy in combatting it; of its explanation for failing to do so successfully; of its assessment of gains and losses in Norway relative to Germany. Members continued to file into the chamber as he spoke, the Conservative benches before and behind him beginning to fill. Amery noticed murmurs of approval and applause coming from them. He took heart. Like Keyes, he found much of the House newly receptive to his argument.

The first part of his speech was a prosecution, detailed and bitter; the second part was an urgent call to action. "We cannot go on as we are," he charged. "There must be a change. First and foremost it must be a change in the system and structure of our governmental machine. This is war, not peace." But a streamlined War Cabinet peopled by Chamberlain's men would not suffice. It must include, or have the backing of, representatives of all parties and of the trade-union movement that was so powerful in Britain. "The time has come . . . for a real National Government." But everyone knew Labour would not join a government led by Chamberlain. The leader of the National Government, said Amery, must possess "vision, daring, swiftness and consistency of decision," all but the last of which Neville Chamberlain manifestly did not exhibit. Winston Churchill, however, had them all. Amery did not name him, as Keyes had done, but simply warned the House: "We cannot go on being led as we are."

Amery's purpose was to overthrow the government, not to name a new prime minister, and now he had arrived at the climax of his speech. Even so, he hesitated to say it: sentences so harsh and wounding they could never be unsaid or forgotten. He was addressing friends and colleagues on the front bench with whom he had worked closely in the past, including the son of his hero. But he went on: "We are fighting for our life, for our liberty, for our all." The newly sympathetic House seemed to agree. He wrote in his memoirs: "I felt myself swept forward by the surge of feeling which my speech had worked up on the benches round me." And so he repeated the words he had researched that morning while preparing his remarks, but even then had doubted he would employ, words that Oliver Cromwell had delivered in 1653 to the Rump Parliament when he had deemed it no longer fit to conduct the affairs of the nation. Amery extended his arm and pointed dramatically at the front bench, at his old friends and colleagues: "You have sat too long here for any good you have been doing. Depart, I say, and let us have done with you. In the name of God, go!"

It was 8:44 P.M. He had spoken for forty-one minutes and had rocked the House. "The most formidable philippic I have ever heard," judged Harold Macmillan. The most dramatic climax to a speech he had heard in fifty years, said David Lloyd George. "These were terrible words," Churchill would write in his history of the war.

There would be other speakers that night, both criticizing and defending the government, but none of them could erase or add much to the impression created by Keyes and Amery. Afterward men gathered in the smoking room and bars and nooks and crannies of the House of Commons. They stayed for many hours to rehash and rethink and resolve their plans. There is no evidence that Churchill participated in any of these conclaves. But then, he had a great speech to prepare, too. The next day, when the debate finally wound down, he would deliver it. He intended a slashing, coruscating defense of the indefensible.

WEDNESDAY MORNING, MAY 8: AGAIN A PERFECT BLUE-SKY DAY. AT THE meeting of the War Cabinet, Chamberlain, who had been offended by Amery's onslaught, nevertheless appeared to be cheerful. Perhaps he took heart from newspaper headlines and editorials predicting he would survive the debate one way or another. Perhaps he fondly and unrealistically believed—as his private secretary did, repeating gossip he had picked up from the Chamberlain entourage—that, if necessary, he could assuage his critics by dropping the most visible former appeasers from his Cabinet—Samuel Hoare, John Simon, Kingsley Wood—and bringing in Labour men to replace them. Halifax was supposed to put this scheme to Herbert Morrison later that day. Certainly the prime minister thought of himself in the same light as the permanent undersecretary at the Foreign Office, Sir Alexander Cadogan, who wrote in his diary that day that Chamberlain was still "the best PM in sight."

In fact Morrison and the other Labour Party leaders were just then discussing whether to call for the vote of confidence when Commons resumed debate in the afternoon. Attlee had reversed field. He now argued that Labour should demand it. He had witnessed the changed mood in

the House the previous night. Probably he had talked with Clement Davies again. "Discontent had gone far deeper than we thought and I was
assured that if a division were called we should get a lot of support from
the Conservatives," he would recall. Greenwood agreed; Dalton did not.
As for Morrison, later he would claim he had played a decisive role at the
meeting, arguing for the vote to be called. Possibly he had come to believe that the demands of the moment trumped whatever understanding
he had reached with Halifax on Monday (today no one knows what the
understanding was, since the meeting went unrecorded); Attlee, however,
later contended that Morrison came only reluctantly to support the vote.
In any event, those at the meeting agreed that Labour should demand one.
Morrison would announce it when he opened the debate that afternoon.
A little later, before the House met, the Parliamentary Labour Party members ratified their leaders' decision.

The "watching committee" gathered on the morning of May 8, too, at
Lord Salisbury's grand residence at Arlington Street. Committee members
did not yet know of Labour's plan, but they needed to decide their own
course of action. "No ordinary reshuffle [of government personnel] will
do," Salisbury warned them. What did this mean, if not that the prime
minister must go? And yet Salisbury shrank from the conclusion that
his own logic suggested. If Labour should demand the vote of censure,
he "beseeched" members to abstain from voting altogether. Ultimately he
wanted to improve Chamberlain's government, not to overthrow it. More
militant members of his committee disagreed. In the end participants
appear to have left this meeting undecided, with Salisbury's advice, but
also Amery's speech of the night before, ringing in their ears.

The three meetings wound down for lunch. Churchill retired to put
the finishing touches to his speech. When he was due to address the Commons, unlike many MPs, he always entered the House with detailed notes
to guide him. He relished the challenge confronting him that day—and
the irony of defending men who had frozen him out for the better part
of a decade.

BY 3:45 P.M., THE CHAMBER WAS PACKED ONCE MORE, backbenches
crammed, some members wearing their uniforms again, and the tension
was nearly as high as it had been at the close of the day before. As scheduled,
Morrison rose to begin the debate. It was three minutes after four o'clock
and, as he understood, the most important moment for his country in the

war so far. A bantam figure, blind in one eye, probably the best political machine-builder Labour has ever possessed, Morrison knew the present government must die if Britain, and not only Britain, was to live. He must puncture the government's pretensions to organization, efficiency and capacity and bring the Conservative waverers to the realization that an alternative had to be found.

The speech he then delivered realized his goals brilliantly. A series of specific unanswerable questions about the Norwegian campaign laid bare the government's pretensions to competence. "Was there a plan in operation for unity of command between the various forces in Norway?" he demanded.

> Is it the case that A.A. guns were sent without predictors, and that they were sent a week late? Is it the case that other guns were sent without ammunition? Is it the case that machine guns were sent without spare barrels? Was there any proper liaison between the port occupied by us at Namsos and the port occupied by us at Andalsnes; were there proper communications between those two points? Is it a fact that the military force was not supplied with snowshoes, the consequence being that the troops were stuck on the roads and were bombed there? Is it a fact that Territorial Brigades were sent . . . which were second Territorial Army units that had never had even brigade training?

His prosecution was relentless, his conclusion inescapable. As Attlee had charged the day before, it was not only Norway that was the problem: "The fact is that before the war and during the war . . . the whole spirit, tempo and temperament of at least some ministers have been wrong, inadequate and unsuitable. I am bound to refer in particular to the Prime Minister . . ." He named other former appeasers, too. When Morrison wound up by calling for a vote of censure, no one should have been surprised.

Chamberlain, however, reacted with astonishment—and with anger, since usually the Opposition gave prior notice if it intended to call for such a vote. But he was confident, for he knew the arithmetic: the Opposition could not possibly outvote him. He sprang to his feet as soon as Morrison had ceased speaking. "The words which the right hon. Gentleman has just uttered make it necessary for me to intervene for a moment or two at this stage." He deprecated the vote because it suggested the country was not united. "But I say this to my friends in the House—and I have friends in the House" (here, according to one who was watching, "a leer of triumph" passed over his face), "I accept the challenge. . . . We shall see who is with us and who is against us, and I call on my friends to support us in the Lobby to-night."

By universal assent both at the time and since, Chamberlain's appeal to "his friends" was not merely misjudged but catastrophic. The prime minister seemed to be reducing the vote of confidence to an issue of party fealty, when everyone else understood it to have vaster implications by far. Clem Davies of the Vigilantes knew immediately who could best articulate the sense of the House that the prime minister had debased it. He "sent word to Lloyd George." So apparently did Morrison; and the Liberal chief whip; and Lloyd George's daughter, Meghan, the member for Anglesey. They all knew who should answer the prime minister, but at first the old man did not want to intervene. Davies "spoke to him furiously in Welsh. . . . [He] said: 'Has the great Achilles lost his skill?'" Whoever finally persuaded him, David Lloyd George answered the call.

He spoke from the corner seat of the Opposition front bench, even though he belonged to the Liberal and not the Labour Party. "As he rises in his place, a stocky figure topped by a pure white mane of hair," wrote a journalist for the American *Christian Science Monitor*, "the old fire comes back quickly to light up his oratory and he begins to wag a minatory finger at the Government front bench across the aisle. . . . [His] voice still has in it the sound of the bells of Criccieth." Some men hoped that Chamberlain would fall—and that Lloyd George would take his place. Many believed this lion in winter would find some role in a new government, even if not the chief role. In fact his speech on May 8 would be Lloyd George's last major political intervention. He could not have wished for a better swan song.

Carefully Lloyd George took the House through the many failures that had preceded the most recent ones in the Norwegian campaign: the loss of Czechoslovakia and Poland; the forfeiture of the short-lived Franco-Russian alliance (1935–1938), which would have presented Germany with a two-front war, if Hitler had dared to start one, and if Stalin had not lost confidence in it and abrogated the pact after the Western democracies buckled at Munich; and, above all, the failure to rearm efficiently and swiftly. "Everybody knows that whatever was done was done half-heartedly, ineffectively, without drive and unintelligently," Lloyd George charged. He tried to separate Churchill from the failures that had taken place in

Norway, for he wanted him to continue to serve: "I do not think that the First Lord was entirely responsible for all the things that happened there." Characteristically, Churchill would have none of it: "I take complete responsibility for everything that has been done by the Admiralty, and I take my full share of the burden." But Lloyd George riposted instantly: "The right hon. Gentleman must not allow himself to be converted into an air-raid shelter to keep the splinters from hitting his colleagues."

His peroration did more than any other speech delivered that day to cut the ground from under Chamberlain's feet: "The Prime Minister must remember that he has met this formidable foe of ours in peace and in war. He has always been worsted. . . . He has appealed for sacrifice. The nation is prepared for every sacrifice so long as it has leadership. . . . I say solemnly that the Prime Minister should give an example of sacrifice, because there is nothing which can contribute more to victory in this war than that he should sacrifice the seals of office."

Churchill whispered to a Conservative frontbencher: "This is all making it damned difficult for me tonight"; and when Lloyd George finally sat down, Churchill delivered his two-word verdict on the speech: "absolutely devastating." There would be additional speeches, including a slashing attack upon the government by Stafford Cripps. But as Cripps himself wrote in his diary late that evening, Lloyd George's effort had been "an almost perfect parliamentary performance. Of all the speeches made on the two days Ll.G.'s was the only one which showed real leadership and fire."

POSSIBLY CRIPPS SLIGHTED CHURCHILL'S OWN EFFORT, WINDING UP FOR the government, for the First Lord nearly turned a sow's ear into a silk purse. Chamberlain's critics knew that Churchill could do it if anyone could. "I wished him luck but added that I hoped his speech would not be too convincing," one of them remembered. Churchill replied that "he had signed on for the voyage and would stick to the ship." Then he left the smoking room for the debate, rolling like a buccaneer. It was a little past ten o'clock at night.

When he rose to speak he concentrated on Norway. The critics said Britain had failed to take the initiative there because it lacked airpower. Whose fault was that? Until 1938, both Opposition parties had opposed expanding the RAF. They criticized because he had canceled the seaborne attack upon Trondheim. All the military experts had advised him to do so. Had he ignored their advice and sent in a British force, and if against all odds it had managed to take that town, "it could not have withstood the immense weight of the attack which was being delivered by the Germans from their magnificent base at Oslo and up the two lines of railway and road from Oslo to the North."

As always, he displayed a quick wit and biting turn of phrase. When a Labour frontbencher suggested that it had been the War Cabinet, not the Chiefs of Staff, who dithered about Trondheim, Churchill snapped, as if in irritation: "Do dismiss these delusions." When Labour back-benchers interrupted him moments later, he snapped again: "All day long we have had abuse, and now hon. Members opposite will not even listen." As for Neville Chamberlain's response to the demand for a vote of censure: "Exception has been taken because the Prime Minister said he appealed to his friends. He thought he had some friends, and I hope he has some friends. He certainly had a good many when things were going well."

But Churchill did not answer the criticism that Norway was merely the awful symptom of a much larger problem. Perhaps he knew that he could not.

THERE FOLLOWED "THE MOST DRAMATIC DIVISION IN WHICH I HAD ever taken part," wrote Amery. When the House of Commons votes, it divides: members either move into the Aye Lobby, a room to the right of the Speaker's seat, behind the government benches, or into the No Lobby, a room to the left of the Speaker's seat, behind the Opposition benches. As they enter the room, they bow slightly to the tellers, party whips, who stand impassively at the door keeping count. Tonight all the Labour and Liberal MPs headed for the No Lobby. So did the dissident Tories, including some who had stood aloof hitherto. Others remained ostentatiously seated. They would abstain from voting, a significant choice in itself. Members in uniform, almost all Conservative, headed for the No Lobby as well, some of them weeping: "I have come straight back from Namsos to vote against the government," one said to Labour's Hugh Dalton. The formidable Dalton wept, too. Another explained later that night to his father that, unfortunately, voting "No" was the only form of protest available to him. He was leaving the next day with his battalion for the front. His troops had no equipment or training, and it was obvious they would pay for that; yet no one in authority would even grant him an audience. As the two files divided, government supporters were yelling at their opponents "Quisling," the name of the Norwegian politician who had betrayed his country and facilitated the Nazi takeover. The critics were yelling back at them, "Yes men," perhaps a slighter insult. In any event, "It was like bedlam," wrote a Chamberlain loyalist. But everyone understood: Britain, the mother of parliaments, was showing the world democracy in action. That was worth fighting for, and even worth dying for. Germans could make no such demonstration.

After voting, the members returned to the chamber to await the tally. Those who sat rested on pins and needles making nervous remarks; those with nowhere to sit milled anxiously in the gangways or by the Speaker's chair. Churchill took up his position on the front bench, near the prime minister. Tension filled the room. Then finally the government chief whip, Margesson, stood before the table in the center of the chamber and read out the results in the voice of a stoic: ayes: 281, noes: 200.

"It took five seconds before I recognized the significance of the figures," wrote one Labour MP. A united Conservative Party would have given Chamberlain a majority of 213; he had a majority of only 81. Forty-two Conservatives had voted against their leaders. About 60 had abstained, which meant they had no confidence in their leaders either—or else they would have voted "aye." A gasp, then a shout: "Resign," yelled the Labour member. Others took up the call. "Resign, resign." Some began to chant: "In God's name, go," repeating Amery's quotation of Cromwell: "Go, go." Amery wrote in his memoirs: "It was not a pleasant moment." "We ought to sing something," a Tory dissident said, and the Labour man sitting next to him broke into "Rule Britannia." Others joined in. Now Margesson signaled for Conservative loyalists, who still composed a majority in the House, after all, to raise a cheer for the prime minister. Their voices added to the din.

Chamberlain blanched when he heard the numbers, then recovered, smiled sardonically, and rose, erect and unyielding, to leave the chamber. At that moment he thought he was finished, but he would not show it. "I felt very sorry for him," one of his most severe Conservative critics wrote. "I thought of him standing in Downing Street [after the Munich accord with Germany] barely eighteen months before, with the cheering crowds surging around him." Now only the frontbenchers followed him when he left the room amid jeers and catcalls. His parliamentary enemies had impaled him on a hook; they were determined he should not wriggle off.

IN GERMANY IT SOON WOULD BE MORNING. IN THE NORTH, ALONG THE Rhine, German soldiers of the Eighteenth Army slumbered tranquilly. They did not know it, almost no one did, but the day about to dawn, Thursday, May 9, would be their last day of peace for a long time. On Friday they would cross the river into Holland, aiming for Amsterdam and Rotterdam, and go north toward the sea. The Sixth Army, just to their south, would head for Brussels and Antwerp. The Fourth Army would push for the Belgian towns of Charleroi and Dinant. As the French and British raced north to confront the invaders, Germany's Twelfth Army would slice beneath them through Luxembourg and the Belgian Ardennes Forest, then cross the river Meuse, near Sedan, France, to cut them off and encircle them.

When Thursday, May 9, Western Europe's last day of peace for more than five years, broke, it dawned bright and cloudless once again.

CHAPTER 2

Finding a
War Prime Minister

WINSTON CHURCHILL'S SEIZURE OF POWER WAS NOT INEVITABLE. ON the night of May 8, as Chamberlain strode defiantly from the debating chamber with exclamations of derision ringing in his ears, his critics did not agree on who should take his place. Some, no doubt, especially among the dissident Tories and Vigilantes, favored Churchill, but others in the Conservative, Liberal and even Labour Parties wanted Halifax, while a few preferred Leo Amery, David Lloyd George, or perhaps even Anthony Eden. King George VI hoped Chamberlain would hang on, but if he must resign, that Halifax would take his place.

The preferences of the men who would enter Churchill's War Cabinet on May 10 shifted over the course of May 9, the day after the debate. At no time did they all favor Churchill. Labour Party leader Clement Attlee said at one point that he preferred Halifax. Later he said he could not distinguish between Halifax and Chamberlain and would not serve under either. At some other point that day, he said only that he would not refuse to serve should Churchill become prime minister. Deputy Labour Party leader Arthur Greenwood told Clem Davies that he "and some of the other Socialist Front Bench," which may have included Attlee, since he was its leader, "would soonest serve under" Amery. Why did they not flock to the First Lord? They did not because, for all his extraordinary qualities, they knew him as a crusading antisocialist, their fiercest enemy during the General Strike of 1926, and an archimperialist who opposed even debating self-government for India—which Halifax had been prepared at least to discuss.

Uncertainty reigned as well among the other men who would soon come together behind the greatest Conservative prime minister of the twentieth century, or perhaps ever. Churchill's longtime friend, the Liberal Party leader Archibald Sinclair, had favored Halifax a few days earlier. On May 9, he began to worry about a pending German attack and reluctantly concluded that it would be better to stick with Chamberlain until the emergency passed. Chamberlain, of course, did not want to step down. If he had to, he hoped Halifax would step up. And Churchill himself, although no doubt nourishing his own ambitions, made clear several times that day that he would serve any prime minister who could put together a truly National Government, which obviously meant Halifax first of all. In fact, the only member of Churchill's first War Cabinet who was unwilling for Halifax to become prime minister was Halifax, and even he vacillated, for he told one of his confidants that he knew he could do the job. If he thought anyone else was capable of doing it, he did not say so.

The convergence of opinion that led to Churchill's elevation developed almost at the last minute, and the process was hardly inevitable. This had consequences. Churchill would remember how contingent his own elevation had been when, later in the war, he thought some of his ministers meant to undermine him. He would recall the evanescence of political loyalty. But he would not remember that Labour had been the decisive factor in Chamberlain's downfall, that it had held the whip hand even if it did not know it. And it never occurred to him that Labour's role in 1940 might in some ways presage its part in the unmaking of his own administration in 1945.

Upon leaving the chamber after the dramatic division a little before midnight on May 8, Chamberlain's first thought was that he must resign at once. To Churchill he said that "he could not go on. There ought to be a National Government." But the old appeasers on his front bench did not agree: "In all humility I do not see where the superior team is coming from," one had written in his diary just before the debate began. "I believe you are well-nigh indispensable as Prime Minister," another informed him some hours after it had finished. More surprisingly, even Winston Churchill did not at that moment believe Chamberlain should resign. His blood was up. He had not delivered his fighting speech for nothing. The riotous scenes following the division only inflamed him further. "This has been a damaging debate, but you have a good majority," Churchill reassured his chief. "Do not take the matter grievously to heart. . . . Strengthen your Government from every quarter and let us go on until our majority deserts us." Churchill wrote that he thought at the time his exhortation had been in vain. But it had not; or perhaps Chamberlain did not really need much exhorting.

At any rate, Chamberlain changed his mind and decided to continue the fight. He left the Parliament Building for Buckingham Palace, where he told a relieved and pleased King George VI that he would continue as prime minister by reconstructing his government, inviting in the leaders of the Labour and Liberal Parties. By the time he went to bed that night he had put the best possible face on the events of the past twenty-four hours. His private secretary, writing in his diary at the end of that extraordinary day and night, faithfully parroted the new line: "The Government got a majority of 81—they had hoped for 100—and were fairly satisfied."

Early the next morning ("tulips almost at their best" in London, as no doubt in Paris and Berlin), with less than twenty-four hours to go before Hitler launched the Blitzkrieg, Chamberlain set about following Churchill's advice. He did not yet contact the Labour or Liberal leaders, but he tried, in a series of telephone calls, to strengthen his government by winning over the Tory abstainers, those who were discontented but had not voted against him. To them he held out various personal inducements; he also promised to drop the other prominent appeasers (Samuel Hoare, John Simon and Kingsley Wood) from his government and carry out a reconstruction. To the outright critics he offered a significant olive branch: at 8 o'clock that morning, he invited to No. 10 Downing Street Leo Amery, the man who had demanded that he "go, in God's name," and asked him to choose any position in the Cabinet that pleased him, not excluding foreign secretary. But this sort of propitiation—some called it bribery—did not work. The Tory abstainers and rebels wanted Chamberlain out. Amery turned down the prime minister flat. Meanwhile, at 9:30, Lord Salisbury's "watching committee" had reconvened at Arlington Street. It "agreed to the following formula," one of its members recorded:

1. That a Coalition Government is essential.
2. That the Labour Party will not enter such a Coalition if Chamberlain, Hoare and Simon remain; and that therefore
3. They must go.

Interestingly, the committee charged Salisbury with delivering this message immediately to Lord Halifax. At that moment, perhaps a majority of its members hoped the foreign secretary would replace Chamberlain as prime minister.

Not so for members of the Parliamentary Labour Party. Stafford Cripps was canvassing its opinion just as Salisbury was delivering his message to Halifax. He quickly realized not only that Labour MPs "did not want Halifax [but also that] . . . many of them were frightened of Winston." He searched out Lloyd George. Would the old lion "take the job on" instead? But while Labour MPs might have welcomed this outcome, a majority of Conservatives never would have done so. In any event, Lloyd George declined. Yet neither man believed Churchill to be Chamberlain's inevitable successor. They discussed his prospects and concluded that he would undoubtedly consent to serve under Halifax, if necessary.

But now Churchill, too, was rethinking matters. He rang Anthony Eden, the anti-appeaser who, like himself, had joined (in Eden's case, re-joined) Chamberlain's government when war broke out in 1939. Churchill wanted to see him "as soon as possible." When Eden arrived at Admiralty House, he found the First Lord shaving. Brandishing his safety razor, Churchill "rehearsed to me the events of the previous evening." If he really had advised Chamberlain to strengthen his team "from every quarter," he no longer believed it possible. Rather, "he thought that Neville would not be able to bring in Labour." But also, he told Eden, "a national government must be formed." The implication was obvious: someone other than Chamberlain must form it. Churchill did not at this moment advance himself.

Eden departed, and Churchill's longtime friend Lord Beaverbrook appeared. The previous day, Beaverbrook, a Canadian-born press magnate and an inveterate political intriguer, had sent Chamberlain an enigmatic note seeming to suggest he should hang on: narrow victories in votes of confidence were not invariably fatal—former prime ministers David Lloyd George and Andrew Bonar Law both had survived them. Now, however, Beaverbrook was asking whether Churchill would serve under Prime Minister Halifax. According to an account he wrote later, he hoped his friend would refuse to do so and claim the top spot for himself. But with Beaverbrook, one never knows; even Beaverbrook may not have known. Upon leaving Churchill he told a former Cabinet minister that he thought Amery should become prime minister.

Beaverbrook and Churchill had no sooner parted than Chamberlain's protégé, the Lord Privy Seal, Kingsley Wood, appeared. From this plump, bespectacled gentleman Churchill learned that the prime minister finally had accepted reality: if he failed to form a National Government of all parties, as he surely would, then he must resign his position in favor of a prime minister who could. It would happen quickly. Now Churchill must have begun to think seriously about the succession. It was not yet noon.

Wood had reported accurately. Chamberlain indeed had reverted to his immediate post-debate pessimism. Perhaps Amery's cold shoulder had shaken him. Perhaps he had feelers out to Labour that already had been rebuffed, or at any rate pessimistic reports from Conservative whips taking the pulse of the House. At 10 o'clock he summoned his foreign secretary and closest colleague, Lord Halifax, to Downing Street and told him that the only way to restore confidence in the government was to reconstruct it, bringing in all parties, but that "the chances of Labour serving under him . . . were negligible." Halifax unhappily agreed. He had been pondering this for days. He thought that Chamberlain must go through the motions of asking, but that a negative response must be expected. And then either he (Halifax) or Churchill must take the top position. He knew that Chamberlain wanted him to take it.

It seemed a natural progression for a man whose life always had combined privilege and authority. Edward Frederick Lindley Wood, Lord Halifax, stood six feet five inches tall. He came from one of the great aristocratic landowning Yorkshire families. Born with a withered arm, he nevertheless developed a lifelong passion for fox hunting, riding to hounds expertly. Religion, too, loomed large in his life. He learned from his father a belief in the need for reunification of the Anglican and Catholic churches, a cause he always favored. But politics called. From 1910 to 1926 he represented Ripon, a constituency so safely Conservative that contested elections rarely took place there. When Prime Minister Stanley Baldwin offered him the viceroyalty of India, he gave up the safe seat and took the title Lord Irwin. (He would become viscount when his father passed away, and then the first Earl Halifax after World War II, as a reward for his services.) In 1931, as a member of the House of Lords, not the House of Commons, he returned to British politics. As minister of education he visited a south Yorkshire village and noticed some boys: "We want a school," he said, "to train them up for servants and butlers." Then he began to focus on foreign affairs. He went fox hunting with the

Nazi leader and Luftwaffe chief, Hermann Goering, and then traveled to the Nazi outpost in the Bavarian Alps, Berchtesgaden, where he mistook Hitler for a footman. Aloof, superior, highly intelligent, he replaced Anthony Eden when the latter resigned as foreign secretary to protest British appeasement of Mussolini. From then on he and Chamberlain worked closely together to fashion British foreign policy. But he appears to have begun to doubt the prime minister's policy of appeasement after Hitler invaded Czechoslovakia.

And now Chamberlain proposed to steer him into the premiership. What did Halifax make of this? From his diary we know that, first of all, he hoped Chamberlain somehow still would prevail. Perhaps from modesty, more likely for calculated reasons, he "put out all the arguments that I could think of against myself." He stressed that as a Lord he would have no contact with the House of Commons. But "the P.M. did not think so much of this." Possibly the question uppermost in Halifax's mind was this: If Chamberlain should step down and government reconstruction become inevitable, what would be the best way to continue taking advantage of Churchill's extraordinary abilities during the crisis, while simultaneously keeping him from running off the rails? Should he, Halifax, become prime minister to restrain him, or would he be better able to do that if he remained in his present position as foreign secretary? Chamberlain thought Halifax should do it as PM, but Halifax was not so sure.

Another thought may have occurred to the foreign secretary. If he took the premiership now, then Churchill would be his heir apparent, and should he, Halifax, fail, then Churchill would replace him. But if Churchill became prime minister first and failed, then Halifax could step forward, and do so with no obvious rivals behind him. Perhaps that would be the smarter move. So many possibilities and all of them fraught: "The conversation [with Chamberlain] . . . left me with a bad stomach ache," he wrote in his diary.

Halifax left No. 10 for the Foreign Office at about 11 o'clock. There Lord Salisbury delivered to him the resolution of the "watching committee"— more pressure for him to take over as prime minister. He spoke with one of his closest aides, who "tried earnestly and long to persuade [him] to accept the Premiership." To this man he said that "he felt he could do the job." But he also said that if he accepted, "Churchill's qualities and experience would surely mean that he would be 'running the war anyway,' and Halifax's own position would speedily turn into a sort of honorary

Prime Minister." Here was yet another reason to turn down the succession. Perhaps he knew in his heart that Churchill better understood how to fight a war than he did. For all these reasons, then, Halifax may well have decided the matter to his own satisfaction before noon.

The Cabinet convened at the House of Commons at 11:45. Chamberlain took the chair at 12:15. Ministers were again discussing Norway. But in Berlin, Adolf Hitler had ordered implementation of a brilliant plan conceived by the chief of staff of Army Group A, Erich von Manstein. This was to feign a repetition of Alfred von Schlieffen's right hook through Belgium in 1914, which would draw British and French forces north, while actually developing the main German attack from below, from the south, a left hook, with panzer divisions emerging from the Ardennes Forest and striking out for the Channel. The British and French would find themselves surrounded. The Führer now was composing the declaration to be delivered the next day to his troops: "The battle beginning today will decide the fate of the German nation for the next thousand years."

UNAWARE OF HITLER'S FATEFUL DECISION, "THE CABINET SAT UNTIL 1:35 in an air of gloom," pondering Norway, recorded Foreign Office undersecretary Alexander Cadogan. Equally unaware, Chamberlain's opponents continued their work. With Clem Davies in the chair, the Vigilantes and "glamor boys" of the Eden Group hammered their nail deeper into the coffin of his premiership. They agreed unanimously "that there must be a genuine National Government comprised of all parties . . . [and] that we would give full support to any Prime Minister who could form such a Government and none to one who couldn't." Then Amery hurried over to Committee Room 8 in the House of Commons, to a gathering of Conservatives who had voted no confidence the previous night. It reached similar conclusions. Before long, the prime minister knew the results of both cabals.

Neither meeting specified who Chamberlain's successor should be. Halifax had his partisans; Churchill by now probably had more, among meeting participants anyway. Everyone accepted, however, that the first job was to overthrow the prime minister. His successor would be determined afterward.

So Chamberlain stood upon the very brink. His Cabinet ministers knew it, as did he—all that morning, while the Germans were preparing to launch, they remained focused upon Westminster. Conservative

Party whips continued to be "very active," offering "vast promises of conciliation" to members judged disaffected but reconcilable, but the prime minister must by now have deemed these efforts beside the point. He now realized that all depended upon Labour. Sometime after the Cabinet finished he arranged for Attlee and Greenwood to call upon him at the end of the afternoon. Already he had arranged for Churchill and Halifax to call at 4:30, before the Labour leaders arrived.

Churchill lunched with Kingsley Wood and Anthony Eden. They told the dominions secretary that "Neville had decided to go." They discussed the future. Wood "thought that W. should succeed and urged that if asked he should make plain his willingness." Chamberlain's protégé had turned against his sponsor, perhaps in part because he knew the latter had offered to throw him, a former appeaser, under the bus to win back the Tory critics. He also warned that Chamberlain favored Halifax and would ask Churchill to support him. If that should happen: "Don't agree, and don't say anything."

Clem Davies lunched at the Reform Club with Attlee and Greenwood. He wanted them to refuse service under Halifax, and to accept only Churchill. But now Attlee, like Sinclair, sensed an imminent German assault, and he believed it would not be wise to overthrow a prime minister on the eve of what might prove to be the decisive battle of the war. Davies and Greenwood argued with him for two hours before the Labour Party leader finally came around. Then he and Greenwood left for the meeting at No. 10.

After lunch Churchill returned to his papers at Admiralty House. After his own lunch Halifax met the French ambassador at the Foreign Office and reassured him that Britain still intended to take Narvik from the Germans (this as the Germans prepared to invade France). Just before 4:30 both Halifax and Churchill left their desks and walked over to the prime minister's official residence for the most important meeting of their lives, and for what may have been the most important meeting of three politicians in twentieth-century British history.

CHURCHILL KNEW CHAMBERLAIN AND HALIFAX WELL AS COLLEAGUES and political rivals, if not as friends. All three had served under Prime Minister Stanley Baldwin during the 1920s. In 1931 Churchill and Halifax had clashed sharply over British policy in India. In 1935 Baldwin appointed Chamberlain to Churchill's old job as chancellor of the exchequer, and Halifax as Lord Privy Seal. He excluded Churchill as punishment for his various transgressions. One can imagine with what pangs Churchill viewed these preferments. He knew his colleagues to be formidable figures, each in his own right, but he knew, too, that they were less brilliant than he. And then Chamberlain rose higher still, replacing Baldwin as prime minister in 1937, and appointing Halifax as his foreign secretary in 1938, after Eden resigned. Only when the war that Churchill had been warning against broke out did Chamberlain finally call for him. Churchill served with unimpeachable loyalty. But on May 9, the wheel had come full circle: they met in the Cabinet Room at 10 Downing Street to discuss whether Chamberlain should step down, and if so, whether Halifax or Churchill should replace him.

Accounts of the meeting vary on details. Halifax kept a diary in which he recorded the events of the day and his thoughts about them; he also described the meeting immediately afterward to Cadogan, who recorded it in *his* diary. Both diaries survived. Churchill provided his own recollections in his magnificent memoir, *The Gathering Storm*. But that was published eight years after the event, and is manifestly incorrect about the meeting in several instances.

Chamberlain began the discussion with a recapitulation of the situation. Only a truly National Government could manage the country now, and he doubted he could form one, because Labour would not enter. If it would not, then he must resign. He would serve under either of the men in the room with him. He did not indicate whom he favored.

At about this point, Attlee and Greenwood appeared. The slight, balding, laconic and occasionally diffident-seeming Attlee did not impress at first glance. But first impressions can be misleading. He was as savvy and effective a socialist leader as Labour ever has had, and he possessed a hard and ruthless streak.

He had graduated from Oxford in 1904 and had qualified for the bar in 1906, but he had never practiced law. Coming from comfortable circumstances, he easily could have padded them, but he felt the need for service to others. Poverty-stricken East London drew him. There he first managed a charitable house for working-class boys in Stepney. Later he served as secretary of Toynbee Hall, the most famous settlement house in the nation. What he saw in the East End convinced him that private charity could never reduce real poverty, and that therefore the state must intervene. He became a socialist, joined the Independent Labour Party, and threw himself into local politics. "He had no swank," said one East Ender, speaking for many in that neighborhood who learned to like and respect the privileged but unassuming outsider. After World War I, during which he saw combat and received two promotions, they elected him Labour member for Limehouse. He won the leadership of the Labour Party in 1935, when Ernest Bevin swung the bloc vote of his enormous Transport and General Workers' Union behind him in order to keep out Herbert Morrison, whom Bevin detested. Many thought Attlee would not last in this position, but they, too, underestimated "the little man," as another Labour stalwart, Hugh Dalton, sometimes slightingly referred to him in his diary (before learning to appreciate his qualities).

Attlee could be "aloof and brutal," one socialist MP remembered. "Cold and icy with a tough tongue," recalled a journalist. "He was a soldier in everything," a former secretary of the Parliamentary Labour Party recollected rather more generously. "Short, sharp, concise." He doodled with pencil on paper at meetings, and said little, but missed nothing. When later in the war he deputed for an absent Churchill as chair of the War Cabinet (by virtue of his position as Labour Party leader and deputy prime minister), it ran noticeably more smoothly and efficiently than when the prime minister presided. He also proved extremely effective at promoting Labour MPs into posts as junior ministers and onto strategic government committees. Middle class, but without airs; socialist, but not a dreamer; effective, efficient and as tough as the English Army: these qualities drew Ernest Bevin, who became his most important political ally.

As for Greenwood—a former schoolteacher and advocate of educational reform and worker education, a former civil servant in the Ministry of Reconstruction after World War I, and an advocate of ethical socialism—he had climbed the rungs of Labour's hierarchy nearly to the top. By 1940, however, his star had begun to fade. One might have asserted that he had seen his best days, except, as it turned out, these were his best days. Perhaps his predilection for drink undermined his career before the war, otherwise he might have become Labour Party leader; probably it undermined it later; but at this critical moment in his country's history it did not undermine it. The early period of the war constitutes Arthur Greenwood's finest hour.

The two men seemed "pale and evidently in a state of tension" to a witness who saw them entering 10 Downing Street that afternoon. It cannot have been long after their lengthy and difficult talk with Clem

Davies at the Reform Club. Now they confronted Chamberlain, Halifax and Churchill, a challenging triumvirate if ever there was one, but they remained resolute. The prime minister asked them point-blank to join his government. "He seemed to have no idea that he was finished," Attlee said later. But this is wrong. Chamberlain knew well what his chances were; he was maintaining a poker face. Amazingly, Churchill intervened to argue passionately, as Attlee recalled, that they should all "come in under Chamberlain." He was, Attlee judged, "quite sincere." Now Greenwood showed his mettle: "We haven't come here to listen to you orating, Winston." Halifax said nothing. But Attlee did: "Our party won't have you," he told the prime minister brutally, "and I think the country won't have you either."

Chamberlain finally had to ask a crucial question: Would Labour serve under a different Conservative prime minister than himself? Attlee and Greenwood thought Labour would, but said they could not speak for the party. Labour's annual conference would begin the next day at Bournemouth, however. They would travel down to ask its National Executive Committee (NEC) two questions and report back immediately when they had answers: "Are you prepared to join a government led by Chamberlain?" and "Would you be prepared to serve under somebody else?" They predicted that the answer to the first question would be no, and that the answer to the second question would be yes.

The two Labour men left No. 10. Chamberlain, Churchill and Halifax remained in the Cabinet Room, where Conservative Party chief whip David Margesson joined them. Chamberlain, accepting finally that he could not go on, tried his best to steer the succession to the man he favored, Halifax. He suggested that Churchill's fighting speech during the debate the previous night had further alienated Labour members. They would not assent to him as prime minister. Then he came round to Halifax's ostensible objection to accepting the top spot: "He looked at [Churchill] sharply and said 'Can you see any reason, Winston, why in these days a Peer should not be Prime Minister?'" It was a trap, because if Churchill said yes, he would be dismissed as a self-promoter, while if he said no, then Chamberlain would propose Halifax. Instead of answering, Churchill took Kingsley Wood's advice and said nothing. As he put it afterward: "Usually I talk a great deal, but on this occasion I was silent. . . . As I remained silent, a very long pause ensued. It certainly seemed longer than the two minutes which one observes in the commemorations of Armistice Day."

Halifax was more forthcoming. On his own account he told Chamberlain: "For me to take it would create a quite impossible position. . . . Winston would be running defense. . . . I should have no access to the House of Commons. . . . I should speedily become a more or less honorary Prime Minister." For obvious reasons he did not speak of the other, more self-interested reasons for his hesitation. He wrote in his diary only that "Winston, with suitable expressions of regard and humility, said he could not but feel the force of what I had said, and the P.M. reluctantly, and Winston evidently with much less reluctance, finished by accepting my view."

Chamberlain had to see someone else at this point, but the crucial meeting had taken place and the crucial decision arrived at, although it remained unspoken. What would proper Englishmen do in such circumstances? Churchill and Halifax went down to the garden behind No. 10 and had a cup of tea in the afternoon spring sunshine.

At 8:30 that evening Churchill dined with Sinclair and Eden, among others. He seemed "quiet and calm." He summed up the afternoon meeting for the table. He thought he must soon take Chamberlain's place. Eden records Churchill saying that the prime minister "would advise King to send for him. Edward [Halifax] did not wish to succeed. Parliamentary position too difficult." Already he had given thought to the shape of his government. He would be his own minister of defense as well as prime minister, coordinating military policies and streamlining military decisions, as critics from all parties had demanded. He knew that many Conservative backbenchers distrusted him as a rebel and loose cannon, however, so he hoped Chamberlain would continue as chairman of the party and as leader of the House of Commons. (In the event, Labour would not accept this last proposition.) He wanted Eden to take the Ministry of War and run the British Army. Later that evening, Churchill's son, Randolph, telephoned asking whether there was any news. Churchill could now tell him what only a select few among the Conservative Party leadership knew: "I think I shall be Prime Minister tomorrow."

AND STILL IT ALMOST DIDN'T HAPPEN. GERMAN ARMIES BURST ACROSS the borders of Belgium, Luxembourg, and Holland at dawn on Friday, May 10. German aircraft supported them. German gliders assaulted the principal Belgian fortress near the Dutch border and key bridges along the Albert Canal. French and British forces rushed north to confront them. They did not imagine Manstein's "sickle cut" to the south. They did not yet realize that Hitler's aim was to trap them from north and south.

Someone woke Churchill at 5:30 A.M. Within minutes, he was dealing with a deluge of telegrams from the Admiralty, the War Office and the Foreign Office. He knew first only about Holland. Half an hour later he learned the Germans were pouring into Belgium, too. At about 7:00 Randolph telephoned again for news. Churchill told him that Allied forces were marching to meet the Germans. The following colloquy took place.

"In a day or two there will be a head-on collision."

"What about what you told me last night, about you becoming Prime Minister today?"

"Oh I don't know about that. Nothing matters now except beating the enemy."

Or so Churchill's son would report the conversation many years later. It may have been a fond recollection, meant to burnish the Churchill legend. For whatever he may have said to his son, and despite the German attack, Churchill did not intend to let Chamberlain off the hook so easily. He did not lightly relinquish positions once he had arrived at them, as he would demonstrate time and again in the coming years. There would soon be a foretaste of this.

The morning passed for Churchill in a blur of meetings: breakfast with the secretaries of state for war and for air at 6:00; Military Coordination Committee (which he chaired) at 7:00; War Cabinet at 8:00. Meanwhile, a continuing cascade of bad news came pouring in: the Luftwaffe had bombed airfields in Belgium and northern France and the town of Nancy; and German paratroopers had landed in Belgium and had also dropped between Leyden and The Hague and near Rotterdam. German submarines had torpedoed a British ship. At a second War Cabinet meeting, at 11:30, he learned that the Germans had bombed many more French towns as well as Brussels, The Hague and additional strategic airfields. And still neither he nor anyone else in the government yet apprehended the genius of Manstein's plan.

To Chamberlain, the German onslaught, terrible though it was, offered an unexpected reprieve. It suggested to him that he must not resign after all, at least until the enemy's offensive had been contained. He instructed the Whips' Office to let his revised intention be known. Eden learned it soon after 10 o'clock that morning: "All changes postponed; it seemed for some time." Most of the old appeasers approved, but not Kingsley

Wood, who told the prime minister so, and then hastened to warn Churchill. The First Lord may have said to Randolph that the only thing that mattered now was the battle with Germany, but he did not meekly accept Chamberlain's decision. Churchill was nothing if not tenacious. Now he attempted to dig in his heels. He still was "pressing for early changes in the government," the Chamberlain loyalist and Lord Privy Seal, Sam Hoare, complained to Eden at the beginning of the 11:30 Cabinet.

Churchill was demonstrating, too, his skill at manipulating such levers of power as came to hand, just as he would when he became prime minister. He must have charged his parliamentary private secretary, Brendan Bracken, to press his case as well—not with Cabinet ministers, but with the leading Tory rebels. Bracken's efforts produced a response from Lord Salisbury of the "watching committee": "Winston should be made Prime Minister during the course of the day." And when Bracken alerted the Vigilantes and "glamor boys" to the change of plan, both groups agreed with Salisbury. Churchill was lining up important forces to impart a message: despite the German attack, nothing had changed; Chamberlain still must go, and the sooner the better. If anything, the military emergency only made change more urgent.

But the prime minister would not go. At the end of the 11:30 meeting, he told ministers that he *had* intended to step down, but not any longer: "He thought it would all have to wait over till the war situation was calmer," Halifax recorded in his diary. According to Anthony Eden, who likewise kept a journal, Chamberlain then said he had communicated his intention to Attlee, "who had accepted." The prime minister had asked Attlee to issue a "notice which would include support of [the] government position."

The prime minister had put his finger on the nub of the matter. In the end, the Tory rebels could not force him to resign; nor could Churchill, whatever his skill and tenacity. For they did not represent a majority of Conservatives, and the prime minister did. Only Labour could force him out now, by refusing to join or support his government at a time when everybody knew that national unity was essential—and Chamberlain thought he had persuaded the Labour Party leader to come in. In fact, Chamberlain had likely misunderstood whatever Attlee had told him earlier that morning. Or perhaps Attlee responded one way at first and then changed his mind. The prime minister had asked for a statement supporting the present government during the crisis. But Davies,

Greenwood and Attlee had hammered this all out the previous afternoon at the Reform Club, when they concluded, finally, that the prime minister must step down despite the imminent German threat. Attlee conferred again with Greenwood, also with Dalton, who likewise had not yet left for Bournemouth. Perhaps these two pointed out to him that the German onslaught altered nothing; if anything it only heightened the need for change. Perhaps they did not need to point it out. The statement Attlee released in answer to Chamberlain's request read: "The Labour Party, in view of the latest series of abominable aggressions by Hitler, while firmly convinced that drastic reconstruction of the Government is vital and urgent in order to win the war, reaffirms its determination to do its utmost to achieve victory. It calls on all its members to devote all their energies to this end."

The statement did not call for Chamberlain to step down immediately, but neither did it endorse his decision to postpone stepping down. Chamberlain could read the tealeaves. Shortly after the Cabinet concluded, according to a *Yorkshire Post* journalist, a group of Conservative MPs, "drawn from those not given to criticism of the Prime Minister," urged him to form a coalition government. However, "these Members left him with the impression that, whatever efforts he might assay to form such a Government, he nevertheless was reconciling himself to resignation."

Chamberlain's Cabinet allies were not yet reconciled. They responded with indignation to the Labour Party statement, but worse was to come. Attlee, Greenwood and Dalton entrained for Bournemouth. As soon as they arrived, they received reports that German airplanes had bombed Canterbury (a false rumor). At 3:30 they met the party's NEC in the basement of the Highcliffe Hotel. There the decision came swiftly and unanimously. Labour would serve, but only "as a full partner in a new Government which, under a new Prime Minister, commands the confidence of the nation." Dalton had insisted on the words "a new Prime Minister." Otherwise, he warned, Chamberlain would try to hang on. It was as Attlee and Greenwood predicted the previous day: Labour's answers to Chamberlain's questions were "no" and "yes."

Labour's statement did not specify who the new prime minister should be. In this dire emergency, Labour would have served under Halifax. Attlee and Greenwood did not know that Halifax had taken himself out of the running right after they had left 10 Downing Street the day before.

But they would not serve under Chamberlain—and in the end they held the whip hand.

At 4:45 Attlee telephoned the prime minister's office and read the resolution at dictation speed to one of Chamberlain's secretaries. At that moment Chamberlain was presiding over yet another War Cabinet, the third of that awful day. He had begun the meeting hoping against hope that Labour would support him. He was about to learn that it would not. As he led a discussion about whether Britain should commence bombing targets east of the Rhine, the secretary brought him Attlee's message. Chamberlain glanced at it for just long enough to read and understand it, then put it down and impassively continued the discussion. But he knew now that the end finally had come. When the Cabinet finished, he took the paper up again and read it aloud to his ministers. Then, according to the minutes, "the Prime Minister said that, in the light of this answer, he had reached the conclusion that the right course was that he should at once tender his resignation to The King. He proposed to do so that evening."

CHURCHILL, HALIFAX AND THE OTHER MINISTERS FILED FROM THE Cabinet Room. Attlee and Greenwood caught the 5:15 from Bournemouth back to London. Churchill returned to his papers at the Admiralty. Halifax went over to the Foreign Office to see Dutch ministers; he promised them that Britain would protect Dutch islands off the coast of Venezuela, where there was oil. Chamberlain made his way to Buckingham Palace, arriving just after the king had taken tea. To him he finally sacrificed his seals of office. "He told me," the king remembered, "that the Labour Party would serve in the new administration of a new Prime Minister but not in one with himself as PM." These were nearly the words of the Labour message. "He then told me he wished to resign." The king, who had enthusiastically supported Chamberlain's appeasement policy, accepted with genuine regret. "I told him how grossly unfairly I thought he had been treated." He would call for Halifax, who, in his opinion, was "the obvious man" to replace the retiring prime minister. Chamberlain explained that Halifax had ruled himself out: "Winston was the man to send for." The king swallowed his doubts and agreed. Churchill arrived a minute or two after 6:00 P.M.

Winston Churchill had wanted to be prime minister since childhood. The prize had seemed attainable when he rejoined the Conservative Party after World War I, and Baldwin appointed him chancellor, a position often regarded as second only to the premiership. But then came the fall. He had spent a decade in the political wilderness, regarded as a Jeremiah, a crackpot and an extremist. Everyone knew he had gifts; practically no one believed he could control them. At this supreme moment in British history, however, with German armies smashing across borders and crushing all that stood in their way, with his country in danger that grew more grave with every minute, Churchill did not doubt himself. He would go to bed that night conscious "of a profound sense of relief. At last I had the authority to give directions over the whole scene. I felt as if I were walking with Destiny, and that all my past life had been but a preparation for this hour and for this trial." With what sentiments, then, must he have entered Buckingham Palace and regarded the king who was about to anoint him?

"I told the King that I would immediately send for the leaders of the Labour and Liberal Parties," he remembered. He would form a truly National Government and a War Cabinet of five members: himself, Chamberlain and Halifax for the Conservatives, plus Attlee and Greenwood for Labour. He would be his own minister of defense. He mentioned other names, men he wanted in the larger Cabinet: Beaverbrook, Eden, and the leader of Britain's largest trade union, Ernest Bevin. The king, perhaps already warming to his new prime minister, judged him to be "full of fire and determination."

Back at Admiralty House, Churchill began putting the pieces together in more formal fashion. First he wrote a letter to Chamberlain, then a message to Halifax, thanking them both for past, present and, above all, future support. He would count on them to help not only with policy but also with politics, for he knew many Conservatives still disliked and mistrusted him. He arranged for Attlee and Greenwood to be met at Waterloo Station and brought to him. They did not know he was prime minister until they got off the train at 9:00 P.M. and his emissary told them. Morrison still did not know. He was waiting for the call from Halifax that never came. But then, also at 9:00, Chamberlain went on air to explain to the nation that he had resigned and that Churchill would become prime minister. Morrison must have listened with mixed feelings.

Attlee and Greenwood did not hear the broadcast. They arrived at Admiralty House, a short drive from the railway terminus, and set to work with the new prime minister. They agreed immediately to the five-man team he had mentioned earlier to the king. They would serve as ministers without portfolio, the better to focus on the war. Chamberlain would become Lord President of the Council, a post that would allow him to range over domestic policy matters. Halifax would remain foreign secretary. They also agreed that Anthony Eden would become minister of war responsible for the army; that Churchill's old friend Archibald Sinclair, who was leader of the Liberal Party, would become minister of air; and that a Labour man, A. V. Alexander, would become First Lord of the Admiralty, a position he had held in a previous Labour government. So there was Winston Churchill's first national War Cabinet, and there were the three service ministers, each from a different party.

Over the weekend, May 11 and 12, Churchill shaped his entire government. It would not remain unchanged for the course of the war, but it would not change unrecognizably, either. Inevitably it reflected his sense of insecurity within his own party as well as Conservative dominance in the House of Commons. To state it briefly: he appointed fifty-two Conservatives and sixteen Labourites. His government included almost all the old appeasers. Only Samuel Hoare lost office, but a month later Churchill appointed him ambassador in Spain. He shifted Simon, who had been chancellor of the exchequer, from the House of Commons to the House of Lords, where he sat upon the woolsack as Lord Chancellor (that is, as head of Britain's judiciary). He rewarded Kingsley Wood for deserting Chamberlain by giving him Simon's old job. He even kept Margesson, the party whip, whom the Tory rebels feared and hated. Of thirty-six ministerial posts, he gave twenty-one to men who had served under Chamberlain.

But he brought in his own supporters, too. He made his old friend Lord Beaverbrook minister of aircraft production. He appointed Leo Amery to the India Office, and some of those "troublesome young men" to junior positions (not enough to satisfy them, however). On the Labour side, he gave Cabinet posts to Morrison, Dalton and Ernest Bevin (aside from Attlee and Greenwood in the War Cabinet)—as he had told the king he would. Within two weeks he had appointed another man of the left (although no longer of the Labour Party), Stafford Cripps, to be ambassador to Russia. He did not reward the leader of the Vigilantes, Clem Davies, a man without a party and therefore relatively powerless in the House—albeit too established a figure to offer anything less than a senior position. In the end Churchill put together a National Government in which Chamberlain loyalists predominated, but which included Tory rebels, socialists and Liberals as well as administrators and businessmen who belonged to no party at all.

On Monday, May 13, Churchill stood before the House of Commons as prime minister to rally the nation: "You ask what is our policy? I will say: It is to wage war, by sea, land and air, with all our might and with the strength that God can give us; to wage war against a monstrous tyranny, never surpassed in the dark, lamentable catalogue of human crime. . . . You ask what is our aim? I can answer in one word: It is victory, victory at all costs, victory in spite of all terror, victory, however long and hard the road may be; for without victory there is no survival."

No one in Britain knew, on that day, that already the great French Army was reeling and staggering from Germany's thunderous, lightning attack. In London, Churchill sounded the tocsin, but in Paris alarm already was quickly turning into panic. The British prime minister had just declared his aim and policy; these would be tested to the maximum, and sooner than even he could possibly have imagined.

PART II

CHURCHILL AND HIS MINISTERS AT WAR

CHAPTER 3

Testing the War Cabinet

Winston Churchill had his team now, composed mainly of Chamberlain supporters, but carefully assembled to balance competing interests. Still, his situation and that of his government were precarious—not only because of the threat posed by Germany (not yet fully appreciated), but also because the former prime minister's loyalists regarded the man who had replaced him as a usurper, and the new government merely as a temporary expedient that soon could be dispensed with. They despised the men on the Tory side with whom Churchill associated, and referred to them as "gangsters" or worse. "Now," wrote one Chamberlain supporter in a venomous, shortsighted and astoundingly provincial vein, "all those reptile satellites . . . will ooze into jobs they are unfitted for . . . I regard this as a greater disaster than the invasion of the Low Countries."

Churchill, too, they continued to loathe and distrust, even though he now occupied the top post. On Monday, May 13, when he entered the debating chamber in the House of Commons for the first time as prime minister to deliver his ringing declaration of aims and policies, they did not cheer him—but Chamberlain instead. They deluged the former premier with letters bemoaning his fall, assuring him of their devotion and begging him to reclaim his old position. "You and you alone," wrote the chairman of the "1922 Committee" (consisting of Conservative backbench MPs) in a typical message, "have the confidence and are the leader of the great mass of moderate Conservative opinion, in the House, in the Party & in the country." On Friday afternoon, May 10, as Chamberlain had made for Buckingham Palace to hand in his resignation, four of his supporters, including R. A. "Rab" Butler, Conservative member for Saffron

Walden and a Foreign Office undersecretary, gathered disconsolately at the Foreign Office. Chamberlain had sold the pass, lamented Butler, "to the greatest adventurer of modern political history . . . a half-breed American" (Churchill's grandparents were American). The four men opened a bottle and toasted the "King over the Water," by whom they meant the former prime minister. Eventually Churchill would win over these four malcontents, but many rank-and-file Tories belonging to a "respectable tendency" within the Conservative Party would remain irreconcilable, not for days, weeks or months, but for more than a year.

Churchill could not even count upon many of the Conservatives or Conservative-minded men whom he had appointed or reappointed to his government. One, Maurice Hankey (a career civil servant of no party, but a supporter of appeasement), whom Churchill retained as chancellor of the duchy of Lancaster, immediately dubbed him "a dictator" and "a rogue elephant." He had "a certain amount of imagination," Hankey conceded, but could not "grip the war," as Chamberlain had done. The only hope, and Hankey judged it doubtful, was for the two "wise old elephants," Chamberlain and Halifax, "to hold" him.

But the wise old elephants had doubts, too. "I have seldom met anybody with stranger gaps of knowledge, or whose mind worked in greater jerks," Halifax wrote of the new prime minister in his diary on May 11, Churchill's first full day in office. "Uneasy as to Winston's methods," he noted on May 12. "There is no comparison between Winston and Neville as a Chairman," he complained the day after that. Chamberlain meanwhile was writing to one correspondent: "I have no confidence that the new Administration will be more effective than the last. Indeed I know they can't be." Anthony Eden thought Chamberlain "was clearly hating it all." And Kingsley Wood, who may have known that Churchill once said of himself, after quitting the Conservatives for the Liberals and then quitting the Liberals for the Conservatives, "anyone can rat, but it takes a certain amount of ingenuity to re-rat," may himself have been intending to re-rat. He told the former prime minister that "he doubted whether this administration would be long lived," and added, not to unwilling or disbelieving ears, that his old chief should hold himself in readiness. Chamberlain "might be wanted again later."

The left voiced discontent, too. It had not forgotten Churchill's past, which, except for his stint in H. H. Asquith's pre-1914 Liberal Cabinet, they viewed as deeply reactionary. But he was a fighter and he had been right about Germany, and so the left trained its fire now not so much on him as upon the former appeasers still in his government. "Why," asked Stafford Cripps, did Churchill "carry the symbols of defeat into what we all hope will be a victory government?" He meant Sir John Simon (although Churchill had placed him out of the way, upon the woolsack in the House of Lords), Kingsley Wood (whom Churchill had promoted to become chancellor) and, above all, Neville Chamberlain. "Why burden the new start with his somber legacy?" Cripps wanted to know, but of course the answer was that Churchill did not dare leave him out, because the Conservative Party would not have stood for it. Another left-winger wrote in a private letter to David Lloyd George: "I cannot feel that Labour did its proper job when the Government was formed." He meant that it had not bargained hard enough for itself, and had not insisted upon excluding the men whom Cripps had named. Lloyd George himself, Cripps wrote in his diary, thought "the war cabinet was a very bad one." In fact, the left would continue calling for Churchill to purge the "men of Munich" from his administration. He defied such demands at his peril, but he could not afford to alienate the "respectable" Conservatives who wanted those same men in.

So the new prime minister had to find a balance between critics on both sides of the political spectrum. Simultaneously, he had to contend with misjudgments, jealousies and generally poor relations among his Cabinet ministers. They had known one another, and had dealt with one another, for many years, not always happily or with respect. Beaverbrook once had written snidely of Halifax, who was devoutly religious, that "he always appears a sort of Jesus in long boots. The long boots are needed because he has had to wade through the mud. But he was not responsible for the mud, oh dear no! [He] could never make anything so dirty as mud, and the last thing he would think of would be to throw it at others." Halifax could sling mud, however, in his diary at any rate. He esteemed Beaverbrook no more than Beaverbrook esteemed him. "In these days one can't be too particular," he sniffed when Churchill brought the press magnate into the Cabinet. "Certainly we shall not have gained on intellect," he wrote disdainfully on May 11, when Churchill excluded Hoare, Simon and Wood and brought in Attlee and Greenwood. "Archie Sinclair at the Air Ministry seems to me a major disaster," Halifax wrote baldly of Churchill's old friend two days after his appointment.

Meanwhile, Chamberlain was advising Churchill against Labour's number two, Greenwood, warning that though he was "amiable and agreeable enough . . . he could [not] contribute much else." But then Greenwood, and indeed all Labour, did not think Chamberlain could contribute much, either. They accepted with great reluctance that he would serve in the War Cabinet at all, and rebelled outright when Churchill appointed him leader of the House of Commons. Churchill wrote dryly in his history of the war: "Mr. Attlee informed me that the Labour Party would not work easily under this arrangement." Churchill withdrew the offer, although he kept Chamberlain in the War Cabinet as Lord President, effectively in charge of domestic affairs. Of course, Labour did not care for that, either.

But then everyone, including Neville Chamberlain himself, knew already what most Labour people thought of him. What the Labour people made of each other was less well known. The famously reticent Attlee did not broadcast assessments of his colleagues in 1940. So far as we can discover, Greenwood did not publicly express his thoughts about them, either. It was common knowledge in the Labour Party, however, that Greenwood drank too much. He had gone on the wagon for a period in 1939, when he had taken over as party leader from Attlee, who was ill, but when Attlee returned, "he had a relapse and started drinking again." Hugh Dalton wrote condescendingly in his diary that Greenwood was "very slow and unimperative." Herbert Morrison thought he knew exactly what to make of Labour's deputy leader, and of the leader, too, for that matter: "Attlee and Greenwood," he muttered, when he learned that Churchill had appointed them, "these aren't the right people to represent the party." Churchill offered Morrison the Ministry of Supply, and after some hesitation he accepted. But he had hoped for a more prominent position in a different coalition altogether. Meanwhile, Ernest Bevin, whom Churchill appointed minister of labor, and who would soon come to play an indispensable role, had despised and distrusted Herbert Morrison, for a variety of reasons, for many years. Someone once remarked in Bevin's hearing that Morrison, an inveterate intriguer, was his own worst enemy. "Not while I'm alive he ain't," Bevin snapped in reply.

THIS WAS THE FRACTIOUS COLLECTION OF MEN CHURCHILL HAD CHOSEN to help him save the country. It would face many crises during the next five years, and none more grave than the one it faced at its inception. For even as the new Cabinet ministers sniped at one another in Whitehall, the German juggernaut hurtled forward on the continent. British and French military experts misapprehended it entirely, just as Erich von Manstein had predicted would happen. They rushed their forces to meet the German thrust west and south through Belgium. They believed Hitler was following the strategy employed by the Kaiser in 1914, the Schlieffen Plan, as Manstein had foretold. How else and where else could Hitler engage his enemies? They thought the Maginot Line ensured the safety of central and southern France. Hitler could not blast his way through that daunting chain of fortresses, and he could not get around it, French generals believed, because the hilly, heavily wooded Ardennes region to its north was impenetrable.

They were tragically mistaken. The main German attacking force, ten panzer divisions, flashed not through Belgium (the forces Hitler sent there, although formidable, were secondary), but through the forests in the Ardennes hills under a canopy of trees, invisible to Allied reconnaissance aircraft. They emerged north of the Maginot Line at Sedan, the weakest point in the French defense system, where they routed the French Second Army. Then, once the Germans were past Sedan and across the Meuse River, their tanks scythed through open French countryside, headed for the sea. They had no time even to collect prisoners, but contemptuously waved aside the French soldiers who had surrendered to them. Now the Allies, having dashed into Belgium to confront the enemy there, must also somehow turn to hold greater numbers on their southern flank. They could not cope with the enemy's swiftness, or with the audacity and originality of its war plan, or with the daring of its best generals. The Germans had encircled them, as Manstein had known would happen.

This was the appalling avalanche descending at lightning speed on the heads of the new prime minister, insecurely installed, and his government of ill-assorted colleagues. They met at the outset in the Cabinet Room of 10 Downing Street (in early September, when the Germans began bombing London, they would have to meet in an underground bunker): the five members of the War Cabinet, the three military service officers, the minister of information, the chiefs of staff, the head of the Foreign Office and a secretary. Churchill sat at the center of the table, Chamberlain to his immediate right, and then Attlee. Halifax faced Churchill across the table, with Greenwood to his immediate left. A pair of double columns stands at the entrance to the Cabinet Room at No. 10, and there is a fireplace behind the prime minister's seat, with a wall of floor-to-ceiling windows facing it. Three brass chandeliers hang from the ceiling high overhead. It is an imposing space; an imposing, if hardly collegial, team had gathered in it; and their world was collapsing about their ears.

The news from the continent grew worse every time they met. On May 17, the Foreign Office man, Cadogan, recorded in his diary that Churchill "sprang up and said he would go to France." And he did go there—six times during that short, awful period between his ascension to power and the French surrender on June 22. He tried desperately to stiffen his ally. Yet defeat continued to follow defeat, and retreat to follow retreat; a jointly planned counteroffensive proved chimerical, and it never was mounted. French and British defenders evacuated one French port after another as the Germans, having reached the sea, now swept north irresistibly. Finally, the British Army, a quarter of a million men, and another 130,000 Allied soldiers, mainly French, had fallen back almost to the Belgian border at Dunkirk, the sole French harbor not yet under German control. There, separated by the Germans from the bulk of the defeated and demoralized French Army, they stood at bay, backs to the sea, with enemy panzer divisions only fifteen miles to the south and closing in, and the Luftwaffe waiting only for Goering's signal to bomb them to smithereens and to strafe the survivors. Evacuation would be difficult, if not impossible, everyone knew; annihilation therefore seemed likely. Belgian resistance was about to collapse, so the Germans would attack from the north, too; France teetered upon the verge of complete surrender. Few believed that Britain could continue the fight against rampant Germany without her allies—and with the cream of her army about to be blown to bits at Dunkirk. Unsurprisingly, then, at this desperate juncture some began to whisper that the time had come to broach to Hitler the possibility of a compromise peace.

ACTUALLY, THE IDEA OF A COMPROMISE PEACE HAD OCCURRED TO A number of more or less influential men long before the fourth week of May 1940. It grew from a variety of sources, chief among them the bundle of motives that went into Chamberlain's prewar appeasement policies, most obviously visceral anticommunism and sympathy for German rage against the injustices of the Treaty of Versailles, coupled, in some quarters, with sympathy even for German anti-Semitism, although not for the totally brutal variety practiced later in the war. That bundle of motives remained strong among elements in the Conservative rank and file, if not among the Opposition parties or in the country as a whole. Other taproots were pacifism, which not all Britons thought inappropriate even in present circumstances; Communist opposition to a war in which they thought workers had no interest, since it pitted British imperialism against the German variety; and simple hardheaded calculation of Britain's chances in the current conflict. Thus compromise with Hitler might appeal to elements in both Houses of Parliament as well as to men and women belonging to all political parties. But it is fair to say that its most influential advocates belonged to the group still inclined to toast "the King over the Water." For a Conservative to broach a compromise peace during the fourth week of May 1940 was to resurrect the bitter argument between the Chamberlainites and Churchillians—before the latter had a chance to consolidate their position, and with Germany now at all their throats.

Still, Lord Halifax broached it. He knew the advocates of an early peace already. As foreign secretary, he had been receiving their petitions, publications and letters since the war began. Occasionally he met them in person. He responded always with unfailing courtesy, if also with skepticism. "The fundamental difficulty," he wrote in a typical response on March 12, 1940, to Lord Brocket, a far-right Conservative who wanted to contact Hitler to ascertain his peace terms, is "the complete lack of confidence that the world generally feels in any promises emanating from the present German Government." But with Germany triumphant everywhere, and with the added awful prospect of Italy jumping into the war to help her fascist ally deliver the coup de grace to prostrate France, without whom Britain's prospects seemed dim, Halifax reconsidered. He thought it might be possible to bargain with Mussolini, to keep him out of the conflict, and to turn conversations with him toward "the wider problems of Europe," as he carefully informed the Italian ambassador, Count Giuseppe Bastianini, on Saturday, May 25. It was an indirect invitation to Italy to disclose what price the Allies must pay to keep her from entering the fray, and to ascertain the price Hitler would demand to end it. Was Halifax also thinking that in broaching these matters he was preparing the way for his own elevation to the premiership? There is no evidence that this was his motivation, but perhaps the thought occurred.

Over three days, May 26 to 28, 1940, the War Cabinet met an unprecedented nine times. It was attempting simultaneously to cope with the emergency about to unfold at Dunkirk; the emergency of a pending Belgian surrender, which would leave the troops at Dunkirk even more dangerously exposed than previously; the emergency of French collapse, explained in person by French prime minister Paul Reynaud, who made a flying visit to London; the emergency of a likely German invasion of Britain; and, above all, although at this point everything was connected, the recommendation made by Halifax (and strongly supported by Reynaud, whose government had come independently to the same idea) that the best way to deal with all these emergencies at once was to bribe Mussolini to keep out, and, through him, to inquire what Hitler's peace terms would be. Whether to approach Mussolini or not truly represented the hinge of fate. Everything that followed would have been different if the Allies had sounded out the Italian leader, and if he then had approached Hitler, and if, as a result, Britain and Germany had ceased to fight in 1940 and begun discussing terms.

On May 25, however, that was what Halifax urged. "We had to face the fact," he warned, according to the War Cabinet minutes, "that it was not so much now a question of imposing a complete defeat upon Germany but of safeguarding the independence of our own Empire." From this it followed, as he put it the next day: "If we . . . found that we could obtain terms which did not postulate the destruction of our independence we should be foolish if we did not accept them." But Churchill realized immediately that Halifax risked too much. His retort was instantaneous: "Peace and security might be achieved under a German domination of Europe. That, we could never accept." Halifax's proposal would put Britain "on the slippery slope," he charged later. If Britain engaged in talks now, she would never start fighting again. Moreover, "there was no limit to the terms which Germany would impose upon us if she had her way." Thus the poles of debate: Halifax favored another Munich-style agreement with the Nazis, hoping to save the British Empire at the expense of continental Europe (and perhaps some British colonies in Africa); Churchill passionately opposed one, convinced that it would not save but rather doom his country, and thus all else.

The five men of the War Cabinet debated the future of Britain and the world over the course of the next few days. They debated, too, their own future as a body. Churchill had risen to power as the champion of a tougher, more dynamic and thorough war effort. He had appointed a War Cabinet to help him organize and fight it. If the War Cabinet voted now to open talks with the enemy, it would be contradicting its own raison d'être.

It would render meaningless the appointment of its leader. It would be reversing the result of the long fight to oust Neville Chamberlain.

But Churchill had no intention of opening talks. The "rogue elephant" preferred outright defeat to talking to the fascists now. He claimed at one point during the War Cabinet debate that "nations which went down fighting rose again, but those which surrendered tamely were finished." And at another: "If the worst came to the worst, it would not be a bad thing for this country to go down fighting for the other countries that had been overcome by the Nazi tyranny." This was precisely the sort of language and sentiment that "respectable" Tories wanted the two "wise old elephants" to restrain; it must never be allowed to shape policy. Halifax wrote in his diary that "it does drive me to despair when he works himself up into a passion of emotion when he ought to make his brain think and reason." The foreign secretary believed it would be a very bad thing if Britain went down fighting, however gloriously. He feared, though he could not say it plainly, that Churchill, romantic and unrealistic, would lead the country to defeat, ushering in German occupation and utter ruin. Halifax would save Britain from that if he could.

The Labour men staunchly supported Churchill. Attlee spoke little during the nine meetings, but his interventions suggest that he never thought Britain should quit fighting. He warned three times that, with France nearly defeated, Hitler would be coming for Britain. During the first meeting of the second day, he spoke explicitly about the measures his country should take when the invaders arrived: "We should have numerous highly mobile units, ready to act quickly on their own initiative. The Division was too big. Spain and Finland had provided examples of what could be done against tanks by brave and determined men." The Labour Party leader had seen combat and had been wounded during World War I; he had risen to the rank of major, and he spoke with authority. He reproached and rejected Halifax indirectly. Then, at the 4 P.M. meeting on May 28, he confronted the foreign secretary head on: "It was necessary to pay regard to public opinion in this country," the minutes say he warned. If the British people learned that their government had opened discussions with the fascists now, "they would sustain a severe shock. . . . There was a grave danger that . . . we should find it impossible to rally the morale of the people." Attlee meant that Britain would be finished if her people lost confidence in the government's determination, and that if it engaged in talks with Italy at this juncture, that was what would happen.

At the War Cabinet meetings of May 26 through 28, Greenwood spoke more pointedly than Attlee, not in the memorable phrases of Winston Churchill, for Churchill was unique, but still with notable clarity and bluntness. "M. Reynaud was too much inclined to hawk round appeals," he charged at one point. (This was an indirect quotation of the words Ernest Bevin had used in 1935 to destroy Labour's pacifist leader, George Lansbury. Greenwood was suggesting that the French premier likewise wanted peace at any price.) "This," he said, referring to the idea of appealing to Mussolini as an intermediary, "was another attempt to run out." When Attlee warned that Halifax risked undermining British morale, Greenwood backed him up: "So far as the industrial centres of the country were concerned, they would regard anything like weakening on the part of the Government as a disaster." He argued that France was finished anyway; the proposed talks would not save her, so there was no point entering into them. Like Churchill, he believed that Britain must not parlay now, but fight—without France, if necessary. "The line of resistance was certainly a gamble," the minutes say that Greenwood asserted, "but he did not feel that this was a time for ultimate capitulation." Halifax interjected heatedly: "Nothing in [my] suggestion could even remotely be described as ultimate capitulation." Perhaps not, but Greenwood, Attlee and Churchill agreed that it must lead there. That this exchange took place at all illustrates how profound the difference was between Halifax and his opponents, both in their understandings of the war and their views of what now was at stake.

It is a measure of the weight of Halifax's influence at this point in the Cabinet discussion that Churchill felt the need to strengthen his hand, despite the support offered him by the two Labour men. On the second day of the three-day debate—Monday, May 27—he brought in his recently appointed secretary of state for air, Archie Sinclair. Ostensibly, Sinclair attended because his Liberal Party must be represented in so important a discussion, even though it had only twenty-five seats in the House of Commons. But, really, Churchill wanted another opponent of appeasement participating in the argument. Sinclair played up admirably, ably backing his old friend. Yet even this was not enough. The decisive boost to Churchill's confidence was provided, probably, by a gathering of the entire Cabinet, excluding members of the War Cabinet, that took place between 6:15 and 7:00 on Tuesday evening, May 28.

To this group of Cabinet ministers Churchill explained the situation without any sugarcoating: British troops were cut off on the continent and surrounded, France was on the verge of defeat, and German invasion of England seemed likely. "It would be said . . . that what was now happening in Northern France would be the greatest British military defeat for many centuries." But he expressed an indomitable determination to keep on fighting. Let the Germans come: "We should mine all round our coast; our Navy was immensely strong; our air defenses were much more easily organized from this island than across the Channel; our supplies of food, oil, etc., were ample; we had good troops in this island, others were on the way by sea . . . and, as to aircraft, we were now more than making good our current losses and the Germans were not."

Churchill made another argument, perhaps more to the point, given the War Cabinet discussions: "It was idle to think that, if we tried to make peace now, we should get better terms from Germany than if we went on and fought it out. The Germans would demand our fleet—that would be called 'disarmament'—our naval bases, and much else. We should become a slave state." The Labour man Hugh Dalton, an old Etonian and Cambridge graduate whom Churchill had appointed minister of economic warfare, listened and understood pretty well what the prime minister had not said as well as what he had: "It is quite clear that whereas the 'Old Umbrella' [Chamberlain] wanted to run very early, Winston's bias is all the other way," he wrote afterward in his diary. Dalton thought the prime minister "quite magnificent." He scribbled in the margins of his diary a direct quotation from Churchill's extemporaneous remarks. Britain would never quit: "If this long island story of ours is to end at last, let it end only when each one of us lies choking in his own blood upon the ground." From the assemblage of Cabinet ministers, Conservative, Liberal and Labour alike, came not a single word of dissent, not one qualifying sentiment. Rather, Churchill wrote that when he had finished speaking, "quite a number seemed to jump up from the table and come running to my chair, shouting and patting me on the back." Dalton was one of those to make so uncharacteristic a gesture from a member of Britain's tightly buttoned, undemonstrative ruling class. But Dalton wrote in his diary that night of Winston Churchill: "He is a darling!"

The War Cabinet reconvened immediately after this extraordinary meeting. Churchill explained to its four members what he had just said, and to whom, and what had been the reaction, and also his great satisfaction at his reception. Halifax must have understood at this moment that there would be no British approach to Mussolini.

Yet there remained another "wise old elephant" in the room, Neville Chamberlain, and everything might have been different even now if he had come out strongly in support of the foreign minister. Instead, he waffled. His first reaction to Halifax's proposal was positive: he thought it could keep Italy out of the war and France in, and therefore, that it was worth pursuing. By the second day, however, he had concluded that France was all but out of the war already and that therefore the "approach to Signor Mussolini would serve no useful purpose." He agreed with a statement Churchill made during the three-day argument: Britain would have a stronger bargaining position after repulsing the imminent German attack than it did now, when Germany appeared and felt triumphant on all fronts. But where Churchill hoped that repelling an invasion would lead to ultimate victory in some presently unforeseeable way, Chamberlain merely thought it could lead to talks with the enemy on a more equal footing—and then to a compromise peace. As he put it on the third day of debate: "If . . . we could hold out we should be able to obtain terms which would not affect our independence." This put him at odds with Halifax, but not over fundamentals. "While . . . an approach to Italy was useless at the present time, it might be that we should take a different view in a short time, possibly even a week hence." In short, Chamberlain objected to the *timing* of Halifax's proposal, not to its ultimate aim. Dalton had been wrong that "the old umbrella" "wanted to run." He wanted to fight—but only for the time being. Like Halifax, Chamberlain hoped for a compromise peace; he just did not believe Britain could get an acceptable one yet.

If Chamberlain had supported the foreign secretary outright, it is hard to see how Churchill, unpopular as he was with the Tory rank and file, could have survived. He would have lost the Conservative element in his War Cabinet. If Chamberlain and Halifax had resigned on this issue—and at one point Halifax suggested that he might—then Churchill could not have continued as prime minister. What would have happened next is anybody's guess, certainly nothing good.

Chamberlain's assessment of the position in late May 1940 may have been more realistic than Churchill's. He knew that Britain alone could never defeat Germany. So did Halifax. Possibly Churchill knew it, too; he may already have been pinning hopes on American entry into the war. But he understood a greater truth, one that his two Conservative colleagues failed to grasp. You could never count upon a deal with Adolf Hitler, and it was indeed better to go on fighting him, even to the death, if necessary, than to try to negotiate one. Precisely because he was a rogue elephant who did not fear but rather understood war and gloried in battle, Winston Churchill comprehended more deeply than the wise old elephants did. Attlee and Greenwood understood, too, because, as Labour men who had seen their German colleagues persecuted, tormented, and murdered by the Nazis, they had long known it was impossible to bargain with Hitler.

Thus the War Cabinet led by Winston Churchill passed its first great test, but only by the skin of its teeth. And, although historians stress the improving relations between the prime minister and his Conservative colleagues in the War Cabinet at this point, in fact Churchill must have continued to harbor doubts, at least about his foreign secretary. Unexpected developments would allow him to act upon them before the year was out.

CHAPTER 4

The Months of Greatest Crisis

During the summer of 1940, Churchill's War Cabinet numbered five, including himself. Over the course of the war he occasionally shuffled its membership, but no more than eight men ever served in it at once, and a core of four or five served nearly from beginning to end, although only Clement Attlee served for the complete period. At the beginning, none of the War Cabinet members except for Halifax held departmental responsibilities, but this arrangement, which was meant to facilitate concentration on the conflict, lapsed as the war ground on—to the consternation of some government critics, as will become apparent.

Because Britain's survival depended upon national unity and solidarity, the War Cabinet had to reflect the most important currents moving the country. Churchill understood this and shaped the body accordingly. He maintained a balance between left and right, Labour and Conservative. Obviously, the spectrum of opinion within the larger Cabinet, and within the government as a whole, which contained dozens of senior and junior ministers, ranged even more broadly. At its best Churchill's coalition government brought together exceedingly right-wing Tories and strongly left-wing socialists, who united in a common purpose.

The War Cabinet functioned as Britain's supreme authority. It dealt, by design, only with the most important topics of the day—the major foreign, domestic and imperial issues raised by the war. A netherworld of carefully structured committees—capped by the Defense Committee, led by Churchill, and the Lord President's Committee, led first by

Chamberlain, but for most of the war by Sir John Anderson, and then by Attlee—ensured that lesser subjects never reached the War Cabinet, and that those which did had been carefully considered already, and side issues dealt with. At first the War Cabinet met daily, but gradually its schedule grew more erratic. At moments of crisis it met as often as necessary. It almost always met at least three times per week: at noon on Wednesdays and Thursdays, when only War Cabinet ministers attended, although other ministers might be invited for particular items; and at 5:30 P.M. on Mondays for the "Monday Parade," when "constant attenders" (such as the minister for air, Archie Sinclair) would be present, along with the chiefs of staff, who would provide military briefings, and other ministers whose particular expertise was relevant that day. Sometimes important representatives of the dominions who happened to be in London would attend the Monday meetings as well.

Churchill modeled his War Cabinet on David Lloyd George's War Cabinet of World War I, but with an important difference. Churchill served not only as prime minister, but also as minister of defense, and, as such, as chairman of the Defense Committee. In this way he maintained control over the war departments (army, air force and navy), the Chiefs of Staff (COS) and military affairs more generally in a manner that Lloyd George never had; moreover, unlike Lloyd George, Churchill never hesitated to contradict his military advisers—when, for example, a member of the COS was briefing the War Cabinet. But although Winston Churchill knew a lot about war, his generals knew more, and the problem was to get him to see that. He bubbled over with ideas, and once he fixed on one, he usually held to it stubbornly, even if it was no good. The diaries of General Alan Brooke, later field marshal and first Viscount Alanbrooke, whom Churchill appointed Chief of the Imperial General Staff (CIGS) in December 1941, are littered with references to his master's "frightful impatience," to his behaving like "a spoilt child" when contradicted, and so on. In Brooke, however, Churchill faced a man as iron-willed as himself, equally adroit and quick-witted, and moreover impossible to intimidate. General Brooke supported Churchill's plans when he thought they were good, acquiesced in the bad ones when he had to (or managed to improve them), and defied his chief when he thought it absolutely necessary. This did not ensure perfection, but rather something equally rare at this level, full and frank discussions. It makes an extraordinary story; surely Hitler's generals did not enjoy similar license.

Until the Germans started bombing London on a massive scale in September 1940, the War Cabinet met at 10 Downing Street. Thereafter it began to meet in a suite of underground rooms in the basement of the New Government Offices at the corner of Horse Guards Road and King Charles Street, just across from St. James's Park. The authorities had chosen the suite as a suitable temporary emergency government center in the spring of 1938, as war loomed. They arranged for it to be fortified and outfitted, including a Cabinet Room. When Churchill visited shortly after becoming prime minister, he said: "This is the room from which I'll direct the war."

Today the site is a museum called the Cabinet War Rooms. Tourists wander through and gain some notion of their claustrophobic atmosphere, for the ceilings are not high, many of the rooms are quite small, and, of course, there are no windows. Churchill broadcast some of his most famous speeches from one of those tiny, windowless rooms. Another room, larger, has a wall lined with a great map charting Allied progress in the war, or lack of it. During the period of the London Blitz, and then during 1944–1945, when Hitler launched the V-1 flying bombs and V-2 rockets, some War Cabinet ministers and important military personnel not only worked but also slept there, in monk-like cells. They could dine there, too. Churchill, however, usually returned to dine and sleep in a specially reinforced annex at 10 Downing Street, and Halifax continued to live at the Dorchester Hotel, as he had been doing ever since a German bomb demolished his house in Eaton Square. When the bombers came, he would take refuge with the other guests in the hotel's cellar.

Almost everyone in the War Cabinet stayed close by the prime minister's residence. When he finally stepped down from the top position, Chamberlain moved just across from No. 10 to No. 11 Downing Street, where he lived until he was overcome by the illness that would kill him and retreated to Highfield Park, his country house in Heckfield, Hampshire. Attlee, who owned a large house in Stanford, in outer northwest London, usually spent the night at No. 11. Anthony Eden often stayed at the War Office, or later, in rooms at the Foreign Office. Lord Beaverbrook stayed for a time at his own grand residence, Stornoway House, at Cleveland Row near the end of Pall Mall, a ten-minute walk away, and when the Germans bombed it, at the offices of one of his newspapers, the *Evening Standard*, just off Fleet Street. Ernest Bevin kept a flat slightly farther afield, at South Molton Street in Mayfair. Two Labour men who were to play important roles likewise arranged for close quarters: Herbert Morrison, with a home in southeast London, generally slept in the basement of the Home Office or at a nearby hotel; and Stafford Cripps bought a tiny flat in Whitehall Court between the War Office and Victoria Embankment. This proximity explains why it was possible for Churchill to summon his war ministers for consultations at a moment's notice, even late at night.

The War Cabinet ministers worked nearly cheek by jowl as well. The Admiralty and the War Office faced each other across Whitehall, the broad boulevard that connects Trafalgar Square to Parliament Square. Farther down Whitehall, Downing Street runs off at a right angle, with No. 10 on one side and the Foreign Office on the other. Behind the Foreign Office runs King Charles Street, and across this street lie the Treasury and New Government Offices—beneath which were the Cabinet War Rooms. The Houses of Parliament sit only a little farther on down Whitehall. It was practically a sealed workspace, although with German bombs periodically ripping through. One understands why Churchill relished getting off to Chequers, the country residence of British prime ministers, on weekends, and Eden to a country house in Sussex called Binderton, and Beaverbrook to his grand country house Cherkley Court near Leatherhead in Surrey. No doubt the others, too, sought country respites during weekends.

Once the War Cabinet ruled out talks with Mussolini that might have led to talks with Hitler, Britain had to confront the possibility of German invasion, a frightening prospect, as Britain had scarcely any trained, well-equipped troops at home. Most British soldiers remained in France; the vast majority squeezed into Dunkirk, just south of the Belgian border, where about a quarter million of them and about half that number of Allied troops faced millions of well-armed, well-led, highly motivated Germans closing in from almost every side. Britain had to have those soldiers home, facing the enemy when the time came. Could she mobilize the armada necessary to transport them from France? Could the RAF protect them from the Luftwaffe when the Tommies stood, as they would have to, with water up to their waists, in queues snaking from the beaches into the sea, waiting to board the ships that would take them back to England? Failure was unthinkable, not merely for the soldiers but also for Britain's chances in the war. Yet failure seemed highly likely, because at this stage the Germans held all the advantages.

The story of how Britain succeeded against all odds in saving the men is well known. She put together a flotilla that included, aside from vessels of the Royal Navy, fishing boats, "butterfly boats," tugboats, yachts, pleasure steamers, Thames lifeboats, "shrimping bawleys," even a London garbage scow (called a sludge hopper). These and others helped, in the face of withering incoming fire, to ferry the men out to the transport ships waiting to take them back to England. And the RAF did prevent the Luftwaffe from gaining control of the airspace above Dunkirk; otherwise, the escape that was taking place below could not have occurred at all. The rescue mission extended over the course of an excruciatingly dramatic week, May 27 to June 4, of which the first four days were most important.

The government called the desperate undertaking "Operation Dynamo," and those in the War Cabinet and the few others attending its meetings who knew what was going on were deeply pessimistic about it at first. "Position of B[ritish] E[xpeditionary] F[orce] quite awful, and I can see no hope for more than a tiny fraction of them now that Belgium has capitulated," the Foreign Office mandarin, Alex Cadogan, wrote in his diary at the end of the day the evacuation began, May 27. "Prospects of BEF look blacker than ever," he wrote gloomily on May 28. Twenty-four hours later he thought the situation had improved, but still that it was ultimately hopeless: "We have got off 40,000 men and [are] taking them, at present, at rate of 2,000 an hr. But the end will be awful." The Royal Navy and the RAF strained to quicken the process. Amazingly, and contrary to all predictions, they managed it. On Saturday, June 1, Cadogan recorded exultantly: "Evacuation marvelous. We have got off 224,000, including about 34,000 'Allies.'" In the end they got off approximately 225,000 British soldiers and about 111,000 Allies, many of them Frenchmen who returned immediately to their native land in the forlorn hope of helping to stem the German tide there.

Britons at the time, and many others since, have called Operation Dynamo a near miracle—although Churchill admitted that wars could not be won by evacuations, however miraculous. (Britain had just evacuated the finally successfully occupied Narvik in Norway.) In fact, many British and Allied soldiers thought the whole thing a chaotic affair on their side, one they had been lucky to survive. They knew that actually, despite the extraordinary variety of craft sent over from England, there had been an insufficient number to ferry all of them from shore to the big ships taking them home, and that they had needlessly lost men as a result; and that there had been too few officers to organize them while they waited on the beaches, which also led to losses; and that they had left behind nearly all of their equipment—tanks, guns, trucks, tractors, ammunition. Revealingly, British authorities forbade the returning soldiers to talk publicly about what had happened for fear of undermining morale on the home front.

Most German officers thought the evacuation hardly mattered. They deemed Britain's ignominious retreat from the mainland to be the capstone of their conquest of Europe. Now the island nation would either sue for peace or face the consequences. Hitler did not worry much about the quarter million men who had gotten away, although of course he was displeased with Hermann Goering for letting them do so. But he focused instead upon the many million more French and Allied soldiers in the process of surrendering to his armies, and then upon the treaty he would force their leaders to sign on June 22. Knowing nothing of the battle so recently fought in the War Cabinet, he appears to have thought it only a matter of time before Britain, too, approached him for peace terms. He would be generous, according to his lights, so long as Britain recognized his conquests thus far.

But Churchill had prevailed in the vital debate in the War Cabinet, and so Britain would not recognize Hitler's conquest of Europe. On the night of June 16, the prime minister appeared before Parliament to sound a warning: "The whole fury and might of the enemy must very soon be turned on us," he prophesied. "Hitler knows that he will have to break us in this island or lose the war. . . . Let us therefore brace ourselves to our duty and so bear ourselves that if the British Commonwealth and Empire lasts for a thousand years, men will still say, 'This was their finest hour.'" The War Cabinet agreed. So did most of the country. Among the populace, a grim determination was taking hold. Churchill gave it voice; they would give it flesh—and blood, and sweat, toil and tears. Those today who emphasize the strength of the Royal Navy and of the RAF, and who therefore discount the likelihood of German invasion, may have the kernel of the military situation, but not of the psychological one. The British people readied themselves. Their leaders did, too, writing to each other, and in their diaries, that the Germans would be coming soon. They said the same in Cabinet meetings and in public. From mid-June until at least mid-September 1940, a pending German invasion remained their primary preoccupation and worry.

THE NEARNESS OF DANGER LED BRITISH OFFICIALS TO SCOUT WILD possibilities, to imagine fantastic scenarios, and to arrive at hasty conclusions. On June 30, soon after the French surrender, Churchill received a suggestion: "If local authorities were instructed to dig trenches across all flat fields more than 400 yards long . . . it should be possible to reduce the danger from air-borne troops to negligible proportions." On this missive the prime minister scrawled: "Let this be done today." Then more sober heads prevailed. The commander of the Home Forces calculated "that the work would take 200,000 men . . . a year to complete." The minister of agriculture, Lord Moyne, voiced "his complaints about the great damage being done unnecessarily to agriculture throughout the country." Moreover, the trenches would deny not only German but also British pilots any place for emergency landings. On top of that Britain's farmers would be furious. Some trenches were dug, but by midsummer the project had ground to a halt.

Suppose, however, the Germans made landfall not from the sky but from the sea, and that they then advanced inland. What could stop them? Churchill wrote to Eden at the War Office about a mortar "which is capable of throwing an ordinary bottle—for example, a beer bottle—150 yards or more. These bottles could be filled with high explosive . . ." He had another idea: "The use of ordinary commercial vans or caravans, of which there are many thousands in the country, as mobile pill-boxes. They could be lined with bullet-proof plate, roughly bolted together and provided with proper slots, etc., for firing." It does not bear thinking on: Dad's Army hurling beer bottles at advancing German panzer divisions, and facing off with them in converted vans. Churchill's primary military assistant and liaison with the COS Committee, General Hastings Lionel "Pug" Ismay, thought that when the invaders came British soldiers ought to wear German uniforms to confuse them. It would have confused Britons, too. Churchill's son-in-law, the Conservative MP Duncan Sandys, recently back in Britain from active service in Norway, actually inquired what would happen if the Germans, when they got to Britain, "let loose prisoners, lunatics and wild animals?" The Home Defense Executive took this query seriously enough to respond: "The prisons point is covered. . . . As far as mental patients are concerned the difficulties of trying to forestall the German ruse would appear greater than those of coping with the ruse itself. . . . Nobody seems to have given specific consideration to the question of wild animals."

Churchill received an avalanche of advice on how to resist invasion. A Conservative MP who had recently returned from France reported that "hordes of refugees fleeing before the German advance contributed largely to her downfall." He advised, therefore, that orders be issued "tonight, not tomorrow or the day after . . . that in the event of a landing by air or sea all non-combatants except those engaged on the spot in essential services necessary for defense should remain in their houses or shelters and should in advance provide themselves with a week's food." "Better have martial law at once," another Conservative advised the prime minister. Secretary of State for India, Leo Amery, representing the views of the "watching committee," which had played so important a role in the downfall of Chamberlain and was still meeting, called for the establishment of "a Committee of Public Safety" (an odd term for a British Conservative to borrow from the Jacobins of revolutionary France) that would be empowered to take dictatorial measures. The people "should be made, under direct orders . . . to take part in the work of defense." From the left, too, came calls for "a People's War" in which all Britons would participate in one way or another. In fact, the national emergency was galvanizing the British left. Its belief in a government with compulsory powers to direct things for the common good finally resonated among all classes. The socialists in Churchill's War Cabinet would give increasing voice to this belief as the war ground on.

Some of Churchill's correspondents claimed expert knowledge on military matters. One predicted a German landing on the east coast; another on the southwest coast; a third that the Germans would not try to land at all to begin with, but focus instead upon "the destruction of the fleet." To such well-meaning advice Churchill usually responded promptly, politely and, if necessary, vaguely. To a Labour MP who wrote seeking assurance that London would never be declared a "free city" as Paris had been, he wrote: "You may rest assured that we should fight every street of London and its suburbs. It would devour an invading army. We hope however to drown the bulk of them in the salt sea." To an old appeaser who still thought compromise with Hitler was possible, he replied much more sharply: "I am ashamed of you for writing such a letter. I return it to you—to burn and forget."(But he retained a copy in his files.)

The prime minister's enthusiasm for unorthodox, even harebrained, schemes for the national defense may have dismayed his colleagues, but his determination to fight on, whatever the odds, undoubtedly inspired them. And of course the War Cabinet under his leadership proved capable of realistic assessment, hardheaded planning, and ruthless action, or else it would never have survived. It rejected the wild schemes, even when they came from Churchill, but it did not reject unorthodoxy out of hand. Any measure that strengthened the country's chances must be considered, no matter how far reaching, even if it interfered with property rights or cherished liberties—and even if it upset long-established hierarchies. For his part Churchill would do whatever he thought necessary to save the country. Pressure was coming from both left and right for the government to assume sweeping powers. The prime minister did not hesitate. On May 22 he deputed Attlee to broadcast on the BBC:

> Today on your behalf, Parliament has given to the Government full power to control all persons and property. There is no distinction between rich and poor, between worker and employer, between man and woman. . . . The Government now has the right to call upon any citizen to do the work that is most immediately required in the national interest. It has power to control any business, factory, mine, shop, or bank, and order it to be carried on in the way desired. It can take property of every kind. . . . The direction of persons to perform services will be under the Minister of Labour, Ernest Bevin.

Thus the trade-union titan advanced toward the center of the stage. Measures that "respectable" Tories might consider heretical did not frighten Ernest Bevin, and he positively enjoyed flattening the faint hearts among them who regarded his policies with apprehension.

BORN INTO POVERTY IN 1881, AS A YOUNG MAN ERNEST BEVIN HAD worked as a carter in the port of Bristol. There, eventually, he joined the old Dockers' Union. Untutored but formidable both intellectually and physically (he possessed a massive head and torso; someone once compared his hands to bunches of bananas), he ascended the union ladder rapidly, gaining (pre-1914) a local and then (post-1918) a national reputation not merely as a powerful advocate for the men, but also as a commanding figure on the anticommunist trade-union left. A sort of human bulldozer, in 1922 he brushed aside and pensioned off the union's aging founder and leader, Ben Tillett, to preside over the establishment of, and to become chief of, a new body into which the old Dockers' Union was merged, the

Transport and General Workers' Union. By the late 1930s this had become the largest labor union in Europe. He sought no political office; the "T&G" was his life. During the interwar period, including even during the Depression, he built it, and strengthened it, and successfully defended it against all comers, whether from the right or the left.

Churchill recognized Bevin's extraordinary capacities and would come to depend upon them. But it was Bevin's position as the country's outstanding trade unionist that made him indispensable. He dominated the T&G, and he played a leading role in the umbrella organization of which it was the largest affiliate, the Trade Union Congress (TUC), which he had led as president in 1937. This body represented nearly 5 million workers. Britain's survival now depended on their willingness to labor without stinting, and to suffer. Neville Chamberlain could never have mobilized them; they hated him and what they thought he stood for. But Winston Churchill could—if he had Ernest Bevin standing by his side.

Bevin was reluctant to stand there at first. He remembered Churchill's strident anti-unionism during the General Strike of 1926 and viewed him as an enemy of British workers. And Bevin had no ambition to play a role at Westminster. "Labour people argued with [him] for fifteen hours at Bournemouth trying to persuade him to take the job," remembered one who had attended the party's annual conference in early May, just as the Germans had launched their attack. And then, when he finally agreed to serve in the Cabinet, he initially hoped to do so without becoming a member of Parliament. Eventually, however, he accepted Churchill's invitation, and the Labour Party's offer of a safe seat in the House of Commons, not merely for the obvious patriotic reasons, but also because, as he put it to a special conference of trade-union leaders shortly after his appointment: "If our Movement and our class rise with all their energy now and save the people of this country from disaster, the country will always turn with confidence . . . to the people who saved them." And he knew what "the people who saved" the country would demand after the war had been won. Already the demand was growing in volume and assurance throughout the nation. It was what he wanted, too: "a new motive for industry, for life," as he explained to another audience, "the whole of your economy, finance, organization, science, everything . . . directed to give social security . . . to the community as a whole."

So Bevin stood with Churchill after all. Upon his appointment, he reckoned Britain's chances of survival at about 2½ percent. "I was faced with an enemy with 200 million [that is to say, most of Europe's working class] at his disposal," he recalled, "and I had to weigh up what it was possible to put against that." He had to act quickly, and he did. "I came in [to office] at 2.30 on the afternoon of Tuesday and on Wednesday at 11 o'clock I produced at least the outline of the basis of my scheme. Then at 3 o'clock the staff gathered round me and examined it in all its details, and by Friday night we had circulated it to the rest of the departments." He was exaggerating, of course—the scheme did not originate with him; he adapted earlier versions. But modesty never was his strong suit; organization was.

In May 1940 the British adult population totaled about 33 million, not including men soon to be drafted into the military. Bevin's job was to coordinate and to stimulate production on the home front in order to match or beat enemy output. But the workforce was hemorrhaging men, for the military had to have them. Bevin had to square this circle. His principles made it harder. He had the power to do so, but he did not relish dictating to workers. As their longtime advocate, he favored voluntary, not forced, labor—not only as a principle but because he thought it more effective in the long run. Moreover, he wanted to maintain trade-union practices wherever possible. Bevin recalled: "You had to work out a very careful time-table to see to it that you did not call your men up too quick; hold them in the factories and the workshops as long as you could. When you see the equipment coming out then put them in the Services in time to get the preliminary training so no time should be wasted." Quickly he realized that Britain's women must step forward—if possible, of their own free will and not as the result of conscription (but he had to conscript them in the end)—to replace the men in shops, mines, mills, factories, and on the land. "I had a headache over that for several weeks," Bevin would say later about conscripting female labor. "I was not so much frightened of the women as I wondered what the old man would say." He had to initiate training schemes. He had to prioritize and then, on the basis of priorities, he had to move both men and women into whatever industry needed them, wherever it was, and he had to keep their goodwill. Without that he knew there would be no increase in production and Britain would lose the war. "I tried to the best of my ability to build up the clubs, welfare, travelling arrangements, to harness the whole of the churches and all kinds of institutions, trade unions, co-operative societies and tried to make their life as congenial as I could under war conditions."

He had accepted a nearly impossible and yet crucial job, and he could not satisfy everyone. Critics on the right thought he favored the workers and their unions; critics on the left thought he tried for too long to maintain the voluntary principle—they wanted government direction for the common good now. Bevin adapted his plans when necessary and plowed forward. In the Cabinet, and then in the War Cabinet, to which Churchill promoted him in October 1940, he overshadowed the self-effacing Attlee and the "unimperative" Greenwood among the Labour contingent, even though he never aspired to replace them as party leaders (he represented Wandsworth Central now, but he was never "a House of Commons man"). For that matter, he overshadowed not merely his Labour colleagues but most Conservatives, too.

One Conservative colleague, however, he did not overshadow. Bevin knew that the Germans could not invade unless they first gained mastery of the skies above the British coastline, and if Britain kept up airplane production, then the RAF probably could keep the Germans away. Bevin thought it would be his job to allocate and direct the laborers building and repairing airplanes. For that, however, Churchill turned to his old friend Lord Beaverbrook, proprietor of the *Daily Express*, the *Sunday Express*, the London *Evening Standard* and two newspapers in Scotland, appointing him chief of the recently created Ministry of Aircraft Production (MAP) on May 14, and promoting him to the War Cabinet on August 2, even before he brought in Bevin. Beaverbrook did not want the labor minister encroaching on his turf. He intended to control manpower where the aircraft industry was concerned. Bevin had to accept it, but he did not like it. Relations between the two men never prospered.

To some, Beaverbrook seemed an unlikely appointment. During the run-up to World War II, he had supported Chamberlain and opposed Churchill. He believed in Britain's splendid isolation. He disliked Chamberlain's grudging guarantee of Poland after the betrayal of Czechoslovakia at Munich in October 1938 because he did not believe his country could or would effectively defend Poland from Germany. Events proved him right; Britain and France did little for Poland when Germany attacked her. From the beginning of hostilities right up until April 1940, Beaverbrook favored arranging a compromise peace with Germany. When Hitler shattered the phony war by striking westward, however, the press lord realized that his country stood on the edge of a frightful abyss. Britain now must fight for her life. For that she needed a prime minister who understood war. Like many others, Beaverbrook turned away from Neville Chamberlain in May 1940.

The press lord had no experience of executive power in government and not much of the House of Commons when Churchill called. He had served as an MP only from 1910 to 1916, and then took a peerage in order to accommodate Lloyd George, whose rise to power in the middle year of World War I he facilitated by helping him establish lines of communication with Andrew Bonar Law, leader of the Conservative Party. The Canadian-born Beaverbrook, who was friendly with both men, not only brought the two together but also put his country house at their disposal. During the interwar era, Beaverbrook did not play a prominent role in the House of Lords, but rather built his great press empire. He knew everybody. Still, the king objected when Churchill proposed appointing him head of the MAP on May 14, 1940. George VI claimed that "the Canadians do not appreciate him." More likely, the king worried about Beaverbrook's inexperience of government office. Or perhaps Beaverbrook seemed to him the kind of dissolute, brash and extravagant "gangster" that almost everyone among the "respectable tendency" of Tories hated and feared. The fact that Beaverbrook had supported the appeasers so recently had nothing to do with it—George VI had supported the appeasers, too.

Churchill, however, insisted. He had known Lord Beaverbrook for three decades, and he felt comfortable with him, although their friendship had waxed and waned. It had waned most recently in April 1938, when Beaverbrook had terminated Churchill's regular column in the *Evening Standard* for attacking Chamberlain and appeasement. During the waxing phases, however, the two had gossiped and schemed, drank, smoked cigars and gambled at cards, to the dismay of Mrs. Churchill, who never liked or trusted the Canadian. FDR's roving ambassador Averell Harriman once observed that Beaverbrook understood that Churchill's "card-sense was almost nonexistent." But Beaverbrook also understood that Churchill admired him because he could do things the prime minister could not, and that winning at cards was one of them. The press lord never let his friend off easy. In May 1943, when he and Churchill and Harriman crossed the Atlantic on the *Queen Mary*, Harriman and Beaverbrook made a pact not to take advantage of Churchill when they sat at the card table. Beaverbrook promptly broke the pact in order to maintain the image Churchill had of him. Harriman wrote: "Winning from the PM at poker is an essential part of their relationship."

Churchill had no long history with any of his other associates, and all his early close friends in the political world had died. Among his Cabinet colleagues, only Beaverbrook had served with him in Lloyd George's government (as minister of information) during World War I. When Churchill appointed Beaverbrook, he chose to ignore their recent disagreement about appeasement but to remember their long-standing connection, and to look to him for friendship as well as for assistance. In May 1940, in his hour of greatest need, he also made him his confidant. The day Churchill became prime minister, the two lunched together and dined together. The next day, they lunched together again; the day after that they conferred all afternoon, and Beaverbrook stayed for dinner. Beaverbrook was helping Churchill to choose his first government.

At the moment of supreme crisis, with France on the verge of collapse, Churchill traveled to Tours on June 13 for what proved to be his final wartime meeting with French president Paul Reynaud. He brought Beaverbrook with him ("In trouble he is always buoyant," Churchill would write later). His old friend played a crucial role. The British contingent of eight arrived to dismal weather, a dismal scene, dismal greeting and lunch, and then dismal news: unless America immediately entered the war, France would bow out. Churchill and his colleagues withdrew to the back garden to discuss the situation. At first, pacing between puddles and under dripping branches, they dithered, but "suddenly Beaverbrook spoke." General Sir Edward Spears, Churchill's liaison officer with the French government, remembered: "His dynamism was immediately felt. 'There is nothing to do but to repeat what you have already said, Winston. Telegraph to Roosevelt and await the answer. Tell Reynaud that we have nothing to say or discuss until Roosevelt's answer is received. Don't commit yourself to anything. We shall gain a little time and see how these Frenchmen sort themselves out. We are doing no good here. In fact listening to these declarations of Reynaud's only does harm. Let's get along home.'"

Churchill readily accepted Beaverbrook's, practical, insightful advice. This moment in the muddy garden behind the prefecture office in Tours distills another aspect of their relationship: Churchill may have been the patron, but he relied upon the recipient of his patronage for counsel.

"URGENCY WAS IN HIS TEMPERAMENT," WROTE A. J. P. TAYLOR, THE GREAT historian, who knew Beaverbrook personally and loved him. Beaverbrook despised committee work, hidebound tradition, red tape and, above all, the time that he judged to be wasted talking with ignoramuses. One morning a couple of months into his tenure in office, a newspaperman arrived by invitation to interview him just as a senior official from the Air Ministry was leaving. "It is the curse of my life," Beaverbrook confided to the journalist as soon as the official had departed, "having to talk to these Air Marshals for an hour or two hours every morning. . . . I can't bear having to sit down and listen to them talking." He wanted action, not palaver. He put three signs above his desk that encapsulated his outlook. They read: "Committees take the punch out of war"; "Organization is the enemy of improvisation"; and "All things in war are simple, but the simple is always difficult."

During the summer of 1940, a sense of urgency was what Britain needed. Her survival depended first of all upon increased and faster production of aircraft, mainly fighters to defend British airspace—not bombers, although the "air marshals" favored the latter, believing (incorrectly) that British capacity to bomb German cities would deter the Germans from bombing Britain. Beaverbrook faced the issue as Churchill hoped he would: squarely, imaginatively, practically and effectively, focused always upon the immediate task at hand, which to him meant the production of fighter airplanes. It occurred to him that he could cannibalize parts from three or four downed aircraft, including enemy aircraft, to make one serviceable machine. The number of repairs swiftly mounted; patched-up fighters would play a crucial role in the Battle of Britain. By its end England had as many cannibalized fighters as fighters built from scratch.

Beaverbrook smashed all the old bottlenecks and obstacles to rapid production. For example, he directed his agents to take spare parts from the airfields when needed, much to the dismay of the Air Ministry, which was hoarding them. Beaverbrook answered: "Better a stringency in spares and a bountiful supply of aircraft than a surplus of spares and a shortage of aircraft." So effective was he during his period of dictatorship (for that is what it was) over the MAP that the problem became not to find sufficient fighters to defend Britain, but to train sufficient pilots to fly them.

He drove his ministry, and all the men who worked directly or even indirectly for it, to the edge of endurance and sometimes over it. Upon appointment he insisted that production in aircraft factories be carried on night and day, seven days a week, for the next month. Then he extended this exhausting schedule indefinitely. He would telephone subordinates at midnight and in the small hours of the morning to demand reports or to exhort them to additional effort. There is a story, apparently not apocryphal, about a Nottingham lace maker whose six-man shop had been converted to produce spare parts for aircraft. His wife roused him at two o'clock one morning. Lord Beaverbrook was on the line from London to congratulate him on his rate of production. But he could also rant on the telephone, and many of his subordinates came to dread it when he rang. One, who was on a tour of inspection, found his airplane had been grounded. Enemy aircraft were about to bomb the area. "Oh, my God, is that all?" the man cried in relief. "I thought it was a telephone call from Lord Beaverbrook."

The figures tell the tale of Beaverbrook's success: manufacture of all types of aircraft doubled between February and September 1940, and for fighter planes it quadrupled. The total output of aircraft for 1940 was twice that of Germany's. It is true that production had begun to rise under the previous minister, Kingsley Wood, so Beaverbrook should not get all the credit, but Wood did not have to deal with German bombing when he was chief of MAP, as Beaverbrook did. Under Beaverbrook, production made good all losses to the German attackers and more.

The figures do not tell how difficult many of his colleagues found this mercurial, high-octane personality. They objected not only to his temperament. Sometimes his judgment failed, and they knew it. For example, twelve-hour days and seven-day workweeks might produce good results over the short term; over the long term they could not be sustained. Beaverbrook insisted that they should be continued, however. At Cabinet meetings he rowed with the chief of the despised "air marshals," Archie Sinclair, the minister for air. Sinclair agreed with his generals that Britain needed bombers, not fighters; and that certain airplanes should be sent to Canada or South Africa, where pilots could train in them. Beaverbrook argued against both ideas, and because he determined how many aircraft were built, where they were built, and what type were built, he always won. During his stint at the MAP, relations with the Air Ministry sank to an all-time low.

Beaverbrook's relations with Bevin began low and continued to drop. The great trade-union leader was suspicious of the owner of the Conservative, imperialist *Express* newspapers even before Beaverbrook entered the government. Now, on top of that, he resented Beaverbrook's control of manpower in the realm of aircraft production and repair. Moreover, he could never accept the labor speedup, the end to trade-union practices, and the ruthless requisitioning of men that Beaverbrook demanded. Perforce the two men had to sit at the same table and to agree to government policies if the War Cabinet was to function. Beaverbrook developed a pronounced respect for his great antagonist, recognizing him as "an immense figure in the country" and "a man of great ability and force of character." Bevin never reciprocated. When the minister for air production tried to insist that workers stay at their jobs even during air raids, the minister for labour threatened to sue his fellow Cabinet minister.

Churchill always had to work at keeping Beaverbrook on board, as he was continually threatening to resign, and had to soothe Bevin, whose distrust of the newspaper magnate never diminished. But he saw them as the two big beasts of his government. "Sir Winston told me several times" his private secretary recalled in 1964, "that if Britain had been invaded in 1940 and we had had to fall back north of the Thames, he would have ruled Britain with a triumvirate of himself, Beaverbrook and Ernest Bevin." The fact is, however, that Beaverbrook proved to be the man for the moment, not for the hour. When the moment passed, when the danger of imminent German invasion lapsed, and when he really could no longer stand the paperwork and committee work any longer, he resigned. Churchill was not done with him, however, and would bring him back into the War Cabinet in a different position later in the war. Then the battles recommenced.

ALL THROUGH THAT SUMMER OF 1940 ONE COULD PRACTICALLY HEAR the motors of the German Luftwaffe revving up, the clanking of the panzer divisions, and the tramp of many millions of goose-stepping soldiers just across the English Channel. Should Hitler send them to invade, the British Home Forces had in early June 1940 only 54 2-pounder antitank guns, 420 field guns with 200 rounds of ammunition apiece, 613 medium and heavy guns with 150 rounds for each, 105 medium and heavy tanks, 395 light tanks, 2,300 Bren light machine guns and 70,000 rifles. Taken altogether it represented a pittance, hardly enough to defend an entire country. At the War Office, the elegant, capable, cautious, newly appointed Anthony Eden "had to think hard," he told a journalist, "whether he dare move, say, an anti-tank gun from one district to another." Memories of the material left on the beaches of Dunkirk haunted him. He hadn't enough soldiers either: only a single trained and equipped brigade to defend all of Britain. He told Lord Halifax that he needed at least a month to pull things together. If the Germans came sooner, the country would likely fall. Churchill made things more difficult for him with a characteristically romantic and stubborn gesture that was also an egregious mistake: the Dunkirk evacuation successfully completed, he sent two divisions of British and Canadian troops back to France to take part in a last-ditch defense. Eden ground his teeth. He wrote to Churchill that in Kent, Sussex and Surrey, which he had just visited, "a holding battalion, a battalion of stevedores, the Hythe Musketry School, an infantry training center and an Officer Training Corps of the R.A.S.C. [Royal Army Service Corps, concerned with logistical matters and not with combat] all form part of the active defense system by night and by day."

By July, the BEF had returned home and Eden felt a little better. He had a first line deployed in the coastal towns, and reinforcements further inland that could move swiftly to trouble spots. He was placing big guns all along the eastern and southern coasts. When a reporter asked him about German invasion, Eden replied that the General Staff still believed "the attempt was coming." He thought the RAF and the Royal Navy could deal with it before the Germans touched British soil. But he did not say what would happen if they could not.

In late June the chiefs of staff warned the War Cabinet that they "could not fix a date before which invasion was unlikely." In other words, it could come any day. Evacuation, especially along the East Anglian and Kentish coasts, should proceed "forthwith." There had already been "a considerable voluntary exodus" from these towns. Now it should become mandatory. The War Cabinet then approved in principle that the evacuation of "useless mouths" from nineteen towns between Sheringham and Folkestone on the east coast should commence the following Monday, July 1. The government would provide railway fare for those who needed it, and a billeting allowance for those who took them in. If invasion took place before that date, however, then people should "Stay Put," because, as an official pamphlet, entitled "If the Invader Comes," went on to explain, "if you run away . . . you will be machine-gunned from the air as were civilians in Holland and Belgium, and you will also block the roads by which our own armies will advance to turn the Germans out."

The War Cabinet also had to decide on a host of related matters if the invader really came. For example, what would be the duties of British police officers and firefighters during a German occupation? At a War Cabinet on the first of July, Attlee, Halifax, and the home secretary, Sir

John Anderson, expressed different views. Halifax thought the government should instruct British police to "act on their own discretion" if the Germans arrived. Anderson thought they should be told not to flee but rather "to stay, to set a good example." This doctrine had been "laid down for years." Attlee disagreed: "Don't like our people put under orders of invader. That's the enemy's job to keep order." On this occasion the Labour man carried the day. The meeting concluded: "Can't be responsible for order that [police and firemen] should act under the orders of the enemy."

Certainly Churchill did not discount the likelihood of German invasion at this point. On June 29, 1940, Halifax learned that the Polish ambassador in Ankara, Turkey, had been told by a reliable source that Germany would invade England by sea "on or about July 8." The next day Churchill warned top naval officers to reinforce the Harwich-Dover stretch of coast, predicting that if they came, "the enemy would go for London and attempt a knock-out blow." He thought, and "it was generally agreed, that 5th July was a likely date for the enemy to move." On July 3 the prime minister warned the War Cabinet that "an attempt to invade this country might be imminent"; to forestall it the RAF should be directed to bomb German ports rather than oil refineries, airports and marshaling yards.

In an undated memo to "Pug" Ismay, his chief staff officer, and to the COS that he must have written at about this time, Churchill elaborated plans for frustrating the invasion. "Our first line of defense . . . must be as ever the enemy's ports," he began. These should be watched and bombed when concentrations of carrying vessels were observed. "Our second line of defense is the vigilant patrolling of the sea to intercept any invading expedition, and to destroy it in transit." He wanted more destroyers on patrol. "Our third line is the counter-attack upon the enemy when he makes any land fall. . . . The enemy [is] at his weakest moment . . . not, as is sometimes suggested, when actually getting out of his boats, but when sprawled upon the shore with his communications cut and his supplies running short." Churchill doubted there would be invasion from the west; the enemy could too easily be intercepted at sea. Likewise, although for different reasons, from the north: "The enemy, who is now crouched, would then be sprawled. His advance would lie in difficult and sparsely inhabited country. He could be contained until sufficient forces were brought to bear, and his communications immediately cut from the sea." This memo shows Churchill in a truer and more flattering light than the one suggesting that motor vans be outfitted to face tanks, and that a mortar be designed to fling beer bottles filled with explosives at them. Yet they derive from the same desperate period.

July 5 came and went—and no Germans. Cadogan at the Foreign Office predicted in his diary that D-day would be July 8, as the Turks had warned Halifax. That day, too, passed in relative quiet. Now Churchill did begin to think the danger had peaked and might be beginning to ebb, at least for the time being. He wrote: "I find it very difficult to visualize the kind of invasion all along the coast by troops carried in small craft and even in boats." No reports had come in of such a flotilla being amassed, and anyway, "it would be a most hazardous and even suicidal operation to commit a large army to the accidents of the sea in the teeth of our very numerous armed patrolling forces." On July 9 he explained to the War Cabinet: "All round the coasts were some hundreds of armed trawlers, motor-torpedo boats and mine-sweepers which could take part in the melee if the invasion were attempted. In addition the Admiralty had with great speed erected around the coast some 150 six-inch guns, in emplacements which would protect them from attacks by dive-bombers. These guns were manned by some 7,000 Naval ratings and marines. A number of land torpedo tubes had been fixed. Another deterrent would be the minefield in the Straits of Dover."

With each succeeding day, Britain's capacity to cope with an invasion increased, and so did Churchill's confidence. He developed a new plan: mines should be sown in the waters behind the invader if he dared come, both to cut off his escape and to prohibit his reinforcement by sea.

As late as mid-September, Churchill still thought it possible, if less likely than before, that the Germans might invade. Nevertheless, as early as mid-July he was beginning to consider how to carry the fight to the continent. He pressed Anthony Eden on the subject. On July 17 Eden gave him a memo looking forward to "the knock out stage" when the three arms of the British military (air, land and sea) would combine to bring total war to the mainland. "Up till now," however, Eden cautioned his eager chief, we have remained at "the reconnaissance and experimental stage of small coastal raids." Churchill did not mind. He was thinking not about the clash of great armies, which of course was impossible at present, but about more subtle methods of undermining German rule in Europe. On July 22 the War Cabinet approved his choice of Hugh Dalton, who was already minister of economic warfare, to lead a Special Operations Executive tasked to conduct espionage and sabotage in the occupied countries. Dalton triumphantly recorded in his diary the prime minister's charge to him on the day of his appointment: "And now . . . go and set Europe ablaze." That was much more Churchill's style. By August 5 he had the War Cabinet discussing not whether, but how best, literally, to "set ablaze" German crops and forests and fields with "incendiary wafers" and 15 million "pellets." For forests, the prime minister favored a method "whereby parachutes were caught up in the branches of the trees, and subsequently ignited." Fifteen days later, with Beaverbrook and Sinclair locked in argument over whether to focus on production of fighter aircraft or bombers, Churchill intervened: "Fighters is [*sic*] salvation," the secretary scribbled furiously in pencil on lined yellow paper, trying to keep up as the prime minister spoke. "Bomber offers means of victory."

IT IS WORTH REMARKING THAT DURING THIS DANGEROUS PERIOD, WHILE Churchill was exhorting every citizen to man the battle stations, Halifax appears still to have been pining for negotiation. He continued to believe that Britain could successfully bargain with Hitler to keep most of Britain's empire, and thus her independence as a great power; he feared that continued war between Germany and Britain would benefit Communist Russia, and that Britain was likely to lose the war in the end anyway. If he could save his country from German occupation, was it not his duty to do so?

The evidence, however, is indirect. Cadogan wrote in his diary on July 2 about the pope "making tentative half-baked suggestions for agreement. Silly old H[alifax] evidently hankering after them." On that same day, Lloyd George learned from his principal private secretary that "the Pope is working furiously for peace. In this connection Halifax who is an Anglo-Catholic and [Joseph] Kennedy [the American ambassador] who is a Roman Catholic [and who thought Britain would lose the war], are believed to be closely associated, working for the same object." Some days earlier, Halifax's undersecretary at the Foreign Office, R. A. Butler—the man who toasted the "King over the Water" on the day that Churchill ascended to the position of prime minister, and who had termed him "a half-breed American"—informed the Swedish minister in London that "no opportunity for reaching compromise would be neglected if the possibility were offered on reasonable conditions."As late as August 1 Butler remained in contact with a small peace party in the House of Commons.

It is unlikely that he would have dared speak to the Swedish minister as he did, or would have maintained the connection with the parliamentary advocates of a negotiated settlement, if he thought his master disapproved.

It is equally unlikely that Churchill, who inevitably found out about Butler's inclinations, and who probably knew about Halifax's "hankering" as well, would ignore them. Butler posed no direct threat to his position, and moreover, as Churchill admitted, he valued the younger man's "delicate manner of answering parliamentary questions without giving anything away." For him mild chastisement would suffice. But Halifax remained a rival, an alternate prime minister. Certainly by now, if not before, Churchill was contemplating ways and means of getting rid of him.

THUS PASSED THE INCREDIBLE SUMMER OF 1940. THE GERMANS DID NOT come, although it still appeared that they might any day. Churchill and his government had established a toehold, but that was all it was. They knew it—and the storm was still about to break.

CHAPTER 5

Shaping the War Cabinet

THE WAR CABINET MET IN THE CABINET ROOM AT 10 DOWNING STREET when it was safe to do so, or in the underground bunker when it was not, reporting, discussing, arguing and usually coming to agreement. Secretaries sat with them, scribbling furiously in order to provide a record, as the five men, or eight, or sometimes more, attempted to fashion a strategy to save their country. They had much to deal with—more than the prospect of imminent invasion. On the far horizon they confronted an increasingly aggressive Japan, unrest in India, a breakdown in relations between King Farouk and the British ambassador in Egypt. On the European front they faced Spanish hostility that might lead to war, Irish hostility that seemed only slightly less dangerous, delicate relations with Turkey, German control of Romanian oilfields. And they had to reckon with the grim possibility that defeated France might now turn positively pro-German.

In particular, the War Cabinet worried about the French Navy. If Britain's erstwhile ally ceded its control to Germany, it would jeopardize British naval supremacy, not only in the Mediterranean but in the Atlantic. During meetings held on July 1, 3, 4 and 5, just as it was making the necessary decisions for defending against invasion, the War Cabinet also authorized and reviewed some hard decisions regarding the French fleet. At dawn on July 3, British authorities seized more than two hundred French ships—including two battleships, four light cruisers, eight destroyers and several submarines—in British waters and ports. At the far end of the Mediterranean they blockaded the port of Alexandria, bottling up a French squadron that included a battleship and four cruisers, effectively erasing the possibility that Germany could take them over. And at Mers-el-Kébir near Oran, an Algerian port, when the French refused to cooperate, British ships opened fire, destroying several vessels and killing 1,297 French sailors, but failing to prevent the escape of one French battleship and two destroyers.

As a demonstration of Britain's determination to take any steps necessary for self-preservation no matter how ruthless (or in this case odious, for at Mers-el-Kébir the French ships could not defend themselves), "Operation Catapult" served its purpose. Few now doubted that Britain would fight on. Hitler took notice. Despite what the War Cabinet believed, he had not yet authorized the final stage of planning for the invasion of his sole remaining enemy. Now, reluctantly accepting that Britain would not cave in as France had, he issued "Directive No. 16 for Preparations of a Landing Operation against England." But "Operation Sea Lion," as it is better known, would only go forward if Hermann Goering's Luftwaffe gained mastery of British skies. In mid-August 1940 Goering unleashed his men and their machines. The Battle of Britain commenced.

In the beginning, the Luftwaffe focused on British airfields, first along the coast, then inland. But Germany had not gained mastery of British airspace when, on Saturday, September 7, the Germans shifted to bombing towns and cities. Eventually Goering concluded that daylight raiding was too dangerous and turned to night bombing instead, but on that first day he sent more than 350 bombers escorted by 600 fighters, aiming at London first of all. "I saw the planes coming over and had mistaken them for flocks of pigeons," one East Ender recalled innocently, and rather endearingly. But these pigeons wreaked devastation: London's "dockland," larder of the nation, exploded in a hurricane of fire. So did the streets and homes of many East Londoners who lived nearby.

The next morning Churchill toured the East End. Aides brought him to a shelter that had suffered a direct hit. What he saw moved him to tears. An old woman said in wonderment: "You see, he really cares, he's crying." The Germans returned that afternoon and night to deliver further destruction. On Monday, September 9, Sir John Anderson, the home secretary, reported the results to the War Cabinet. One of the secretaries, Lawrence Burgis, took notes, employing idiosyncratic and nearly illegible shorthand. The notes were meant to provide the basis for the official minutes and then to be burned, but sometimes Burgis kept his notes against all rules, and to the benefit of future historians (although deciphering them is a great chore).

Anderson reported to the War Cabinet, as Burgis scrawled hastily in his execrable and coded handwriting, that damage had been "widespread," especially in the East End of London. "Two hundred fires required London Fire Brigade action. . . . Public utilities damaged. . . . Fulham Power Station . . . delayed action bomb. Hits on hospitals . . . incendiary bomb in roof." But then Churchill reported on his own trip to the district. "Spirit of people marvelous," he reassured the War Cabinet. Its inhabitants could "stand up to this & a good deal more. . . . King going round this A.M. Damage put right quickly—mains, gas, water, electricity."

Everyone knew that the bombing was meant to be the prelude to invasion. Burgis recorded Churchill musing at one point that same day: "If invasion comes off tonight or tomorrow . . ." The prime minister trailed off. Later he said that, whether the Germans came or not that day or the next, "100,000 [residents] south of Thames," in addition to the thousands who had already left their homes, should be moved within the next twenty-four hours. "Non-compulsory but strongly urged," he directed.

Two days later the War Cabinet met to discuss invasion again. Burgis's account, almost verbatim (but which I translate from his coded abbreviations, correcting his punctuation) provides a sense of how, at this stage, War Cabinet members managed to work together quite effectively, whatever their private opinions of one another.

EDEN: Saw Commander in Chief this morning.

1: Said extension of German shipping down coast extreme. . . .

2: Wants . . . 36 Bofors guns [to shoot at low-flying attacking German aircraft] . . .

3: [Bigger] Guns on coast given to his command. . . . [M]ove 2 or 3 into SE area.

Invasion anywhere else not the same thing . . .

ATTLEE: Troops in reserve to go to south coast.

EDEN: Commander in Chief had in mind: keep tank . . . [and] troops in Maidstone area for action in Dungeness.

CHURCHILL: [HMS] *Rodney* stay at Rosyth.

ALEXANDER: Expected this . . . in face of size of attack have matter in hand.

But also, in the last analysis, Churchill now actually doubted that Hitler would launch the invasion. Burgis recorded him saying at the end of this meeting: "Unless he can beat fighters of RAF then he will console himself with atrocities on our civil population & Egypt." This was a fair prediction.

IT WOULD BE WRONG TO THINK THAT EVEN IN THIS DIRE SITUATION rivalries and jealousies in the British War Cabinet simply disappeared. Its members worked together because they had to if Britain was to survive, but never without difficulties. On August 7 Halifax repeated an old line to Eden: he did not trust "Winston's judgment." A few days later Beaverbrook announced to startled dinner guests that he judged "there were three ministers who were rotten—Greenwood, Sinclair and Duff Cooper [minister of information]." On the 19th, Churchill, dining with Eden, likewise expressed anxiety about Greenwood—and about Attlee as well. On the 21st he complained that three men carried the entire government on their shoulders: himself, Beaverbrook and Eden (the latter not even a member of the War Cabinet yet—and why no mention of Bevin?). On September 6 Beaverbrook warned the prime minister that Labour was "preparing to unhorse the government as soon as it appeared to be tired." In fact Churchill was tired already and confided to Eden that he "had never felt so lonely." Months later he told the younger man that "during the summer I would wake with dread in my heart."

That was in private, and spoken to one whom he would designate his successor, and who would, moreover, later marry his niece. In public the prime minister exuded vitality and confidence, as contemporary diaries and letters attest. References to his good humor, his scintillating conversation and his growing mastery of the House of Commons—including even its Tory skeptic members—have become a staple of the literature. This, actually, was the period when Churchill solidified his hold over his colleagues in the government and in Parliament and over the nation as a whole.

Unforeseen and unpredictable developments aided this process. At the beginning of June, the press had carried stories speculating about Neville Chamberlain's health. "He has not been too good lately," David Lloyd George's principal private secretary observed on June 3. Chamberlain suffered from abdominal pain that only grew worse as the summer lengthened. "Neville has had to go and have an operation to his inside,"

Halifax reported on July 30 to one of his correspondents. That procedure was exploratory. A second operation revealed terminal colon cancer. In late August Beaverbrook told a journalist that Chamberlain would never return to government, inadvertently revealing as much about himself as about his ailing colleague, of whom he spoke with great callousness: "He's done, he's finished, you need not reckon with him anymore as a force in politics—he's got cancer of the bowels—he's finished—you can wipe him out in politics!"

Churchill had the same information as Beaverbrook, but responded quite differently. He wrote to Chamberlain with kindness: "After operations of this kind . . . one very quickly recovers enough energy to do half a day's work, but it takes some time to get to full efficiency. The great thing is not to try to start too soon and then have a set-back." But Chamberlain did try. He attended the War Cabinet meetings of September 9 and 11, although rarely speaking, as he was simply too ill. His symptoms, he reported, "required attention every hour or so and in between gave me sensations which though not painful were so intensely disturbing as to prevent my attending to anything else." Moreover, the Blitz meant that he could not sleep. Churchill advised him to leave London to recuperate, and Chamberlain went. Later the prime minister arranged for him to receive Cabinet papers.

On September 22, Chamberlain, facing reality, offered his resignation. He wrote regretfully in his diary that the nature of his illness meant he must finally relinquish hopes of "another Premiership," evidence that he had never considered Churchill's ascendency to be permanent. Initially, Churchill refused the resignation, writing to the man who had helped keep him in the political wilderness all through the 1930s and who still coveted his job: "Let us go on together through the storm. These are great days." He would continue to write chatty and kindly messages until the very end. Meanwhile, Chamberlain remained unrepentant, even obtuse, about his prewar positions. To the old appeaser John Simon he wrote in a firm hand: "I regret nothing I have done and I can see nothing undone that I ought to have done." He died on November 9, 1940.

Chamberlain's resignation opened a spot in the War Cabinet. Churchill had brought Beaverbrook inside on August 2, ostensibly to fill the gap until Chamberlain recovered. Now acknowledging that Chamberlain's absence would be permanent, he kept Beaverbrook in place but promoted the home secretary, Sir John Anderson, a career civil servant, to fill

Chamberlain's post as Lord President of the Council. He brought Herbert
Morrison from the Ministry of Supply to the Home Office to replace Anderson, that is to say, into the Cabinet but not into the War Cabinet. Still,
this represented another step in Morrison's rise to great prominence and
responsibility. Churchill then raised Bevin to War Cabinet rank, and in
order to balance the new Labour addition, promoted Kingsley Wood, the
Conservative chancellor of the exchequer, to the War Cabinet too. Thus
he had expanded the inner circle from five to eight members.

Churchill kept in close and amicable touch with Halifax about the
changes. Nevertheless, the Cabinet reshuffle had weakened the position of
the foreign secretary. The three Labour members, including the powerful
Bevin, would support the prime minister against the Conservative old
guard at the very least. The newly appointed Anderson belonged to no
party and would not cause trouble. Wood, a Conservative, had "ratted"
on Chamberlain in May and owed his current position to the prime minister, so he, too, was a safe bet. And Beaverbrook, whom the "respectable
tendency" considered a "gangster," remained one of the prime minister's
closest friends. Thus, while carefully cultivating Halifax, simultaneously
Churchill was isolating this remaining Municheer.

And he was strengthening his own position within the party. When
Chamberlain grew too ill to remain Conservative leader, a successor had
to be found. There remained Tory skeptics, including the party chairman
and the party general director, who did not want Churchill. They said he
should remain a national leader and not become a sectional one. But as
the official Conservative report put it: "This view was not . . . shared by
[the chief whip], nor by the Prime Minister to whom it was reported. Mr.
Chamberlain's opinion was also asked and he said that he did not think
that the argument had any force." Moreover, by now Churchill's critics
represented a distinct minority within the Conservative Party. His marvelous speeches in Parliament and to the nation, his inspirational dogged-
ness and defiance, had swept almost everything and everyone in Britain
before him. When, on Wednesday, October 9, 1940, he entered the Caxton
Hall in London to accept the party leadership, all the Tory MPs and peers
and parliamentary candidates accorded him "a tumultuous reception, the
meeting rising to its feet and cheering enthusiastically."

He accepted the position on his own terms. As he explained to the
meeting after it had ceased cheering: given that he was a Tory who led a
coalition government, he had taken the position as Conservative Party

leader because, in his words, "I could discharge my task with less difficulty if I were in formal relations with the [Conservative] majority of the members of the House of Commons." But it was not merely a matter of convenience. Although Churchill was a man of the right, he was determined that ideology would not divide his government. As Conservative Party leader he could set the tone. "This is no time for partisanship or for vaunting party claims," he warned his audience. "But this I will say. The Conservative Party will not allow any party to excel it in the sacrifice of party interests and party feelings which must be made by all if we are to emerge safely and victoriously from the perils which compass us about." One cannot help wondering what the increasingly isolated Halifax thought of it.

Two months later came a second death that would affect the War Cabinet. On December 7, far off in Washington DC, the British ambassador, Lord Lothian, came down with a toxic infection. The stricken man refused medicine because he was a Christian Scientist. Five days later he was dead. He had occupied a crucial position as spokesman for beleaguered Britain in the country most able and likely to help. His replacement must be equally adept. Churchill thought first of David Lloyd George: "His knowledge of munitions problems and his fiery personality marked him out." But Lloyd George turned him down on grounds of ill health (he may also still have been thinking that he would take over when "Winston [went] bust," which he judged likely).

Over the course of the next week Churchill canvassed opinions about the ambassadorship. More than once he and Halifax discussed who might serve. Then, on December 17, Halifax received a visitor: "Beaverbrook came to see me to say that he thought I ought to go [to Washington]. Whether his feeling was due to genuine conviction . . . I am not quite sure." Halifax was right to be suspicious. Likely the minister of aircraft production was preparing the ground for a more weighty invitation. Churchill wrote to his foreign secretary the very next day: "Dear Edward: Before proceeding further about the American vacancy I shd like to know whether you yourself wd care to undertake this high & perilous charge. I feel I ought to put this question to you before considering lesser alternatives."

"It is an odious thought," Halifax reflected. He deemed Americans vulgar. The next evening he had an audience with the prime minister and read aloud to him a letter explaining why he would make a poor choice for the post. It should not be a Conservative like himself representing England in Roosevelt's America, he argued, but a Liberal, perhaps Archie Sinclair; or, if not a Liberal, then perhaps Anthony Eden, or the minister of food, Lord Woolton, the former a liberal Conservative, the latter a man of no party, but possessing liberal inclinations. In any event, it was wrong to insist "that A or B was the only man. . . . The US policy would evolve very rapidly . . . under the pressure of their own appreciation of facts, provided whoever we sent was discreet and adequate." To Eden, the previous night he had rehearsed another argument against going, probably the one he really believed: "He thought what little use he might be . . . lay in restraining W.C.," Eden wrote in his diary.

"I thought I had shaken Winston off," Halifax confided to his diary on December 20. Vain imagining—Churchill wrote him that morning to insist that he go, telling him: "I have no doubt whatever that the national interest will be best served at this juncture by your becoming our Ambassador to the United States." Poor Halifax made one last desperate attempt to change the prime minister's mind. He brought his wife to argue the case on his behalf. She said, as Halifax recorded, that "although at the present moment Winston was at the height of his popularity and could do no wrong, he might later on strike a bad patch and there was nobody else who could be at such a time more loyal and perhaps able to help him with certain sections of opinion than I should."

When Churchill heard this, did he think back to the War Cabinet discussions about approaching Mussolini? With which section of the Conservative Party would that initiative have resonated? And how would it have helped Churchill? Not surprisingly, Lady Halifax did not budge him. And what now could Halifax do, short of making a spectacle of himself? He could do nothing except agree to go to Washington.

CHURCHILL REPLACED HALIFAX AS FOREIGN SECRETARY WITH ANTHONY Eden, a man whose views on foreign policy usually coincided with his own. The previous foreign secretary probably had sealed his fate when he had argued that Britain should approach the Italians to ascertain Hitler's peace terms. That suggestion was decisively rejected, but tentative peace feelers had continued to filter into London. Churchill wrote to Eden, after reading one of them: "I am absolutely opposed to the slightest contact." Eden wrote back: "I . . . agree and am in fact relieved at your decision." No doubt Churchill felt equally relieved by his new foreign secretary's fighting spirit. And yet, much like Halifax, Eden nourished prime ministerial ambitions of his own, and Churchill knew it. This provided an additional dimension to their relationship, and a particular kind of tension when, as was inevitable, they found themselves in disagreement over some aspect of Britain's wartime foreign policy.

Eden came from a landed, eccentric, aristocratic family. From his father he inherited an artist's eye and a hair-trigger temper that, unattractively, he had learned to let loose only against subordinates; from his mother he received striking good looks and, when it pleased him to deploy it, an irresistible charm. That he possessed additional extraordinary qualities soon became apparent. Upon graduating from Eton in 1915, he had enlisted in the King's Royal Rifle Corps. He had taken part in some of the worst battles of World War I, winning the Military Cross for rescuing his wounded sergeant under fire. At age twenty, he received promotion, becoming the youngest brigade major in the British Army. After the war he attended Oxford University, where he read modern languages and gained a first-class degree. Then he entered politics, ascending the greasy pole with unusual rapidity. He won election to Parliament as Conservative member for Warwick and Leamington in 1923; accepted the post of PPS from Foreign Secretary Austen Chamberlain in 1926; rose to become undersecretary of state at the Foreign Office in 1929; became Lord Privy Seal in 1933; and finally, in 1935, was appointed foreign secretary (at age thirty-eight) under Stanley Baldwin.

Many celebrated him as the coming man. He gained a following among the "troublesome young men" of the Conservative Party who wanted Britain to stand up to the dictators and who judged Eden would do so as prime minister. Others took a more jaundiced view. The journalist Malcolm Muggeridge thought Eden rose so fast because he was handsome: "an elegant appearance . . . equipped him for dazzling advantage." R. A. Butler deemed him "half mad baronet, half beautiful woman." Many said there was something "feminine" about him, possibly because he was vain, thin skinned and prey to gusts of emotion—and he loved flowers. He had the good looks of a movie star and wore the clothes of a fashion model: pinstriped trousers, a white linen vest under a lounge suit, a fur coat with an astrakhan collar, and a black felt homburg hat, in which he appeared so regularly that it became known as an "Anthony Eden." Fittingly, he lived for a time in a London house that once had belonged to Beau Brummel, the Regency dandy. But also he collected art with an expert eye (and despite a relatively thin wallet); he filled that house with the paintings of Corot, Monet, Degas, Picasso and Braque, among others. He knew the classics of English, French, German and Persian literature, all of which he could read in the original; he doted on his two sons; he was unhappily married.

Eden was both highly strung and a ditherer—until he made up his mind, after which he was adamantine. He was also modest and yet ambitious; an exquisite aesthete capable of sustained, concentrated, high-caliber work; and an opportunistic politician who yet possessed a streak of principle. In 1938 he had resigned his position as foreign secretary to protest Chamberlain's appeasement of Mussolini. But then, to the disappointment of those "troublesome young men," he made no further difficulty, because he did not want to undermine his chances of a return. When war broke out, Chamberlain grudgingly brought him halfway back, as secretary of state for the dominions, without a seat in the War Cabinet. Churchill, when he overthrew Chamberlain, returned Eden to the heart of power, first at the War Office, and now for a second stint at the Foreign Office.

Eden's greatest strength was his capacity for work. He rarely went into a meeting without all the relevant information at his fingertips. He had, too, the true diplomat's rare ability of teasing out an agreement between opposing sides that no one in the room previously had discerned. These skills complemented Churchill's own. The prime minister had an eye for the big picture, but not for details. Eden saw the trees, if not always the forest. Churchill enjoyed brilliant flashes of piercing intuition. He had little tolerance for the methodical, painstaking work at which Eden excelled. Eden often soothed the older man and restrained his impulsive or romantic gestures. But not always: occasionally his skills and qualities rubbed up against the prime minister's and caused friction. Their intricate five-year-long wartime pas de deux describes yet another problematic relationship in a War Cabinet that would show itself to be full of them.

BY THE END OF 1940 CHURCHILL HELD AN INFINITELY STRONGER political position than six months previously, even though the German onslaught in the air had commenced. He had assumed leadership of the Conservative Party, to cheers. Almost all the leading appeasers were gone: Simon to the Lords, Hoare to Spain, Chamberlain to a premature grave, and finally Halifax, soon to Washington. Of the original group in

Chamberlain's War Cabinet only Kingsley Wood remained, and Churchill found him useful as a conduit to, and interpreter of, opinion among the "respectable tendency" of Tories.

He had now the core of the War Cabinet that would see him through: Attlee and Bevin for Labour, Eden and Beaverbrook for the Conservatives. Of course, there would be others of greater or lesser importance. Beaverbrook, by his own choice, would leave and return more than once. Even now the members of the War Cabinet did not love each other. They were as much "a team of rivals" as the group Abraham Lincoln assembled to help him prosecute the American Civil War. But taken together, they represented a formidable group. True, at this point none of them could see a way to win the war; neither could their leader. But so long as the RAF remained strong, and the British Navy, too, Hitler could not successfully invade and conquer. It was not stalemate; the balance favored Germany by far. But the reconstituted and strengthened War Cabinet would find a way to hold on until fortune brought new possibilities.

CHAPTER 6

The War Cabinet at Work

BRITAIN HAD BEEN AT WAR FOR NEARLY A YEAR AND A HALF NOW, her situation parlous but not desperate, and Winston Churchill was in his element at last. He had no rivals in his reshaped, powerful but edgy War Cabinet, or in the Conservative Party whose headship he had assumed, or in the country as a whole, of which he was undisputed master and leader. His position, wrote a well-placed observer, was "astonishingly unassailable." As prime minister and minister of defense he controlled military as well as domestic policy, presiding over not merely the War Cabinet but also the most important meetings of the Chiefs of Staff (COS), where a secretariat of superlative skill and efficiency supported him. He was sixty-six years old (he would turn sixty-seven on November 30, 1941), healthy and seemingly tireless. "War is real champagne to him," Leo Amery wrote, not without admiration, of the man who loved champagne.

Churchill followed a routine, insofar as that was possible during wartime. He would wake every morning at eight after sleeping for six hours—but stay in bed until the last possible moment. He would consume a big breakfast, which might include pheasant or partridge or steak—and wine—while still abed. And he would work in bed—he had a custom-designed wooden tray for his books and papers, which facilitated this. The papers came in locked boxes, whose contents were arranged according to a system he had devised. The boxes contained files, which he took in order: first "Top of the Box" folders with information about the war; then "Foreign Office Telegrams"; then "Service Telegrams" between the service chiefs and their principal officers in the field; and finally "Periodical Returns," which included reports on domestic matters such as production, technical developments, manpower and the like. Other boxes, differently colored, held files containing intelligence reports, parliamentary reports and miscellaneous reports on matters of current significance. He worked on the files in bed in the morning and in bed at night before he went to sleep. (When he had time he also read all the important newspapers before he fell asleep.) And from his bed he would dictate to one of three highly trained woman typists who had become expert in deciphering his grunts, mumbles and murmurs and his endearing, but strangely intermittent, upper-class speech impediment when pronouncing "l"s and "s"s. The typists were so fast and accurate on their silent Remington typewriters that they could produce verbatim transcripts that he simply signed and dispatched, many of them bearing a stamped injunction in red: "Action This Day!"

Oddly, Churchill despised paperclips and pins. His secretaries learned to replace them in incoming documents with green tags stuck through holes they had punched in the papers. Churchill referred to the hole-puncher as a "klop." He hated the sound of crackling paper, and so the secretaries learned to insert carbon sheets between pages noiselessly. The secretaries traveled with him wherever he went, ready to transcribe his every word. He had only to bark a command to set them to work. Only when he was in an automobile, where typewriting was difficult, was he likely to go unrecorded.

When he stayed in London, which was most of the time, he would rise from bed at midmorning to attend a meeting of the COS; otherwise he rose at noon to attend the War Cabinet. And invariably he returned to bed before five o'clock in the afternoon for an hour-long nap. It was that replenishing interval that enabled him to work long into the night, actually into the next morning, much to the dismay of colleagues who had no opportunity to sleep during the day. He took a full bath after rising in the morning and another following the nap in the afternoon, as if he were starting a second day. Eden records meeting with him one day at about five o'clock, right after the afternoon nap: "He was in tearing spirits. Said he could not remember where he was on waking, he had had such deep sleep, and he was striding about his room in vest and drawers with cigar in his mouth, whisky and soda at his side and calling for Nellie to produce his socks!" In this manner Churchill squeezed two working days into every twenty-four hours.

When he got up he dressed in raffish three-piece suits, handkerchief in breast pocket, bowtie at his neck, watch chain visible; or he wore pin-stripe grey wool "siren suits," one-piece outfits made especially for him by Turnbull and Asser, the fashionable clothiers. A "siren suit" zipped up the middle. It was generously cut, with breast pockets and roomier pockets to the side, fold-over cuffs, and pleats to the trouser fronts. He had, as well, velvet bottle-green "siren suits" for eveningwear and for sleeping. Some called these his "rompers." He hated laces and always wore zippered shoes. At important occasions he might don a full and imposing naval uniform or another uniform associated with the armed services, although there is a photograph showing him wearing a silk kimono decorated with dragons while standing next to the American general Dwight Eisenhower. The kimono covers one of the "siren suits."

If dress reveals the man, then Churchill's dress suggests at the very least a man possessing an eccentric and fearless sense of style.

Churchill's days were filled with meetings, travel, inspections, inter-views, speeches and preparations for all this and more. He could devote little time to his three daughters—Diana, who turned thirty-one in 1940; Sarah, then twenty-six; and Mary, then eighteen—and his son Randolph, then twenty-nine, although he often referred to them with pride. He slept apart from his wife; nevertheless, evidence suggests that he and Clemen-tine generally formed a happy and effective couple. Together they would lunch quietly at 10 Downing Street or in its steel-reinforced annex, which was safer, especially during the Blitz, and later in the war, in the period of the V-1 flying bombs and V-2 rockets, but sometimes they would pre-side over larger luncheons in either location, to which they invited guests. These luncheons provided him with some respite from the pressures and tensions of the day. He would exercise his wit; she would roar with laugh-ter when he did so. She did not obviously defer to him, but rather took opportunities to chaff him, even in company.

They ate well, even as the nation consumed strictly controlled rations. A typical luncheon at No. 10 began with a fish course, followed by a main course of tournedos with mushrooms, braised celery and chipped pota-toes, and then a dessert course of peaches and cheese; sherry came before the meal, wine with it, brandy afterward. According to a guest on the day they ate the tournedos, Churchill "drank quite a lot of port and brandy and smoked a big [Cuban] cigar which he lit at least ten times." On an-other occasion, the first course was macaroni and cheese, but the prime minister objected, saying, "This is only a barbed wire entanglement to prevent us from attacking the main position," which was an Irish stew. Churchill's "delightful informality" charmed the recorder of this observation, a newspaper editor who lunched occasionally with him during the war. He described the prime minister joking with his guests, talking informally with them about the war, and uttering unprintable jibes about his political opponents, as well as the occasional aphorism, e.g.: "Opinions differ. That is why we have check waistcoats."

"I know no one with such perfect manners as a host," Eden wrote in his diary after visiting Churchill at Chequers, the country residence of British prime ministers. Churchill insisted "upon escorting me to my bedroom and lighting my fire." R. A. Butler, the departed Halifax's former defeatist number two at the Foreign Office, who was now returned to Churchill's good graces, painted a droll picture of the prime minister at his country residence to which he had been summoned a little after Eden's visit. "There was a tiger-like noise on the stairs and the P.M. appeared in his siren suit . . . 'You are to tell nobody you are here. . . . Anything I want from you, you must keep very private. I shall not talk now.'" Butler continues: "He then proceeded to talk at great length about the news, and to read me bits from the evening paper."

Like Eden before him, Butler spent the night and part of the next day with the prime minister at Chequers. After dinner, during which Churchill expressed himself forcefully and objectionably about South Asians ("gross, dirty and corrupt"), he read to his guest "at great length and with incredible gusto" a portion of a speech he intended to deliver in the House of Commons, "asking me whether I thought he was lacking in force or vigor! I said I thought he was not." He handed the entire speech to Butler and asked for critical comments: "You shall have the whole night—shitting up, cowwectng it, revishing it in pencil, and will shpeak to me in the morning."

CHURCHILL COULD BE HUMOROUS AT MEETINGS OF THE WAR CABINET and in his dealings with ministers. When, early during his tenure as prime minister, scientists urged Britons to adopt a more balanced diet, Churchill called them "food faddists" and exhorted his minister of food, Frederick Woolton, to ignore their recommendations and to listen to the British soldier instead. "All he cares about is beef," Churchill observed approvingly of the British Tommy. This was when everyone expected a German invasion at any moment. Nevertheless, Churchill found time to write to

Woolton: "Almost all the food faddists I have ever known, nut eaters and the like, have died young after a long period of senile decay. . . . The way to lose the war is to try to force the British public into a diet of milk, oatmeal, potatoes, etc., washed down on gala occasions with a little lime juice." Woolton seems to have stimulated Churchill's funny bone. At a Cabinet meeting about a year later, the minister of food recommended rationing all tinned food. The Cabinet accepted this, but, as Eden recorded in his diary, "Winston kept murmuring at intervals during [the] rest of business: 'I shall never see another sardine.'"

When he thought Woolton strayed from the proper line, Churchill could handle him deftly. Early in 1941, in his zeal to ensure that all Britons had enough to eat, Woolton emphasized Germany's threat to the food supply in a broadcast on the radio. He proclaimed stringent restrictions on the serving of meat, fish, eggs and cheese by restaurants and hotels, and announced draconian punishments should they break them. Churchill wrote to his food minister: "I do not like this rather dictatorial publicity." Woolton wrote back: "I am doing my best in circumstances of great difficulty." Churchill replied soothingly: "Believe me I realize all the difficulties with which you are manfully contending." Still, he advised that Woolton should exhort the public to eat smaller portions and the restaurants to dress up scraps in tasty ways; he should not threaten wholesale arrests.

Here is Winston Churchill as manager of men, a role not much appreciated at the time, or often studied by historians. In fact, he worked hard to encourage his team and to keep it in good temper. The papers of his colleagues contain many notes written by him. He exhorted and encouraged them when necessary, congratulated them when appropriate, and sympathized with them in their troubles. Not only did he congratulate and encourage them, but he also continually had to attempt to check them, or to make excuses for them, or to soothe them—or those they had offended. For he presided over a political coalition of tough and prickly individuals, strong personalities unaccustomed to turning the other cheek when criticized or contradicted.

One example, taken from many, is from Churchill's reaction to a speech Ernest Bevin had made to the annual gathering of the Works Management Association in Birmingham in April 1941. Bevin had dealt roughly with local Conservative MPs who had attacked his policies in the House of Commons. When questioned about the speech afterward, Bevin told the prime minister that he had engaged merely in "good humored badinage," but as one of Churchill's advisers put it, "Mr. Bevin's idea of badinage is elephantine." The organization of backbench Conservatives, the 1922 Committee, thought so too. It rushed to defend the MPs whom Bevin had criticized. Churchill, upon reading the speech, had to agree. He wrote to Bevin: "It seems to me very difficult to prevent ill-will rising if you attack in this extremely personal manner Members who support the Government in which you take a leading part." Bevin replied characteristically: "I adhere to every word I said." In the end it was Churchill, not Bevin, who had to mollify the 1922 Committee.

Churchill dominated his War Cabinet, but he did not always get his way, even in important matters. An example, taken from a slightly later period (June 15, 1942), is highly revealing. The government had just learned from Edvard Beneš, Czechoslovakia's president in exile, of "savage cruelties" perpetrated by German troops upon his countrymen after the assassination of a leading and particularly brutal Nazi, Reinhard Heydrich. (The cruelties included the indiscriminate murder of more than 1,300 innocents and the razing of two villages.) On a moonlit night with good visibility, Churchill reported, British bombers could "wipe out" three German villages in retaliation. He favored letting the bombers do it. The bellicose Ernest Bevin did, too, saying, as the official meeting minutes put it, "German responds to brute force & nothing else." Amery wanted even more blood. He wished to know why highly populated towns rather than sparsely populated villages could not be obliterated. These were the out-and-out hawks. But Eden would admit only that "there might be a deterrent element in this." And then Attlee introduced a moral consideration: "Doubt if it is useful to enter into competition in frightfulness with Germans." Morrison backed up his Labour colleague, warning against the cycle of frightfulness that would ensue if Britain bombed the villages: Germany's response would be to retaliate upon defenseless British communities, and then "public wd say 'why did you draw this down onto us?'" Sinclair introduced a practical consideration. Bombing civilians would represent a "diversion of effort fr. military objective," an argument Anderson picked up: "It costs us something & them nothing," by which he meant that if Britain carried out bombing raids on defenseless towns or villages, she would lose an opportunity to bomb important military objectives, while Germany would only lose civilian lives. Now Eden, too, swung decisively against the proposed action: "Waste of a moonlight night. Bigger diversion than I had thought." Churchill insisted, "My instinct is all the other way," but in the end he had to defer: "I submit (unwillingly) to the view of Cabinet against."

This particular discussion reveals Churchill's ministers in a characteristic light when considering affairs outside Britain. The prime minister, combative as usual, demanded swift, dramatic action; Bevin, the sledgehammer, supported him. Then most of the others chipped in to moderate the tone. Attlee once said to Eden that he thought their main achievement in the War Cabinet had been to restrain the prime minister from his wildest schemes. Thus, unexpectedly, did they fulfill the function that the old Chamberlainite, Maurice Hankey, originally had prescribed for the two "wise elephants" Chamberlain and Halifax. Still, it is a measure of how quickly total war had eroded traditional scruples in Britain that, even given the horrendous nature of Nazi excesses, the War Cabinet could discuss killing noncombatants at all—and that some of its most important members could seriously entertain doing so.

During this period, Lawrence Burgis's handwritten notes can convey a sense of the ebb and flow of discussion and the range of subjects covered in the meetings of Winston Churchill's War Cabinet. Especially early in the war, they sometimes provide a more thorough impression than can be gleaned from the official minutes, which are typically abbreviated. Burgis showed that usually Churchill opened with a few remarks, perhaps reporting on a trip he had taken, or welcoming the return of a minister who had journeyed abroad, or a prime minister from one of the dominions who was participating in War Cabinet deliberations while he was in England. Then the service chiefs would explain the military situation. Churchill and others with specialized knowledge would interject, and this could lead to broad-ranging discussions, for the Cabinet had to consider nearly every part of the globe, although not necessarily its military aspects. Reading these exchanges, it becomes obvious that the prime minister had assembled a team of levelheaded, tough-minded, experienced, hard men. They examined a subject from all angles. They sifted and weighed possibilities. Despite their many differences, usually they focused on their common purpose, which was to win the war.

Five months before the Japanese attacked Pearl Harbor on December 7, 1941, Churchill met Franklin Roosevelt on a warship off the coast of Newfoundland at Placentia Bay. There the prime minister attempted to court the president, while his navy chiefs consulted and became acquainted with their American counterparts. Churchill desperately wanted increased American commitments of material support, especially for the Battle of the Atlantic, which was being waged to maintain supply lines, without which Britain must fall. Instead, he got the eight-point Atlantic Charter, parts of which he accepted mainly in order not to offend FDR. Point Three, for example, declared that all peoples had a right to self-determination: Churchill hoped that this principle would apply to Europeans conquered by Hitler but not to the colonized peoples of Africa and Asia, including South Asia—that is to say, not to the British Empire. Point Four gestured toward world free trade, which Churchill knew many British Conservatives opposed. Point Six pledged the two countries to work for a world free of want and fear. Roosevelt saw this as a natural corollary to his domestic policy, "Freedom from Want," but Churchill responded unenthusiastically. It was Attlee, acting as prime minister in London in Churchill's absence, who drafted the positive British response to this particular point with the backing of his Labour colleagues in a hastily summoned midnight meeting of the War Cabinet, and who then cabled it to Britain's leader.

Upon his return home, Churchill discussed the implications of the Newfoundland meeting with the War Cabinet. Halifax, temporarily returned to Britain, and Mackenzie King, the Canadian prime minister, took part. Burgis noted:

> CHURCHILL: I'm anxious about [the] situation. [The] US [is] asked to put up with [the] inconveniences of war without the stimuli. . . . [FDR is] a creature of politics. [He] may not feel able to give [sufficient aid] if Hitler does not attack [the] US. [It is] going to be awkward. . . . I can't say we should contemplate a peace with Hitler. We might get ten years. I'd not touch it—die rather. Can convey [to FDR] . . . they [the USA] are in great danger.
>
> EDEN: [We should tell them that we] can't finish Hitler without you.
>
> CHURCHILL: I've said we can't win this war without you . . .
>
> BEAVERBROOK: Something must be done. [The] US [is] sitting down. . . . Methods must be taken to move them. . . . Republican Party voting against administration and that brings them to gradually voting against war.

The Cabinet discussed the "methods to be taken," as Beaverbrook had termed them:

HALIFAX: Wonder whether . . . useful to ask President privately whether [it would] help or hinder [if we] say publicly: "It will be a difficult job for us to finish Hitler alone."

CHURCHILL: I've said that. "Give us the tools and we'll finish the job."
Look up exactly what I said.

MACKENZIE KING: [We should say that the] danger [is] so great—if they do not come in [there will be] no salvation for anyone. . . .

MORRISON: If US get[s] impression [we are] finding [it] difficult to win the war . . . [then the] more we press them the more they will withdraw.

AMERY: You [Churchill] are admired by whole US. You say something [it will] make more difference than anything the President might say.

Amery's flattery may not have been apt. But Roosevelt recently had won reelection by promising American parents that "your boys are not going to be sent into any foreign wars." Any speech Churchill delivered must somehow appeal to American public opinion, in which isolationist sentiment remained strong. With the advice of his War Cabinet in his mind, no doubt, the prime minister traveled a few weeks later to Harrow, the private school he had attended as a boy (Amery had also gone there), ostensibly to hear and sing the old school songs. But he made a speech, too. "Never give in," he urged his audience of pupils and masters, "never, never, never . . . except to convictions of honor and good sense." No doubt he wanted Americans to read this speech and conclude that a country so staunchly led deserved all the help it could get. Thus had the War Cabinet helped him to hone his message.

BRITAIN OCCUPIED A DIFFICULT POSITION IN 1941, BUT A TOUGH AND thoughtful War Cabinet that did not shrink from harsh measures, and that would not countenance bloodthirsty ones, guided her through the storm, while a skillful, humorous, solicitous and democratic prime minister led them. It sounds too good to be true and, in fact, sometimes it was. Even Winston Churchill could dither. Even he could back out of agreements to which his colleagues thought he had committed—and do it with ill grace. Even Winston Churchill could pout and throw a temper tantrum, as the following example reveals.

It occurred during a series of linked meetings from December 3 to 5, 1941. Six months earlier, Hitler had invaded Russia, anticipating swift victory. Now it was becoming clear that he had gravely miscalculated. The chiefs of staff reported almost daily to the War Cabinet about developments on the eastern front. The Soviets' continuing resistance pleasantly surprised them, although they did not know how long it could last. Yet Britain finally seemed to have an ally with staying power, albeit one that both Conservative and Labour Cabinet ministers abhorred.

At a Defense Committee meeting on December 3, Lord Beaverbrook suggested that Anthony Eden, who was about to embark upon a journey to Russia to meet with Stalin, be authorized to promise quick delivery of five hundred tanks and five hundred aircraft. Churchill agreed, and Eden deemed this suggestion "most useful." The next day at the War Cabinet, however, the foreign secretary ran into difficulties. In Eden's words, first Morrison "annoyed me more than a little, by saying that he hoped I should not be unmindful of my country's interests while I was away!" Then Kingsley Wood backed Morrison, opposing letting "anything leave these shores." More weightily, the Chief of the Imperial General Staff (CIGS), General Alan Brooke, warned that Britain could not send five hundred tanks to Russia anyway: "Best we could do was 300." Moreover, he "did not recommend such a gift as we should be seriously denuding this country and prematurely disclosing a new pattern of tank." He went on to paint a "picture of possible tank battles in this country such as were taking place in Libya. These [descriptions]," Brooke noted in his diary with grim relish, "gave Kingsley Wood the shivers." Nevertheless, Eden, bargaining hard, got Churchill to agree to "a gift of some 300 tanks and 300 aircraft" for Russia.

The meeting broke up temporarily for dinner. Eden dined with friends and returned to the reconvened gathering. He quickly discovered that someone had been working on the prime minister during the interval. Brooke recorded in his diary: "The PM had swung right round again, tanks and aircraft had been put aside, the gift was now to consist of 10 squadrons of aircraft [120 airplanes] to be made available immediately after the Libyan offensive was finished." One can imagine Eden's dismay, as this was less than half the number of aircraft originally agreed upon, and no tanks, but he had not yet plumbed bottom. The chief of the air staff, Charles Portal, now weighed in. Britain could promise some aircraft, but not a definite number and not on a definite date. At this, Churchill (not Eden) lost his temper. Had he not met his military advisers more than halfway? "Anthony soothed him temporarily," Brooke recorded, which says much about the foreign secretary's role and relationship with the prime minister. Still, Churchill broke out again before lapsing into silence. He "looked at his papers for some 5 minutes, then slammed them together, closed the meeting and walked out of the room!" So there had been "no decision" at all, as Eden recorded glumly in his diary later that night.

Nor was that the end of it. Another meeting took place the following morning. Brooke wrote: "We were greeted by a memorandum from the PM couched practically in identical terms with those we had asked him to accept last night!" Churchill had reversed course and disappointed his foreign secretary in order to please his military advisers.

Such ups and downs and bickerings and confusions represent a more accurate record of war meetings than historians usually describe. Even the participants would later gloss them over. In his memoir, Eden did not mention Churchill's overnight conversion to Portal's position. Instead he presented the prime minister's earlier temporary decision about ten squadrons as final—and as a hopeful sign for Anglo-Russian relations. He wrote: "Even more important was the offer I was authorized to make of ten squadrons of the Royal Air Force to operate on the southern flank of the Russian armies. These squadrons were to be withdrawn from the Libyan battle at the earliest moment when success had been gained."

But when Japan attacked Pearl Harbor, Churchill withdrew the reduced offer of even ten squadrons. He needed them for the Far East.

SOCIAL AND CLASS DIFFERENCES COULD ALSO INTERFERE WITH SMOOTH sailing in the War Cabinet. An autodidact Labour minister might inadvertently reveal insecurity when dealing with a figure who had attended a great public school and university. The home secretary, Herbert Morrison, the son of a South London policeman, appears to have been compensating, for example, when he showed off his knowledge in a note to the Lord Chancellor, Sir John Simon. The latter had attended the exclusive public school Fettes in Edinburgh, attained a first at Oxford and served as president of the Oxford Union. "May I say how much I enjoyed reading your speech of yesterday?" Morrison wrote to him safely enough in a note of congratulation early in 1942. "There was only one thing which marred it, and that was the stupid printer's error giving the date of the publication of *Areaopagitica* as 1694 instead of 1649." In fact it was first printed in 1644.

Or the reverse: a member of Britain's upper class might reveal his snobbery—if inadvertently, and only in his diary. At a Buckingham Palace dinner, Frederick Woolton, who had himself climbed the social ladder from the lower middle class of Salford, outside Manchester, to chairman of Lewis Department Stores and a seat in the House of Lords, observed disapprovingly: "Bevin continued to sit as the King joined the group. During dinner he broke one of the liqueur glasses. . . . [T]he King [treated] him rather like a child who really doesn't know any better." Many years later in an interview, Anthony Eden showed himself a snob too. The former World War I army officer simply assumed the right to judge and to place men he deemed to be his social inferiors: "Morrison was a good rifleman," he recalled of the home secretary, "the kind of man you promote to lance corporal one week and he may lose his stripes the next, but he will be back up again soon. Cockneys make the best soldiers." Then, realizing how this sounded, Eden asked the interviewer not to use the quote. It is easy to imagine the unspoken tensions, hesitations and resentments that must have been part of the atmosphere at War Cabinet meetings.

Moreover, jockeying for position, apple-polishing, toadying and the clash of personalities among ministers continued as always—although everyone denied it. On January 22, 1941, Beaverbrook addressed the 1922 Committee. According to the meeting's note taker, "during the course of his speech [he] assured members that perfect harmony existed between his colleagues and himself." He did not mention that "a quiet scrap was going on [just then] between the two B's—[himself] . . . and Bevin," over control of manpower and conscription of labor, or that he had recently offered his resignation to the prime minister: "For some time I have been most uncomfortable and I have asked for my release on that account," he wrote to Churchill.

Beaverbrook employed flattery, and even something like bribery, to bend Cabinet colleagues to his will. He tried hard to split the Labour ministers from his great antagonist in the War Cabinet, Bevin. For example, he attempted to ingratiate himself with A. V. Alexander, a Labour man who was therefore Bevin's natural ally. Before the war, Beaverbrook's newspapers had attacked Alexander, who then led Britain's co-operative movement. Now, sitting at the same table as his erstwhile foe, who had been raised up to be First Lord of the Admiralty, Beaverbrook scrawled him a note: "I will do all I can to help you as dictator of ships—I believe you will do the job better than anybody else." That year he invited Alexander to his country house, Cherkley Court, for Christmas. "'The Beaver' has got A. V. Alexander just where he wants him," reported a well-placed observer. He did, too. Alexander defended Beaverbrook from attack at the

War Cabinet. Beaverbrook scribbled him another note: "It is surprising that the Co-op Boss should make a defense for his old opponent. But to make it in such generous terms has touched me so deeply and warmed me so completely that I give you my affectionate devotion."

He flattered Herbert Morrison in the same way, although Morrison hardly needed splitting from Bevin, who was also Morrison's nemesis in the Labour Party. Perhaps Beaverbrook thought he could build up the one in order to diminish the other, or at least to make the other's road harder. "You stated your case most splendidly this morning," he wrote to the home secretary in late 1941. "It was in fact the best argument I have heard in my 18 months of Ministerial service." A month earlier, he had written, "You made a most excellent impression on the House of Commons. Perhaps it was the best speech you ever made." Does this not sound faintly patronizing? Yet eventually Beaverbrook felt able to write to Morrison (against much evidence to the contrary): "Churchill apart, you are today by far the biggest figure in the country. . . . I hope to live under you as Prime Minister."

Meanwhile, even as he was building up Morrison, Beaverbrook was flattering, soothing, and whispering to Bevin, his own great enemy in the War Cabinet. In this case, however, he came up against a brick wall. In one note, also written in late 1941, just at the time he was writing to Morrison, the millionaire newspaper magnate praised the great trade unionist's "leadership of men and women in the industrial centers." "Can we make a platform for you where I can stand at your side?" he inquired. "I am sure you can do so if you determine to build it." This seemed to Bevin a suggestive but also a dangerous idea. He replied: "I have no policy except the policy of the Government as a whole arrived at through the Cabinet, therefore I do not know what you mean by making a platform for me. I have no intention of building any platforms during the war outside the platform of the Government itself."

Beaverbrook may have mounted a similar campaign to woo Attlee, although no letters between the men survive from the pre–Pearl Harbor war years. (One rather smarmy missive written by the press lord to Labour's leader in 1943 may be found in the Beaverbrook Papers, however.) In any event, Beaverbrook would have found Clem Attlee to be at least as impermeable as Ernest Bevin. Attlee despised Beaverbrook's modus operandi. Immediately after the war, he spoke words of warning to young Labour MPs who were about to enter the House of Commons for the first time:

"There are many people to whom it will be easy to talk. Chief among these is Beaverbrook. He is a magnet to all young men, and I warn you that if you talk to him no good will come of it. Beware of flattery."

And yet Beaverbrook remained a generous host and friend to Churchill. In June 1941, out of the blue, so far as one can tell, he sent to Churchill five dozen bottles of Deidesheimer Hofstuck 1937. Churchill was delighted to receive this fine Riesling wine, despite its country of origin. He wrote to Beaverbrook: "Thank you so much for your exhilarating gift."

EVEN IN EARLY 1941, WITH CHURCHILL AT THE ACME OF HIS POPULARITY, some continued to doubt him. David Lloyd George's Principal Private Secretary was a doubter. The prime minister "is said to be very arrogant these days and once he has made up his mind there is little chance that he will alter it," he reported to his chief. And two months later: "Winston these days has got a sort of dictator complex; his attitude is 'Do not criticize me. I am the great one.'" But the Principal Private Secretary had an agenda, albeit an increasingly unrealistic one: to convince Lloyd George to organize a parliamentary coup against Churchill just as he had against H. H. Asquith during World War I (with Beaverbrook's support), and to take the top spot once again. His observations may have been accurate, but they must be taken with a grain of salt.

But it was not only men nursing private hobbyhorses who were finding fault with the high-riding prime minister. "Everything of importance has to be referred to him," an important official in the Ministry of Aircraft Production grumbled. "There is nobody to control him," worried Churchill's friend Lord Trenchard. Even Churchill's strongest supporters shared such concerns. Eden's diaries are sprinkled with them: "The worst Cabinet we have had yet," he noted on the evening of May 26, 1941. "Winston was nervy and unreasonable." A few weeks later: "I find W's dictator moods irritating." And some months after that: "W. wants to move all the pieces himself." The Foreign Office adviser, Cadogan, worried, too: "Winston very obstinate," he recorded in a typical diary entry, this one after a May 1, 1941, War Cabinet meeting. Three weeks later: "What he does is jump to decisions—ill-considered—and then say that it shows weakness to recede."

Eventually, these private, or semiprivate, grievances reached Churchill's wife, Clementine. Appalled, she wrote her husband a famous letter of warning: "My Darling . . . One of the men in your entourage (a de-voted friend) has been to me & told me that there is a danger of your being generally disliked by your colleagues & subordinates because of your rough, sarcastic & overbearing manner. . . . It is for you to give the Orders, & if they are bungled—except for the King, the Archbishop of Canterbury & the Speaker—you can sack anyone & everyone. Therefore with this terrific power you must combine urbanity, kindness & if possible Olympic calm. . . . Besides you won't get the best results by irascibility & rudeness . . ."

Clementine's letter hit the mark. Churchill did not suffer fools gladly, and usually he thought that anyone who disagreed with him was a fool. He did possess dictatorial tendencies. Unfortunately for him, but fortunately for the country, he had not chosen a War Cabinet that bore them easily. "I hear," Lloyd George's PPS wrote to his master yet again, "that some of his immediate colleagues are at times upset about this attitude." Even Chur-chill's least assertive colleagues (comparatively speaking) were more than capable of sticking up for themselves. For example, A. V. Alexander, the First Lord, to whom Churchill had shown much solicitude, sent him a note in response to a prime ministerial memo criticizing the navy: "I think you will wish to withdraw your minute. . . . I do not accept any of the 'find-ings' in the third paragraph. . . . Do not let us wound each other if we can avoid it." And Woolton, with whom Churchill had dealt so successfully and delicately early on, wrote in his diary after a less sensitively handled incident: "I told him . . . that if he continued to make public comments in the strain of those he had made today he would have to find another Minister of Food. He's a bully and it's necessary to deal brutally with him." Herbert Morrison, never to be confused with a shrinking violet, reported robustly to a journalist in 1942: "When he was crossed Churchill would glare at the offenders . . . saying nothing at all. . . . Well you must stand up to him." Beaverbrook and Bevin stood up to Churchill all the time; At-tlee, too, had a spine of steel. Critics who complained, as some did, that Churchill surrounded himself with yes-men were mistaken.

When Churchill did manage to curb his rough tongue, however, other complaints emerged. Like Eden and Cadogan, the career civil ser-vant Maurice Hankey littered his diary with dyspeptic descriptions of the prime minister's failings: hubris, sentimentality and lack of judgment among them. A recurring theme was that the prime minister spoke too often and too long. He would "harangue" his colleagues. Hankey did not like Churchill, but his criticism cannot be discounted; too much independent confirmation exists. Worse still, Churchill never learned to curb this tendency. Friends, colleagues and biographers all agree that he always loved to hear himself talk. Churchill's War Cabinets made Australian prime minister Robert Menzies, who had been attending them during a stay in London, "very cross." He bumped into Hankey in the street and "made some acid remarks about . . . the complete ignoring of time by the War Cabinet." (Hankey recorded this with delight.) Two weeks earlier Eden had grumbled: "Cabinet in evening when Winston spoke to us at tremendous length of all aspects of military situation."

Four years later, the problem had gotten so bad that Attlee finally wrote a blunt protest to the prime minister. He typed it himself so that his secretaries would not know of his disgruntlement (widely shared and long-held among Cabinet ministers and the chiefs of staff), but Churchill then went and talked it over with his wife, and with Beaverbrook, among others, and soon enough, Attlee's letter became common knowledge among cognoscenti. Attlee, by then deputy prime minister, had written: "I consider the present position inimical to the successful performance of the tasks imposed upon us as a Government, and injurious to the war effort." He charged that because Churchill rarely read notes prepared for his guidance, "often half an hour or more is wasted in explaining what could have been grasped by two or three minutes reading of the document. Not infrequently a phrase catches your eye which gives rise to a disquisition on an interesting point only slightly connected with the subject matter. The result is long delays and unnecessarily long Cabinets."

BRITAIN WAS WINNING THE WAR BY 1945, WHEN ATTLEE WROTE HIS letter, and so in the end everyone discounted the prime minister's drawbacks and personal foibles. That had not been the case earlier, however. In 1941, Britain clearly was not winning the war, and no one knew how she could win it. The nation had survived the Battle of Britain to everyone's immense relief, but that had been a defensive endeavor. She had enjoyed great success early that year against Italian troops in North Africa and against the Italian Navy in the Mediterranean, but then Germany had recouped the Axis position in North Africa, conquered Yugoslavia and Greece, and chased the British from Crete, meanwhile taking 13,000 British prisoners. Britain remained safe behind the moat of the English Channel, although the military experts still thought a German invasion likely. But nowhere on the continent could British troops engage the German Army on advantageous terms, and nowhere had Britain beaten the Wehrmacht. Churchill therefore placed much hope in his country's long-range bombers. He thought they would devastate German industry and German cities and eventually bring her to her knees. In fact, the Germans shot down the bombers in such numbers that Britain temporarily broke off the bombing campaign in November 1941. As one historian put it, "It was doing more damage to themselves than to the Germans." Britain had acquired a significant ally in the war when Hitler committed the folly of invading Russia. But no one yet knew how great this folly was.

Therefore, as spring turned to summer and summer to autumn in 1941, uneasiness about Britain's position in the war began to spread. Critics latched onto Churchill's arrogance and tendency to pontificate. Just as in April 1940, opponents had demanded that Chamberlain and the appeasers sacrifice the seals of office to a smaller, harder, more effective group of men, so now a similar murmur began to be heard, with Churchill's government as the target. Essentially, the detractors charged that although Churchill had embodied the national will to resist and survive in May 1940, and had staved off near-certain disaster, and indeed continued to inspire with great oratory, he no more than his predecessor knew how to organize victory or to put together a ruthlessly efficient team for winning the war. The criticism had not yet reached the dangerous level it had attained before Chamberlain's fall, but it was not as insignificant as Churchill might have liked it to be—or thought it was—either.

Clem Davies, the independent backbencher who played so large a role in the downfall of the appeasers only twenty months before, led the charge again. To the Liverpool Constitutional Club he explained that, Churchill's rise notwithstanding, the country needed a more efficient and streamlined War Cabinet. It should be composed of men who had no departmental duties but focused exclusively upon broad matters, with a proper minister of defense under them doing the duties Churchill had delegated to himself, and with the ministers of war, navy and air under him. Also it needed a minister of production directing the ministers of construction, labor, transport and food, and having control over all raw materials. "The people of the country were first class," *The Times* reported Davies concluding. "It was direction and leadership and organization that were lacking."

Churchill dismissed Davies's critique with contempt, seeing him as a disappointed office-seeker. That moved Wilfrid Roberts, the Liberal

member of Parliament for North Cumberland, to warn in a public speech
that "the Prime Minister, although welcoming debates in the House of
Commons, shows a certain sensitiveness about criticism. I think that is
a mistake." Roberts served as PPS to Archibald Sinclair, minister of air.
He was a member of the very government whose leader he had just criticized. This made his intervention all the more significant. Sinclair wrote
a letter of abject apology to Churchill promising to sack Roberts. "Keep
him and teach him to spell," the prime minister replied airily. He remained confident. But meanwhile, one Conservative MP warned a Cabinet minister that "the House was beginning to be critical about some of
the P.M.'s actions and decisions." "Disgruntled back-bench Conservative
MPs are meeting privately at dinner parties to concert a plan of campaign
to be followed in Parliament," claimed a journalist. "The promoters are
anti-Churchill." The Conservative member for South Croydon, Herbert
Williams, reiterated Davies's larger point at a public meeting: "Although
Mr. Churchill possesses the capacity for inspired speech, he is not so good
as a manager of the war effort." And in another address, reported in *The
Times*, Davies said "it was a real peril to this country that Mr. Churchill
should be regarded as a man beyond challenge. . . . It was bad for him and
bad for the country. . . . Mr. Churchill must get a better team round him
if this country was to be better served. We had tolerated in our Government Departments inefficiency. . . . Until we got a Prime Minister who
would say, 'If you don't do your job you will be fired,' things would not
improve."

Now the press joined in the agitation. Churchill remained "the only
man who can answer the call of the nation. . . . [H]e has the power [and]
the courage," noted the *Sunday Pictorial* of November 2, 1941. But: "We
need a War Executive Council of six men working under Mr. Churchill,
with none of them tied to a government department." "The growing assault is not on Churchill," *Cavalcade* reassured its readers. But: "The critics
want the load of placemen shifted off his back. . . . [B]ig changes pend both
in the War Cabinet and the Administration."

Things had gone far enough at this point to seriously worry an old
ally and friend of the prime minister, the naval officer Robert T. Bower,
who served as the Conservative member of Parliament for Cleveland.
Bower could think only to get in touch with Leo Amery. Churchill
had long since given up "the arduous exercise of listening" to small-fry
such as himself, but the secretary of state for India, who was a friend of

Churchill's of even longer-standing than Bower, should attempt to warn him: "There are ominous signs of a situation like that just preceding the fall of Chamberlain. . . . Sentiment in the lobbies and in the pubs and clubs and back streets . . . can roughly be summed up by saying [of Churchill] . . . '*Vox et praeterea nihil*,' ['He is voice and nothing more']. There is every sign of diverse oppositions crystalizing into something serious."

On December 7, 1941, Japan attacked the American naval base at Pearl Harbor, drawing the United States into what now became a truly worldwide war. Churchill immediately headed for Washington, DC, to confer again with President Roosevelt. He believed that with America in the war, victory finally was certain, although the road to it would be long and hard. But he left behind in England an uneasy Cabinet and uneasy Parliament. For the first time during his premiership men were calculating odds and playing parlor games as they had in May 1940, asking one another who among them could both successfully challenge the prime minister and put the country on a real war footing—and gradually, opinion began to coalesce around a single individual. Churchill would return from the United States in January 1942 to confront the first serious challenge to his position as prime minister. It came from the man he had appointed ambassador to Russia, who had just recently returned. Many thought or hoped that he had come home to claim the top position for himself.

CHAPTER 7

Spearhead of the Left

THE INFLUENCE OF THE POLITICAL LEFT PEAKED IN BRITAIN DURING World War II. The war seemed to legitimate its insistence upon activist government. Many Conservatives accepted the need for some controls and guarantees during the national emergency in areas such as wages and prices, but an enlarged, energized and newly confident left now was demanding much more. Most of the Labour Party wanted the government to ensure housing, employment, education, medical care, and old age and other pensions for all Britons, not just during the war but afterward. Many wanted the state not merely to control aspects of the economy during wartime but for all times, by nationalizing the means of production (coal mines, first of all), distribution (starting with railways) and exchange (the Bank of England). Such measures would represent an early installment on a program that socialists thought would end long-standing class divisions and privileges. Increasingly they claimed that this was what the war was all about—that such government actions were the ransom that wealthy Britons must pay for deliverance from the German threat. When Communist Russia entered the war on Britain's side, such demands only increased in volume and popularity. The Soviets did not succumb to the German juggernaut as almost every other country had. Many concluded that this meant the Soviet system, the socialist system, spelled the difference.

Labour was an obvious beneficiary of the swing to the left in Britain during the war. But Labour belonged to Churchill's Grand Coalition. Party leaders knew they must compromise on all the measures now clamored for, or the coalition would fall. They walked a political tightrope, and some of their supporters deemed their balancing act a betrayal of principles. In 1942, some of the Labour malcontents, along with a few radical Liberals, bolted to form a new socialist party that would not compromise. They called it the Common Wealth Party, and within months they were running candidates in by-elections—and winning them (they won five by-elections in all during the war). The Communist Party also benefited from the swing to the left. Communist Party membership peaked in Britain in 1943 at about 60,000, and Communist influence in the trade unions, always out of proportion to party membership, grew ever stronger, particularly among miners, engineers, transport workers (despite Ernest Bevin's influence), firemen, foundry workers and those in the electrical trades. At the end of the war, two Communist candidates would win parliamentary seats in the general election.

If any single individual stood to gain from this leftward swing in public opinion, it was the man whom Winston Churchill had appointed to be his ambassador to Russia on May 31, 1940. Stafford Cripps had supporters in the Labour Party (although not among the leadership), in Common Wealth, and among the Communists as well. For a time in 1942 he seemed to embody and to speak for Britain almost in the same way Winston Churchill had two years before. Stafford Cripps became the spearhead of the British left at a time when it was scaling new heights of popularity. The prime minister would have to face him down.

IT IS HARD TO IMAGINE A MAN LESS LIKE WINSTON CHURCHILL IN HIS personal tastes, predilections and appearance than Stafford Cripps. Increasingly stout, Churchill may still have looked robust, but he was not fit, although he had great recuperative powers. The taller, leaner Cripps looked fit, but he never was robust. Churchill gloried in the good things life offered him. Cripps enjoyed life, too—during the prewar era he had had a high income, a splendid country manor house, a close-knit and happy family and many friends—but he looked and acted to a degree like an ascetic. He followed the "Alexander technique," a method of using movement and posture to alleviate pain and various afflictions, and as a result he always stood straight as a post. For some reason, he chose to wear unflattering, rimless spectacles. Because he suffered from colitis, he followed a strict vegetarian diet, lunching "on two nuts and half a carrot"—"parrot food," someone called it—which was hardly what the roast-beef-loving prime minister liked to eat. Churchill drank a great deal—estimating at one point during the war that he had consumed a pint of champagne every day since his twenty-first birthday, and wondering on another occasion if all that liquid would fill a railway carriage (it would not). Cripps, in contrast, forswore alcohol entirely. Churchill famously loved cigars; Cripps, for reasons of health, gave them up. "He has all of the virtues I dislike," the prime minister once mused, "and none of the vices I admire."

Perhaps not surprisingly, the two men did not see eye to eye with regard to religion. Churchill once admitted that he could never be termed a pillar of the church but merely a flying buttress, since he preferred to support it from the outside. Cripps was a devout Christian. One day in September 1942, he spoke at an Albert Hall rally on the same platform as the Archbishop of Canterbury. He entitled his speech "The Challenge of Christianity," and ended it with the following question: "Will we as Christians put our faith and God's purpose before all our selfish desires, before our worldly possessions and comforts and before all else, so that we may help to accomplish that Kingdom of God on earth which Christ initiated and for which He died 2,000 years ago?" Then he rushed from London all the way to the pulpit of St. Matthew's Church in Moorfields, Bristol, a train journey of perhaps three hours in wartime conditions, to deliver a broadcast on the need for organized Christianity to champion the poor and oppressed. And always he appeared the model of probity and high-mindedness. Churchill found it hard to take: "There but for the grace of God goes God," he once muttered as Cripps strode by.

Most importantly, the two men occupied opposite sides of the political spectrum. Churchill, whatever his idiosyncrasies and transgressions, led the Conservative Party, to which he had belonged for twenty years. He was a man of the right. In 1940 Cripps stood unapologetically as a man of the far left. An exceedingly successful barrister (although first trained as a chemist), he had joined the Labour Party in 1928, served as paymaster general in Ramsay MacDonald's second Labour government from 1929 until it fell in 1931, and represented Bristol East in the House of Commons. In 1932, much influenced by Marxism (except with regard to religion—he never relinquished his Christianity, which, indeed, seemed only to grow stronger in him), he helped to found the Socialist League, a left pressure group within the Labour Party. The League campaigned for the unity of all British socialists, including Communists. In 1933 Cripps assumed leadership of the League, which he largely bankrolled. He speculated publicly that, once elected, a socialist government really intent upon abolishing capitalism might have to postpone the next election in order to secure its power. He called the League of Nations an "International Burglars Union" dominated by European imperialists. He voted against British rearmament because he thought Chamberlain would be more likely to send British troops to fight Communist Russia than Nazi Germany. Whatever Cripps favored politically, Winston Churchill and most other Conservatives were likely to oppose.

And not only Conservatives: Labour's leaders believed there was only one road to socialism for Britian, the parliamentary one. Most of them despised and feared both communism and Communists, whether at home or abroad. In 1937 the National Executive Committee of the Labour Party voted to disaffiliate the Socialist League and to expel Cripps unless he toed the more moderate party line. In response, Cripps dissolved the League, which momentarily sufficed to restore him to Labour's good graces. But he did not change his tune. Two years later he mounted a new campaign, demanding a "Popular Front" of antifascists still including Communists to combine against Chamberlain and force his government from office. This time the Labour Party did expel him. Cripps became a man without a party, but he retained his seat in East Bristol, a constituency that would remain loyal through every vicissitude.

Cripps in fact became one of the most prominent politicians in the country. He had a deserved reputation for honesty, decisiveness, efficiency, generosity and rectitude. The far left, within the Labour Party as well as without, recognized him as a leader and thought he would serve one day as prime minister. But at the center of the party, men like Attlee, Bevin, Morrison and Dalton, while acknowledging his great abilities, feared he was squandering them on ill-judged crusades. They considered him unreliable. They would not let him back in until he promised to behave, which Cripps would not do.

Meanwhile, some Liberals and Conservatives had begun to discern his extraordinary qualities. The eminent lawyer Walter Monckton, a confidant of the former king, Edward VIII, for example, considered Cripps to be a man of destiny. He and Cripps became fast friends. But most Britons, probably including Winston Churchill, believed the maverick MP to be a Communist fellow traveler. Churchill, at least, had no use for him. When, in May 1940, shortly after forming his government, Churchill sent Cripps to Russia as British ambassador, he thought he was simultaneously sending coals to Newcastle ("left understands left," as Bevin once notably, and mistakenly, claimed) and ridding himself of a public nuisance. He meant for Cripps to stay away for a long time: "He was a lunatic [now] in a country of lunatics and it would be a pity to move him."

For all their differences, however, the two men shared important qualities. Both possessed powerful intelligence and astonishing capacity for sustained work; both inspired admiration, devotion, even something approaching awe among their followers and, at the very least, great respect (often tempered by great impatience) among their colleagues; both thought they knew best what was good for their country, to which they were selflessly devoted; and both assumed it was their destiny to lead others. For all these reasons, an eventual head-on collision between the two men seemed preordained.

CHURCHILL MAY HAVE THOUGHT HE WAS SENDING CRIPPS TO PURDAH when he sent him to Russia, but, in fact, he was facilitating his restoration to the political mainstream. He did not realize that Cripps already had begun to rethink his political position and that the stint in Russia would further clarify it for him. Cripps had favored a Popular Front early in 1939, and British Communists did too—but later in that year, unlike the Communists, Cripps "would put socialism aside," as one Labour man recorded with surprise after talking with him, to concentrate on the most important matter, which was getting rid of Chamberlain. He would cooperate with anti-appeasement Conservatives to achieve this goal; he would cooperate even with Winston Churchill. So he no longer believed, as the Communists professed to, that one Conservative was as bad as another. Moreover, as war with Germany drew ever closer, Cripps abandoned all thoughts of the revolutionary defeatism advocated by British Communists, determining instead to do whatever he could to defend his country against the Nazis.

When war broke out, Cripps acted upon both these aperçus by quitting his lucrative law practice so that he could devote himself full-time to the nation. Consulting with David Lloyd George and publishing his alternative Cabinet in the *Daily Mail*, he tried to play a part in bringing down Chamberlain. He still would not rejoin the Labour Party, but he accepted from the hands of Winston Churchill the appointment as ambassador to Russia because he judged he could be useful to his country there. He thought he could better interpret Soviet policies to Britain, and Britain's to the Soviets, than the typical Foreign Office diplomat. More particularly, he believed that the Nazi-Soviet Pact of 1939 could not endure, since the Nazis and Communists were natural antagonists. He hoped, as ambassador, to be able both to hasten the pact's end and to ensure that Britain benefited when the end came.

Cripps did not arrive in Russia as a starry-eyed supporter of communism, then, if ever he had been one, but as a patriotic Briton serving his nation. In any event, the longer he stayed in Russia, the less starry-eyed he became. "One thing has been proved here," he wrote to his daughter within a few months of arrival, "and that is that you cannot leap into Utopia in one bound." He did not question the necessity of the Revolution of 1917, or that Russian Communists strove within the Russian context for an egalitarian society such as all socialists desired, but he realized quickly that Russian practices would not necessarily translate to other countries, and certainly not to his own. "Here," he wrote from Moscow to a British friend, "nothing is ever said frankly and freely because none of them dares to talk." It followed that he could never agree with British Communists who wanted to import the Russian model to Britain.

A similar reorientation took place in Cripps's understanding of Russia's foreign policy. He had come to realize that, contrary to Communist claims, Russian diplomacy did not break new ground, and that principles of international working-class solidarity did not inspire it. Rather, Joseph Stalin and his subordinates practiced cold-blooded realpolitik just as the czars had done, and for the same purpose: to protect Russian interests as they understood them. That explained the pact with the Nazis as well as Russian interventions in Poland, Finland and the Baltic countries. On the one hand, Cripps sympathized with the Russian approach. He believed that legitimate security concerns prompted it. On the other hand, he parted company with British Communists who continued to insist that it sprang from high idealism. He knew that it did not.

Cripps felt politically isolated and underutilized in Moscow. Stalin and his minister of foreign affairs, Vyacheslav Molotov, kept him at arm's length because they did not wish to provoke Germany by treating with the representative of Germany's enemy. Predictably perhaps, Churchill and the Foreign Office back home often disregarded Cripps's advice and announced new policies without consulting him. The archives contain a series of protests written by the increasingly irritated ambassador. London noted these. "I am sorry for him," wrote one Foreign Office mandarin to another. "Reading between the lines one can see his disillusionment which has made him peckish. I hope you may be able to soothe him." But London failed to soothe him—or to make better use of him.

Cripps understood that the prime minister and the Foreign Office did not trust him. He did not trust them either. He thought the Foreign Office practiced a reflexive anticommunism that had needlessly driven Stalin into Hitler's arms. He abhorred Churchill's long history as a crusading anticommunist. Now he strove to teach his masters in London that Soviet policies lay rooted in deep and well-founded suspicion of the West. He wanted to modify Britain's Russia policies accordingly. The government did not modify them. So Cripps began ignoring London's instructions when they conflicted with his own plans. The prime minister grew ever more exasperated with his ambassador.

And then Cripps could not keep his hand entirely out of British domestic politics, either, even from a distance of several thousand miles. Special Branch, Scotland Yard's intelligence unit, took note when he sent telegrams to British trade unions "saying that he was kicking his heels in Moscow and urging them to create enthusiasm amongst their Members of Parliament for an improvement with their relations with Moscow." Churchill's reaction to such exhortations may be imagined.

More importantly for the long run, along with many in the Labour Party and on the left more generally, Cripps believed that Britain should announce her war and peace aims, both to contrast them with those of her enemies and to provide inspiration at home and abroad. Churchill resisted this call: he held that such a pronouncement would open a Pandora's box of political disputation. That would constitute a diversion from the task at hand, which was killing Germans. But also he was out of sympathy with the call, which he thought was inspired by woolly-minded idealists. This was an early sign of the gap that would grow ever wider between his conservatism and the aspirations of a majority of British voters.

Cripps, languishing in Moscow, nevertheless took it upon himself to write a statement outlining his socialist vision of a postwar Britain and a postwar world and then to circulate it among certain well-placed friends back home. The statement said, in part:

> Those who seek to build a world order, based upon peaceful and prosperous foundations, must be prepared in the first instance to make a reality of their own democracy, both in its political and economic spheres. In the past, pretenses and shams have often cloaked the actual rule of a

privileged few under the high-sounding titles of popular government. We must have done with all such unrealities. . . . The interests of the community and of humanity override the selfish interest of the individual not merely in theory but in the hard facts of everyday life.

He would extend these principles beyond the borders of his own country: "Throughout the Empire we must show ourselves ready to apply to others the same standards of liberty and freedom as we so strongly claim should rule our own lives." Thus he added his voice to, and tried to help shape, a swelling chorus. If Churchill saw Cripps's document he gave no sign. But the longer the prime minister refused to discuss postwar options, the more alienated Cripps (and not only Cripps) became.

RELATIONS BETWEEN PRIME MINISTER AND AMBASSADOR MOMENTARILY improved after Germany invaded Russia on June 22, 1941. Cripps, who had been predicting this development all along (although he was not at first confident that Russia could withstand it), believed he had been vindicated. He welcomed Churchill's famous speech about the invasion, which, while retracting none of his earlier criticisms of communism, offered the Russians all support within Britain's power: "Any man or state who fights against Nazidom will have our aid. . . . It follows therefore that we shall give whatever help we can to Russia and the Russian people." Eden, who had replaced Halifax as foreign secretary, flew out to Moscow and with Cripps negotiated a mutual assistance pact with Britain's new ally. This treaty marked the apogee of Cripps's diplomatic career. Moreover, Cripps developed an enduring respect for the debonair foreign secretary. He thought they worked well together.

But then on September 22, Churchill sent Lord Beaverbrook to hammer out details. He could not have sent someone less likely to get along with Stafford Cripps if he had tried, although, as it turned out, Lord Beaverbrook got along well enough with Joseph Stalin.

Beaverbrook had resigned as minister of aircraft production in April 1941, and Churchill had appointed him minister of supply in June. He arrived in Moscow in late September accompanied by FDR's representative, the American roving ambassador Averell Harriman. Upon meeting Cripps, Beaverbrook embarked upon the customary campaign of flattery: "He told me that he and Anthony [Eden] were the only two Crippsites in the Cabinet," Cripps recorded in his diary, and he "mentioned to me the need for me to join the Government." It didn't work. Cripps gave Beaverbrook credit for one thing—"He is dead keen to win the war"—but Cripps knew he wanted a different kind of postwar Britain than Beaverbrook did. He deemed the latter to be "about the most reactionary person possible." When Beaverbrook asked him where they differed politically, Cripps replied baldly: "on the attitudes towards management and Labour questions."

That was for starters. Beaverbrook's subsequent conduct widened the gap. According to Hugh Dalton, who may have been repeating malicious gossip, Beaverbrook "took possession of Cripps's office in the embassy and turned him out of the room. When he wanted him he opened the door and bellowed, 'Cripps!' When dining out he demanded that an orchestra should be produced." Beaverbrook certainly thought Cripps was a sanctimonious prig. The Russians kept offering drinks and toasts, but the teetotal ambassador always refused to join in. Beaverbrook drank and toasted with gusto. He also thought the Russians despised Cripps for being an upper-class theoretical socialist, but respected him—Beaverbrook— because he was a tough-minded, no-nonsense newspaperman. Anyway, Beaverbrook had Churchill's blessing and full support while Cripps did not, so he had the authority to exclude Cripps from most of his meetings with Harriman and the Russians. He did not even inform him of what transpired at them.

This was not the way to work with Stafford Cripps. For months he had been thinking he could better serve his country at home anyway. The week before Beaverbrook arrived, he wrote to Eden: "I am not prepared to . . . put myself permanently out of British politics for the sake of a diplomatic career." On October 1, with Beaverbrook now in Moscow, he wrote to Eden again: "What do you think of the idea that I return to England . . . on October 15?" Eden kept replying that the prime minister wished him to stay. Cripps hung on with increasing frustration for some months more, but he understood Churchill's true motivation. "I am pretty sure the major part of Winston's desire for me to remain here arises from the domestic political situation and not from his view as to the needs of the position out here."

Cripps had that right. Autumn 1941 was when the mood of the country and of the House of Commons darkened: when men began calling again for a smaller, more efficient War Cabinet; for Churchill to give up his position as minister of defense; and for a declaration of war and peace aims on the lines of the one Cripps had recently released. Moreover, this was when they began feeling increasing gratitude for the Soviets, who were bearing the brunt of the war against Germany and unexpectedly still in the fight. "'Thank God for Russia' is a frequent expression of the very deep and fervent feeling for that country which permeates wide sections of the public," the Home Intelligence branch reported. British Conservatives found, for the first time, that anticommunist and anti-Soviet rhetoric had little or no impact, or had become actually counterproductive. So did Labour Party leaders, who remained as reflexively anticommunist and suspicious of the Soviets as ever.

Cripps's views on Russia and communism had evolved, but the British public did not know it. To many, including many who were not Communists, he was more a hero than ever. They believed that he had primary responsibility for the Anglo-Russian mutual assistance agreement; that the Soviets respected and worked well with him; that he, better than anyone else, even in the socialist Labour Party, could forge an understanding with Russia that would be good for Britain. Of his disputes with Churchill and Beaverbrook, his disillusionment with certain Soviet practices, and his initial doubts about their powers of resistance, they had little inkling. The press began to speculate about his future: "Someday Sir Stafford will return from Moscow," wrote one journalist. "He will have a great following. His sense of power, never modest, will be developed fully. He will be dressed up in the garb of leadership—and he will find somewhere to go!" Another wrote: "He would return to Westminster with greatly increased prestige as the man who successfully handled our relations with the USSR through a most difficult period. He would have the advantage of coming fresh to the scene, his reputation uncontaminated by any of the failures and controversies of the war years." What would be the result? "Shrewd political observers talk of him as the next P.M.," a third journalist observed.

Cripps's friends from both sides of the political spectrum were also pressing for his return. They believed that a great future lay before him. "I wonder if Stafford fully realizes the vacuum that is deepening in British 'left' political leadership, & that now for the first time he might be able to rally sufficient support young and vigorous enough to start building an alternative political block," wrote one socialist, who thought Labour Party leaders reflexively anticommunist, and Communists reflexively pro-Russian. From the Conservative side, his friend Walter Monckton, the eminent barrister, wrote bluntly: "I have discussed you as a leader with the most diverse people, from Nancy Astor up and down. I find them all attracted by the possibility. I wish, therefore, you would begin to turn over in your mind whether it would be easy and safe in the national interest for you to hand over your Embassy to someone else? . . ."

Cripps no longer needed such prodding; he was thinking seriously about his future now. "I am quite convinced that I couldn't possibly go into the War Cabinet or any other job for the Government except upon the condition of many changes of personnel and policies," he informed his wife. How likely was that? He may already have been eyeing Churchill's job. Churchill may already have suspected as much. He told Eden on November 14 that Cripps could come home after all. Then, said the prime minister, "[I will] put my fist into his face."

But Churchill did not let Cripps come home just then. In fact he might have kept him in Moscow indefinitely, calculating that Cripps would cause less trouble there than in Britain, and that Cripps's highly developed sense of responsibility and patriotism would hold him in situ. But Japan attacked Pearl Harbor. America entered the war. Churchill sensed that the mood in London, and hence his own position, were improving. Finally he could afford to grant the difficult and importunate Cripps his heart's desire. It took another few weeks, but Cripps sailed from Murmansk homeward bound in the middle of January 1942. He may not have known what his next step would be, and only generally what he wanted to do when he got there, but many in Britain thought that *they* knew.

CHURCHILL SEEMS ALWAYS TO HAVE KNOWN PRECISELY WHAT HE WANTED to do. Now he wanted to continue as prime minister. He moved quickly, although at first unsuccessfully, to contain the threat Cripps posed to his position. He could not immediately prick the Cripps bubble. But for the duration of the war he largely kept the initiative and the upper hand in his dealings with the former ambassador. The prime minister proved himself yet again a skillful manager of men, and also a master of political maneuver.

Cripps arrived in Britain on Friday, January 23, 1942. Churchill invited him and his wife, Isobel, to Chequers for lunch on Sunday, the 25th. "Well Stafford, how have you returned? Friend or foe?" he inquired of his guest. Cripps replied: "a friendly critic or a critical friend." The sparring continued over a lengthy meal and postprandial conversation that touched on many aspects of the war and on India. Churchill drank four different wines and several brandies. Cripps, of course, abstained. Eventually the prime minister came to the main point. As his critics had been arguing, war production remained insufficient, despite all efforts to increase it. He would attempt to satisfy them, and to solve the problem, by creating a Ministry of Production. The new minister would have a seat in the War Cabinet. All of this Cripps approved. Then came the surprise: despite the objections of both Attlee and Bevin, Churchill had decided to appoint Lord Beaverbrook to head this new ministry. That would open the Ministry of Supply, Beaverbrook's present job. Churchill would be glad for Cripps to take it. He would have a free hand there—mainly; in some respects, however, Supply must be subject to Production. Moreover, although the minister of supply would have a seat in the Cabinet, he would not sit in the War Cabinet.

Churchill must have known that Cripps's first reaction would be negative: How could the former ambassador welcome a position subordinate to the hated Beaverbrook? How could a man possessing so great a popular following relish serving as a member of the second rather than the first eleven—that is to say, in the Cabinet but not in the War Cabinet? But Churchill knew what he was doing. He was willing to bring Cripps into the government in part to satisfy a growing chorus, in part to make better use of the former ambassador's manifest abilities. He did not want him in the War Cabinet, however, where he might appear as an alternative prime minister. The offer may have served a more Machiavellian purpose as well. Cripps must take time to consider it. That would mean that he could not gracefully participate in a critical three-day debate on the government's conduct of the war concluding with a vote of confidence (on which the prime minister was insisting) in the House of Commons the next Thursday, January 29. Churchill was muzzling a potentially dangerous critic. And if, after the debate had finished and the votes been tallied, Cripps declined to enter his administration, Churchill may have reasoned, well then so much the better.

Cripps did decline. His written refusal of Churchill's offer arrived on the same day as the vote of confidence after the three-day debate. During that debate, many members, while protesting their loyalty to the prime minister, voiced great anxiety about the situation in the Far and Middle East and South Asia, about the Cabinet and War Cabinet, about Churchill's combined role as prime minister and defense minister, about war production, and more specifically about the failure to help Russia as much as promised in the arrangements worked out by Lord Beaverbrook. This last matter in particular was a subject Cripps knew a lot about, but he kept silent. He knew as well as Churchill that it would be unseemly for him to discuss, let alone to criticize, the conduct of a government that had just offered him a Cabinet position. In the event, only the tiny Independent Labour Party voted "no confidence" in the government: two of its parliamentary members acted as tellers, the third entered the No Lobby alone. Four hundred and sixty-four members voted "aye."

It seems an astonishingly lopsided victory until one recalls that the House contained 640 members in all. No doubt many members could not attend, but some undoubtedly chose not to, so as not to vote, and some, including about twenty Labour members, abstained from voting, although they were present in the chamber. An experienced observer estimated that fifty Tories had intended to abstain, but that Churchill's winding-up speech, delivered in "a minor key," and during which he soberly predicted "misfortunes still to come," evoked in them a reflexive party loyalty. Another witness, more shrewd, and himself a member of the government, wrote: "The criticism of the Prime Minister was not factious, but arises from uneasiness which Members cannot hold within themselves. . . . Many of us in authority have to stamp upon our own uneasiness and say nothing."

Cripps had not been silenced altogether, however. The day after his return to Britain he gave a press conference about Russia so interesting that, according to Lloyd George's PPS, who attended, the journalists "almost forgot to take notes." When he finished, they "showed their appreciation by a terrific display of applause." During the week, while Commons debated government conduct, Cripps made the political rounds, taking counsel with friends and colleagues, including even Beaverbrook. And he wrote to Churchill declining the post just as House members were voting. Perhaps his timing suggests his attitude, and how he would have voted if he had thought it proper to participate in the debate and ballot.

In his letter to Churchill, Cripps aligned himself with the critics who wanted a more thorough reorganization of Britain's war-planning and war-making machine. He argued that the minister of supply, not the minister of production, should control allocation of raw materials and have power to set priorities. He protested against Supply's exclusion from the War Cabinet. He could not join the government, given these restrictions on his power to make necessary changes, but must remain instead merely "a frank and I hope helpful critic." Churchill replied: "I shall always be ready to receive your friendly advice." Later that night Churchill told Beaverbrook he "rejected out of hand any plan to bring Cripps into the War Cabinet at that moment."

So the ex-ambassador remained outside, with his nose pressed to the glass, looking in, planning his next move. Touché, and for the present a draw, although perhaps with slight advantage to the prime minister.

CHURCHILL WOULD REMAIN IN BRITAIN'S TOP POSITION UNTIL JULY 1945. But in February 1942 it would have been reasonable to doubt his staying power, given that he was attempting to deal simultaneously with a world war, an increasingly doubtful and fractious Parliament, and a public whose political sentiment was moving ever to the left. He had effectively gagged a potential leader of the critics during the recent debate, and he felt secure enough to keep him out of the War Cabinet, but he had not muzzled him permanently. Cripps was a magnet for press reporters speculating about his intentions. The gossip did not abate even when the former ambassador withdrew from the public eye to a newly purchased farmhouse (he could no longer afford the grand manor house) to ponder his future. And when he reemerged on February 8 to deliver a broadcast on the BBC about Russia, he succeeded, as he no doubt intended, in stoking speculation further.

"I hope that all you who are listening are settled comfortably by your radio, warm and well-sheltered and with a feeling of gratitude, even though some of you have been bombed out of your homes," he began. "You have had snow and cold during this winter, but not the cold of Russia, where thirty to forty degrees below zero are no exceptional experience. You have known the tragic horrors of prolonged aerial bombardments, and still more of you will have had your houses and your possessions destroyed; but you have not experienced the brutalities and the savage violence and rapine of the Nazi invaders."

That was one theme of his broadcast, to contrast Russian and British conditions: it was worse over there. Another theme was exhortation: for the Allies to win the war, every Briton must work harder, as the Russians did; and make further sacrifices, as the Russians were doing; and vow that "not a moment shall be lost through any failure of mine." He mentioned America once during his talk, and only in passing. People listening to their radios that February night could have been forgiven for concluding that Britain's future depended upon her citizens' hard work—and upon her connection with Russia. And while the man most commonly understood to be Britain's best link with, and interpreter of, the USSR did not in any way suggest that he could work better with the Soviets than the current prime minister could, that did not keep people from thinking it. Churchill would have listened to Cripps's broadcast with grudging admiration, but also with increasing irritation.

Cripps broached another subject in his talk, with great delicacy given its sensitivity, namely, Britain's war and peace aims. This cannot have pleased the prime minister either. "We are anxiously reaching out to that time when the new world for which the peoples are longing, and for which almost every man and woman is daily hoping, begins to show itself in clear outline on our horizon . . . a world of new values, cleansed of the old evils and offering a full and free manhood to the peoples of every class, religion, nation and color . . . that positive achievement which we are determined shall issue from this ghastly war, [which is] itself the brutal negation of every teaching of our Christian civilization." One who heard him reported, approvingly: "His reference to Christianity . . . shows that he has not swallowed all Stalin's doctrines. . . . The trouble in the past has been—so the talk goes—that there has been no one to replace Winston. Now Cripps is the man!"

All things being equal, however, Churchill still could deal with Stafford Cripps. To serve in his place as minister of supply, he chose Andrew Rae Duncan, a powerful businessman for whom Chamberlain had arranged a seat in the House of Commons in January 1940. Chamberlain had also appointed him president of the Board of Trade, a position in which Duncan had continued to serve under Churchill until October of the same year, and to which Churchill had reappointed him in June 1941. The prime minister intended to stick with Beaverbrook as minister of production, even though Ernest Bevin, who may have wanted the ministry for himself, continued to object strenuously. Churchill promised to safeguard Bevin's powers as minister of labor, and Bevin acquiesced, at least for the moment. The prime minister also made a number of other small changes to the government, of which the most notable was bringing in Harold Macmillan as undersecretary of state for the colonies. It was a minor reshuffle only, and Cripps remained out in the cold, which was where Churchill wanted him.

Then war developments dangerously complicated matters. On February 12 three German ships (two battle cruisers and a cruiser) left Brest, heading for their German home ports. They sailed up the English Channel in broad daylight, hugging the French coast, joined by an escort of smaller ships and fighter airplanes flying at mast height to avoid detection by radar. The British did not discover them until almost too late, itself a great humiliation, and then managed to damage only one seriously, and even that one not fatally. All three ships reached home port in Germany.

Parliament buzzed with this news; indeed, the whole country did. If Britain's vaunted navy could not catch three German ships sailing up the coast of France in broad daylight, how could it protect the country from invasion? But the episode did not merely cast the British military in a bad light. Churchill "cannot excuse himself because he has always been talking war," expostulated Lloyd George's PPS. In discrediting the prime minister, the fiasco emboldened detractors who previously had been whispering that he had nothing beyond a magnificent voice. As the PPS continued excitedly: "People . . . were saying this was the end of Churchill. . . . Names are already being discussed in high places." It is easy today to minimize the unease felt then; it was not so easy in 1942. Even government ministers wrestled with this dilemma: they knew Churchill had saved the country two years before; but they thought that his arrogance, windiness and inability to delegate jeopardized it now. The minister of food, Frederick Woolton, tossing fitfully in bed all night, finally "came to the conclusion that it might be my duty to resign from the Government in order to break it."

That was February 13. Two days later news arrived of the fall of Singapore, a military disaster in comparison with which the escape of three German ships was a mere pinprick. The Japanese captured 130,000 men, three times as many British and British imperial troops as the Germans had taken in France. One military historian wrote of the British situation in the Far East at this point: "There was only abject defeat, surrender to numerically inferior enemies who had proved themselves better and braver soldiers."

Now Woolton, who despite his heartburning had done nothing to precipitate matters, wrote in his diary that Churchill was "heading for a downfall" anyway. Stormy scenes took place at the Palace of Westminster. Liberal MPs vented their frustrations at a private meeting. "A regular hullabaloo" took place at a private meeting of Labour MPs. Even at the private meeting of Conservative MPs belonging to the 1922 Committee:

Mr. Calderwell said he hoped the Prime Minister was being kept in touch with the general opinion of Members, namely that further drastic changes in the Gov't were desired & that Members were not satisfied with the present position. . . . Flt Lieut Raikes said that he did not agree with the Prime Minister holding the office of Minister of Defense as well as that of Prime Minister. Mr. Strauss . . . suggested that all the Members of the present War Cabinet should place their resignations in the hands of the Prime Minister so that he should have a free hand in selecting men of the highest ability, irrespective of party. Sir Cuthbert Headlam thought that the 3 Service Ministers should be in the War Cabinet.

It was one thing for Liberal and Labour MPs to voice discontent about a Conservative prime minister. It was another for Conservatives to do it themselves. But then, many of them had never liked or trusted Winston Churchill. He had just won a vote of confidence by 464 to 1, but he could not feel confident now.

RELUCTANT AT FIRST TO MAKE SUBSTANTIAL CHANGES, FINALLY Churchill moved quickly, even as the rumor mills continued to grind, and the various players plotted and planned—some for advantage in a reworked government, a few perhaps for the premiership itself. Many predicted that Cripps should or would have it, but other names bubbled to the surface, too: most prominently Eden's and Beaverbrook's. One Labour MP and junior government minister who held himself aloof from the plots wrote despairingly in his diary: "Parliament is given over to intrigue." Churchill was lucky that the critics did not coalesce behind a single leader, such as Cripps, and luckier still that Cripps did not possess the ruthless qualities and single-mindedness of, say, Lloyd George when he had moved to depose Prime Minister Asquith during World War I. Cripps, who was talking with family and friends about mounting a parliamentary coup, did nothing concrete.

Churchill, for his part, did not approach his most dangerous rival, but on February 16 he talked with Eden, who had repressed his own ambitions for the duration of the war and who argued that Cripps must be included in any new War Cabinet, if only to contain him. On February 17 the prime minister conferred with Beaverbrook (for whose ambitions see Chapter 9), who, predictably, expressed strong opposition to bringing in Cripps. Churchill also sounded out Attlee. The leader of the Labor

Party most emphatically opposed bringing Cripps into the War Cabinet. As one historian later explained: "Having excommunicated Cripps in the peace, he [was] not going to make him assistant Pope during the war." Churchill took it all in and made up his mind. By the end of February 18, or possibly sometime during the small hours of the morning on February 19, he knew he wanted a thorough reconstruction of his government—and how to do it.

The relative small-fry first: within the larger Cabinet he would weed mercilessly (it took some weeks to complete the cull), especially at the junior levels, replacing various assistant secretaries, parliamentary secretaries and undersecretaries with men he deemed more suitable. Sometimes he replaced their superiors as well: for example, David Margesson, Chamberlain's chief whip, whom Churchill had appointed to the War Office in 1940, he now fired unceremoniously, along with Maurice Hankey, another former appeaser who had been serving as chancellor of the Duchy of Lancaster. He then made nearly a clean sweep of former appeasers by dropping from the War Cabinet its sole remaining Chamberlainite, Kingsley Wood, although he retained him as chancellor of the exchequer. So one effect of the reconstruction of February 1942 was to rid the War Cabinet of, and to demote, virtually all the remaining "men of Munich."

Next Churchill went after what he considered to be dead wood on the Labour side. He had resolved to dismiss Arthur Greenwood. Aside from staunchly opposing Halifax's proposal to approach Mussolini in May 1940, the minister without portfolio had contributed little. But Churchill also knew that Labour loyalists would react with outrage when he sacked the deputy leader of their party. His method of mollifying them reveals his mastery of the political game: he would sack Greenwood but simultaneously promote Labour Party leader Clem Attlee to become secretary of state for the dominions—and deputy prime minister (which would mollify not only Labour supporters but Attlee himself).

Churchill's method of dealing with Cripps best illustrates his political cunning. He decided to bring his rival into the War Cabinet after all, and, though he did not want to, as Lord Privy Seal, which had been Attlee's previous job. Attlee would then be reconciled, because his own promotion meant he would outrank the newcomer. But at the same time Churchill decided to bestow upon Cripps his own position as Leader of the House of Commons. It seemed a great concession, but one suspects that Churchill did not view it that way. The role of the Leader of the House is to be a general interpreter of government policy to House members, and of House opinion to the government, and Churchill may have thought that Cripps could not do the second part of this job. After all, he was not a clubbable figure; for obvious reasons he did not enjoy the House smoking room or bar, and he was no "House of Commons man," although he had some followers there. He belonged to no party, which meant that he had no claque of men to automatically support him. His relationship with the Labour Party, which had expelled him, remained prickly at best; he had hardly any relationship with most backbench Conservatives or Liberals. As Leader of the House, Cripps would come into contact every day with members who disliked and distrusted him, and he would faithfully have to report back their sentiments, grievances and the like. Churchill may have thought that there would be a honeymoon period, but that the back-benchers would ultimately sour on their new Leader, begin to hound him and eventually bring him down.

And finally Beaverbrook: if his longtime colleague and comrade continued to oppose the most important changes Churchill intended to make, then he would replace him as minister of production with Oliver Lyttelton, another high-powered old friend who had served most recently as minister of state in Cairo, and who was, like Beaverbrook and Duncan, a man with one foot in politics and the other in business. Moreover, Churchill judged correctly that Lyttelton would object less strenuously to certain restrictions on his powers as minister of production that Bevin was insisting on and that Beaverbrook found insupportable.

On the morning of February 18, Churchill talked over the main aspects of the reconstruction again with Beaverbrook and Eden. The latter wrote in his diary that Beaverbrook was "vehement against Cripps as Leader of the House," but then he did not know Churchill's plan to ultimately sidetrack him, if indeed a plan it was. Anyway, Churchill did not change the plan, although, perhaps to satisfy Beaverbrook, he asked Eden whether he would take the House leadership post in addition to his post as foreign secretary. Eden requested, and Churchill granted him, time to consider. When the two men left, Churchill ate lunch. A sign of the importance with which he viewed the situation was that he forewent his afternoon nap. Instead, with reluctance that may be imagined, but also perhaps with secret pride in his own craftiness (if we are right in judging it so), he summoned the former ambassador. Cripps had only just finished addressing the Empire Parliamentary Association on the subject of Anglo-Soviet relations in a packed Committee Room 14 of the House of Commons, where, according to Chamberlain's former minister of war, Leslie Hore-Belisha, he had met "with great approval." It was 2:30 in the afternoon. Within minutes, Churchill had offered and Cripps had accepted the two posts—Attlee's old position, Lord Privy Seal, and his own, Leader of the House of Commons. Eden might still be considering whether he could fill the latter post while continuing to serve as foreign secretary, but it would not be offered him now.

So that was one part of the reconstruction done. Churchill next summoned Attlee, whom he had to reconcile to the departure of Greenwood and the inclusion of Cripps. They were discussing these subjects and the reconstruction more generally when, at 5:30, Eden reappeared, hotfoot from yet another consultation with Beaverbrook. The latter had reversed himself and now was arguing for a War Cabinet of just four: the prime minister, Eden, Attlee (although in fact he despised the Labour Party leader, as would soon become apparent) and Cripps, although still not as Leader of the House. The three talked over this new possibility, but came to no conclusion. They broke up for dinner and agreed to reconvene at 10:30 that night.

Churchill sat at his desk sketching out combinations and permutations. When Eden and Attlee returned at the appointed time, he had alternative War Cabinets for them to consider. He handed over two sheets of paper, one containing five names, the other seven. Greenwood's name did not appear on either list; Attlee's did, on both, and his pleasure at seeing perhaps for the first time the words "Deputy Prime Minister" next to it may be surmised. Cripps's name appeared on both lists as well, but now at least Attlee had been squared, and he would not oppose the changes. Eden's name also appeared on both lists. The three mulled and discussed some more. Then Beaverbrook arrived.

As it happened, Churchill now had in the 10 Downing Street Annex nearly a quorum of his current War Cabinet, and the ensuing discussion provides further insight into their personal relations. But first he brought his friend into an empty room, where he showed him the two sheets of paper with the lists of names. Beaverbrook did not care for either. He said, "Take the five and leave me out. I want to retire." This was true. The millionaire lord had unexpectedly emerged as Russia's strongest advocate in the government (Cripps remained its most popular advocate in the country), and he found it tough sledding. He believed that Russia held the key to the war, and also perhaps to his own future. He wanted to supplant Cripps and campaign for more and faster aid to Russia, which he could do only from outside the government. In addition, perhaps he did not relish facing the socialist Bevin in a Cabinet strengthened by the socialist Cripps. He knew that the two had been consulting since the latter's return from Russia, and that they would present a formidable combination in the War Cabinet. Also, as he had argued earlier, he thought Eden, not Cripps, should become Leader of the House of Commons. As for his opinion of Attlee as deputy prime minister, he said to Churchill: "His abilities [do] not warrant the position. His contribution towards fighting the war has been nothing, save only as leader of a party who is always seeking honors and places for his followers. . . . We want tougher fellows at a time like this. Fighting men." His old friend listened without sympathy. "The Prime Minister invited me to go into the next room and give my views there."

When Beaverbrook entered the room he saw Attlee and Eden (and also Minister of Information Brendan Bracken and James Stuart, who was Margesson's replacement as Conservative Party chief whip), but he did not hesitate. "I repeated what I had just told the Prime Minister, adding that Cripps was being appointed Leader because he had made a successful speech in a Committee Room of the House that day. But as Attlee had made a very bad speech to the Labour Party, this criterion provided an additional reason why he should not be Deputy Prime Minister." This seems entirely gratuitous, but Beaverbrook may have known something Attlee would rather he did not. According to Eden, earlier that afternoon the Labour Party leader had been "vehement in his denunciation of Max [Beaverbrook] and would not allow him any value in any post." Now the soon-to-be deputy prime minister looked at Beaverbrook and asked innocently: "What have I done to you that you treat me in this way?" Beaverbrook replied: "Why should I not talk frankly? You criticize me and I make no objection." Attlee answered him quite falsely: "I never did."

The meeting broke up after midnight. Before they parted, Beaverbrook informed Churchill that he would not join the new government. The most important reason for this he did not mention: that he intended to go all out for more and quicker aid to Russia. But what he did tell the prime minister was also true: he could not stomach Attlee as deputy prime minister or Cripps as Leader of the House. In any case, he could not serve as minister of production so long as he lacked control over aircraft production, ship production and manpower, and Bevin would not relinquish his hold over this last. Churchill, who had Oliver Lyttelton up his sleeve, said the selections would stand. He offered Lord Privy Seal, Attlee's old post, to Beaverbrook, who declined it immediately (luckily, since Churchill had already offered it to Cripps, who had already accepted it). He offered to put him in charge of all foreign supplies; Beaverbrook declined again. In that case, Churchill instructed, Beaverbrook must sign a statement saying he had refused a position in the government on grounds of ill health. To this Beaverbrook assented. A few days later Churchill persuaded him to go to America, to coordinate the pooling of Allied resources. Churchill told him: "We will gain in tranquility, but we will lose in activity." He was right about the second point, but completely mistaken about the first. The checkered story of the Churchill-Beaverbrook wartime relationship was far from finished.

BY THE END OF FEBRUARY 1942, CHURCHILL HAD ARRANGED A GREAT shift in the balance of power in his War Cabinet. Cripps, infinitely more able and ambitious than Greenwood, but much less predictable and controllable, joined Attlee and Bevin on the socialist side. Lyttelton, highly capable but less dynamic and ambitious than Beaverbrook (not surprising, few were), joined him and Eden on the Conservative side. Sir John Anderson, the seventh man in the War Cabinet, belonged to no party. To put it succinctly: Cripps in, Beaverbrook out, socialists and Conservatives at numerical parity.

Churchill had overseen this reconstruction partly in order to satisfy public opinion, and more importantly, to strengthen his government, and thus his own position, politically, but he could not have liked it. The left had gained strength, the right had lost it, and Stafford Cripps had climbed another rung in his ascent toward the very top. Moreover, the strains of this period were taking a personal toll, as would soon become apparent. The prime minister had played a relatively weak hand well, and his cunning might bear fruit in the future: nevertheless, this latest round had gone to Cripps.

CHAPTER 8

Coping with
Mr. Cripps

IF IN FEBRUARY 1942 WINSTON CHURCHILL THOUGHT HE HAD EARNED A respite from his critics after reconstructing the government, he was mistaken. One Labour journalist, whose reaction may be taken as typical for those belonging to his party, cheered the "decided shift to the Left" that Churchill had engineered, but cautioned that "the changes by themselves have settled very little." He looked to Cripps, not to the prime minister, "to satisfy the insistent demand for a drastic regeneration of the war effort." A Liberal journalist worried that "the one man apart from the Prime Minister, whose driving power and capacity for getting things done commanded general confidence," namely Beaverbrook, had been dropped. Conservatives lamented the evident leftward trend in the government; a few worried about the loss of Beaverbrook, too. One industrialist told a Conservative MP it was "the best news for the indolent manufacturer" that he had yet heard.

So Churchill had no time to bask; quite the opposite, and the unrelenting pressure beating down upon him finally began to show. Never impassive, now he wore his emotions on his sleeve. Circumstances had forced him to play the role of butcher of his government, but in personal matters he had a soft heart. Entering the House of Commons smoking room, he came upon one of the ministers he had sacked, John Moore-Brabazon, who had replaced Beaverbrook as minister of aircraft production in December 1940. He put his hand on this man's arm, observed Beverly Baxter, a Conservative MP and journalist who happened to be in the room at the time, "and said 'Oh, my dear' and the tears welled out of his eyes."

But reconstructing the Cabinet was the least of it. His country's misfortunes in war hit him harder. In the Far East, the seemingly unstoppable Japanese invaded and took Burma: this meant that Ceylon and India lay under threat, even perhaps Australia. Meanwhile, in the North Atlantic, losses to German U-boats mounted perilously. The bad news beat down upon him, and he nearly broke. On March 9 he arrived at a luncheon in his honor to speak in closed session about Britain's position in the conflict. One who attended thought his face "baggy and bloated," his eyes "bulging." This man noted that organizers had provided three bottles of champagne for the prime minister. Upon entrance Churchill downed a cocktail right away, and "on the luncheon table in front of him was a bottle of White Label Whiskey. It was full when he started and half empty when he ended." And finally: "To round off the meal he had a bumper glass of liquor brandy." As the chairman of the meeting spoke of the burdens Churchill carried, "the Prime Minister gave way to his emotion; tears came into his eyes and rolled down his cheeks." Then, when Churchill addressed the gathering, "tears stood in his eyes" more than once. As he finished, "his face flushed, his eyes bulged more than ever, their whites turned red and were flooded with tears."

But he never thought of giving up. Rather, he held on, waiting and working for a turn in fortune. Stafford Cripps may have thought his day was about to dawn, but if so, then he was underestimating the tenacity and cunning of a man who had immense reserves of both.

Churchill would soon demonstrate this, and with regard to Stafford Cripps first of all. His strategy for diminishing his rival—if rival he was, and if strategy it was—had not yet had time to ripen, but choosing him to be Leader of the House had set the most acute antennae vibrating, even in far off Washington, DC. "The thing that interests me," Lord Halifax noted in his diary, "is Stafford Cripps being put to lead the House of Commons rather than Attlee. I wonder why that has been done." Within days, a close reading of *Hansard*, the printed verbatim report of parliamentary proceedings, might have provided a possible answer. Cripps addressed the House for the first time as Leader on February 25. "This great lawyer and great humanist revealed at once the qualities of Parliamentary leadership," gushed a journalist who witnessed the event, but who may have missed its most significant aspect. In the course of a speech devoted to Britain's world situation and the government's plans for coping with it, the Leader of the House of Commons found time to condemn dog racing and boxing matches, and then, when questioned, horse racing, too. He judged these pursuits "completely out of accord with the true spirit of determination of the people in this crisis in their history." He went on to censure "personal extravagance . . . together with every other form of wastage, small or large, and all unnecessary expenditure."

It was vintage Cripps, and because he practiced what he preached, no one could accuse him of hypocrisy. Indeed, many lauded his twentieth-century version of puritanism. Nevertheless, it is hard to imagine that he was representing the views of Winston Churchill, or even of a majority in the government, let alone the country. He was "miles ahead of the band, especially when he talked about dog racing and boxing," David Lloyd George's PPS judged, and went on to report that the Conservative chief whip had been "amazed; he had not been consulted and so far as I can learn no one else had [been either]." "Poor Stafford," his sister-in-law once observed, "he wouldn't know how to talk to a working-man if he met one." In the House of Commons he had not been addressing workingmen, but rather many who represented them. Still, the result might have been predicted. Lloyd George's PPS wrote: "Because of what he said about dog racing . . . he had a row with Herbert Morrison [the home secretary, who held a seat in the Cabinet, and who more than any other man in government had his finger on the pulse of working-class London]. Morrison did not like it." The PPS concluded: "It looks as if Cripps means to make the wheels go round, but I do not think if he does it this way he will be very popular for very long." Churchill had much to contend with now, but if he had read this report he would have smiled.

What further irksome encouragement to self-denial Cripps might have delivered next must remain unknown, for events intervened. He served not only as Leader of the House but also as Lord Privy Seal. In this position he had no departmental duties, but power to range broadly over government policy. He ranged all the way to India, which had long been the object of British left-wing sympathy and was currently endangered by Japan, and which was moreover a land where strong nationalist and independence movements had already threatened grave disruptions. Cripps, along with many on the left, believed a British statement promising independence would rally South Asians to England's cause. He wanted to go to Delhi to present such a statement, and to persuade nationalist leaders that a postwar elected constituent assembly could implement it, so long as any province on the subcontinent had the right not to participate. In the meantime, there would be only two conditions: while the war continued, India would be governed by a representative Cabinet presided over by the British viceroy, and Britain would continue to direct India's strategic defense.

Bevin's description of Churchill at this point—"sitting collapsed in his chair and plaintively saying: 'I suppose this is another of the concessions that I must make for the sake of national unity'"—may describe his general attitude, but must be modified in this instance. First of all, even the prime minister had begun to realize, however reluctantly, that the days of old-style British imperialism in South Asia were drawing to a close. His American and Russian allies had no sympathy for it. Besides, in the face of well-organized opposition to her rule, and given also the demands of world war, Britain no longer had the strength to maintain it. Churchill therefore grudgingly came to accept that Cripps—who had visited India shortly before the outbreak of the war; and who had forged strong links with the Indian National Congress, and more particularly with one of its leaders, the Hindu Indian nationalist Jawaharlal Nehru; and who also had gotten to know prominent Muslims—might be the best Briton to negotiate a graceful end. He would not celebrate it, but nor would he fight it, so long as it happened after the war. This was his position for the moment, at any rate.

Exhausted and stressed though he might be, Churchill remained canny as ever. "The emergence of Cripps has put WC in the background," one important member of the House had just observed. Churchill could never rest there. Why, then, would he object if his most dangerous rival left the country to embark upon a necessary but difficult mission? To the contrary: so long as Cripps remained abroad, he would be out of the public eye; he would be in the War Cabinet but not of it. If he failed in his high-stakes undertaking, then perhaps at last his star would begin to fade. Churchill agreed to the Cripps mission for more than one reason.

The mission's progenitor would have been aware of all of them. But as a socialist, an internationalist, a humanitarian and a patriotic Briton who wanted to win the war and who thought a mollified India would contribute significantly to that victory, he felt he had to go. Was Cripps entirely selfless? One of his secretaries wrote: "If he brought this Indian settlement off, C. would certainly replace Winston." It is inconceivable that this thought did not occur to Cripps, too. It certainly occurred to others. The minister of food, Frederick Woolton, who met him for the first time at just about this moment, for example, drew one conclusion: "The premiership is his goal."

Cripps left for Delhi on March 22 and returned to Britain on April 11. During the interval, Britain's enemies continued everywhere to advance, and her own troops to fall back. At home, discontent, including discontent with the prime minister, scaled new peaks. "One hears nothing but abuse of Winston wherever one goes," the old appeaser Maurice Hankey reported gleefully, "in Clubs, Government offices, Parliamentary lobbies, Fleet Street, private houses." Lloyd George's PPS confirmed this impression: "The stock of the Prime Minister is very low." Churchill knew it. At the end of March he told the editor of *The Times*: "I am an old man. . . . No man has had to bear such disasters as I have."

Had Cripps succeeded in India, then he really might have come back to unhorse the prime minister. His stock would have been stratospheric; the prime minister's was plumbing new depths. But Cripps proved unlucky. Despite waging a skillful and indefatigable campaign with Hindu and Muslim leaders, he could not persuade the former to accept his proposal. The sticking point proved to be postponing independence until after the war had been won. Mahatma Gandhi, apostle of nonviolence and India's most famous nationalist, said this point amounted to offering a "postdated check"; he would not accept it. Cripps publicly castigated the Indian leader for refusing seven-eighths of a loaf. In this manner he deflected criticism from himself but stored up troubles for his country—and for Gandhi's. Bitterly disappointed, he headed home. He did not return in disgrace, but neither did he return as the man who had solved Britain's South Asian riddle. His balloon had not been punctured, but a little air had escaped from it, and perhaps was continuing to escape. For Churchill, who did not love the idea of Indian independence anyway, Cripps's failure would have been one bright spot during a very dark period.

GERMANY DELIVERED YET ANOTHER DEVASTATING BLOW TO BRITAIN (and to Churchill) on June 21, this time in North Africa. A fierce battle had raged there for weeks. Now, although leading numerically inferior forces, General Erwin Rommel, commander of the German *Afrika Korps*, captured Tobruk in Libya, and nearly 35,000 more prisoners; British and imperial troops fell back past the Egyptian frontier all the way to El Alamein, only fifty miles from Alexandria and eighty from Cairo. Churchill, who had traveled to America to argue against opening a Second Front against Germany on the European mainland in the near future, and in favor of opening one in French West Africa ("Operation Torch") instead, received the bitter news in the White House in the presence of President Franklin D. Roosevelt. He now faced the appalling prospect of British expulsion from, and Axis conquest of, the entire Middle East. He knew that he would face, too, yet another row at home.

He had that right. Parliament reacted swiftly when the news about Tobruk and the British retreat reached it. On June 25, twenty-one MPs from the three major parties and every part of the political spectrum—from far right to far left—placed a motion of "no confidence in the central direction of the war" on the Order Paper, the list of House business that is published every day when the House of Commons is sitting. They wanted not to overthrow Churchill but to force further reconstruction of his government. Most of them wanted him to relinquish the Ministry of Defense. Some of them wanted reorganization of the War Cabinet. All of them wanted more incisive leadership, primarily in planning and fighting the war, but also on the home front.

The debate would take place over the first two days of July. As so often since 1939, men were whispering to one another in the hallways of the House of Commons, and twisting arms and convening secret meetings to plan strategy. And the government was taking defensive measures: sending out its whips, in this case from all parties in the coalition, to twist arms too, and to offer blandishments or threats, and generally to rally support. Two pro-government men learned that the critics intended to talk matters over in a private room at the Dorchester Hotel after a cocktail party on the night of June 26. They showed up uninvited and persuaded two MPs to withdraw their signatures from the Order Paper, so that now it contained only nineteen names. But still the vote would take place; it could not be deferred. Nor did the government fear losing it; what it feared was that the number of abstentions would be high, and that this would be taken (not least in America) as a sign that while Parliament still might hesitate to say so, really it no longer had confidence in Churchill's leadership.

Gossip swirled during the run-up to the debate. "There never could have been a Motion put on the Order Paper which has caused more consternation and enquiry," reported Lloyd George's PPS. He learned that the leader of the 1922 Committee had persuaded most Conservatives, including some who would much rather have abstained, to swallow their anxieties and vote to support the government. He kept close tabs on dissident Liberals, but they could bring few votes to the table in any event. He discovered that Attlee and Bevin had tamed the vast majority of Labour rebels. Reluctantly (for he still hoped Lloyd George would supersede Churchill), he came to the conclusion that the critics were "mishand[ling] the thing."

On the day that Churchill returned to Britain from his visit to Washington, newspapers reported the results of a by-election in Maldon, a village in Essex. The government candidate, a Conservative, had been trounced two to one by an independent socialist who advocated closer ties with, and more aid to, Russia, and who wanted the government to issue a declaration of its war and peace aims—in short, a backer of the program now associated in the public mind with Stafford Cripps and the left. A piquant twist: the successful candidate, Tom Driberg, worked as a journalist on a newspaper owned by Lord Beaverbrook, who was said to be "much amused" by the election result. This by-election gave further evidence, should anyone still doubt it, that unease with the direction of the war extended beyond the halls of Westminster.

Meanwhile, Cripps's attitude toward the government and the prime minister had evolved. He must have realized that his own stock had fallen to a degree. He no longer believed, if ever he had, that he could simply supplant Churchill. But he did still believe that the prime minister needed supplanting. On June 17, a few days before the fall of Tobruk, but with discouraging news arriving daily from the Far East and North Africa, he attended a dinner in his honor at the Savoy. There, R. A. Butler recorded in his diary, Cripps "told the astonished company that he wanted an election." A general election in Britain in 1942 would certainly have led to another government reconstruction, as it would have altered the parliamentary balance. It might well have further weakened Churchill's position—and strengthened his own. Later in the evening, Cripps, who belonged to no party and had little to lose if the current party system broke up, explained further: "What he had in contemplation was a joint Government consisting of Oliver Lyttelton [the former minister of state in Egypt who had favored appointment of a popular, if anti-British, prime minister there, and whom Churchill recently had brought home to be minister of production], Anthony Eden and himself." Butler added that Cripps "did not deny that Churchill was the best for the strategic war period . . . [but] implied that in due course Churchill would be pushed aside, because he did not understand the home front." (Actually, this last observation was not a bad prediction.)

Ironically, with Churchill in America, it fell to Cripps, as Leader of the House, to plan the government's defense at the debate preceding the no-confidence vote. But imagine Cripps's dilemma: he wanted to restructure the government and eventually to sidetrack the prime minister; he sympathized, to a degree, with the case of the critics; but instead he must marshal the government's defense. Perhaps it is no wonder he "did it badly," according to Anthony Eden. Not himself a "House of Commons man," Cripps did not know who should lead off speaking on the government's behalf. Ultimately he chose Oliver Lyttelton, one of the two men he thought might help him supplant Churchill. Lyttelton had belonged to the House of Commons for only two years. He knew it no better than Cripps did. When on the first day of the debate Lyttelton launched into his defense of the government, he quickly found himself in trouble, "simply," Anthony Eden judged, "through not being familiar with [House] personalities and practices." Lyttelton so little caught the prevailing mood that during his speech members interjected thirty-five times, almost always critically.

In the end, it did not matter much. When the debate began on July 1, Sir John Sydney Wardlaw-Milne, the Conservative member who moved the vote of no confidence, committed an egregious blunder in an otherwise hard-hitting indictment by suggesting that Churchill give up the Ministry of Defense to the Duke of Gloucester, the third son of King George V. The House broke into disbelieving laughter. Everyone else knew the duke could fill no such role. As one MP put it: "It is true that the Duke of Gloucester might have had more toy soldiers in his youth than the average child, and might have displayed certain abilities there." The mover had ruined his case and his cause. According to witnesses, Churchill, who had returned from America in time for the debate, sat at the front bench, grinning like a Cheshire cat.

The seconder of the motion, the Conservative member for North Portsmouth, Sir Roger Keyes, the former admiral who had played an important role in elevating Churchill to the premiership in May 1940, spoke next. Everyone assumed he wanted to play an important role again, elevating someone else this time, but he surprised them: Keyes had no confidence in the government not because Churchill had too much power, but because he had too little. He argued not that Churchill should be deposed, but that he should be able to more quickly and more often countermand the misjudgments of his chiefs of staff. An incredulous member interrupted to point out that the mover of the motion wanted less Churchill, while the seconder of the motion wanted more. The critics had handed victory to the government before its first advocate had even taken to the floor. It did not matter then that Lyttelton botched its defense.

To compound matters, the critics bungled yet again on the second day of the debate by choosing their most effective advocate, the left-wing Labour MP Aneurin Bevan, to speak first rather than last. Bevan and Cripps had cooperated in the prewar campaigns for socialist unity and a Popular Front to oppose Chamberlain. They remained close political colleagues. With what tangle of emotions did the new Leader of the House watch his erstwhile comrade in arms eviscerate the government and its chief? Quite brilliantly, Bevan charged that "the Prime Minister wins debate after debate and loses battle after battle. The country is beginning to say that he fights debates like a war and the war like a debate." Bevan held everyone's attention; no one laughed derisively at him. If Churchill had had to follow Bevan in his winding-up speech, the atmosphere would have been quite different and more difficult.

Instead, he followed a rather sad figure, the National Liberal Leslie Hore-Belisha, whom the critics had chosen to conclude for them because he had served before the war, and during its earliest stages, as Chamberlain's secretary of state for war. But this former Cabinet minister, who wanted nothing more than to be a Cabinet minister again, emphasized that Britain was fighting with inferior military equipment—for some of which he was himself responsible. Churchill, who followed Hore-Belisha as the last speaker before the vote, made sure to connect these dots for his audience, in case they had not connected them already.

"This long Debate has now reached its final stage," Churchill began. "What a remarkable example it has been of the unbridled freedom of our Parliamentary institutions in time of war. I am in favor of this freedom, which no other country would use, or dare to use, in times of mortal peril such as those through which we are passing. But the story must not end there, and I make now my appeal to the House of Commons." He went on to rebut every charge and criticism, as only he could. He gave no sign of fatigue, or depression, or pent-up emotion. There were no tears on this occasion. Rather, he provided the House with numbers: of men in the various theaters of combat, and of guns and aircraft (without divulging anything the enemy did not already know); and with shrewd assessments of the quality of Britain's weaponry, including the improved weapons that had come on after Hore-Belisha's retirement. Without minimizing losses and defeats, he insisted that the outlook for Britain and her allies, taken all and all, remained positive. He did not scruple to warn that this kind of debate gave comfort to England's enemies, but he did so in typically elegant language: "If democracy and Parliamentary institutions are to triumph in this war it is absolutely necessary that Governments resting upon them shall be able to act and dare, that the servants of the Crown shall not be harassed by nagging and snarling, that enemy propaganda shall not be fed needlessly out of our own hands, and our reputation disparaged and undermined throughout the world." He timed his speech to end precisely at 5 P.M., so that no one could plant seeds of doubt afterward. There was more than a grain of truth in Bevan's charge that he fought debates as if they were wars.

And when the division took place immediately after Churchill ceased speaking, he won yet another parliamentary victory, this time 475 to 25. As in February, it seemed a clear-cut triumph, but again as in February, the figures mislead to a degree. He had carried the House because it still shrank from deposing the man who had rescued Britain in 1940. But he had not allayed its doubts. "THERE NEVER WERE SO MANY VOTES CAST FOR THE GOVERNMENT WITH SO MUCH APPREHENSION," Lloyd George's PPS wrote to his master in capital letters. He estimated that Churchill's speech had persuaded between fifty and eighty Conservatives to oppose the motion who otherwise would have abstained; and that about forty men from all three parties had abstained nevertheless.

That the vote had done little to dissipate uneasiness was further demonstrated less than two weeks later, to one individual at any rate. Minister of Food Frederick Woolton received the chairman of the 1922 Committee, who had played an important role in rounding up Conservative votes for the prime minister. Despite what he had done for Churchill before the vote, this individual remained uneasy. "They are wondering how long he will last," Woolton wrote in his diary after the meeting. The chairman "came to see whether I had any views about succeeding him. The Party wouldn't mind having me, if I would take it on[,] because they know I don't want to hang on after the war is over." Woolton ended almost plaintively: "I don't want to be Prime Minister." (But he appears to have reconsidered his position later.)

MEANWHILE STAFFORD CRIPPS REMAINED WAITING IN THE WINGS. He may no longer have thought he could replace Churchill by himself, or even as part of a triumvirate—in the near future at any rate—but he still wanted to, and he still did intend to shape events. He continued to worry about the direction of the war. He believed that under Churchill Britain was waging it unscientifically and inefficiently and still could lose it. He thought he knew how to fix things. On the very day of the no-confidence vote, he sent Churchill a long memo. If Churchill had accepted it, he would have been going a long way toward satisfying his parliamentary critics. In the memo, Cripps recommended promoting younger, more imaginative army commanders and creating a Military Directorate of three to supersede the Chiefs of Staff. The new group's sole job would to be to advise the defense minister (Churchill) about planning, strategy and tactics. Cripps also suggested that the minister of production should exercise increased powers, including oversight of a newly created Ministry of Materials and Machine Tools. He wanted to streamline bodies concerned with scientific research and development relating to the war. Finally, he proposed reconsidering Britain's bomber policy. It suffered, he thought, from "a rigidity of view in the Air Ministry, which is particularly exemplified by the Minister." "The Minister" happened to be Archibald Sinclair, Churchill's old friend and ally.

Churchill did not answer Cripps right away. Instead he made plans for additional international travel, initially to Moscow, where he would meet Stalin for the first time, and then on to Cairo, where he would help plan countermoves to Rommel as well as other measures. Of course, important military and diplomatic considerations prompted these journeys; but it is significant that Churchill took more of them than any other head of state during the war. In 1942, international travel could be difficult and uncomfortable, even dangerous, but for Churchill it almost always proved a tonic, partly because his hosts treated him as a great man when he arrived, and partly, one must suspect, because while he was away he did not have to deal with the carping at home (and also because occasionally he would take over as pilot of his airplane—he greatly enjoyed this, although it unnerved everyone else). But putting off Cripps proved difficult. With the prime minister poised for departure, Cripps wrote to him again: "I have for the last week or two been working on a note for you elaborating the earlier one. I was going to let you have it this week and ask you to have a talk with me about it." Given Churchill's travel plans, this would now be impossible. But perhaps the prime minister could read the note during his travels. This second document would have upset Churchill whenever and wherever he read it, for it merely reiterated and amplified Cripps's earlier recommendations.

Upon returning to Britain, the prime minister consulted with "Pug" Ismay, his chief of staff, and with the secretary to the Cabinet, E. E. Bridges. Then, on September 2, he wrote to Cripps rejecting almost everything Cripps had proposed. Cripps's daughter recorded in her diary the next day: "D[addy] . . . and the P.M. base their views on foundations too different for them to be partners for an indefinite time." By now Cripps had to be wondering whether he could serve usefully in Churchill's War Cabinet at all. He would make a last attempt to press his case in yet another lengthy and closely argued brief, but by then events had further diminished his influence.

For Cripps, in his role as Leader of the House of Commons, had misunderstood the House of Commons yet again. This time the government had arranged a two-day debate on its policies in India—and apparently nobody wanted to debate. On September 7 Churchill addressed a chamber that emptied even as he spoke. When Attlee rose to speak, Churchill, too, departed, as did most of the remaining members. Finally only sixteen still sat in the great room. The next day, in response to a question, Cripps remarked: "It does cause me, as Leader of the House, very seriously to think when Members cannot wait even . . . to hear the first two leading speeches in the Debate." Such conduct had been disrespectful, he charged. And, he concluded accusingly, "I do not think that we can conduct our proceedings here with the dignity and the weight with which we should conduct them unless Members are prepared to pay greater attention to their duties."

Members had deserted the chamber for two reasons: first, because Conservatives agreed with the government's India policies (which, since the failure of Cripps's mission, no longer envisioned immediate postwar independence), and therefore did not see any reason to debate them; second, because they wanted lunch, and Churchill had begun to speak just when they wanted it most. They typically left the chamber at lunchtime no matter who was speaking. Cripps must have known this, but the practice offended him. When he dared to complain, however, he unleashed the furies. Commons met the next day, September 8, and hostile questioners immediately threatened to overwhelm him. "By what right did the right hon. and learned Gentleman rebuke hon. Members yesterday?" asked one MP. "Is there some special onus on the House to be present [when the PM or deputy PM speak]?" asked another. "Are not ill-informed criticisms of this House likely to have a bad effect on the country?" inquired a third. "May I ask the right hon. and learned Gentleman whether he thinks that it is in keeping with the dignity of the House that he, as Leader, should fling this sort of accusation about?" queried yet a fourth. Cripps compounded matters by refusing to back down: "The onus is on the House" to maintain at least a quorum, he insisted.

Churchill's PPS, whose job was to keep the prime minister informed about Conservative backbench sentiment, reported to him that "Members felt that the collapse of the Debate so soon after your speech was the best vote of confidence you have yet had. In consequence they bitterly resented the lecture on attendance given by the Lord Privy Seal which completely spoiled the effect." The 1922 Committee told the party chief whip, who told the prime minister: "The House of Commons had received a bad blow to its prestige. . . . Sir Stafford's statement should not be allowed to rest unanswered." Labour MPs likewise felt insulted. Greenwood conveyed their outrage to Attlee, who also reported to Churchill. The prime minister must have smiled again. He had been holding his difficult colleague at arm's length for some time now, and at last the strategy for undermining him had borne fruit. In making Cripps House Leader, he had knowingly passed him a poisoned chalice. Finally, Cripps had drunk deeply of it.

At the War Cabinet on September 9, Churchill confronted Cripps directly about the incident. The exchange between the prime minister and the Lord Privy Seal went as follows, according to the minutes:

PM: Why encourage criticism?

LPS: Didn't. Regretted lost opportunity to express support.

PM: Silent support is prhs best. H/C [House of Commons] in v. good mood—better to have left them alone.

LPS: General effect was bad.

PM: Disagreed.

LPS: . . . They might wait—at least until PM had finished his speech.

PM: Didn't worry me—luncheon engagements etc.

Cripps's stock nose-dived. One Labour member wrote in his diary: "His attack on MPs recently is bitterly resented by all groups. . . . I think Cripps' chance of getting the succession is less than it was." Churchill felt free to speak his mind at last. At one of his luncheons, a journalist who dined occasionally with the prime minister recorded that "he made some rather biting references to Sir Stafford Cripps, and spoke of the way in which Cripps 'lived on pea and lentil, with an occasional orgy on a carrot and a pumpkin as a New Year's dinner.' He said that Stalin roared with laughter whenever Cripps' name was mentioned and made fun of Cripps' vegetarian diet."

The climax could not be long postponed; nor could its outcome be any longer in doubt. Cripps's friends recognized as much. One of them wrote to another: "Stafford . . . has reached the position of final humiliation. . . . Churchill . . . can ignore him." Cripps recognized it, too. He wrote to the prime minister, perhaps slightly disingenuously, given that at first he had intended to replace him: "When I joined the Cabinet seven months ago I hoped that I might be able to help the country by cooperating with you in the direction of the war effort . . . [but] there has been a change in our relationship and I do not now feel that you place reliance upon my help." He did not threaten to resign, but the implication was clear. In Churchill, however, he faced a master of the double-edged reply: "I was certainly not aware of any change in our relationship since you first took office seven months ago." Churchill believed Cripps's resignation at that moment would weaken the government just when Britain and America were preparing to launch Operation Torch. And he thought, mistakenly, that Cripps meant to weaken it, meant even to bring it down. He thought Cripps still wanted to replace him.

The prime minister summoned Cripps to 10 Downing Street at eleven o'clock on the night of September 30 to ask him not to resign. Cripps had hesitated to take that final step, but the ensuing interview seemed almost designed to push him into it. Churchill employed not the carrot but the stick, which was ill-advised at any time when dealing with Stafford Cripps. He charged that the Lord Privy Seal attracted criticism "from all quarters. . . . If he went out he would have no future, neither Tories nor Socialists supporting him." Cripps did not take it lying down. As he told Eden afterward, he had "retorted," citing "instances of how badly [the] war was run." For three and a half hours the prime minister and the Lord

Prime Minister Neville Chamberlain, 1938. As he lay dying two years later he wrote to a friend: "I regret nothing I have done and I can see nothing undone that I ought to have done."

Lord Halifax in his office at the British Embassy in Washington, DC. In 1940 he had favored discussions with Italy that might have led to negotiations with Germany. Churchill sent him to America.

The future Prime Minister in 1939 and the man who would become his heir apparent, Sir Anthony Eden.

Prime Minister Winston Churchill in 1940 with his friend and adviser Lord Beaverbrook.

Clement Attlee and Arthur Greenwood in 1940: leader and deputy leader of the Labour Party.

Ernest Bevin, Minister of Labor, in 1941. In the end he had to conscript female as well as male workers, he said: "I was not so much frightened of the women as I wondered what the old man would say."

Members of the War Cabinet and ministers in the garden at No. 10 Downing Street on 6th October 1941. Sitting (from left to right): Ernest Bevin, Lord Beaverbrook, Sir Anthony Eden, Clement Attlee, Sir Winston Churchill, Sir John Anderson, Arthur Greenwood and Sir Kingsley Wood. Standing (from left to right): Sir Archibald Sinclair, A. V. Alexander, Lord Cranborne, Herbert Morrison, Lord Moyne, David Margesson, Brendan Bracken.

Stafford Cripps in 1941. In the middle of the war he thought he might take the Prime Minister's place.

Herbert Morrison, "The Cocky Cockney", also had aspirations of becoming Prime Minister.

A section of the Birmingham crowd assembled on 21 June 1942 to hear Lord Beaverbrook demand the "Second Front Now." Beaverbrook thought he might capitalize on such support to become Prime Minister.

The wartime Prime Minister.

Churchill's triumphant cross-country progress during the general election campaign of 1945. Everyone thought he would win.

Privy Seal went at it, first with hammer and tongs, then more calmly, but still "without agreement."

The next two days saw a flurry of meetings squeezed into the interstices of already hectic twelve-hour schedules. First, on October 1, Cripps consulted with Eden, the colleague he may have respected most. The foreign secretary tried unavailingly to soothe him. Then he consulted with Oliver Lyttelton, to whom he presented his resignation as "decided upon." At eleven P.M., Eden saw Churchill and Attlee at 10 Downing Street. Churchill still thought Cripps was trying to trigger a crisis. He could not get the example of Lloyd George and Asquith out of his head. Lyttelton appeared and reported accurately that Cripps had told him he definitely would resign. This confirmed Churchill's suspicions: "W. up in arms and unwilling to treat," Eden wrote later that night in his diary. He and Attlee attempted to calm the prime minister. Whatever Cripps had thought and planned in February, they told him, the former ambassador no longer believed he could emulate Lloyd George. He had lost too much ground for that, and he knew it. They suggested that Churchill appoint him either to coordinate supply in the United States or to head the Ministry of Aircraft Production (MAP), without a seat in the War Cabinet. This would simultaneously harness Cripps's great organizational powers and, by removing him from the center, render null his capacity for making trouble. Churchill approved this plan.

Although it must have been well past midnight, the two War Cabinet ministers went looking for Cripps. A brisk five-minute walk would have brought them from Downing Street to his two-room flat on Whitehall Court. There they put the choices to him. Eden wrote in his diary that Cripps "seemed to like the idea of both, especially the latter [MAP]." To Cripps, either job represented an honorable way out of the current impasse. He retained grave doubts about Churchill's leadership, but he no longer thought he had power to replace or even to influence him. Back at Downing Street, Eden and Attlee reported their progress to Churchill, who professed his satisfaction.

Next morning, however, the prime minister had second thoughts. At a pre-lunch meeting, Churchill asked Cripps to agree to postpone making any move until after Operation Torch. Cripps had his letter of resignation in hand; he replied that he must check again with Eden. As soon as Cripps left him, Churchill rang the foreign secretary, and by the time

Cripps reached the Foreign Office Eden knew what to say: he warned his friend that the government could not at this moment withstand the political crisis that would follow his resignation. Cripps "argued that my [Eden's] course left all difficulties unresolved and that [the] truth was that he was convinced we should all get on much better without W. anyway." They were back to square one, but with this glaring difference: when first Cripps had occupied square one in February, his political star had been ascending; now, in October, it practically had set. He had no power to shift "W.," however ineffective as prime minister he judged him to be, and he understood as much. Cripps showed Eden his letter of resignation. Another problem surfaced: the letter was a scorcher. "I told him that no PM could accept it," Eden recorded.

In the end, Cripps simply caved. He wrote a second letter, a tamer one, but also agreed to postpone his resignation because it was in the national interest for him to do so. He would await the results of Operation Torch, as Churchill wanted. Here is conclusive evidence of Cripps's high-mindedness, unworldliness and political naïveté. Churchill, with Eden's help, had completely outmaneuvered him. Suppose Operation Torch went badly. Then Cripps would be resigning along with everyone else. If it went well he would resign alone. Churchill and Eden had persuaded him to accept this proposition: "Heads you lose, tails you lose along with everybody else."

When the coin came up heads, then, nobody lost but Cripps. First Operation Torch succeeded in French West Africa, and then General Bernard Montgomery, commander of British ground forces, beat Rommel in North Africa at El Alamein on November 11. This was Britain's first triumph over German forces on land. At Westminster the critics ceased to carp, at least for the moment. Churchill famously announced that even if the two victories did not presage the beginning of the end of the war, they presaged the end of the beginning. The nation rejoiced. And when a few days later Cripps resigned from the War Cabinet and accepted the MAP, hardly anybody noticed. Mass Observation, a British social research organization, discovered that 43 percent of the men and 67 percent of the women responding to a poll were unable to give an opinion of Cripps's action.

Churchill could now safely manage the postponed reshuffle. Its most notable aspect was the promotion of Home Secretary Herbert Morrison into the War Cabinet in place of the demoted Cripps. In this manner the prime minister maintained the same ratio of Labour supporters to

Conservatives as before. Eden took over temporarily as Leader of the House of Commons. And Cripps finished out the war usefully, but in relative obscurity, as minister of aircraft production, with a seat in the Cabinet but not in the War Cabinet.

In the great, if never publicly acknowledged, contest for primacy carried out between Winston Churchill and Stafford Cripps during most of 1942, then, game, set and match to the prime minister.

CHAPTER 9

The Cat That Walked Alone

WINSTON CHURCHILL EXHIBITED PATIENCE AND CUNNING IN HIS DEALINGS with Stafford Cripps. With Lord Beaverbrook, another member of his War Cabinet who would likewise pose a significant challenge to his position, he exhibited those attributes again, as well as insight, great forbearance and sympathy. Beaverbrook represented a different kind of test for Churchill than Cripps ever did, because he only flirted with the idea of mounting a coup, or at any rate of taking the top spot should the prime minister fall. Nevertheless, he caused the prime minister more anxiety and general trouble than Cripps did. While the Canadian-born Beaverbrook was scintillating, dynamic and effective, he also could be obstreperous, conniving and stubborn. You knew where you stood with Cripps; you never knew what Beaverbrook might say or do. He made mountains out of molehills, but also he leveled real mountains. He was a less likely rival to the prime minister than Cripps only because he was more ambivalent about trying to attain the throne. Since he never showed himself to be high-minded, idealistic or naïve, however, but almost always only shrewd, calculating and hard, he also represented the greater danger.

Beaverbrook did not so much crave the top position—although occasionally he thought he could fill it better than anyone else—as crave excitement. He wanted to be where the action was. Once he had found it, he usually wanted to shape whatever followed from behind the scenes. He did not wish to be the prime mover, although, again, the time would come when he thought that for his country's sake he *should* be just that. Rather, he mainly wanted to be the man upon whom the prime mover relied. He sought a leader to follow, a hero worthy of his support. In the wartime Winston Churchill, he found one.

Beaverbrook ladled out flattery to Churchill just as he did to everyone else. "Your broadcast has surpassed anything, and all America is under your influence today." Or: "What you mean to the people in this crisis is beyond reckoning; beyond any figure in our history. . . . [T]he victory, when it comes, will all be yours." And: "I send this letter of gratitude and devotion to the leader of the nation, the savior of our people and the symbol of resistance in the free world." Even: "You are the only guardian of mankind." Such effusions suggest not only the hero-worshiping aspect of Beaverbrook's personality but also the manipulative side, for Beaverbrook always wanted Churchill's support in the War Cabinet. Whatever Churchill made of these effusions (and it is hard to think that he did not enjoy them), they constitute a strand linking the two men and provide insight into Beaverbrook's character.

Yet, from the distance of nearly three-quarters of a century, Beaverbrook appears in his professional capacity to have been hard, above all: manipulative, yes; dynamic, yes; but mainly driven—and therefore often harsh, argumentative, stubborn, ruthless, even cruel. If the war taxed him, it also liberated and justified him, because he could drive not only himself but also others to the absolute limit. Given the circumstances, few dared protest. His secretary thought "there was a touch of sadism" in him. He intimidated and browbeat those he could, and fought with the rest. John Moore-Brabazon, who lost his job at the Ministry of Aircraft Production (MAP) during the Cabinet reconstruction of February 1942, recalled that with Beaverbrook, he "always felt tongue-tied and rather like a little boy trying to conduct an adult conversation with the headmaster of his school." Beaverbrook's self-description in a letter to Churchill explains his effect: "I am the victim of the Furies. On the rockbound coast of New Brunswick the waves beat incessantly. Every now and then comes a particularly dangerous wave that breaks viciously on the rocks. It is called the 'Rage.' That's me."

Regardless, Beaverbrook kept demanding more authority and additional work. After all, the country was in danger, and he knew he could produce the goods. He always did: aircraft when he was at the MAP, tanks when he was minister of supply. Over the course of time, Churchill would offer him the Ministry of Food, the Ministry of Fuel and Power and Light, the Ministry of Agriculture and perhaps other ministries, as well as various other assignments. He valued Beaverbrook's advice and often took it. Even during the intervals when Beaverbrook did not belong to the government, so long as his friend was in the country Churchill continued to consult with him regularly and to depend upon him. He belonged to the circle of intimates—which also included Brendan Bracken and "the Prof," Frederick Lindemann, a science adviser—who regularly drank, smoked and schemed into the small hours of the morning with the prime minister.

But sparkle and amuse though he might over brandy and cigars, no one except Churchill trusted him. "Beaverbrook is an intriguer first, last and always," wrote one who had watched him for many years, "and he is the more dangerous because his intrigues are governed by no principle that I have ever been able to discover—always by personal aims and an insane passion to pull strings." Someone else said of him: "He is two percent genius and ninety-eight percent crook." He could not work in groups, even when Churchill put him in charge of them. He kicked against all traces, above all those that kept him from exercising complete power in his own sphere. When his frustration boiled over, he would send Churchill a letter of resignation. Since he was often frustrated, he resigned a thousand times. One of his best letters put it this way: "I am not a committee man. I am the cat that walks alone."

His thousand resignations did not reflect a secret desire for the quiet life, although no doubt they testify to his hatred at being balked and to a more general fury at interference, inefficiency, sloth and incompetence during a period of great peril. He resigned to let off steam, expecting that Churchill would not permit him to stand down. But he also resigned because he judged that Churchill approved the tactic. He thought: "You wished me to stay in office, to storm, to threaten resignation and to withdraw again." In short: "I made a practice of submitting my resignation. It became a deliberate act of promotion. The object was 'urgency and speed.'"

He thought he knew what the prime minister wanted of him then, but the prime minister only partially grasped what Beaverbrook desired in return. To understand why Beaverbrook was constantly resigning (and at some level, Churchill surely did) was not to understand the man at heart. But then no one really did, or could. Except for compliance with his wishes, Beaverbrook himself did not always know what he wanted. Churchill struggled to find the proper tone to use with him, the better to harness the Canadian's great capacity for work and organization. He would cajole him: "You are in the collar and you have got to go on." He would attempt to pacify him: "Part of my job is to try to smooth things down and keep the team pulling together. . . . Let us keep plodding on . . . and see how things look in another year. I think they will look much better." He would appeal to him: "No one knows better than you how much I depend on you for counsel and comfort." Or, patience wearing thin at one resignation too many, he might respond simply: "I refuse to accept [it]." Patience wearing even thinner, he might finally chastise him: "Your resignation would be quite unjustified and would be regarded as desertion." In this letter he went further: "No Minister has ever received the support which I have given you."

It was true. Churchill worked to conciliate Bevin and Attlee, and to sustain Woolton and Alexander, and to encourage Eden and all the others, but he tried hardest and longest to keep Beaverbrook by his side. When the latter complained that his Cabinet colleagues blocked and conspired against him, Churchill wrote: "There is no question of a cabal by yr colleagues against you, & I shd not allow it if there were." When niggling critics, as Beaverbrook deemed them, made his path difficult, the prime minister wrote in sympathy and support: "You must not forget in the face of petty vexations the vast scale of events and the brightly lighted stage of history upon which we stand." For every letter of resignation that Beaverbrook sent him, Churchill wrote a carefully couched and almost always heartening reply. And when he thought face-to-face conversation would be more effective than another letter, he arranged for that, too: "We can talk about this tomorrow driving . . . to luncheon, if you like."

What Churchill never expected was that Beaverbrook might start to think he could be a more effective prime minister than he himself—as Stafford Cripps did, and at just about the same time.

Because Beaverbrook had played a role in the downfall of Prime Minister Asquith and the elevation of Lloyd George in 1916, some thought of him as a kingmaker and king-destroyer, and even as a potential king himself, even during the summer of 1940, and even with Churchill at the apogee and singing Beaverbrook's praises for what he had accomplished at the MAP: "He's done astonishing things. . . . He's done miracles." That did not stop the leader of the British Communist Party from predicting that Beaverbrook would soon smash Churchill's government. And it did not stop a rival press magnate from warning Anthony Eden a few months later that "Max . . . had an eye to the succession. . . . Max was doing an immense amount of propaganda for himself."

In fact, during this period of supreme crisis, Beaverbrook acted with perfect loyalty to Churchill, and professed it on numerous occasions both publicly and privately. But despite the flattery, which he applied with a trowel, usually he held negative opinions of his colleagues—opinions he could never keep to himself. Soon enough, then, he was telling a journalist that Herbert Morrison "never accomplished anything"; that Bevin had no sense of urgency; that Sinclair "was a nice man," but did as the air marshals told him to; and as for Greenwood: "Well you know all about him" (referring to his problem with drink). He never disguised his impatience when someone talked too much, even if it was Churchill doing the talking. Halifax described a War Cabinet meeting of October 1940 as "more disordered and disorderly than anything I have ever seen. . . . Max Beaverbrook was in despair."

So the inconsequential chatter about his intentions persisted, fed in part by his own conduct. Then Germany's invasion of Russia altered everything. More even than the Japanese attack on Pearl Harbor, Germany's assault upon Russia represented the war's great hinge, although most Britons, including the military experts, did not recognize it as such immediately. They were grateful that Hitler had turned his baleful eye away from them, but they did not believe it would be turned for long. How could the Soviet Army, whose leading generals Stalin recently had purged, withstand the German panzers better than the vaunted French Army had done? Even Stafford Cripps warned Churchill that the Russians probably could not do it.

Beaverbrook placed a different emphasis on events. He did not know how long Russia could hold out, either, but this he knew: the longer the better. Russia possessed nearly inexhaustible reserves of manpower, which, properly equipped, might cause the Germans infinite trouble. Therefore, everything Britain could do to sustain Russia must be done. That the Soviets had enlarged their western border at the expense of Poland and the Baltic countries and Finland, that Stalin had purged not only his general staff but also numbers beyond counting, that he had pursued policies leading to untold misery and death, did not matter. That Beaverbrook himself always had been anticommunist did not matter, either. With Russia in the war and on Britain's side, anything was possible; without her, Britain faced stalemate, at best, or even defeat. The logic was simple: everything for Russia, and no stinting. The British government should sponsor "Tanks for Russia" weeks. It should send food, ammunition, guns and other supplies, difficult and dangerous though the journey to Murmansk might be. The same man who as minister of aircraft production fiercely opposed sending pilots and planes to Canada and South Africa for training purposes, because Britain could not spare them (even though they would return to Britain eventually), enthusiastically supported Churchill's intention to send three hundred Hurricane airplanes to face the Germans in Russia. Already Beaverbrook was beginning to think that Britain should send troops to the Continent to draw off German soldiers from attacking Leningrad and Moscow. He thought that colleagues who voiced qualifications, or who wished to limit British aid, revealed their shortsightedness, or worse.

There was an additional dimension to Beaverbrook's thinking. He realized that the Russian connection would stimulate production in British factories. Up to that point, British Communists, who possessed great influence in the trade unions, had condemned the war as one between rival imperialisms. They had dragged their feet when Beaverbrook, at the Air Ministry or Ministry of Supply, had called for longer hours and speed-ups to increase production. But the German invasion of Russia transformed their outlook. Now, with the motherland of socialism under attack, they supported Beaverbrook's production drives wholeheartedly. For the first time, the Conservative imperialist millionaire lord and the Communist shop stewards, who served as intermediaries between workers and trade-union leaders, saw eye to eye. Perhaps this new association planted certain seeds in Beaverbrook's mind, for surely he understood that the War Cabinet minister who championed aid to the Soviet Union, and who also had the shop stewards behind him, might become leader of a powerful movement.

His newspapers echoed his cry of all possible support for Russia. This led to trouble with his colleagues in the government. What was his connection to the press campaign? He denied that there was any. Not surprisingly, the War Cabinet remained unconvinced. Ministers thought he was trying to influence government policy from outside. Most of them never had trusted him anyway. Beaverbrook offered to resign; Churchill refused to accept his offer. But we may see here the first sliver of a wedge that eventually could separate the two.

Churchill never really trusted his ambassador to Russia, Stafford Cripps. But despite all, he did count on and admire Beaverbrook, who might have been born to be his emissary to Joseph Stalin. Beaverbrook had demonstrated his skills as a go-between when he had represented Lloyd George and Conservative Party leader Andrew Bonar Law to each other during the previous war. On September 22, 1941, Churchill sent his friend to Moscow as head of a twenty-three-man British team joined by eleven Americans led by Averell Harriman. Beaverbrook knew his mission: to keep Russia fighting hard. He was going "not to bargain but to give," he said. "It was to be a Christmas tree party and there must be no excuse for the Russians thinking they were not getting a fair share of the gifts on the tree."

This was the mission so resented by Stafford Cripps, whom Beaverbrook and Harriman excluded from all the important meetings and practically ignored. Beaverbrook charmed his Russian host, however, exchanging jokes with him, some of them at Cripps's expense. He told Stalin that Cripps was a bore.

STALIN: "In that respect is he comparable to Maisky [the Russian ambassador in London]?"
BEAVERBROOK: "No, to Madame Maisky."

Stalin threw back his head and laughed. But joking (and toasting and feasting and drinking, of which there was a great deal, and of which the puritanical Cripps disapproved) aside, the essence of the mission was as Beaverbrook had conceived it: to offer a bonanza of supplies to keep Russia in the war. He avoided all difficult subjects. Time after time he cheerfully renounced aid that America had promised Britain so long as it went instead to the Soviets. So generous were his renunciations that at one point the Russian interpreter jumped excitedly from his seat and exclaimed: "Now we shall win the war." In the end, even Stalin, whom Beaverbrook was fascinated to observe sketching wolves in the margins of his notepapers while listening to the foreign emissaries, expressed satisfaction. Beaverbrook wired to Churchill: "The Russians are deeply grateful and absolutely confident. I am satisfied that we have a faithful friend now." Churchill wired back: "Heartiest congratulations. . . . No one could have done it but you." Stafford Cripps, who was present in Moscow, might have thought he could have done it. But Cripps remained entirely out of the loop.

ON OCTOBER 10, 1941, THE PRESS-LORD-TURNED-DIPLOMAT RETURNED
to London in triumph, bearing twenty-five pounds of caviar. "He was on
top of the world," report his most recent biographers. Gossip about his
ambition to become prime minister increased. For the first time since the
beginning of the war, such rumors may have had a basis in reality.

Late 1941 was a season of discontent for, and with, Winston Churchill.
The backbench MPs Clem Davies, Wilf Roberts and Herbert Williams
were calling for reorganization and streamlining of the government in
the interests of efficiency. Many wanted Churchill to give up his position
as minister of defense. Certain organs of the press had joined in. Stafford
Cripps's friends were importuning him to come home to challenge the
prime minister. Cripps himself, smoldering in Moscow over his treatment
by Beaverbrook, was angling to return, and he wanted to force big changes
when he got there.

The difficult political situation for Churchill meant an opening—
for Cripps certainly, if he returned in time to capitalize upon it, but also
for Beaverbrook, whether he intended to exploit it or not. By now many
thought he did. "I have just had a talk with a Labour Man . . . [an] MP . . .
closely associated with the Ministry of Supply," wrote Lloyd George's Principal Private Secretary. "His information was that the Beaver was definitely
out to succeed Spencer [Churchill's middle name]." The Principal Private
Secretary reported the next day: "Another contact said . . . everybody was
interested in one man and one man only and his name was Beaverbrook."
Meanwhile, whatever Beaverbrook's intentions, his newspapers were
trumpeting him shamelessly. "You are getting Beaverbrook's newspapers;
Beaverbrook's aeroplanes; Beaverbrook's tanks; Beaverbrook's mission to
Russia," the Principal Private Secretary continued. It was "Beaverbrook
propaganda" of course, he admitted, "but it's all Beaverbrook."

Beaverbrook certainly envisioned a pivotal role for himself, as he made
clear in a speech over the BBC on October 12. Perhaps predictably, he
praised Stalin to the skies and the Russian resistance to Hitler. But he also
went on to imply that the war depended upon the personal relationship
he had established with the Soviet leader, on the one hand, and with British production workers, on the other. They had heeded him, he claimed,
when as head of the MAP he had called for increased production. Now
he pressed them to work even harder—not only for their own country,
but also for Stalin's. Britain and Russia shared a common destiny, he told
them. It was not very different from the speech broadcast over the BBC

a few months later by Stafford Cripps when he returned from Russia. Beaverbrook got his in first. He did not so much as mention Cripps.

Now he thought he could vault over Cripps to become Russia's foremost champion in Britain. He thought, too, that he could vault over the leaders of the Labour Party, who remained staunchly anticommunist no matter how fiercely and successfully the Soviets fought the Germans. Lloyd George's Principal Private Secretary again: "B. got it into his head that he could *lead* the Labour Party" (emphasis added). Of course he could not do that; he could never have become the party's titular head and he must have known it; but he really may have thought that a pro-Soviet newspaper magnate supported by the shop stewards and factory workers could lead the labor movement as a whole. He may also have thought that he could lead such a movement and still remain loyal to the current prime minister.

Or not: the evidence is ambiguous. On October 20 he submitted to the Defense Committee of the War Cabinet a memorandum entitled "Assistance to Russia." He wrote: "If we do not help them now the Russians may collapse. . . . It is folly for us to wait. . . . We must strike before it is too late." When the committee discussed his memorandum, Beaverbrook said, according to the note-taker: "He wished to take advantage of the rising temper in the country for helping Russia. Others didn't. He wanted to make a supreme effort to raise production to help Russia. Others didn't. He wanted to fulfill in every particular the agreement made in Moscow. Others didn't. He wished the Army to act in support of Russia. The Chiefs of Staff didn't." And he issued a warning: if his colleagues refused to support him, he would have to "consider his position."

The note-taker looked up at this: "Hullo," he thought. "This chap wants the top job."

HISTORIAN A. J. P. TAYLOR, A FRIEND OF BEAVERBROOK'S, ARGUED THAT the press lord never strove consciously or actively to overthrow Churchill, but may have fantasized about doing so during his sleepless nights throughout parts of 1941 and 1942. Beaverbrook's most recent biographers believe the prospect of leadership clearly attracted him during this period, but they have reached no firm conclusion about how actively he sought to gain it. The journalist Tom Driberg, one of Beaverbrook's employees, who won the by-election in Maldon as an independent socialist and then served as a Labour MP for nearly thirty years, wrote in his portrait of Beaverbrook that "at various times in 1941 and 1942 he believed himself to be the coming Prime Minister of Britain." An old friend of Churchill's read Driberg's book and queried this: "I should not have thought that [Beaverbrook] suffered from '*folie de grandeur*' or that he could have imagined himself displacing Churchill at the moment in question, although he (rightly) prided himself on being a 'Hidden Hand'." Driberg did not back down—Beaverbrook had read his study in manuscript, he explained to Churchill's friend, and had forced him to excise portions "under the threat of legal proceedings. But it is perhaps significant that he could not make us cut the plain statement of his ambition . . . no doubt because he guessed that we could bring witnesses to prove it." The witnesses Driberg had in mind included his fellow journalist and Beaverbrook employee Michael Foot, who became a Labour MP in 1945 and went on to become leader of the Labour Party from 1980 to 1983.

What of Churchill himself? Did he think his old friend wanted "the top job" on October 20, 1941, when Beaverbrook threatened to resign if his colleagues did not support more and faster aid to Russia? Possibly he did, for he "at once tackled him," wrote a member of the Defense Committee, Oliver Harvey, an adviser to Foreign Secretary Anthony Eden. He "saw him," Harvey recorded, employing a poker term. If Beaverbrook resigned from the government, Churchill warned, then "they would *all* 'have to consider their positions'" (emphasis in original). He meant that Beaverbrook's resignation could bring down the entire government. Surely his old friend did not want that? "B. blustered and growled," Harvey continued, "and finally acquiesced." After the meeting, Churchill told Eden that he did not believe his old friend would resign, but he did not underestimate the deadly threat that such a resignation would pose. If Beaverbrook quit over the issue of aid to Russia, and then mounted a public campaign to press for it, that "would mean war to the knife against him." Churchill preferred to think that Beaverbrook was merely engaging in his usual tactic. The worrisome aspect was that this time he had offered his resignation not in a private letter but in public.

Beaverbrook and Churchill both quickly reverted to form. During the autumn and early winter of 1941, the former sent the prime minister a flurry of resignation letters, and the latter refused them all. Beaverbrook did not insist. But he had transferred his ferocious energy and focus from production for the British war effort to production and every other form of aid for Russia. At War Cabinet meetings he argued that, in solidarity with her Soviet ally, Britain should declare war on Finland, which, despite the armistice that had concluded the Winter War of 1939–1940, had resumed fighting Russia on the same day Germany invaded her in June 1941. He also thought Britain should recognize Russian conquest of the Baltic States. "Unless we accept the principle of strategic frontiers we have no right to Gibraltar [Britain's strategic frontier at the western end of the Mediterranean]," he argued with impeccable if unwelcome logic. His colleagues refused to accept the parallel. Beaverbrook complained: "Attlee, backed by some of his friends, blocked this policy over and over again."

It may have been at this point that he honed the contempt for Labour's leader that would surface during the Cabinet reconstruction in February 1942. Certainly he now concluded that Attlee and the other Labour leaders had lost touch with their rank and file, who, he was certain, wanted a stronger pro-Russian policy. He even suggested to the War Cabinet that Churchill appeal to the country on this issue. He never thought he could be leader of the Labour Party, but he may have calculated that a general election, during which he campaigned for more aid to Russia, and Labour's leaders campaigned against, would weaken them and strengthen him as well as others who shared his views. Interestingly, only a little later Cripps reached a similar conclusion about his own chances after a general election. Churchill, who was at least as suspicious of the Soviets as Attlee, however, never took the idea seriously. A general election would await victory over Germany.

Meanwhile, the domestic political situation continued to deteriorate. But when Japan attacked Pearl Harbor on December 7, 1941, and Churchill embarked for America and consultations with President Roosevelt five days later, he took Beaverbrook with him. He believed that no other Briton could press the Americans harder and more effectively for increased war production than his old friend, and events proved him right. Beaverbrook may have made his greatest contribution to Britain's wartime cause not in London as chief of the MAP in 1940, but in Washington at the end of 1941 and beginning of 1942, by persuading American policymakers to drastically increase their production targets.

Churchill and Beaverbrook's return to Britain on January 14, 1942, preceded that of Stafford Cripps from Russia by only a few weeks. Beaverbrook aspired to be his country's greatest champion and interpreter of the Soviet Union, but that was a role Cripps already had played and was determined to play again, despite his disillusionment with Russian-style communism. Beaverbrook may already have begun to think of himself as a potential successor to Churchill, although he did not say it out loud, or perhaps even admit it to himself. At this point, Cripps definitely entertained this possibility, and said as much to his intimates. Beaverbrook and Cripps had clashed in Moscow; they were destined to clash in London as well. Churchill would have to find a way to reconcile them, or, if that proved impossible, to make use of them somehow anyway, and simultaneously to protect himself from these two ambitious men.

Early 1942 was the period of the of no-confidence vote in Churchill's government called by the Independent Labour Party, which garnered only two ballots; of the prime minister's abortive attempt to appoint Beaverbrook minister of war production and Cripps minister of aircraft production; of Bevin's refusal to cede an inch of turf to any production minister, let alone to one named Lord Beaverbrook; of the three German ships sailing up the coast of France; of the fall of Singapore; and of Cripps delivering the speeches and press conferences on Russia that further enhanced his reputation and fueled his ambition. Churchill must have felt more beleaguered than ever.

These developments forced his hand. Churchill had to have Cripps, at least for the moment, because the country demanded it. He had to have Bevin because the Labour Party demanded it; he had to have Labour; and he had to have Attlee, who was leader of the Labour Party. He could have kept Beaverbrook, if only his friend had been willing to compromise with Bevin about his powers as minister of production and with Attlee about aid to Russia. But his friend would not do it. As noted earlier, the prime minister let him go with great reluctance on February 18, 1942.

AT FIRST, THE PRESS LORD THOUGHT IT A BLESSED RELEASE. BY NOW everything about government service exasperated or angered him. He could not work with Bevin or Attlee or Cripps, or indeed with practically anybody at this point. The RAF, largely his creation, had won the Battle of Britain and, despite the German ships jaunting along the French coast and the country's renewed jitters inspired by them, the threat of invasion had eased. American planners had accepted his production targets. He could persuade himself that he already had done his job. "I have a deep respect for the Prime Minister," he wrote to Eden on March 3. "I will not do or say anything to weaken his authority."

But Beaverbrook could be only Beaverbrook, and perhaps the note-taker at the meeting the previous October had been right—maybe

Beaverbrook really was thinking about "the top job." Exactly two weeks after promising Eden he would never weaken Churchill, Beaverbrook had lunch at the Savoy Hotel with Leslie Hore-Belisha, the former Cabinet minister who would wind up the House of Commons debate for the sponsors of the no-confidence motion in July. "Max . . . said he had decided to oppose the Gov't," wrote Hore-Belisha in his diary. "He would provide any money required for the creation of an opposition." Hore-Belisha does not say in his diary how he responded. Then Beaverbrook invited Sir Arthur Salter, the independent MP for Oxford University, to dinner at his country house. Salter had recently returned from a successful stint in America, where Churchill had sent him to stimulate US shipping production. Beaverbrook wondered: "Would Sir Arthur join him in forming an anti-Churchill party?" Salter said that he would not. Beaverbrook dined also with Harry McGowan, chairman of Imperial Chemical Industries. McGowan asked him whether he would rejoin the government. Beaverbrook replied: "Never, unless I join as Prime Minister."

Simultaneously, Beaverbrook was telling Eden that he "considered himself free to advocate his Russian views" because he was outside the government. In a letter of March 17 to Churchill (containing further protestations of loyalty, although written on the same day that he hosted Hore-Belisha), he listed those views: recognition of Russia's new borders along the Baltic; additional tanks and airplanes to be sent to Russia; and "an expedition into Europe," by which he meant a Second Front against Germany mounted across the English Channel. He unleashed his newspapers. Churchill read their pro-Russian articles with irritation. It was at about this time that he learned his friend had said to one of his aides: "It is either the Premiership or nothing now" (the aide later said he could remember hearing no such statement). Whether Beaverbrook uttered it or not, the prime minister could have been excused for thinking that his old friend was perhaps a greater troublemaker outside the government than he had been while inside it.

Churchill had brought one cuckoo into the nest by appointing Cripps to his War Cabinet; he had expelled (or rather permitted the self-expulsion of) another, Lord Beaverbrook. He did not think Beaverbrook would actually conspire to bring him down. He accepted the press lord's many protestations of loyalty and friendship. But he also knew that such protestations carried little weight at the highest level of British politics ("There is no friendship at the top," Lloyd George is supposed to have once said, and Churchill agreed). Churchill had sent potential political enemies abroad before (e.g., Hoare to Spain, Halifax to Washington). If his original intention in sending Beaverbrook to America had *not* been to get him out of the way for a while, then surely it became one of his aims now. As he had said to Beaverbrook shortly after accepting his resignation, he hoped at least that with him out of government his War Cabinet would gain in "tranquility."

The prime minister did not gain it, however, even when Beaverbrook crossed the Atlantic Ocean, ostensibly to coordinate supply with the Americans, as Churchill had asked him to. The Canadian traveled first to Lisbon and then by flying boat to Port of Spain, Trinidad, where on March 24, 1942, he told reporters: "I am simply a sick man needing rest." He already regretted resigning and accepting Churchill's new assignment. Turning the matter over in his mind, he had concluded that it amounted to demotion. Churchill was putting him on the sidetrack, but Beaverbrook still wanted to be near the center of action. Failing that, he wanted to take action himself. Six days later, he was broadcasting from Miami, Florida: "The hopes of humanity . . . are all centered on the fight that Joseph Stalin and the Red Armies are making against the invaders of Russia. . . . His armies need more tanks, more airplanes, more anti-tank guns and more anti-aircraft guns and plenty of motor-cars with good big guns—mobile guns." He was repeating the arguments he had made in the War Cabinet—arguments that the War Cabinet had rejected, in part, if not in toto. Then for the first time in a public speech he broached the Second Front: "Among the free peoples of Britain, the Empire and the United States . . . the cry goes up now for offensive action. This is the proper mood for great nations who are resolved to remain great."

The "sick man needing rest" had the bit between his teeth. He traveled north to Washington for discussions with President Roosevelt and others, not so much about supplies, but rather about recognizing Russia's expanded borders and arranging more and quicker aid for her. This was not disloyalty, as such, but nor was it helpful. On March 25 Beaverbrook called at the British Embassy and spoke with Halifax. "What a remarkable little man he is," the ambassador recorded immediately afterward, "humorous, puckish, dynamic, opportunist." The Canadian told him: "I am completely loyal to Churchill who I think is the greatest leader we could have had." But note the past tense, and then the note of creeping doubt: "I hope nothing will ever force me to take a different view." In his "secret diary" written on the same day, Halifax recorded Beaverbrook also saying to him in meditative voice: "I might be the best man to run the war. It wants a ruthless, unscrupulous harsh man, and I believe I could do it." To the military theorist Liddle Hart only a week earlier, just before his departure for America, he had complained that Churchill possessed "no grasp of mechanized warfare" and remained stuck conceptually in "the wars of Marlborough."

While still in Washington, Beaverbrook received and accepted an invitation from the Newspaper Proprietors Association of America to deliver an address at their annual banquet in New York City in April. From Roosevelt he learned that the administration favored opening a Second Front in Europe as quickly as possible. He knew that Churchill believed there must be at least a yearlong preparation. So Beaverbrook returned to Florida pondering. He moved to Sea Island, off the coast of Georgia, and sat at the water's edge considering further. He paced the beach. He asked himself: Why could not the greatest navy in the world mount and protect a cross-Channel Anglo-American armada? And why could not the combined forces of the British and American armies establish a lodgment on the continent once the armada had brought them there? He answered himself: they could do it. Only the political will was lacking, not in the United States, but in Britain. He decided to come out full throttle for immediate establishment of a Second Front in his New York speech, whatever the prime minister might think. Again, it was a strange method of demonstrating loyalty: it may have indicated a desire to weaken the prime minister—or it may have indicated merely a desire to prod him in the right direction. In any event, Churchill's response was predictable. Beaverbrook sat in a beach chair under an umbrella dictating a draft of the speech to his secretary and paused and said to him: "He won't like it, will he?" meaning the prime minister. "No sir," said the secretary, "I don't think he will."

Churchill did not know what Beaverbrook was planning. He still thought his friend could cause more trouble for him in England than he ever could in the United States. When Roosevelt proposed returning him to London with one of his top advisers, Harry Hopkins, and General George Marshall, Roosevelt's military chief of staff, to make arrangements for an early cross-Channel expedition, Churchill demurred. His friend must remain in America coordinating supplies. It occurred to him that perhaps Beaverbrook could be induced to remain there a long time. He considered appointing him to replace Halifax as Britain's ambassador to

America. He thought, too, about making him British czar of Allied supply, stationed for the duration in Washington, DC. It had come to this: he
enjoyed Beaverbrook; he valued and admired him; he relished the stim-
ulation Beaverbrook provided; but he doubted now that their political
relationship, or perhaps even their friendship, or perhaps even his premiership, could survive proximity. Then, after Beaverbrook delivered his
speech in New York City, Churchill had to wonder whether any of those
could survive at all.

ON APRIL 20, BEAVERBROOK STOPPED IN WASHINGTON ON THE WAY TO
New York and saw Halifax again. "I wish I knew what was going on in his
mind," the ambassador wrote. "He told me that he thought Cripps was a
key point for the moment in British politics, but within three months if
further military setbacks came then the tar brush might have gone over
him and it was possible that people would ask for something quite outside!" Halifax did not comment, but it was not hard to guess what was in
Beaverbrook's mind. Roosevelt's adviser Harry Hopkins, who saw him the
next day, guessed it immediately: "He was quite convinced Max Beaverbrook thought the Government was going to fall one of these days, and
that he would be the next Prime Minister," wrote Halifax, to whom Hopkins had confided this assessment. Halifax agreed, adding astutely: "But
I think that Max is yielding to wishful thinking."

Wishful thinking or not, Beaverbrook was playing a double game, still
probably without admitting it to himself. He would do nothing to shake
the prime minister but only argue as a private citizen for the pro-Russian
policies in which he believed; by arguing for those policies he could not
help but shake the prime minister, which at some level he surely recognized. Assuming a deterioration of Cripps's stock, if the prime minister
fell, for whatever reason, or was pushed, then Beaverbrook would be a
leading candidate to replace him.

On April 23, bronzed from the sun and looking fit and wearing evening dress with a white carnation in his buttonhole, Beaverbrook strode
to the rostrum on the stage of the Waldorf Astoria ballroom in New York
City to deliver his address—and to shake the prime minister. He spoke
into microphones that broadcast his speech from coast to coast, paying
lavish tribute to his former chief: "Churchill is the embodiment of the
spirit of Britain today." Then he planted seeds of doubt—while ostensibly
trampling upon them: "I am told . . . that [Churchill] will fall before the

summer is out. You must help me to kill that bad rumor." Everybody knows that there is no better way to give a rumor currency than to deny it.

Beaverbrook did not offer unambiguous support to Churchill later in his speech, either. He did heap further praise upon him, and upon the gallant British soldiers and sailors and airmen, and upon the British people, who had borne enormous sacrifices over the past two years. But his main point was that "somewhere along the two thousand miles of coastline . . . held by the Germans," American and British soldiers should establish a Second Front now. "The day has come when in almost every quarter in Britain the cry goes up, 'Attack!'" His words directly contradicted Churchill's thinking. So did these: "Communism under Stalin has produced the most valiant fighting army in Europe. Communism under Stalin has provided us with examples of patriotism equal to the finest annals of history. Communism under Stalin has produced the best generals in this war." And, more egregiously: "Persecution of Christianity? Not so. There is no religious persecution [in Russia]. . . . Racial persecution? Not at all. Jews live like other men. Political purges? Of course. But it is now clear that the men who were shot down would have betrayed Russia to her German enemy."

Back in England, Beaverbrook's newspapers carried the speech on their front pages and reprinted it as a pamphlet. Churchill read it. Journalists asked Churchill about it, and he replied: "I would rather have him preaching the Second Front than a negotiated peace." It was an adroit answer, but in fact the prime minister felt great dismay. His friend caused him grief no matter which side of the Atlantic he occupied. Churchill decided to call him home after all and to keep an eye on him. Later he would reconsider. Perhaps he should send Beaverbrook to Cairo, or to Moscow, or to the West Indies, or back to Washington, DC, again.

For when he returned to Britain, Beaverbrook did not sit still. According to his biographer and employee, Tom Driberg, the man who had won the Maldon by-election, Beaverbrook hired a publicity agent "to start a whispering campaign throughout Britain. His whisperers were to say: 'Churchill is on the way out . . . Beaverbrook's our man . . . Send for Beaverbrook.'" Or possibly he did not hire the publicist; an admirer did, and Beaverbrook terminated the campaign when Churchill complained about it to him. The two accounts of this episode conflict, and Beaverbrook never discussed it publicly (but it may be indicative that he allowed Driberg to print the less creditable version in his book). Accounts of another incident conflict as well. Later in the spring, Beaverbrook approached his great enemy, Ernest Bevin, to discuss what would happen if Churchill fell. The trade unionist cut him off. It was not a subject he would entertain. But was Bevin correct to report to Churchill, as he did, that Beaverbrook was conspiring against the government? Or was Beaverbrook not conspiring, but wanting only to gossip and to speculate? That is how Churchill interpreted it. The prime minister continued to believe that his friend would never actively scheme against him. He thought Beaverbrook extremely troublesome, but not actually disloyal. He may have thought, too, that if he did fall from power, Beaverbrook would make an acceptable replacement. Beaverbrook told one of his journalists that just before he had gone to America, the prime minister said to him that if he did ever take over the top spot, then "I, Churchill, will be willing to serve you."

Whatever his ultimate objective, Beaverbrook threw himself into the campaign for opening a Second Front on the European mainland without delay. The British government was vehemently opposed to this; Churchill and his generals thought opening a Second Front in 1942 was far beyond current Allied strength. They opposed doing so in 1943 as well, overcoming American arguments in favor, much to Russia's distress, and much to the distress of Russia's mounting number of friends in Great Britain. "Operation Overlord," the Allied invasion of France, took place in June 1944. Today most people outside Russia think Churchill was right to insist on waiting. But he never convinced Beaverbrook. The Canadian provided funds for a national organization, the Centre of Public Opinion (CPO), to carry the campaign in favor of a "Second Front Now" around the country. His newspapers publicized CPO meetings. Invitations to speak poured into his office from all parts of Britain. There were forty for the remaining months of 1942 alone. An alphabetical list of them compiled by a secretary began with the Aberdeen British-Soviet Unity Campaign and ended with Vicar of Victoria Park Parish, East London. The millionaire lord who was also a press lord, a Conservative, an imperialist and a former appeaser received invitations to speak from Anglo-Soviet Friendship Councils, district committees of the British Communist Party, Communist-dominated trade unions, factory works committees, shop stewards committees and workers' production committees, for British Communists and fellow-travelers, above all others, favored the "Second Front Now."

Most famously, Beaverbrook accepted an invitation to address the Birmingham Committee for Anglo-Soviet Unity on June 21, 1942, the anniversary of Hitler's attack on Russia. Somebody filmed it; today a video of the event may be seen online. To view it is to understand how Beaverbrook could have thought that he might lead a popular left-wing movement, how he could even have thought that he would be popular enough to replace the prime minister should Churchill fall. Before he spoke, 10,000 workers and members of the Home Guard and other bodies, banners flying, bands playing, marched past the stage and rostrum, many giving him (and the Lord Mayor of Birmingham, and Mrs. Lawrence Cadbury, chair of the committee and wife of the chocolate manufacturer) the Communist clenched-fist salute. They marched beneath a Russian flag of hammer and sickle flying above the Birmingham Council House. A Russian and a British flag, sewn together, draped the rostrum from which he delivered his speech. He looked out upon 30,000 people (50,000, according to another account) packing Victoria Square in front of him and launched in:

> Now is the need for urgency. No unnecessary delay in sending forth our second expeditionary force to fight on the Second Front. We must work, every one of us, work with all our strength. Work in the factories and the foundries and the shipyards of Britain. Do you recall Tanks for Russia Week? Remember it and do it again. Tanks for the Second Front. Airplanes for the Second Front. Ships for the Second Front. . . . What we have got Russia is entitled to share. What we can give should be sent to them willingly, gladly, rejoicing as we go. . . . We may have to share our bread with the Russians . . . and sugar too. Men we must give, equipped with tanks and airplanes. . . . The [naval] blockade did not win us the war. . . . The bomber will [not] bring the war to an end. . . . The Army will win this war. . . . [It] is in my opinion equipped, ready for the job and wanting to do it. . . . Let the Ministers launch that movement now.

The audience roared its approval. Beaverbrook was at the peak of his powers and riding the crest of the wave. What might he not aspire to, given his reception at events such as this, and given the national response to his campaign?

BEAVERBROOK IN FACT STOOD THAT DAY ON THE VERY PEAK OF THAT wave, but it had crested and was about to break. He may have known it even as he spoke. Moments before he strode to the rostrum, one of his journalists pulled him aside. Word had just arrived that Rommel had

taken Tobruk in Libya. Beaverbrook's eyes clouded over at the news, probably because the news was bad—but possibly also because he understood
in a flash that this development doomed all his hopes. He would deliver his
defiant lines. But Churchill would never agree to launch a Second Front
in Europe with Suez in danger; he would do everything in his power to
protect Britain's position in the Middle East. Even the men and women
presently cheering in Victoria Square would place Russia on the back
burner when they learned of this most recent defeat. They would demand
action to avenge it, but in Libya, not on the European mainland. "On the
morning of June 21st the Second Front was a near certainty," Beaverbrook
was to say. "By the evening the odds were 100 to 1 against."

As a result, the odds against his becoming prime minister approached
the same ratio. He had persuaded himself that as the chief spear-carrier of
an irresistible movement he, too, was, or might become, irresistible. Now the
spear had broken in his hands. Without it he could be only Churchill's friend
and ally and, perhaps eventually, colleague again, but not his successor.

He did not wind up the campaign for a Second Front Now, but nor
did he any longer drive it with his unique implacable ferocity. To almost
all the organizations that had issued him invitations to speak, he sent
polite refusals. To a very few he sent discreet telegrams of support, but
nothing more. He no longer saw the campaign as a vehicle for his career
but only as means of pressuring the government to do what he judged to
be right, and he knew the government would not do it just yet. His newspapers continued to advocate the Second Front. In July he lobbied MPs
for the Second Front at a cross-party dinner of which he was host. On one
occasion he spoke for it at the House of Lords. He remained sufficiently
associated with the diminished movement that when Churchill went to
Russia in August 1942, to break the news to Stalin that there would be no
Second Front that year, he did not invite Beaverbrook.

Because he had relaxed to a degree about the Second Front, the press
lord no longer had to juggle ambition for himself and loyalty to Churchill.
He dropped the one and took up the other. He finally faced facts. To an
American friend he wrote: "Churchill's prestige stands as high as two
years ago. . . . He has no rival." To another: "His position is unassailable."
He had always been decisive, and until he had gotten the idea of becoming
prime minister into his head, he had always been a realist, too. Now, Beaverbrook reverted to form. He finally quit indulging in "wishful thinking,"
as Halifax had termed it.

As in the summer of 1940, so once again in the summer of 1942 Beaverbrook demonstrated unambiguous loyalty to the prime minister. Ten days after the rally at Birmingham, during the first day of the debate in the House of Commons on the no-confidence motion so disastrously moved by Wardlaw Milne, and even more disastrously seconded by Sir Roger Keyes, Beaverbrook delivered to the House of Lords a full-throated defense of "the Government to which I used to belong." Critics complained that the British Army in North Africa had been both under-equipped and poorly equipped. Beaverbrook, with more facts and figures about British production in his head than any other man, demonstrated conclusively that this was not so. Britain had more guns and tanks in North Africa, and better ones, too, than Germany and Italy combined. Blame for the defeat at Tobruk could not be laid at the government's door, then, let alone at Churchill's, but only at the feet of the generals who had botched things in the field. Perhaps he already knew that the prime minister intended to replace General Claude Auchinleck with General Harold Alexander. Within days, Churchill also appointed Bernard Montgomery, who would lead the successful British counterattack.

In this speech, Beaverbrook also specifically defended the prime minister's unshakable intention to continue serving as minister of defense: "If you want divided authority and all the delays and disputes that flow from it, if you want to substitute indecision for decision, then we can agree on the separation, for that is the way to get it." He defended him, too (and thus himself), from critics who charged that tanks had been sent to Russia to the detriment of Singapore and Tobruk. "Well, it is nonsense, it is not so; it is quite impossible," he said, first because Britain had tanks to spare now, which was in part his doing, and second because Churchill would never have made such a mistake: "Do not tell me he neglected to send weapons to the battle front: that is beyond the possibilities."

In April 1943 Beaverbrook accepted an invitation from Roosevelt to travel to America again. He fascinated FDR, as he did almost everyone who did not hate him. Almost simultaneously, Churchill discovered a need for additional Anglo-American talks on war strategy, so he would travel to America, too. While there, Churchill insisted that his friend be excluded from all military discussions. He tried unsuccessfully to keep him from private talks with the president, although, by this stage of the war, such talks would not have been terribly dangerous. Montgomery had won the battle of El Alamein, and British and American forces had landed in North Africa, successfully implementing Operation Torch. The first American troops had begun arriving in Great Britain. Churchill had felt confident enough to make his famous "end of the beginning" speech. A. J. P. Taylor wrote, of spring 1943: "Victory was in the air." Beaverbrook could never threaten the prime minister when it was not he but Churchill riding the crest of the wave, and both men knew it. On the *Queen Mary* going over to America, the two played cards as if nothing had ever come between them. Beaverbrook won, as usual, as Averell Harriman noted.

Beaverbrook remained persona non grata among former colleagues and members of Parliament, however. That never changed. When, after the July 1942 no-confidence vote and his loyal speech in the House of Lords, rumors began to circulate that Churchill intended to reappoint him to the War Cabinet, they reacted strongly. Bevin told Halifax, who had again returned briefly to Britain, that "he would certainly resign if there was any truth in the reports that Winston intended to bring him back into the Government." Attlee, too, "spoke in strong terms against Max Beaverbrook." So did Cripps. The objections were not limited to the Labour Party. Even the Conservative chief whip wrote to Churchill: "A rumor of this nature has a very disturbing effect upon a very large section of opinion in the House." Churchill assured them all that he had no intention of bringing Beaverbrook back.

It was a fib. He wanted him back desperately. No one else in government could do for him what Beaverbrook could. "Winston is undoubtedly a very lonely man," wrote Lloyd George's PPS. Then, too, as we have seen, the tide of war had turned in Britain's favor. Churchill and the Americans began serious planning for the Second Front during the summer of 1943. The prime minister told his friend about it. With his position absolutely secure again and Beaverbrook back on his side and satisfied about the Second Front, Churchill finally could do what he had long wanted to do: in September 1943, he offered the Canadian reappointment to the government as Lord Privy Seal, confident that Beaverbrook would accept.

Churchill still had to keep a weather eye out for Beaverbrook's enemies. To assuage them, he stipulated that the position did not entail a seat in the War Cabinet. Now all the blocks fell into place except for one. Stafford Cripps, presently minister of aircraft production, objected strongly. Churchill handled him with the aplomb he had shown all along. He wrote: "It is not usual for a Prime Minister to consult all his colleagues . . . on the advice which he tenders to the Crown in respect of His Majesty's servants.

For good or for ill in our system in this country he must bear the responsibility himself." Then he let Cripps down lightly. To this typewritten letter he appended in his own hand: "I hope we can have a meal together soon."

Beaverbrook accepted the appointment. His exclusion from the War Cabinet did not matter. He and the prime minister could and did resume talking and scheming and drinking and smoking long into the night. Churchill would rely on him more than ever, never more so than during the run-up to the general election of 1945.

It may seem today that neither the challenge posed by Stafford Cripps to the prime minister, nor the challenge posed by Beaverbrook, ever amounted to much. Most obviously, neither man led a political party; in fact, neither man could be termed a party loyalist. This meant that neither man ever commanded a voting bloc at Westminster. It is also the case that almost nobody trusted Beaverbrook, and that while many trusted Cripps, only a few in the House of Commons trusted his political sense. Finally, neither man ever actually threw down the gauntlet; they only maneuvered for place and thought about throwing it down.

One or the other of them might have become prime minister, however, if he had played his cards differently, or if Churchill had, or if the war situation had continued to deteriorate. After all, in 1940 Churchill, too, had suffered from drawbacks very much like those of Cripps and Beaverbrook, and he had made it to the top. As with them, so with him: he had had no party machine at his back; few had trusted his political wisdom; he, too, had long hesitated to throw down the gauntlet to Neville Chamberlain. In short, his usurpation of power in 1940 did not seem more implausible at the time, perhaps, than the prospect of usurpation by Cripps or Beaverbrook did in 1942, however that prospect may seem to us now.

It is useful to remember that Churchill's colleagues did not treat him with the reverence he so often receives today. They did not know how posterity would view him. They saw him at the time as a great and brilliant man, no doubt, but also as a difficult and flawed one. He seemed to them too fond of his own voice, too dictatorial, too sure of his own judgment. Some thought he drank too much. Some worried about his health. In short, they viewed him as a human being, imperfect like all human beings. During late 1941 and early 1942, not everyone viewed him as the inevitable and irreplaceable prime minister, even if that is how most of us view him three-quarters of a century later. Churchill had to maneuver with great cunning to defend his position from Cripps; he had to demonstrate a steady hand and steadier nerves to keep it from Beaverbrook. He could not count on the loyalty of either man, even though Beaverbrook was a friend of long-standing. There is no loyalty at the pinnacle of politics: only calculation, ambition and ideology.

Churchill dealt with Stafford Cripps by giving him enough political rope to hang himself. He dealt with Beaverbrook quite differently: first with great patience and insight, then perhaps less astutely by sending him across the sea. For better or for worse he never believed that his old friend was working actively to bring him down. He did not need to hang him with a rope, therefore, but only to string him along until something turned up. He wanted not a rope at all, really, but rather a pin to let the air out of Beaverbrook's balloon. In the meantime, the prime minister and his military advisers persuaded the Americans to postpone the Second Front. Britain signed a treaty of friendship with the Soviets, but without committing to an immediate invasion of Europe. Churchill was in America when he learned about Tobruk. Ironically, this bad news for Britain was good news for him, at least in one sense: it was the pin to puncture Beaverbrook's bubble. It ended the threat that the Canadian posed to his premiership, because it ended the campaign for the Second Front Now, and therefore Beaverbrook's hopes for the top job, however seriously Beaverbrook cherished those hopes and however he may have intended to realize them. The prime minister had only to wait some more, until further developments enabled him to bring his old friend back into the fold. Once again, he had gotten what he wanted.

CHAPTER 10

The Impact of Professor Beveridge

IN JUNE 1940, AFTER NEGOTIATIONS WITH MUSSOLINI HAD BEEN RULED out and a fight to the finish against Germany agreed upon, socialists and Conservatives in the War Cabinet knew they must learn to cooperate and compromise with one another or Britain would lose the war. Ministers on the right agreed, however reluctantly, that in order to prosecute the war most efficiently, the government would have to assume new powers enabling it to intervene in the economy. Ministers on the left accepted that the government would not intervene so often and deeply as they thought it should.

Nevertheless, even during 1940–1942, the period of Britain's greatest peril, the Grand Coalition experienced ideological conflict. The left sensed the tides of history flowing with it. Leftists in and out of Parliament never ceased calling for Labour ministers to demand further reforms and government interventions. Attlee, Bevin and the others ignored such demands at their peril; they could not ignore them completely. Conservatives attempted to counter them by endorsing less far-reaching measures. Centrists such as Eden, Woolton and R. A. Butler (the former defeatist Foreign Office undersecretary) took the lead here. Indeed, Butler eventually steered through Parliament a sweeping reform of the educational system, although it was not as sweeping as many on the left might have wanted.

Such Tory moderates notwithstanding, the fact remained that generally socialists and Conservatives held very different views about how the country should be organized—not only while the war was being fought, but afterward as well. Many weighed in from both sides, or wished to, on what should be the lineaments of postwar Britain. When America joined the war and victory began to appear likely, ideological conflict in the War Cabinet, in Parliament and in the country as a whole only sharpened. Churchill struggled heroically to contain it. He met with mixed success.

AT THIS STAGE OF HIS LIFE WINSTON CHURCHILL INSTINCTIVELY FAVORED the right over the left in every ideological debate, but he disliked any sort of conflict in his War Cabinet. He thought giving voice to differing approaches to domestic policies diverted ministers from the main task, which was winning the war; moreover, it had the potential for disrupting the War Cabinet's hard-won unity. Domestic policy, in any event, did not much interest him now. He preferred to focus on the strategic matters raised by the war itself, or upon anticipated challenges to Britain's postwar international position. In October 1940 he transferred discussion about home-front economic policy from the War Cabinet to the Lord President's Committee, chaired, after Neville Chamberlain's retirement, by Sir John Anderson, a career civil servant who belonged to no party.

It was a shrewd choice. "He is agreeable and always agrees with you," Beaverbrook once observed of Anderson to Churchill, although he himself disliked the man. In Cabinet meetings, Beaverbrook and Brendan Bracken, whom Churchill had selected to replace Duff Cooper as minister of information on July 21, 1941, would pass snide notes to one another. They called Anderson "Pomposo." The urbane Eden never indulged in such behavior, but confided to his diary about Anderson: "A good committee man, but zero in Cabinet." The prime minister may have judged that such a figure was unlikely to initiate comprehensive measures. He did not seem aware of an inbuilt bias in his own approach. With the Nazis at his throat it was relatively easy for an advocate of temporary or limited reform—that is to say, a Conservative or a Whitehall mandarin such as Anderson—to deprecate visionary talk. It was not so easy for men who had gone into politics in order to champion the working class, and who possessed a transforming vision for Britain, even though the Nazis were reaching for their throats, too.

Not surprisingly, then, even though Churchill had the Lord President dealing with domestic issues, the muted approach did not satisfy a rapidly growing chorus demanding that more attention be paid to what Britain should look like after Germany had been defeated. Churchill threw the chorus a small bone: at the end of 1940 he appointed his increasingly bleary War Cabinet colleague Arthur Greenwood to study this subject. The Lord Privy Seal would have "a small staff of five or six," mainly junior ministers, to help him. Churchill warned Greenwood: "It will not be possible for any of the Ministers in charge of Departments mainly concerned with the conduct of the war to pay real attention to postwar reconstruction. To those Ministers I must reluctantly add myself." He thought of Greenwood's committee as a safety valve, and as he probably expected and privately hoped, the committee met several times but made slow progress.

The progress was so slow, however, that eventually even Churchill felt he had to do something about it. During the Cabinet reshuffle of February 1942, he finally sacked Greenwood and replaced him with Sir William Jowitt, a less bibulous yet remarkably pliable figure who had once been a Liberal MP, then attorney general in the Labour government of 1929–1931 ("after a painful interview with Lloyd George" to explain why he was resigning from the Liberal Party), then an unsuccessful National Labour candidate, and now finally a Labour MP as well as paymaster general in the Grand Coalition. Jowitt once had said that he "wished to have some convictions." Perhaps Churchill appointed him to replace Greenwood because he deemed him, as perhaps he deemed Anderson, unlikely to have too many about far-reaching reform.

If so, then certainly Jowitt tried to please: "I find it difficult to find out what he has been doing. I suspect very little," one Cabinet minister commented. But Jowitt did commission the Home Intelligence Division (HID) to undertake a survey of "Public Feeling upon Post-War Reconstruction." In this way, a man who was eager to satisfy quite inadvertently placed the prime minister in an unsatisfactory position. For the HID Report, issued in November 1942, revealed an extraordinary radicalization of popular sentiment since the days of Neville Chamberlain. Now a majority of Britons expected five great changes on the domestic front after Germany had been defeated:

i. There must be work at a living wage for everyone who is capable of doing it.
ii. Private profit must cease to be the major incentive to work; everyone must work primarily for the good of the community.
iii. There must be financial security for everyone who is unable to work.

iv.   There must be decent homes for everyone at a cost which will not
      reduce people to poverty.
v.   The same education must be available to everyone so that all will
      have an equal chance.

The findings of the HID Report confounded many Conservatives but
confirmed what politically acute observers on the left had been registering
and pondering since the spring of 1940: popular sentiment was swinging
dramatically their way. The HID findings also dovetailed with those of
another committee that had been taking testimony for two years. When
that second committee released its report, *Social Insurance and Allied
Services*, in December 1942, a month after the HID Report came out, it
exploded a bombshell that dwarfed that of the first committee.

THE CHAIR OF THE SECOND COMMITTEE WAS WILLIAM BEVERIDGE, A
former civil servant and former head of the London School of Economics
who was now master of University College, Oxford. Ernest Bevin had
appointed this distinguished and hugely ambitious figure to be an undersecretary in the Ministry of Labor in September 1940, but had quickly
discovered him to be a difficult colleague. He attempted to get rid of his
prickly, egocentric undersecretary by sending him to Arthur Greenwood
(who at that point was still in charge of the Reconstruction Committee)
to lead an inquiry requested by the trade unions on coordinating social
services. Beveridge, refusing to be sidetracked, turned his new assignment
into a broad-ranging survey of the social services' deficiencies. His committee interviewed hundreds of witnesses and consulted many experts,
including trade unionists and socialists. The result was that for the first
time in his life, Beveridge, who had previously advocated social reform
as a strategic and practical necessity for his country, now became fired
up with a vision of social justice as an ethical ideal. Basically, he now
believed what the HID had reported a majority of Britons believed: that
for ethical as well as pragmatic reasons, government should and could
guarantee full employment and, via generous welfare programs funded by
state, employer and worker contributions, protect every Briton from cradle
to grave against want, ignorance, squalor and ill health. Even before he
issued his report, Beveridge courted the limelight on the airwaves and in
the press to publicize his views and maximize their impact. He intended

to lift the lid on debate over postwar reconstruction that Churchill had been trying to clamp shut.

While Beveridge was taking testimony and writing and polishing and publicizing, Conservatives grew uneasy. Tory backbenchers representing districts with coal, gas and electricity interests feared he would recommend nationalizing them. MPs representing "country districts hate it too," warned the party chief whip, referring to Beveridge's prospective report. A committee of Tory diehards wrote a secret paper for Churchill attacking the idea of even a minimal interpretation of social security, arguing it was not the state's business to provide it. Rather, when the war was over, the government should first lower taxes, and then get out of the way. They claimed that 90 percent of Conservative backbenchers supported them.

Beveridge also worried Tory ministers, even those who were themselves reform-minded. R. A. Butler met him for dinner in August 1942. "He said that we lived in revolutionary times," remembered Butler, who had become minister of education by then, "and he proposed to make his contribution to the revolution. . . . One cannot help being very nervous of Sir William Beveridge's views." Butler attempted to distinguish his own approach from that of his crusading dinner companion: "We believe in leading up and not leveling down, in diversity and not in uniformity."

Mounting anxiety about Beveridge affected even Churchill, who tore his gaze from Britain's overseas battlefields to focus momentarily on this uncongenial character and his unwelcome plans. The prime minister deemed Beveridge "an awful windbag and a dreamer." He wrote to his chancellor: "I hope you are giving full consideration to our postwar financial position. Nothing could be more dangerous than for people to feel cheated because they had been led to expect attractive schemes which turn out to be economically impossible." Kingsley Wood needed no such prompting. He assured Churchill that he intended to scrutinize Beveridge's cost projections and that he would never let the government promise more than it could pay for. Then he told Butler that he hoped Beveridge would make "as many high-minded and fantastic suggestions as possible," presumably because they would be easy to shoot down.

Labour ministers feared Beveridge, too, although for different reasons. Actually, one of them shared Conservative reasons: William Jowitt, living down to Churchill's hopes for him, told the secretary of his committee, E. E. Bridges, that Britain could not afford expensive measures; he

intended to submit to the Cabinet "a document designed to show how bare
the cupboard was." Among War Cabinet Labour ministers, Bevin, who
disliked Beveridge personally, thought his proposed family allowances
would undermine trade unions when they bargained for higher wages. He
also thought Beveridge set employee contributions to social security too
high. Mainly, however, he and Attlee and Morrison (who had just replaced
Cripps in the War Cabinet) worried that Beveridge would create a political problem for them. They knew that the Labour Party as a whole would
welcome a report that complemented its own views on reconstruction,
and that the Labour left would demand implementation at once, as a first
installment of socialism. Conservatives, however, with whom they had
to work in the Coalition, would oppose. Labour ministers feared finding
themselves caught in the middle.

On November 16, 1942, the War Cabinet met to discuss the troublesome don, the trumpet blast he intended to issue, and the political strife
he would thereby provoke. Beveridge had announced his publication date
for later in the month. Bevin objected to Beveridge trying to set the schedule: "Shouldn't accept *his* date for publication. Tell him he presents and
Government decides publication. Then fix a different date" (emphasis in
original). The War Cabinet agreed. It also instructed the minister of information, Brendan Bracken, to refuse Beveridge's request that he arrange a
press conference to "enable him to expound his Report." Beveridge wanted
to address House of Commons Lobby correspondents. The War Cabinet
decided he should be given no such opportunity. "Let us have a little order
and discipline," Churchill expostulated. Kingsley Wood took the hardest
line, quoting a recent headline in the *Daily Telegraph* against Beveridge:
his politics placed him "half way to Moscow."

Ten days later the War Cabinet met again. Members now had before
them copies of the Beveridge Report, which had not yet been released to
the public. With the issue no longer whether to let Beveridge promote the
report (and himself), but rather what their first impressions were of its
contents, party divisions immediately surfaced.

CHURCHILL: Cost.
WOOD: £100M. immediate.
CHURCHILL: . . . If we promise this largesse, far ahead of U.S. standards,
        they may say "we are being asked to pay for this."

ATTLEE: U.S. reaction may be good—they may be impressed by our
　boldness. . . .

CHURCHILL: Most serious reaction is on finance. Rate of taxation.

WOOD: These recommendations must be considered in relation to claims
　of other services on the money available.

EDEN: Reminder too . . . of necessary expenditure on armaments after
　the war.

The non-party man, Anderson, also opposed the Beveridge Report,
but he worried about public reaction if the government simply rejected
it. "Could we not welcome it in principle?" For the moment, his political
antennae were more sensitive than those of his Conservative colleagues.

The government finally allowed Beveridge to release the report on
December 2. As many had feared, it created a sensation. *Social Insurance
and Allied Services* became one of the most popular and well-read official
publications in British history. Seventy thousand copies sold within a few
days. All sides of the House of Commons clamored to discuss it, Labour
to express support, most Conservatives to express reservations. The War
Cabinet scheduled a three-day debate in the House to begin on February
16, 1943. But first it had to define its own position. Jowitt's committee
would review the report and make suggestions, and Anderson would convey these to the War Cabinet for further discussion.

AND CHURCHILL WOULD MISS ALMOST ALL OF IT, IN ORDER TO CONCENTRATE
on what really interested him and on what he deemed the most important issue: the war. On January 12, 1943, he flew to Casablanca to meet
Roosevelt; from there he traveled to Marrakech, Cairo, Turkey, Cyprus
and Algiers. The purpose of the trip, he told the House of Commons on
February 11, shortly after his return, had been to plan with various allies
how "to make the enemy burn and bleed in every way that is physically
and reasonably possible." We may deduce that he had not spent much time
considering the report by William Beveridge. And then he fell ill. A slight
cold turned into pneumonia and he took to his bed.

In the weeks before the Beveridge Report debate, Jowitt's committee
began to fashion a possible government response. Perhaps following Anderson's lead, it suggested welcoming most of Beveridge's proposals in
principle, opening talks with relevant committees, but postponing any
legislation until after the war. Meanwhile, in Churchill's absence, Attlee,

as deputy prime minister, presided over several difficult War Cabinet meetings. Agreement to follow Jowitt's plan did not end discussion—or reconcile differences. Labour and Liberal ministers wanted the government to accept Beveridge's main prescriptions now, even if without promising a date for implementation; Conservatives wanted to welcome them as a useful guide to reform and leave it at that.

The War Cabinet of February 12 proved particularly contentious. "Children's Allowances," mused Kingsley Wood about one of Beveridge's recommendations. "No hope to be extended of speedy introduction because of long time necessary to work out details—this applies to the scheme as a whole." Morrison, who favored acceptance and prompt implementation, countered: "Inexpediency of grudging assent. If we are going to pay Bill, we might as well get the credit for it." When Wood voiced another reservation—"We can't be committed on pensions"—Archibald Sinclair, the Liberal, reiterated Morrison's point: "Spirit of announcement—must endorse not only principles but early action on these principles. Safest thing is to give House of Commons a firm lead." Wood remained unconvinced. Near the end of the meeting, he raised concerns about old-age pensions specifically: "We must avoid increasing amounts for people who don't need them." Attlee provided Labour's answer: "Say impossible to define classes which are in no risk of ever needing social security. Administrative difficulties."

Meanwhile, Churchill was in bed with a fever. That did not stop him from communicating about high strategy with Dwight D. Eisenhower, who was the United States' commanding general of the European theater; General Bernard Montgomery, British commander of the 8th Army in North Africa; Marshal Stalin; and many others. Sick he might be, but he remained consumed by the task of making "the enemy burn and bleed." Still, as the date of the House debate drew near, he found time to consider the Beveridge Report more carefully. He did not think Britain could afford "airy visions of Utopia and Eldorado." At the same time, like Anderson, he recognized how popular the report had become. Therefore he approved the approach now recommended by Jowitt: welcome but don't commit. He wrote a memo pointing out that the current Parliament had been sitting since 1935, and therefore that it no longer represented the electorate and should not pass controversial legislation. Moreover, it was impossible to predict Britain's postwar financial situation. The Coalition should "get everything ready" for the next prime minister and his government, "and leave them a free hand to take up or reject a scheme." On February 15, he rose from his sickbed to preside over the last War Cabinet meeting before the Commons debate and to put these arguments to the Cabinet ministers.

This meeting proved even more contentious than the last one had been. Attlee met Churchill's first point head-on—during World War I, an older Parliament than the one currently sitting had passed important bills: "If P.M.'s line is taken, it will provoke demand for General Election." He half feared that was Churchill's intention. Despite the HID Report indicating a popular swing to the left, and despite the popularity of Beveridge's scheme, which Labour supported and most Conservatives opposed, all the Labour ministers thought they would lose a general election if one took place. They could not imagine that the country would vote against Winston Churchill's party. But that meant, in the final analysis, that all Churchill had to do in an argument with them was stand fast.

Still, Attlee and his socialist colleagues put up a fight. The Labour Party leader had produced a cogently argued response to Churchill's memo. At the War Cabinet meeting, he and his allies repeated its main arguments:

> ATTLEE: You can't make plans even, without reaching some decisions. . . .
>
> CHURCHILL: No promises—no commitments—every conceivable preparation.
>
> ATTLEE: Preparations all involve decisions of policy . . .
>
> CHURCHILL: I would agree to legislation by this Parliament to prepare for postwar: but not to legislation taking decisions binding the future.
>
> MORRISON: If we accept the view that we can have no enabling legislation dealing with postwar problems—we shall be in an indefensible position.
>
> CHURCHILL: [I] don't mean to ban legislation enabling you to make preparations.
>
> WOOD: We don't propose to say this week that we *shall* introduce legislation. [Emphasis in original.]

Because Churchill had placed Anderson in charge of committees dealing with the home front, Anderson would speak first for the government in the debate the next day. He sought clarification on Wood's point. "What I want to know is whether I am to say that legislation will *not* be proposed to this Parliament" (emphasis in original). Although the National Liberal

Ernest Brown answered Anderson—"That would be fatal"—and the minutes record that "Minister of Labour [Bevin] and others agreed," Churchill
and Wood had their way: Anderson would not promise legislation to introduce any aspect of the Beveridge Report.

PARLIAMENT CONVENED TWENTY-FOUR HOURS LATER TO CONSIDER THE
following motion, approved by the War Cabinet and introduced by Arthur
Greenwood, who had now returned to the back benches but was still Labour's deputy leader: "That this House welcomes the report of Sir William
Beveridge on Social Insurance and Allied Services as a comprehensive
review of the present provisions in this sphere and as a valuable aid in
determining the lines on which developments and legislation should be
pursued as part of the Government's policy of postwar reconstruction."
When he rose to state the government's position, Anderson ploddingly
followed instructions: "A time will come when difficult decisions will have
to be taken. . . . The time for such decisions is not yet." He may have been
a superb committeeman, as Eden judged, but he could not hold the House
of Commons. A Labour member shouted: "It is not much use listening
to him." This individual had concluded already that the government was
stalling, and that Labour Party leaders who were accepting the government line had betrayed their followers. Socialist backbenchers interrupted
continually from this moment on. They maintained a rowdy accompaniment while "Pomposo" tried to speak. At one point, a Conservative
member rose on a point of order: "There are some of us who want to hear
this speech, but there is a continual muttering going on the whole time
from the Opposition benches." Yet the unruliness was not confined to one
side of the House. A Labour member wrote bitterly in his diary that night
that Anderson had spoken "to a running and approving murmur of Tory
die-hard cheers, that the Government would shelve the whole matter."

Newspapers the next morning recorded an acute political crisis.
Tories, who feared explicitly opposing Beveridge's wildly popular plan,
accepted the government motion, since it committed to nothing, but
Labour backbenchers intended to table an amendment demanding implementation of Beveridge's scheme as quickly as possible, even during
wartime. Liberals and some dissident Tories would join them. It would
be the biggest parliamentary "rebellion" since May 1940. At a closed-door
meeting of the Parliamentary Labour Party, Attlee and Morrison unavailingly urged the rebels to drop the amendment. They found themselves

precisely where they didn't want to be: between their own party on the left and their Conservative ministerial colleagues to the right, and unable to shift either side.

The War Cabinet convened a little later that day with the ideological divide between socialists and Conservatives widening perilously. When Attlee and Morrison reported on the unsatisfactory conclusion to their recent meeting, Wood merely reiterated that the government was following proper procedure: it would welcome the report, consult with appropriate committees, and prepare legislation. Churchill reiterated that the War Cabinet must confine itself to matters raised by the war. Implementation of Beveridge's recommendations would depend upon Britain's financial position when the war was over.

Tempers flared.

ATTLEE: [We] didn't come into this Government on basis only of dealing with War. [We] always understood that we would concern ourselves with preparations for postwar problems. Moreover the public are very much interested in their postwar conditions. This Government must either govern or get—through [a] General Election—a Government that will. [But he was bluffing. He feared the results of a General Election.] We have e.g. concluded a 20-year Treaty with Russia. That commits the future: we can't exclude other things on ground of no jurisdiction.

CHURCHILL: Peril to financial security: irresponsible commitments. We must get our soldiers home and into employment. I'm not fighting this issue on "No Mandate" basis. Deal with this on merits of this Bill. Suppose you draft and even introduce it: you can't bring it into force during the war. . . . Everyone wants it: but can you pay for it? You can't pass the Bill before you know where you are. . . .

MORRISON: If this Government leaves its successor with no legislative preparation for postwar period we shall be treacherous to the country.

Finally, and characteristically, the minister of labor intervened to settle matters. As a trade unionist, he believed in loyalty. The War Cabinet had agreed the previous day to the course recommended by Jowitt's committee. He might not like it, but he would stick to it. However, there still was room for maneuver.

BEVIN: We arrived at agreement on Monday. I stand by that. . . . [P]roceed
at once with preparations including preparation of Bill. . . . If when
we reached that stage [and the] war was still on, we would be ready
to go forward with Bill, reserving date of operation, subject only to
review of all financial implications of other projects. . . .

He had cleverly amended Jowitt: the government should prepare legislation; propose legislation while continuing to fight the war; promise
to implement legislation even if still fighting the war, subject to finances;
and leave open the date of implementation. The prime minister accepted
this solution:

CHURCHILL: If [the] approved day [for implementation] can be left blank
I wouldn't oppose introduction of Bill. Though I think it would be
unwise—occupying much Parliamentary time and provoking much
controversy. So long as we reserve the right to decide at end of war
when to bring it into operation. . . .

This last sentence worried the leader of the Labour Party.

ATTLEE: We can have no arrière pensée about a negative commitment, in
regard to legislation.

Churchill did not reply. With this papering over, the War Cabinet had
bridged the chasm.

THE HOUSE MET LATER THAT AFTERNOON TO DISCUSS BEVERIDGE FOR
the second time. Kingsley Wood, speaking for the government, had no
more parliamentary sense than Anderson. He paid mere lip service to
the paper bridge. He seemed not merely to favor but to relish delay. The
government *could* implement reforms during the war, he acknowledged,
but first it must discuss Beveridge's proposals with the relevant ministries, which would take time, and then it must prepare legislation, an even
lengthier business. Moreover, there could be no guarantee of implementation after all that, because "it is right and proper and only fair to the
country and to our people that the financial aspect should be carefully
considered and weighed." At this Arthur Greenwood interjected: "It will
need a very long war if all these items are to be settled before the war is

over." The man who had introduced the government motion welcoming the Beveridge Report in the first place was now criticizing the government position. In the end he would vote for the amendment to the very motion he had introduced. No better indication of Labour disillusionment with the government's approach to the Beveridge plan could have been offered.

Labour Party leaders found themselves in a tight spot. They thought Churchill could always trump them by calling and winning a general election, and they thought they had managed to compromise with him at the War Cabinet; nevertheless, Labour backbenchers thought their leaders had sold them out. And the rebels still insisted on proposing their amendment. Bevin tried to resolve matters at a meeting of the Parliamentary Labour Party the next morning, February 18, before the third and final sitting of the debate. But the great trade unionist did not know how to take the temperature of a roomful of suspicious Labour MPs. He lectured and chastised and stormed. "He says," wrote one who was there, "the party amendment is a vote of censure on him, that they never gave him an opportunity of speaking before it was put down, that this is not the kind of treatment he has been accustomed to, that this is not the way they do things in the unions." He succeeded only in putting up their backs. The movers of the amendment would not withdraw it, and a majority of their colleagues continued to support them.

That afternoon, as MPs of all parties began filing into the Debating Chamber, tensions ran high. A Labour Cabinet minister spied one of his party's left-wingers "rushing about with a maniacal glint in his eye. He reminds me of the chap who was determined to set fire to the house and burn it down for his own delight." Beveridge, with his great beak of a nose and longish, thinning white hair, appeared in the lobby looking, according to Harold Nicolson, the National Labour MP, "like the witch of Endor." "Well are you enjoying this?" Nicolson asked him. "I am having the fun of my life," Beveridge replied. "My Report . . . may bring down the Government."

When debate recommenced, Labour and Liberal speakers demanded that the government commit to swift action on Beveridge's recommendations. Conservatives, not liking the report but still not daring to oppose it because it was so popular, tepidly supported the government motion welcoming it. Given the speeches of Anderson and Wood, they believed the government would not be implementing Beveridge's proposals anytime soon. Then, at the end of the debate, Herbert Morrison rose to put the official case for the final time. He occupied an especially difficult position, because he had supported implementation of the report both in the War Cabinet and in public speeches. Now he must advocate a different course of action. But he belonged to a coalition that had found a basis for compromise, although previous government spokesmen had failed to articulate it. Morrison would. According to the *Manchester Evening News*, he was "the most dangerous debater on the Labour side in the House of Commons." Today he would show it. He had helped bring down Chamberlain's government with a devastating speech; now he would help save Churchill's with a brilliantly supportive one.

MORRISON BEGAN BY POINTING OUT THAT BEVERIDGE HIMSELF DID NOT expect the report to be implemented until after the war.

HON. MEMBERS: No.
MORRISON: Yes, with great respect. It would be a good idea to read the
    Report. [He referred to the relevant passage.] Therefore hon. Mem-
    bers are wrong. . . . That, I think, clears that point. [Interruption.]
    I go farther. It not only clears the interruption; it demolishes it.

He argued, as Anderson and Wood had, but in a characteristically pungent manner, that no responsible government should commit to reforms, however desirable, without taking financial considerations into account. He had learned this lesson as leader of the London County Council a decade earlier, and he would not abandon it now: "There has been too much of parties in Opposition, or semi-detached opposition, giving reckless undertakings and making rather wild promises and then not carrying them out when they are in power. I will not be a party to any such political jiggery-pokery."

Most significantly, he transformed the tone of the government's defense. Where Anderson and Wood had emphasized the negative, Morrison reminded members that the government already had accepted in principle five of Beveridge's six fundamental points and sixteen of his twenty-three recommendations, including universal health care (although retaining private hospitals), children's allowances of five shillings per week (Beveridge recommended eight shillings), free meals for schoolchildren without means testing, and old-age pensions (starting at a level higher than Beveridge recommended)—a formidable list.

Labour members complained that the government had paid only lip service to the report. Morrison seemed to demonstrate, to the contrary, that the government accepted and believed in it; the reforms it already had accepted in principle and that he had just listed proved that. He explained the need for consultation before implementation in a manner beyond the parliamentary skills of the civil servant Anderson, or Chancellor Wood: "This is a country in which if you do things without giving reasonable opportunities for consultation with the persons who are affected . . . they will be very cross and there will be trouble. I speak feelingly. I was accused of not consulting my trade union friends when I brought in the compulsory Fire Prevention Order on which I was in rather a hurry, because the country was in danger of burning down. But they complained, and not without justification entirely, that they had not been consulted." A member asked whether, after consultations, the government would "undertake to bring in the necessary legislation." Morrison did not prevaricate: "I was coming to that. All these preparations lead up to the preparation of the Bill or Bills. I cannot go further than what has been said. We cannot give a date when the Bill will be produced . . . but we are going to lose no essential time, subject to the prior claim on our labors, which is the successful prosecution of the war."

He had not contradicted Anderson and Wood, but most of his audience thought he had, if only implicitly. When he concluded that "the Government [has] acted with speed. We have reached among ourselves reasonable agreement with a big progressive outcome," a majority of Labour members decided that the government favored Beveridge's recommendations and would implement them as soon as it could, possibly before the war was over. They would vote for the amendment—they could hardly do otherwise—but only a few on the far left would want to press the rebellion further. The home secretary had rehabilitated not only the government in their eyes, but the Labour Party leadership, too, at least for the time being.

Herbert Morrison had delivered a bravura parliamentary performance. Everyone knew it and said so. This success built the confidence of a man who had not lacked it to begin with. It fed his ambition. If before delivering the speech he had stood not quite on a par with other Labour ministers in the War Cabinet, he did so now. Increasingly, the prime minister would have to take him into account. And the debate over Britain's postwar future was only just beginning.

CHAPTER 11

The "Cocky Cockney" and the Debate over Postwar Britain

THE RUN-UP TO THE HOUSE DEBATE OVER THE BEVERIDGE REPORT, capped by the debate itself, marked a watershed in British wartime politics. Previously, discussion of postwar reconstruction had been relatively muted—at least in comparison with what was to come. From then on it grew ever more intense, culminating in the claims and counterclaims of the general election of 1945. This was not Beveridge's doing alone. By the end of 1942 the tide of war had turned, with Allied victories at Stalingrad in Russia, El Alamein in North Africa, and Guadalcanal in the South Pacific. Britain no longer seemed likely to lose. But that meant that, much though Churchill might want to, he could no longer dismiss concern about the shape of postwar Britain as a mere distraction. The realistic prospect of victory, however distant, legitimized serious discussion of the shape of things to come.

From the autumn of 1942 until the lead-up to the general election, the man who most often and most tellingly put Labour's case for socialist reconstruction was Herbert Morrison. During the debate on the Beveridge Report, he had stepped firmly not merely onto the national stage but to its very center; afterward, he stayed there, an easily recognizable figure with his one blind eye, his rumpled suits, his untamable quiff of hair. During the interwar period, politically conscious Britons had already known him as a dominant figure in London politics. He had served as a borough councillor and mayor, building a powerful political machine in London, leading it to victory on the London County Council in 1934, and had then demonstrated what "municipal socialism" could mean by unifying all London transport under a single municipal authority, the London Passenger Transport Board. Britons also knew him as a leader in the national Labour Party, for which he represented South Hackney in the House of Commons. He had played a prominent part in framing Labour's socialist program, which he tried to design to appeal to all classes, not only the working class. He served on the party's most important committees, always emphasizing practical measures as incremental steps toward the great goal, and advocating public corporations (such as the London Transport Board) as the best form of government control. Finally, he had a reputation for being reasonable and democratic and for being an effective administrator. He listened carefully, asked intelligent questions, drew the logical conclusions and acted on them swiftly.

Some in the Labour Party distrusted him, however. The Labour left believed that his Fabian version of socialism, with its emphasis on government boards, represented a top-down approach and provided no scope for democratic input from workers on the shop floor. A powerful contingent of trade unionists nursed more visceral suspicions. They believed, probably correctly, that while Morrison was minister of transport in Ramsay MacDonald's second Labour government, his ambitions had nearly trumped his principles. In 1931, with the economic depression at its worst and the government divided over what to do, Morrison, said his doubters, had wanted to stick with the prime minister, who was about to dissolve the Cabinet, form a "National Government" composed mainly of Conservatives, and then call a general election and campaign against his own party for "a doctor's mandate" to fix things, mainly by cutting government spending. But MacDonald, they said, wouldn't have him. Ernest Bevin led this contingent of doubters. He deemed Morrison an irremediably slippery character. When Morrison stood for leadership of the Labour Party in 1935, Bevin and his trade-union allies made sure Attlee would beat him. As a result, Morrison could not hope to dominate the Parliamentary Labour Party as he had dominated the Labour contingent on the London County Council. But he continued to nurse his ambitions, and so far he always had realized them sooner or later.   .

In May 1940, Churchill enabled Morrison to take a giant step in that direction by choosing him to be minister of supply, and then, six months later, home secretary. The second appointment, which took place at the height of the London Blitz, proved crucial. The prime minister recognized that this quintessential London man, this "cocky Cockney" (although since he had been born in south London, not east London, he wasn't a Cockney, strictly speaking), could best organize the capital's civil defense, just as he had organized London's municipal services and transportation providers before the war. He thought also that Morrison could best represent the great city to the government, and the government to the city, and that he could do for Britain's provincial cities what he could do for the capital.

Events proved Churchill right. Wherever the Germans bombed, there soon appeared Herbert Morrison, offering sympathy to the survivors, listening judiciously to their complaints and recommendations, promising quick action, fulfilling his promises. He worked hard and successfully to improve London's bomb shelters, to open new ones deep underground, to systematize access to them, and to improve their amenities. "By the spring of 1941," wrote his biographers, "most Londoners sheltering underground were sleeping in reasonably civilized dormitories." He also ordered production of indoor shelters—which eventually became known as "Morrisons"—for people who preferred to stay at home when the bombs fell. He established "fire-watchers" to assist fire brigades and nationalized the fire brigades. He responded with equal flair, compassion and organizational skills throughout the country, and by the end of his tenure in the position he had reorganized Britain's entire civil defense system, making it infinitely more efficient than it had been before. In November 1942, Churchill promoted him to the War Cabinet. He commended Morrison's "courageous and resourceful leadership" at a rally in Hyde Park, and the people cheered. Within the Labour Party, only some powerful trade unionists and a few on the left continued to nourish suspicions and resentments of him.

Morrison took his place in the War Cabinet, sitting at the right end of the oval table, with Eden to his left, and Bevin—whose dislike had not abated over the years, but rather ripened into loathing—to the left of Eden. Churchill sat on the other side, between Attlee and a secretary. Years later, Eden reported to an interviewer that whenever Morrison spoke at these meetings, Bevin would provide a *sotto voce* accompaniment of jibes and taunts. He found sitting between the two men "rather uncomfortable." Morrison heard Bevin but never responded. Hurt and offended he must have been, but it did not deter him; he proved as effective in the War Cabinet as he had been everywhere else. "Morrison was certainly not reticent or shy," Eden remembered. "He was always well briefed and put his case well."

By late 1942 the home secretary had his department running smoothly. He judged that with Russia and America now in the war, Britain would win, and he knew that Beveridge would soon release his report. Morrison never neglected his many duties as home secretary, or for the Labour Party, but finally he felt able to turn his mind to postwar problems. In December he launched a series of speeches on this subject. Two months before the Beveridge Report debate, he already was answering Conservatives who judged that a welfare state would be too expensive, arguing in a speech in Swindon, for example, that a "cautious, niggling worldly wisdom, counting chances while children went hungry, would be a miserable foundation for our future life together as a family." Three days before Commons debated the Beveridge plan, he went further in a speech at Nottingham. The government already had agreed, for practical reasons, to maintain some price controls during the transition to peace. Morrison wanted much more: "rationing in appropriate forms for the sake of fairness at home, and for the sake of keeping the ship of State on an even keel. We must have raw-material controls too. . . . We shall also want price control." In this manner, he predicted, Britain would contain "the forces of selfishness and sectionalism."

Meanwhile, the party leader, Attlee, had his hands full, not only with government work but also with managing his disputatious party and colleagues; he largely remained quiet about postwar matters. Bevin, rude though he might be to Morrison, had been schooled in loyalty by the union. Heeding Churchill's exhortations not to rock the Coalition, he, too, avoided visionary speeches about reconstruction. So, by and large, did Cripps during this period; his moment in the sun was temporarily eclipsed. The result was that when Morrison rose to defend the government in the debate on Beveridge's report, he already had a reputation not merely as a successful and popular home secretary, but also as the Labour War Cabinet minister most willing to voice his party's aspirations for the future. When he then satisfied Labour MPs that the government would implement Beveridge's proposals as soon as it could, he further cemented that reputation. This placed him well for future efforts. Obviously, it also put him in a position to advance his career. He would soon be doing both.

AND WHAT ABOUT WINSTON CHURCHILL AT THIS TIME? AFTER FEBRUARY 15, when he chaired the last War Cabinet before the Beveridge Report debate, he returned to his bed, sick with pneumonia, temperature rising dangerously to 102 degrees. Nevertheless, except for an interlude during which he read *Moll Flanders*, his illness did not stop him from composing and dispatching one memo or letter after another to generals, diplomats, dictators, presidents, prime ministers and King George VI. His correspondence ranged over the Allied invasion of Sicily ("Operation Husky"), now scheduled for June, the ongoing campaign in North Africa, the great battles raging in Russia, Gandhi's hunger strike in India, and the Free French in West Africa. Then: "A gentleman, Mr. Thomson, kindly presented me with a lion." Churchill made sure the zoo could take it: "I do not want the lion at the moment either at Downing Street or at Chequers, owing to the Ministerial calm which prevails there. But the Zoo is not far away and situations may arise in which I shall have great need of it." In his multivolume history of World War II, the chapter dealing with this period mentions all of the above, and not a word about Beveridge. However, Churchill did receive a letter from Beveridge around this time and wrote a brief reply on the first day of the debate: "Thank you. . . . I hope an opportunity for a talk with you will occur in the future, but of course I have to give my main attention to the war."

He could not ignore entirely the issues Beveridge finally had succeeded in raising, however. Lying on his sickbed, he received a verbal report about the debate from his PPS. The Conservative chief whip sent him a breakdown of the government's House supporters and opponents. Among Liberal MPs, all but three had voted for the amendment to the government motion. Aside from Labour's ministers and their subordinates, practically the entire Parliamentary Labour Party had done the same. Only the Conservatives had supported the government motion unamended, and Churchill knew what most of them really thought of Beveridge. The vote for the amendment to the government motion proved to be the biggest parliamentary rebellion during his premiership. Churchill finally realized he would have to publicly address the subject of postwar reconstruction after all.

Here was a crucial moment in Churchill's premiership, although it is rarely treated as one. It was the moment when he might have taken hold of the growing movement for far-reaching postwar reconstruction. But that would have required recognizing the extent of the groundswell then taking place, accepting its sweeping aims (or at least many of them), and carrying a majority of his party with him. Churchill only partially grasped the extent of the upsurge, and at heart he neither sympathized with nor accepted its aims. He simply did not believe in many government controls. He was not much interested in postwar reconstruction, and he continued to deem its most enthusiastic partisans woolly-minded idealists.

Still, Churchill knew he had to do something. When he was well enough to go to Chequers, on March 3, he began working on a speech. He wrote a draft while sitting in the bathtub, working the taps with his toes. He would rise from the tub and stride across his room naked except for a bath towel, reciting portions of it. On March 11 he summoned R. A. Butler to discuss it, especially the section on education. Butler, in his account of the visit, made clear that it was a version of the address on postwar reconstruction that Churchill would deliver over the radio nine days later.

Recovered from his illness, Churchill went on air on the evening of March 20, 1943. He began by assuring listeners, perhaps not altogether accurately, that when he had been ill he nevertheless had "followed attentively all the time what was happening in Parliament and the lively discussions on our home affairs when peace comes." He took a page from the book of Herbert Morrison, whose speech he undoubtedly had read: "Nothing would be easier for me than to make any number of promises and to get the immediate response of cheap cheers and glowing leading articles. . . . I am resolved not to."

But he did want to co-opt and redirect the groundswell of left-wing opinion in the country, so he announced a "Four Year Plan." He announced that he supported creation of a National Health Service. He said he favored higher education for anyone capable of benefiting from it, and full employment, and maintenance of price controls for a period of transition after the war. As for social security: "You must rank me and my colleagues as strong partisans of national compulsory insurance for all classes for all purposes from the cradle to the grave." At first blush, this seems hard to distinguish from what Labour supporters wanted. Arthur Greenwood probably spoke correctly when he said at the Labour Party Conference a year later: "The Prime Minister's broadcast . . . flabbergasted a lot of British listeners."

Some thought the speech recalled the days before World War I, when as a Liberal Churchill had worked with David Lloyd George to establish Britain's first social insurance programs. There may be some truth in this. A close reading of the speech, however, suggests a different conclusion: that it was an elaborate exercise in fobbing off. Churchill spoke of postwar reform, but he provided no details and avoided contentious matters. When he came to the National Health Service, for example, he did not mention whether it would abolish private hospitals and private medical practices, as many in the Labour Party wanted. When he spoke of education, he did not mention abolition of "educational class privilege" in the "public schools"—that is, the historically private independent schools, such as Eton, his own alma mater, Harrow, and the like—again as Labour advocated. When he spoke of full employment, he said that the state would plan for it—but also that private enterprise must play its part "to the utmost." As for postwar controls, he did no more than repeat government policy: there should be controls on some prices during the transitional period from war to a peacetime economy. Moreover, he unmistakably distinguished his approach from that of the socialists: "Our people would be the last to consent to be governed by a bureaucracy. Freedom is their life blood." Most importantly, he continued to insist, as he had done at the War Cabinet before the debate on Beveridge's proposals, that no plan, not even his own, would be implemented until Germany had been beaten and a new government elected in Britain to assess the financial situation.

It seems clear that Churchill wanted to be associated in the public mind with the extraordinarily popular Beveridge plan, but without alienating the base of the Conservative Party, and without denying his own convictions. He went as far as he could, but it was not far enough in the eyes of many. His main motive was not to outline schemes of postwar reconstruction, but rather to "simplify and mollify political divergences and enable all our political forces to march forward to the main objective in unity and, so far as possible, in step." To the War Cabinet, he said: "Last thing I want is endless buzz of ardent discussion of postwar problems." But he had not said enough to quiet the buzz. If anything, the buzz grew louder and more intense.

INDEED, IT GREW LOUD EVEN INSIDE THE PARLIAMENTARY CONSERVATIVE Party (PCP). In April, shortly after Churchill's speech, Tory right-wingers founded a National League for Freedom (NLF). This organization argued that all government intervention leads inevitably to totalitarianism, a view famously encapsulated one year later in Friedrich Hayek's *The Road to Serfdom*. Members may have feared that Churchill was traveling down that road. In 1944, one would cite Hayek in a letter to him: "Anyone who has read Professor Hayek's book . . . will realize the danger of the tendency

towards more and more State control." The immediate purpose of the
NLF, as it announced in the introduction to its first pamphlet, was "to
fight the growing threat to British liberty represented by the host of Government officials who today shut down businesses, pry into private affairs,
issue endless forms . . . and are slowly strangling not only trade but liberty." Its members utterly opposed Beveridge's schemes and Churchill's
gestures toward them, halfhearted though these gestures may have been.
They wanted to roll back government controls as soon as the war ended.
Probably they represented majority opinion within the PCP, if not within
the Conservative Party as a whole.

Some younger Tory MPs welcomed Beveridge's report, however. These
members, consisting of about forty men, most of them relatively young,
told Churchill's PPS that a Conservative minister of their generation, R.
A. Butler, for instance, would have better represented the government in
the Beveridge Report debate than Kingsley Wood had. Then they tabled a
motion requesting the appointment of a minister of social security to prepare the legislation Beveridge had adumbrated. The day before Churchill
broached his "Four Year Plan," they set up their own permanent committee, the Tory Reform Group (TRG). They believed that Conservatives who
opposed Beveridge's proposals were committing political suicide. In their
initial press announcement they claimed that "Social Reform is a tradition
which the Conservative Party desires to see maintained." The TRG began
releasing bulletins dealing with current political questions, for example
on land and agriculture, on coal, and on employment policy. It advocated
a Tory "middle road." These members did not think the prime minister
was taking it.

Churchill's radio address did not even quiet his Conservative colleagues in government. Butler was buzzing about education, which Churchill had set him onto, thinking it would divert him from demanding
sweeping reforms in other realms. Eden had said well before Beveridge
released his report that "social security must be the first object of our
domestic policy after the war." Now he was saying: "If we imagine that all
controls can be swept aside or that we can return to the economic anarchy
of the old days . . . then we shall bring not only discredit but disaster upon
ourselves." Even Lord Beaverbrook was buzzing about plans for Britain
after the coming victory. That old buccaneer had produced a characteristically brash and blunt outline of the postwar Conservative reforms he
favored just before the debate on Beveridge. He opposed socialism but

recognized there could be no going back to 1939. He advocated a paternalistic capitalism, with state-sponsored public housing and public health as well as co-education and abolition of "public schools." "Labour of every type attaching to a factory," he wrote in a memorandum "becomes a charge on it, and must take precedence over every other form of charge. . . . Now and henceforth the first charge shall be the labour[er] instead of the shareholder." He sent a copy of this memo to a more representative figure in the party than himself, the chairman of the 1922 Committee: "Is it the suggestion," asked this gentleman, aghast at Beaverbrook's last proposal, in particular, "that a firm should employ six hundred workmen where five hundred will do?" Undeterred, Beaverbrook composed a short statement reiterating his main points: "The program is not Socialism. The program is not Fascism. Nor is it a return to prewar conditions. . . . Industry must take the responsibility." He was recommending "a new capitalism which will provide for production and consumption expanding as fast as daring and initiative can provide the way."

The minister of food, Lord Woolton, a non-party figure who would join the Conservatives immediately after the war, contributed to the buzz as well. "Nationalization, Private Enterprise: What do these things matter to the man in the street?" he wanted to know. Like the TRG, he advocated a middle road for Conservatives to follow. "By means of private enterprise or by means of Government action," Britain should, after the war, "provide houses for the people of this country so that they may live decently." It should "put a floor into wages and into conditions of employment, so that whilst employers shall gain their freedom to make what they like and what they can sell, only such people as are worthy of respect as employers shall be able to employ labor in the commercial world." He asked: "If we license public houses [i.e., pubs] . . . is there any reason why we should not license employers and premises so that labor may know [which] employers . . . have prescribed to a standard for the rest?"

Unlike Eden and Butler, who knew their political futures lay with the Conservative Party no matter how frustrating it sometimes seemed to them, Woolton may have briefly flirted with the idea of leading a separate centrist party. He sent a copy of his speech to a former member of the board of directors of Lewis Department Stores, on which he, too, had served (as chairman for four years before the war), and told him he planned to deliver three more addresses. This man, who recently had started a Conservative Research Center for progressive Tories, advised against publishing the speech until autumn, by which time Woolton should have the next three clear in his mind. Then "you come out . . . and nail your colors firmly to the mast. . . . This speech is your entry into politics as the leader of a centre party. . . . [Y]ou are setting the stage admirably." Woolton duly addressed the TRG. His former colleague wrote: "A compact little group of fifty MPs with an organization behind them might be of use to you."

Did Churchill think that his minister for food was buzzing too loudly? Perhaps wanting to nip a potential threat in the bud, but more likely realizing that his hopes for quieting debate had failed, and wishing to appeal at least to advocates of moderate renewal, he appointed Woolton in November 1943 to a newly created post, minister of reconstruction, with a seat in the War Cabinet. (He had thought first of appointing Beaverbrook, but Labour ministers rose up in opposition.) Once in his new post the former minister of food abandoned his dreams of leadership—without telling his friend from Lewis Department Stores, who inspired a series of articles puffing him in the provincial press. The embarrassed Woolton disavowed them—and his friend—in an obsequious letter to the prime minister. But he still believed in the middle road. Two days after his promotion, he had a long session with the same chairman of the 1922 Committee whom Beaverbrook had outraged. More in sorrow than in anger, he tried to indicate to this gentleman where the Conservative Party was going wrong:

> I asked him to consider whether, as a party, they agreed with me in the steps that I had taken to preserve infant health by making milk readily accessible to all nursing mothers, by insisting that those simple "luxuries" of the rich, such as orange juice and cod-liver oil, which have caused rickets to disappear from the nurseries of the well-to-do, were not an equal necessity for the children of the poor. . . . I pointed out that in none of these things . . . simple and humble as they are, have the Conservative Party ever raised a voice in the House of Commons by way of support.

He laid out the moderate path he thought Conservatives should follow with regard to trade unions and regulation of industry and conditions of employment. What the 1922 Committee chairman thought is unrecorded. Perhaps not much: R. A. Butler deemed the committee head "too stupid to do anything but intrigue."

As for Labour, its rank and file now was buzzing louder than ever. But Churchill had the Labour ministers on a hook. They cherished socialist goals as much as the rank and file did, but they also believed in the Coalition. They thought Churchill would yank the hook if they pushed their program too hard, dissolving the Coalition and calling a general election, which the Conservatives would win. By and large, they held their tongues in public about the shape of things to come—except for Herbert Morrison. He had no doubt that a Labour minister should boldly call for more than his socialist colleagues dared to, and for far more than middle-of-the-road Tories and Churchill were. In speeches he delivered prior to the debate on the Beveridge Report, Morrison had indicated what he thought Labour's postwar policies should be. After the debate, he continued in the same vein, only more sharply and in more detail.

DURING THE MONTHS AFTER THE DEBATE, THE "COCKY COCKNEY" cemented his reputation as the voice of Labour socialism with a series of hard-hitting addresses. On May 3, 1943, he told an audience in Birmingham that his party always had favored the measures Beveridge now proposed. Finally the Liberals had come round, and so had the Conservatives (by voting to welcome Beveridge's proposals). Therefore, "the real question [today] . . . is the great issue of the relation between the State and industry." Labour must win this argument, too. It must persuade the country that the state should "find some means, by public ownership or some form of public control, to ensure that [centrally organized industries] are operated in the interests of expanding national wealth and a policy of full employment." Without Labour victory in this argument, there would be no public ownership; without public ownership, there could be no full employment; and without full employment, predicted Morrison, "Beveridge and a whole lot of other things [would] in the end go down the drain."

Possibly somebody told Morrison to ratchet back after this speech. If so, he refused. But he seemed to be answering someone when he said, six days later in a speech at Bromwich, "So long as we keep things in the right perspective I believe that this concern about the future does not hinder but rather helps the prosecution of the war." Then he returned to his central message: "Control has helped to get maximum production in war. It has helped us solve problems of prices and wages. . . . It will have to help solve many of the very similar problems that will face us after the war. The choice will be between control and chaos."

Morrison had a talent for putting complex matters into language all could understand. In this same speech he warned his audience not to be fooled by "people who . . . tell you that we have fought the war for freedom and that the irksome restrictions and regulations and control that the war has brought should be completely done away with." He was preempting a likely Conservative argument:

> Now what do you think would happen if we took off all the controls? . . . There would be a mad scramble with everyone competing against everyone else. . . . Prices would go skyrocketing up, the man with the long purse would do the best for himself, the rich man would get his motor car before the poor housewife got her new pots and pans, the millionaire would get his mansion before the bombed-out docker got his new house, some of the key requirements of government and industry would be delayed far longer than they ought to be.

This was the kind of argument that Labour supporters were longing to hear. Unlike Winston Churchill, Herbert Morrison was not merely paying lip service to the groundswell; he identified heart and soul with its desire for a radically reconstructed postwar Britain.

He returned to the charge at Dundee a few weeks later. "We shall have won this war by a system of fair shares—which means control; by a system of finding what we needed wherever we could get it—which means control; by a system of allotting our resources to the most urgent need on a basis of first things first—which means control. All these things will be needed after the war."

In London, he gave a speech called "A Restatement of Some Socialist Principles" in which he attempted to work out "a right relation between the State and industry." He favored socialization of "centralized business," of monopolies, cartels and all other enterprises that had power over "public wellbeing and public policy," but not of small businesses, which "pay a real social dividend." In fact, characteristically, he assured small business owners that under a Labour government there would be "a good deal of business activity carried on among us without State operation or control." This was vintage Morrison, attempting to reassure the "useful classes," as he called them, that socialism would not hurt them, that the new economic order would be in their interest, too, not just in the interests of the industrial proletariat.

Morrison said only what he believed. He wanted Britain to become a more just, humane and egalitarian country, and he believed that socialism would make it so. He wanted his party to state this unambiguously. But also, he wanted to become its leader and eventually prime minister. When he gave these speeches, he raised his profile and positioned himself for the coming struggle for leadership, and of course he knew it. By mid-1943, observe his biographers, "no other figure in the Labour movement . . . so symbolized . . . [the] will to make sure that it was Labour which shaped Britain's postwar destiny." Attlee did not yet perceive Morrison as a threat, but Ernest Bevin, who remained steadfastly loyal to both Attlee and Churchill, did. He determined to puncture Morrison's balloon.

He got his chance soon after January 1943, when Morrison arranged to be nominated for treasurer of the Labour Party. Morrison hoped this position would serve as a springboard to the leadership—if not now, then after the next general election, which he thought would be followed by a ballot for party leader. It came as a blow, therefore, when Arthur Greenwood threw his hat into the ring, too. Greenwood's colleagues at the top knew, as Hugh Dalton put it in his diary, that "the poor old chap couldn't even sign his name after midday," but he remained popular in the Labour Party as an old warhorse whom Churchill had treated shabbily. Still, Morrison thought he could beat Greenwood in a straight fight. But then a third candidate, nominated by the miners' union, appeared as well.

At the Labour Party Annual Conference in June 1943, where the election would take place, politicking grew intense. Morrison had the support of the vast majority of delegates from local branches of the Labour Party. His allies trawled for votes among trade-union leaders, not without success. But the third candidate divided the anti-Greenwood vote, and then at the crucial moment Bevin delivered the coup de grace by throwing the bloc vote of his massive Transport and General Workers' Union behind Greenwood, ensuring the latter's victory and Morrison's defeat.

The home secretary took his loss hard. But he remained at the height of his powers, and irrepressible. Within a week he was back out on the stump. "Tinkering and patching with our social system is not good enough. The basic question is who will control industry," he exhorted another London audience. He had picked himself up and started in all over again, redoubling his efforts as Labour's boldest spokesman for postwar socialism. The setback, he must have assured himself, would be only temporary.

MEANWHILE, CHURCHILL HAD A WAR TO RUN. ON MAY 4, 1943, HE SET off aboard the *Queen Mary* for the United States for further military discussions. Amazingly, William Beveridge had booked passage on the same ship. Churchill could not avoid inviting him to lunch. So the two men finally had a chance to talk about the famous Beveridge Report after all. It did not go well. Churchill's doctor recorded in his diary: "When the PM summoned to his table an acquaintance in whom he had little interest," a few words would be exchanged. After that, though, Churchill "would make no further attempt at conversation, sitting all hunched up and scowling at his plate with his thoughts a long way off." In this particular instance, the doctor concluded, "at about half-past-two the bleak little function just petered out."

Churchill addressed the US Congress, on May 20, to thunderous applause. A week later he headed for Africa for discussions about the campaign there, and the need for a quick, decisive victory over Italy. He did not return to Britain until June 5. Then in August he set sail again, this time for the now-famous Quebec Conference, where at last serious planning for Operation Overlord, the Second Front in France, would take place. From Quebec he traveled again to Washington, DC, for further discussions. This time he did not get back to London until September 20, and then he would be off for Cairo and for a conference in Tehran with FDR and Stalin in November. Meanwhile, nervous or angry Conservatives who hated what Morrison advocated kept complaining about him. When Churchill got home, in addition to all his other concerns he had to juggle these men and, finally, Morrison too.

The home secretary's speech in Dundee on the necessity of postwar controls had agitated Conservatives. One of them gave notice that he intended to raise a question in the House of Commons. Did Morrison speak for the government? Churchill, perhaps comparing his rapturous reception by Congress in Washington to the troublesome Parliament in London, got Morrison on the telephone: "Why are you so provocative? . . . Why do you put me in a jam like this?" Morrison told a journalist: "We had a hell of an up-and-down about it." He added: "But it was all in quite good humor." Perhaps so—or maybe not. In the House, Churchill quoted Kingsley Wood, reminding Conservatives that even that orthodox chancellor once had said that "a considerable measure of control of our economic life will have to continue after the war." Then Churchill spoke his mind: "In a National Coalition formed to carry on the war, a certain diversity of opinion, or at least of emphasis, is indispensable to political sincerity. I earnestly hope, however, that party controversy will be avoided. . . . This is a time when all combative impulses should be reserved for the enemy." It was hardly an endorsement of his minister—and yet that did not satisfy his minister's critics. Another Tory raised his voice: "Will the right hon. Gentleman consider suggesting to the Home Secretary that he should join the National League for Freedom?"

Nor, in fact, was Churchill himself satisfied. He thought a speech here or there was one thing, but that a series of them on a central theme, which he now realized Morrison had delivered, amounted to a campaign. Moreover, he did not sympathize with the campaign. He took the home secretary aside. This time, the two men "rowed." Morrison reported to another Labour minister: "Hitherto the PM has not minded [my] speeches on postwar control at all, but now he is angered by them." This did not stop Morrison from continuing to make them, however, or from continuing to make trouble for the prime minister in other ways.

IN FEBRUARY 1943, THE LABOUR MINISTERS HAD ACQUIESCED GRUDGINGLY in the decision on the Beveridge Report forced by Wood and Churchill: there would be no rulings about reconstruction until the end of the war, when Britain's financial situation would be clear. Morrison had sold this to Labour MPs in his famous speech in Parliament during the Beveridge debate by emphasizing that the government would make decisions as soon as it could, but he cannot have liked doing so. In May, he wrote a paper, entitled "The Need for Decisions," that revisited this fraught subject. In early June, Attlee and Bevin reworked the paper, and the three men, a potent combination whenever they managed to cooperate, discussed it. On June 26 they submitted a powerful memo to the War Cabinet calling for a complete revision of the government's position. They wanted it "to make now the best forecast it can of the financial and economic position of the country after the war, and on that basis to take a major decision as to the items which it is prepared to carry through into law before the end of the war." They listed the items they thought should be considered: the use of land, development rights, compensation, water supply, the financing of the building program, and the reorganization of transport, heat and power. Also they wanted information on the budgetary implications of postwar reforms in such areas as social security, education, agriculture, full employment, the future of domestic industry, export trade, health and colonial policy. "Official plans are not enough," they argued. "Nor is the taking of decisions upon them 'in principle.' . . . We urge therefore the taking of early decisions on reconstruction planning intended for wartime legislative implementation where necessary."

Churchill sent the paper to Wood for comment. The chancellor did not like it. His reply detailed the many times and ways in which government ministers—including, most obviously, the prime minister, but also Morrison himself during the Beveridge debate—had stated that decisions could *not* yet be made. But he provided no new justification for postponing them. The prime minister sent Wood's memo to Attlee, who returned an acid reply: "I have read with interest the observations of the Chancellor of the Exchequer which seem to me to beg the question we have posed. I shall welcome an early discussion."

It did not take place. Churchill had set off for Quebec. Six weeks later, with Churchill again absent, Morrison wrote in frustration to his party leader: "I appreciate the Prime Minister's intense preoccupation with other matters, but I really do not think the discussion of the broad question of principle involved in our paper ought to stand over for very much longer." But it did stand over for the rest of the summer and on into the fall. During this period, Kingsley Wood died suddenly and unexpectedly, and Churchill, briefly back in England, appointed the Lord President, Sir John Anderson, to replace him as chancellor. Attlee would then replace Anderson. "The little man will be no loss," Eden noted unkindly of Wood in his diary. But perhaps Churchill would miss him. He had lost his strongest ally in the fight against early implementation of Beveridge's proposals.

Churchill finally found time to write a response to Attlee in late October. Perhaps Wood's absence was taking a toll on him. But so was the continuing leftward swing in the country as a whole. One indication: at almost every by-election, the newly formed socialist group, Common Wealth, gathered strength. Although every party in the Coalition, and the Communists besides, opposed the group, its by-election candidates almost always polled respectably. Common Wealth won victories in three constituencies, ousting a National Liberal and two Conservatives in the process (of the two other Common Wealth MPs, one had left the Liberal Party, and the other had previously been an Independent). Needless to say, the organization favored swift implementation of Beveridge's proposals and much more. Churchill felt impelled to cede further ground: "Any decisions which are needed for the supreme objects of food and employment in the years immediately after the war must be taken now," he admitted, "whether they involve legislation and whether they are controversial or not."

When the War Cabinet met to discuss Churchill's response to the Labour paper, the prime minister surrounded himself with his party's heaviest hitters: Beaverbrook, Butler, Anderson, Lyttelton (the former businessman whom Churchill had first appointed as minister of state in Cairo and then as minister of production), and Frederick Lindemann (Lord Cherwell), his confidant and scientific adviser, whom he had made paymaster general. But Labour put up a strong team, too, including Attlee, Bevin, Morrison, Cripps, and Dalton (minister of economic warfare and chief of the Special Operations Executive). Everyone knew already that the left had the wind at its back. In the end, all the Conservatives agreed to Churchill's concession. Perhaps they thought it would be sufficient to stem the left-flowing tide.

Yet Morrison pressed for more, broaching indirectly the possibility of nationalizing certain industries. He said he hoped the government would "not be precluded from considering such changes in the organization of particular industries as would increase their efficiency and thus enable them to provide fuller and more continuous opportunities of employment." He then said he "would like the Prime Minister to consider certain suggestions, which he would send to him, for modifying some passages in his Memorandum in order to meet these two points." This seems almost too cheeky, but the Labour ministers knew they had public support. Two days later, Morrison was crowing to the editor of the *Manchester Guardian*: "The PM . . . [is] willing now to admit that there must be certain practical measures to be taken in good time."

DURING THE FINAL YEAR AND A HALF OF THE WAR, LABOUR WOULD continue to advance and the Conservatives to retreat. Given the country's mood, they could do no less. It was shortly after the meeting on "Decisions" that Churchill appointed Woolton to head the new Ministry of Reconstruction. The establishment of such a department marked yet another concession in and of itself. There followed a series of famous White Papers: on health, employment, town planning, land use and more, all of them surrendering further ground to Labour's position. Another notable example of ground ceded was the prime minister's apparent conversion to the Keynesian doctrine of countercyclical spending during periods of economic slump: "What is proposed for public authorities," the prime minister explained in May 1944 to his colleagues, as if a light bulb had just been lit in his brain, "is the exact opposite of what would generally be done by private persons: when things look bad, they should not draw in their horns but push them out and launch forth into all sorts of new expenditure." But he cannot have liked it.

In a January 1945 letter to Attlee, Churchill, testifying to the great weight Labour now wielded in his government, observed that "a solid mass of four Socialist politicians [Attlee, Bevin, Morrison, Cripps] of the highest quality and authority, three of whom are in the War Cabinet, . . . exercises a dominating force." But he never sent the letter, in part perhaps because for all that Labour continued to advance, it did not really dominate. So long as the war lasted, Labour ministers, including even Morrison, feared pushing too hard for anything, lest they provoke a general election they were sure they would lose. For all the leftward swing in public opinion, they—and not only they, but also their Conservative colleagues, including the prime minister himself—still believed Britons would never vote against the man who had saved the country in 1940—or against his party. Ironically, Labour men did not realize that Churchill never even seriously considered calling a wartime general election, because he did not want to break up the Coalition either; he considered a multiparty government essential until Germany surrendered. These complementary inhibitions set the limits to wartime ideological conflict over domestic issues, but the conflict never ceased, and in fact only grew fiercer, as victory appeared more likely.

Churchill, whose extraordinary qualities included great political savvy, defeated the threats to his leadership posed by Cripps and Beaverbrook. He did not defeat Morrison, but then Morrison never directly challenged his position as prime minister. And yet Morrison came to personify, more than Attlee, Bevin or even Cripps, a Fabian socialist movement that was about to reach its climax. The tide had been running left since 1940. Even Winston Churchill could not stem it, as the general election of 1945 would make painfully clear.

PART III

SUNDERING THE WAR CABINET

CHAPTER 12

Churchill on the Downslope

WINSTON CHURCHILL'S WARTIME CAREER DOES NOT DESCRIBE A perfect arc but rather a rough one. From the moment Neville Chamberlain brought him into the government in September 1939 until sometime after the crises of the spring and summer of 1940, he experienced a breathtaking ascent. Churchill propelled and directed this upward movement, establishing himself not merely as Britain's prime minister but as her indispensable man. Particularly during 1940–1941, he spoke, in language as beautiful as Shakespeare's, what everyone wished that they could say. The nation recognized him as the embodiment of its will to survive. And so, despite the occasional hiccup, he reached the apex of the arc—probably on December 7, 1941, when he learned that America would enter the war against the Axis Powers. From that great height he could see at last a clear path to likely, if hard-fought and costly, victory.

But an apex must be followed by a descent. With national survival no longer at stake, Churchill had to deal with parliamentary critics and rebellions. They were inconsequential at first but increasingly threatening, or at least conceivably threatening. He had to fend off potential rivals for the leadership. His fierce concentration lapsed as well, and he experienced physical illness, the "black dog" of depression, and occasional bouts of lassitude and lachrymose self-pity. There still would be triumphs, and not small ones. He did not know he was on the downslope; nor did anyone else. At times, he, and they, must have thought the direction remained upward. But in fact, Winston Churchill was destined to plumb the depths

in July 1945, only two months after Germany surrendered. He had wished
to maintain the Coalition after victory in Europe; he could not, and therefore had to call a general election. He entered the campaign supremely
confident he would triumph. Everyone agreed with him; even his opponents thought he would win. But the voters turned his party out, giving
an enormous parliamentary majority to Labour instead. It was Winston
Churchill's turn to relinquish the seals of office. Shocked beyond measure,
he entitled the last volume of his memoir of the war years *Triumph and
Tragedy*.

There had been warning signs, but he had missed them.

CHURCHILL HAD NO INKLING OF THE WRETCHED DENOUEMENT TO HIS
wartime premiership when on Monday morning, May 15, 1944, he and
his old friend Jan Smuts, prime minister of South Africa, King George VI,
and, accompanied by the chiefs of staff, various top British and American
military personnel, and the entire War Cabinet, assembled in a room at
St. Paul's School on Hammersmith Road. The school served at that time
as the London headquarters of General Bernard Montgomery; students,
faculty and staff had relocated to premises in Easthampstead Park, near
Crowthorne in Berkshire, back in September 1939. At the front of the room
in which the group gathered stood a stage, and on that stage stood a great
map of the Normandy beaches, tilted at an angle so that everyone could
see and understand its geography. General Dwight D. Eisenhower, now the
Supreme Allied Commander in Europe, mounted the stage with pointer in
hand; the august assemblage sat in rows of seats before him. Then the American military chief announced what everyone had come to hear: Operation
Overlord, the long-awaited Allied assault upon France, the one that would
open the Second Front for which the Russians, in particular, had long been
calling, would commence in three weeks, weather permitting.

During the interval between the briefing and the invasion, the War
Cabinet spun its wheels. On May 22, the Foreign Office official Alexander
Cadogan wrote in his diary: "Cabinet 5:30, put off till 6 because nothing
on agenda. But the shorter the agenda the longer the ramble and they
hadn't finished when I left at 7:50." Eight days later, he wrote: "5:30 Cabinet, as usual put off till 6:30, as there was nothing on agenda. . . . We
rambled incoherently till 8:45." Winston Churchill had never been good at
running meetings. He harangued, speculated, pontificated. He preferred
his own voice and thoughts to those of any other man or woman. The

pending operation on the continent exacerbated his indiscipline. "Oh for N. Chamberlain on these occasions," lamented Cadogan, who recalled the late former prime minister as an admirable chairman, at any rate.

During this period Churchill could not disguise his nerves. The commander of the Imperial General Staff, Alan Brooke, judged him to be "in a very highly strung condition." And why not? Alan Brooke himself admitted to being at this time "really torn to shreds with doubts and misgivings," and he oversaw only military matters. Churchill had to take not only the military realm but also the political into account. If Operation Overlord failed, the Allies would not lose the war, but they would suffer a grievous setback. Morale would plummet among the war-weary people of Britain; it would plummet in the United States, too, which could affect FDR's prospects in the pending presidential election. There would also be great disillusionment in Russia. Stalin might consider making a separate peace with Hitler, who would be feeling a new lease on life. Churchill, the War Cabinet, the generals—indeed everyone—had been straining for four years to make Operation Overlord possible. Now that it was in the offing it must not fail.

The tension had an effect, and not only in poorly run and unproductive meetings. Churchill's colleagues sprinkled their diaries with references to his furious diatribes and rages during these weeks. He could not abide the French leader, Charles de Gaulle, and did not hide it. He savaged the ministers who opposed him, about de Gaulle, or about anything. Restless, anxious, but also characteristically mischievous and bold, he wanted to be present when the landings in France took place. He overrode the inevitable opposition of his generals and Cabinet colleagues. It took the king, finally, to dissuade him from this crazy venture. Underlying everything must have been his apprehension of the carnage to come, especially if Operation Overlord did not unfold as planned. On the eve of D-Day, June 5, just before midnight, he paced the underground map room of the annex to Number 10. He knew that the first Allied soldiers were about to begin gliding and parachuting into Normandy. He said to his wife, Clementine: "Do you realize that by the time you wake up in the morning twenty thousand men may have been killed?"

When he went to bed that night, only a few in Britain knew precisely what was in the offing. Ten hours later, everyone knew. On the 9 A.M. broadcast the BBC announcer quoted the German Overseas News: "Early this morning, the expected Anglo-American invasion began when airborne forces were landed in the Seine estuary." At the House of Commons, MPs waited in an agony of suspense for the prime minister to provide more information. He arrived, Harold Nicolson wrote in his diary, at three minutes before noon, "white as a sheet." First he reported on the Allied campaign in Italy, which was going well. The troops of American general Mark Clark and British general Harold Alexander had liberated Rome. The House cheered. It was welcome news, but not what members had come to hear. Then Churchill gave it to them: "I have also to announce to the House that during the night and the early hours of this morning the first of the series of landings in force upon the European continent has taken place. . . . The fire of the shore batteries has been largely quelled. The obstacles that were constructed in the sea have not proved so difficult. . . . Everything is proceeding according to plan." Thankfully the Allies did not suffer 20,000 dead on D-Day, as Churchill had feared they might, but rather about 3,000.

CHURCHILL WENT FROM NERVE-WRACKING TENSION TO HIGH SPIRITS AND boundless optimism: he stood upon an uptick of an arc. That arc, however, otherwise generally pointed down. On June 10, he and Brooke and Smuts, who was not merely an old friend and colleague but also the only politician whom he both trusted and considered to be his equal, crossed the Channel in a British destroyer to lunch with General Montgomery (who had relocated his headquarters from St. Paul's School to a chateau in Normandy). He toured Britain's "limited bridgehead" on the continent. Returning to England aboard the destroyer *Kelvin*, and watching the shore recede, and imagining the German troops only a few miles inland, he suggested to the captain: "Since we are so near, why shouldn't we have a plug at them ourselves before we go home?" The captain obliged: "And in a minute or two all our guns fired on the silent coast." Then the destroyer turned about and aimed for England, at speed.

That was the triumphant, buoyant and audacious side of the story: Churchill exulting in a great military victory and directing potshots at the enemy himself. There was another side, domestic and political, that did not bode so well for the prime minister, however. Perhaps because of his high spirits, he chose to ignore it, or did not even see it. But then, very few did.

He had agreed reluctantly to bring over from Algiers his bête noir, Charles de Gaulle, on June 4, only two days before D-Day, to inform him of the pending operation. The two men would meet in Churchill's special train in Droxford, near Portsmouth. The British prime minister would be accompanied once again by Smuts, and also by the rough diamond, Ernest Bevin, for whom he had developed considerable, if wary, respect. Foreign Secretary Anthony Eden would motor over from his country house to join them. On the appointed day, the foreign secretary arrived early enough to walk with de Gaulle down the railway line toward Churchill's train. "The Prime Minister, moved by his sense of history, was on the track to greet the General with arms outstretched," Eden recalled. The French leader, formal and stiff, did not respond, and the ensuing meeting did not go well. But it is a brief exchange that took place afterward, between the supporting cast members, and not the principals, that is revealing for the state of the coalition government.

With Churchill otherwise occupied, Bevin and Eden found a moment to consult. Perhaps they stood on the track, perhaps in a corridor of the railway carriage: one man trim and elegant, the descendent of a long line of baronets, the other rough-hewn and bulky, the son of an agricultural laborer who had deserted him and his mother. At this critical moment of the world conflict, these two crucial, ill-assorted and yet mutually respectful ministers at war did not speak of de Gaulle or of relations with France, or even of Operation Overlord, which they and their colleagues had been dreaming of, and planning, for years. Rather, they spoke of politics. Bevin told Eden he thought a coalition should continue to govern Britain after the war. Eden agreed. Bevin wondered whether "the old man" would want to lead it. Eden did not know. If Churchill stepped aside, Bevin averred, he himself "would not care which office either of us held." Eden replied, "Neither would I." Bevin stipulated only one condition: nationalization of the coal mines. Eden agreed to it. It sounds as if the two men were dividing between them the top positions of a post-Churchill coalition government and deciding upon its first domestic priority. A few minutes later, Smuts, who had noticed the brief colloquy, asked Eden what it had been about. When Eden told him, Smuts merely remarked, referring to Bevin's price for continuing to work with the Conservative: "Cheap at the price."

It is worth noting when a prime minister's closest colleagues whisper behind his back about future arrangements in which he will not be included, even if the arrangements come to nothing. Here is one piece of the evidence Churchill did not see, or chose to ignore: that men could now imagine a postwar government in which he did not figure. It was a sure indication that despite Britain's improving military situation, he was on the downslope of the arc.

The odd thing is that, despite their little conference, Eden and Bevin did not see it either. They stood together in Droxford, not quite conspiring against their leader, but at least drawing castles in the air. Neither of them wanted Churchill to stay on; they thought he had seen his best days. But at the same time neither of them thought Churchill could be denied the premiership after the war if he still wanted it; and at this point both were prepared to serve under him if he did want it. Ironically, this attitude may have been harder for Eden, the Conservative, to bear than for Bevin, the socialist. As long ago as September 1940, Churchill had promised to step aside in Eden's favor once Britain's enemies had been defeated. As he had said on more than one occasion, he would be an old man then. And he had written a famous letter to the king in February 1942 advising him to appoint Eden as prime minister in case of his death. Still, it is not clear that Churchill ever seriously thought that victory in war should signal an end to his premiership, and the closer to victory Britain drew, the less attractive such a prospect seemed. By 1945, he thought, as he wrote in his memoir: "I had the world position as a whole in my mind, and I deemed myself to possess knowledge, influence, and even authority, which might be of service. I therefore saw it as my duty to try [to continue as prime minister] and at the same time as my right. I could not believe this would be denied me."

Eden could only grind his teeth and vent his frustration in his diary, although even here he did not write straightforwardly that he longed for the top job (although surely he did), but merely that, with regard to Churchill, "there is certainly deterioration," a judgment confirmed by many other diarists. Churchill could not run meetings; he drank to excess; he would often browbeat his colleagues. Yet none of them, whether Conservative, Liberal or Labour, believed there really would be a postwar government led by anyone else. Even British voters, who soon would cast their ballots in record numbers against Churchill's party, assumed that Churchill would be Britain's prime minister when the war was over. Practically no one grasped where on the curve Winston Churchill now truly stood.

ONCE HE DECIDED NOT TO STEP ASIDE AT THE END OF THE WAR, Churchill hoped to become prime minister of a postwar coalition government, not a Conservative one. He was in tune with Eden and Bevin to this extent. He told Smuts that, for all their sniping and rivalry, his War Cabinet colleagues constituted "the most capable Government England has had or is likely to have." A normal general election would break it up. Churchill conceived an expedient: a general election, and then a new coalition to reflect the new balance of power in the House. It did not occur to him that he would not be its prime minister.

Churchill still distrusted, disliked and disagreed with many Conservatives—who returned the favor. Now that Chamberlain, Halifax and Kingsley Wood were gone, he had not a single orthodox senior Conservative colleague in the War Cabinet (although he did have several unorthodox ones). He did not identify with a single political party, either, but rather with two: primarily with the Conservatives, to which he belonged—but also and to a lesser extent, and as perhaps his Four Year Plan had indicated, with the Liberals, to which he once had belonged. (During the general election campaign of 1945, he would say: "I am as much a Liberal as I am a Tory.") Not surprisingly, when he proposed that plan back in 1943, he had made a prediction: "It will have to be presented to the country, either by a National Government formally representative as this one is of the three parties in the State, or by a National Government comprising the best men in all parties who are willing to serve."

He knew that although many rank-and-file Conservatives might prefer a return to party politics, they would go along with him on the new coalition idea. They would never cross "the man who won the war"; he was their side's greatest electoral asset. Churchill thought Labour would go along, too, for the opposite reason. Its leaders remembered that David Lloyd George, who also had "won" a world war, had called a snap "khaki election" in 1918. Lloyd George, who had led the section of the Liberal Party that did not remain loyal to Asquith, the man he had replaced as prime minister, consulted with his Conservative partner in the wartime coalition government, Andrew Bonar Law, as to which candidates should receive a "coupon," the imprimatur of their support. Then they scored a landslide victory, wiping out Asquith's couponless followers. It spelled the end of the Liberal Party as a major force in Britain. Labour Party leaders feared that if Churchill called a "khaki election" and bestowed his own "coupons" at the end of World War II, he might destroy their party also, or at any rate damage it badly. Churchill would have been pleased, had he known, that in September 1943 Morrison and Minister of Economic

Warfare Hugh Dalton spoke to Lord Halifax, who was visiting in England
again from the United States, "about the importance of having a National
Government continuing after the war"; and that a few days earlier, Dalton
had put the same point to Attlee, who had agreed with it. Bevin came to
it as well, as he indicated to Eden. In the autumn of 1943, all of them reasoned as Churchill suspected they must: better half a loaf, gained through
continuing the coalition under Churchill, than no loaf at all.

In the end, however, Labour's leaders changed their minds. They felt
pressure from an energized and expanding left. The Communists and the
new body, Common Wealth, and Labour's own left wing would not be satisfied with merely half a loaf. If that was all Labour offered, then all three
might make common cause in demanding more. Labour's leaders feinted
right: they did try to appeal to the middle class—or, as Morrison called
them, employing old Fabian terms, "workers by hand as well as brain . . .
the 'black coats.'" But they moved more decisively to the left, seeking to
co-opt, to channel and to satisfy, at least partially, the militants. Morrison
embarked upon his series of speeches about the need for postwar controls.
He and Attlee and Bevin pushed "The Need for Decisions" on a reluctant
War Cabinet. They called for, and the War Cabinet accepted, with more
or less reluctance, various Keynesian measures of demand management,
including some postwar controls detailed most notably in a White Paper
on full employment published in 1944. During the general election campaign a year later, Labour's leaders would claim that, but for their efforts,
the government never would have recommended such an approach. They
did enough to assuage the Labour left and Common Wealth, as the election results would demonstrate, while limiting the appeal of the even more
militant Communists. But partly as a result of their actions, party divisions within Churchill's Coalition grew wider, not narrower, as the war
drew to a close—and the prospects of a second coalition dimmed.

Despite having favored it to begin with, in the end Labour's leaders
turned decisively against the idea of a postwar coalition. In August 1944,
Attlee told a special committee of his party's National Executive Committee that he believed "a moment will come when the PM will say to
[me] that he hopes, having gone through the war in Europe together, we
can go on together through a general election on an agreed program. [I]
would then reply that [I am] afraid that this is impossible and that, when
the general election comes—and we should do nothing to hasten it—we
must offer the country the choice between two alternative programs."

Other party leaders made similar statements. Winston Churchill's fondest hopes notwithstanding, they had numbered the Grand Coalition's days and begun to count them down.

IN THIS SENSE, LABOUR FORCED THE GENERAL ELECTION OF 1945, WHICH it did not even think it could win, upon a reluctant Winston Churchill. The leaders preferred outright opposition and a united Labour Party to a new coalition and Labour divided. But they could not force its timing, although they had a preference. They judged, as Attlee had indicated in August 1944, that the later the general election took place, the better it would be for them. They wanted an interval between the German surrender and the vote, during which Churchill's prestige might deflate somewhat. Churchill's PPS put it this way: "The greater the delay the more time they have to spread their poison in an endeavor to discredit you." In addition, they favored delay because they wanted an up-to-date electoral register. The old one might disenfranchise Labour voters, who probably had been more peripatetic during the war than Conservatives. The general election should not take place until the new register, now in preparation, had been completed.

Conservatives, in contrast, preferred speed, not delay, if a general election must come, and not merely to take advantage of electoral rolls that might favor them. Whereas Labour hoped time would diminish Churchill's popularity, Conservatives hoped to cash in on it before that could happen. "The general opinion was in favor of an early election," the same PPS reported to Churchill in April 1945 after monitoring discussion on the subject by Conservative House Members. A meeting of Conservative election agents took an identical line, as the party chairman recounted: "There were only one or two who thought that advantage would be gained by postponing until the autumn." The prime minister took the temperature of his senior non-Labour and non–Liberal Party colleagues. Almost unanimously, they favored continuing the Coalition until Japan had been defeated, and calling a general election at that point. But, if Labour should demur, then, as Woolton put it: "Demand election at earliest." One Conservative Cabinet minister, the acute R. A. Butler, objected: "Unless our tactical position vis a vis the Socialists is stronger than it seems at the moment, I would prefer an October election." No one paid attention to him.

In any case, the matter must wait upon military events. No one proposed holding a general election before Germany surrendered. In the fall of 1944, Hitler had loosed upon Britain the V-2 rockets. With enemy forces closing in on Germany from all directions, he ordered desperate counterattacks both east and west, all of them ultimately futile. The loss of life was tremendous for both sides. By February 1945 the western Allies had entered the Rhineland. By late March they had crossed the Rhine and headed into Germany proper, millions of them. From the other side, Russian troops entered Warsaw in early January and, to the south, they poured into Austria at the very end of March. Finally they, too, in their millions, pressed onward into Germany. By April 24 Russian forces had encircled Berlin. On April 30, as they approached his bunker amid fierce fighting, Adolf Hitler committed suicide. Germany surrendered a week later.

Again Churchill rode the crest of a wave. On May 8 he drove through streets teeming with joyful crowds to Buckingham Palace for lunch with the king. Then he went back to Downing Street and addressed the nation over the radio: "After gallant France had been struck down we, from this Island and from our united Empire, maintained the struggle single-handed for a whole year until we were joined by the military might of Soviet Russia, and later by the overwhelming power and resources of the United States of America. Finally almost the whole world was combined against the evil-doers, who are now prostrate before us." Only Japan still resisted, and she could not hold out long (Churchill, who had knowledge of research on the atom bomb, did not mention it). "Advance, Britannia," he concluded this radio address, his voice breaking. "Long live the cause of freedom! God save the King."

From Downing Street he traveled the short distance to the House of Commons in an open car. The delighted crowds, ever growing, nearly blocked his path. It took him more than half an hour to cover the several hundred yards from door to door. When finally he made it into the debating chamber, wrote Harold Nicolson to his son, "the House rose as a man and yelled and yelled and waved their Order Papers." Churchill repeated the speech he had just delivered on the radio. He addressed further multitudes later in the afternoon from a balcony of the Ministry of Health building, overlooking Whitehall; and after dinner, with the throngs undiminished, he spoke from another balcony above Parliament Street, where, according to the newspaper magnate and proprietor of the *Telegraph*, Lord Camrose, "the crowd roared and roared again." Then it broke into song: "Land of Hope and Glory," and "For He's a Jolly Good Fellow."

Downslope of the arc? Every appearance suggested the contrary, and not only to him. Churchill could be forgiven for thinking he would win any British election. With Labour refusing to commit to the Coalition, why then continue to postpone the contest?

IN LATE APRIL, CHURCHILL HAD SENT EDEN AND ATTLEE AS BRITAIN'S chief representatives to the founding conference of the United Nations in San Francisco. That meant that when Germany surrendered, Morrison and Bevin had to speak for Labour back at home. Sometime during May 8 to 10, Labour's worst-matched pair met to hash out the position. But really they knew it already, and for once they agreed about it. The left, and not only the left but also the solid center of their party, were clamoring for a return to politics as usual. The mass of Labour supporters relished the prospect of confrontation with the Conservatives now. To ignore this sentiment would be to risk splitting the leaders from the rank and file, perhaps driving a significant number into the arms of Common Wealth or the Communists. The Coalition must be wound up. It had been brought into being at a desperate moment to save Britain. That it had done. For reasons already explained, Bevin and Morrison hoped the winding-up would take place later rather than sooner. But the need for another decision, this one about when a general election should take place, was obvious to them.

On May 11, at 12:30 P.M., the two entered 10 Downing Street to put this to Winston Churchill. He didn't like the idea of breaking up the government, but he did not fear doing so, if necessary, either. Morrison reported to Attlee that he "warned the Prime Minister that [the] present register is in a bad way and that this and other imperfections must be faced by him." Accordingly, he pushed for an autumn poll. Bevin backed him. Churchill did not commit to any date, but he realized he must choose soon. "I have not finally settled between June and October," he telegrammed to Eden in San Francisco immediately after the meeting. But "a decision must be made within the next three or four days."

It took a little longer than that, and there would be a few twists and turns. Attlee rushed back to England on May 16. Churchill met him on the night of his return, and then again the following day. Did the Labour Party leader remember the meetings five years before in the same room at Downing Street, when he had told Chamberlain that Labour never would serve under him? How could he not? But Attlee did not think the present circumstances comparable. He did not realize that he still held the advantage; he thought Churchill did, because Churchill would soon be "the man who won the war," just as Lloyd George had been in 1918. Therefore, when the prime minister ruled out the autumn election on a date he knew Attlee favored, and suggested instead, as his Conservative colleagues had recommended, the stark alternative of either a spring election or an election after Japan had surrendered, whenever that might be, Attlee did not demur, but merely promised to take it up with his senior colleagues.

Attlee met with those colleagues on the following morning, May 18. Dalton and Bevin agreed with Attlee that the prospect of a spring election was too dangerous. Labour had no option but to go on with the Coalition until the defeat of Japan, as Churchill suggested, soothing the left as best it could, and preparing for a general election all the while. Morrison, however, disagreed emphatically. He did not want to wait for the Japanese surrender, which he assumed might not occur for years (he had no knowledge of the atom bomb research), and he predicted that the party as a whole would not want to wait either. Attlee proposed a compromise. Labour would stay in the Coalition, as Churchill wanted—but only if the prime minister promised to speedily implement the proposals for social security and full employment outlined in earlier White Papers. It was like framing "The Need for Decisions" memo again. Perhaps he alone, perhaps he and the other three, worked out on paper the language the prime minister must accept if Labour was to stay until victory in the Far East had been won. As it happened, the Labour Party was about to convene its annual conference at Blackpool in northwestern England—just as in 1940, when the negotiations with Chamberlain had been taking place, it had been meeting at Bournemouth. Once Attlee had his paper, Bevin, Dalton and Morrison entrained for the conference.

Attlee returned to 10 Downing Street for a final session with the prime minister, document in hand. Churchill read and accepted it immediately. He thought that in return for promising to implement social security and full employment, Attlee had promised to persuade Labour to stay in until the defeat of Japan: "I certainly had the impression when he left that he would do his best to keep us together," Churchill later wrote. Attlee, for his part, believed, as he left for Blackpool, that in return for Labour's continuing participation in the Coalition, Churchill would implement the proposed reforms and then call an election sometime in the autumn. He did not tie this to the defeat of Japan. His understanding of the agreement and Churchill's were mutually exclusive.

At Blackpool, Attlee put the case as he understood it. But first the National Executive Committee of the Labour Party voted against delaying the election until autumn, and then, on May 21, so did the conference as a whole. The majority could not wait to get to grips with the Conservatives. Even Bevin and Dalton swung round to that position, and finally Attlee accepted it as well. With Morrison's help, he composed a letter to Churchill reflecting the more militant view: "It is precisely on the problems of the reconstruction of the economic life of the country that Party differences are most acute. What is required is decisive action. This can only be forthcoming from a Government united on principle and policy." Again, it was an odd echo of the events of 1940: just as Attlee had telephoned Chamberlain with Labour's decision before delivering the letter saying his party would not serve under him, so now he telephoned Churchill to say pretty much the same thing.

Churchill regretted it. He blamed Morrison for forcing the issue. He thought Attlee had betrayed him. He wrote to the Labour Party leader: "I have concerned myself solely with trying to create tolerable conditions under which we could work together. It is clear from the tone of your letter and the feelings of your Party that these no longer exist." But it never occurred to him that he was on a slippery slope headed downhill. He simply did not recognize the weight of public opinion in favor of the reforms advocated by the left.

On May 23, 1945, with regret, no doubt, but also with supreme confidence, he submitted his resignation to the king, who immediately charged him with forming an interim "caretaker" government to rule until a general election should take place. Churchill selected from the previous administration leading Conservatives such as Eden, Beaverbrook and Lyttelton (current minister of production); several representatives of the rising generation of Conservatives, such as Butler and Harold Macmillan; and the non-party men Anderson and Woolton. Amazingly, he invited Cripps, who had not yet returned to the Labour Party, to join, too. "I can't do that, much as I admire the old man. We do not think alike," Cripps reported afterward to Eden and Lord Cranborne, whom he came upon standing outside the door to the Cabinet Room at No. 10 just as he was exiting. Then a faint echo of earlier hopes for a coalition *sans* the great advocate of coalitions: Cripps whispered to the two Conservatives, "It might have been different if it had been Anthony who'd asked me."

Churchill advised the king to dissolve Parliament on June 15. Polling day would take place three weeks later, on July 5, with a few local variations. The counting of ballots would begin on July 26. This second three-week interval would permit time for the votes of overseas soldiers to be transported home. To the chagrin of Labour Party leaders—but to the delight of their own rank and file, and also to the delight of most Conservatives—Churchill had called a snap "khaki election" after all.

STILL, HE WAS SENTIMENTAL ABOUT HIS ERSTWHILE COLLEAGUES. "We had been through so much together," he wrote in his memoir. On May 28 he invited former government ministers to an "at home" at No. 10, in the Cabinet Room where they had so often met. The Cabinet table around which they were accustomed to sit had been draped to serve as a buffet. Practically all the former Labour ministers, as well as most of the Tories and Liberals and non-party men—more than forty individuals in all—gathered around it. "The temper was friendly but electric," Churchill would recall. His guests would have stood, with drinks and canapés in hand, when he came before the table to address them, tears streaming down his cheeks. Recent events notwithstanding, Churchill referred to Attlee as his "good friend." But they all were friends. "He said," Hugh Dalton recorded in his diary, "that we had all come together, and had stayed together as a united band of friends, in a very trying time. History would recognize this." Recording the prime minister's exact words, Dalton wrote: "The light will shine on every helmet," and his own reaction to them: "I feel the moment a bit too." Perhaps he was remembering the day in 1940 when, in the same room, Churchill had explained to him and others how desperate Britain's plight was, and yet how utterly determined he was to fight on.

Two important Conservatives did not attend this emotional gathering, however. The previous evening, Lord Beaverbrook had hosted a small party at his country house in Surrey. After "an excellent dinner with a magnum of champagne and lots of brandy," the group had settled in for "a long political conversation. . . . The evening was fun, with a real buccaneering, racketeering atmosphere," wrote one who took part. The gossip swirled; snide comments ruled. Bevin, Eden and Anderson came in for particular abuse. Charming, clever Brendan Bracken, the Churchill acolyte, and irascible, incorrigible Lord Beaverbrook, Churchill's intimate, set the tone and dominated. The guest who wrote in his diary about it afterward predicted, more presciently perhaps than he could have known, that "of course they [Beaverbrook and Bracken] . . . will do the Conservative Party countless harm, at this election and afterwards."

The next day Beaverbrook bid farewell to his overnight guests. He would stay in the country, and so would miss Churchill's "at home" that afternoon. Bracken motored up to London, but he did not attend the event at Downing Street, either. Those two had little time for sentiment, but plenty for politics. "I am anxious to drive and intending to display restless activity until after the election is over," Beaverbrook had warned the Conservative chief whip a few months earlier. Bracken had similar intentions.

CHAPTER 13

Aftershock

THEY WERE NO LONGER A "BAND OF FRIENDS." IT SEEMS FAIR TO ASK whether they ever truly had been, so acrimonious did the general election campaign of 1945 become. Perhaps the pent-up emotions loosed after victory over Germany promoted ill temper during the political contest that immediately followed. Certainly Beaverbrook, and perhaps Bracken, had something to do with the ugly tone. And certainly Churchill felt let down by his former Labour and Liberal partners, whom he thought had deserted him, and was determined to pay them back. He had offered his tribute to them during the "at home" at No. 10. But the party was over now, and he always had been a tough and exuberant campaigner. "He was mostly consensual," wrote one in a position to know, but "when he was partisan he was very, very partisan." During the campaign of 1945, Churchill went out on the stump and let off fireworks. So did many former members of his War Cabinet, from all parties. So, for that matter, did some of the audiences, literally.

Churchill's first radio broadcast set the tone. He prepared it over the weekend of June 1–3 and delivered it Monday evening from a little room at Chequers hung with small paintings by the quintessential English landscape artist John Constable. As he spoke into the microphone, he gestured more broadly than he did in conversation, as if he were addressing a large audience. He chopped at the air with his hands, chopping at Labour, too. Its members "had been for some time eager to set out upon the political warpath—and when large numbers of people feel like that it is not good for their health to deny them the fight they want. We will therefore give it to them," he said.

Evidently he had been reading Friedrich Hayek's *Road to Serfdom*:

My friends I must tell you that a Socialist policy is abhorrent to the
British ideas of freedom. . . . Socialism is . . . an attack . . . upon the right
of an ordinary man or woman to breathe freely without having a harsh,
clumsy, tyrannical hand clapped across their mouths and nostrils. . . .
No Socialist Government conducting the entire life and industry of the
country could afford to allow free, sharp, or violently worded expressions of public discontent. They would have to fall back on some form
of *Gestapo* . . .

This last word he pronounced with a soft "g," perhaps to make it sound
more sinister.

It was a disastrous overture to the campaign, "by common consent a
strategic blunder," as Butler would later call it. Many knew that Labour's
leaders had denounced the Gestapo before Conservative Party leaders
did—after all, the Gestapo had first gone after their comrades in the German labor and socialist movements (as well as the Jews). Everyone knew
that during the war many Labour supporters had sacrificed their lives
defending "British ideas of freedom." Everyone also knew that for the past
five years, Churchill had worked with, and often praised, the very men
he now claimed would impose dictatorship over the country. Churchill's
wife, Clementine, who was more politically sensitive at this moment than
he was, begged him to take out the reference to the Gestapo before he gave
the speech. He would not.

It fell to Clement Attlee, leader of the Labour Party, to make the first
public reply to this ill-judged broadside. Churchill is supposed to have
once said of Attlee that he was "a modest man with much to be modest
about." It was a serious underestimation, if he ever made it (Churchill
denied that he did). Attlee could never be discounted. His reply to Churchill's accusations, also delivered on the radio, was devastating:

When I listened to the Prime Minister's speech last night in which he
gave such a travesty of the policy of the Labour Party, I realized at once
what was his object. He wanted the electors to understand how great
was the difference between Winston Churchill the great leader in war
of a United Nation, and Mr. Churchill the Party leader of the Conservatives. He feared lest those who had accepted his leadership in war might

be tempted out of gratitude to follow him further—I thank him for having disillusioned them so thoroughly—the voice we heard last night was that of Mr. Churchill, but the mind was that of Lord Beaverbrook.

Thus the modest man unhesitatingly picked up the gauntlet thrown down by a great man.

During 1940 to 1945, Attlee had never conspired against Churchill. He had held aloof from Cripps when the latter dreamed of a centrist triumvirate to replace the prime minister. He had made no time for Beaverbrook when the Canadian fantasized briefly about ascending to the throne. Indeed, he disliked Beaverbrook, with whom he had clashed often and openly, especially over Russia, and he distrusted Beaverbrook's influence over Churchill, an influence he thought the recent radio broadcast demonstrated. Unlike many of his colleagues, Attlee did not gossip or scheme. He had always acted as a loyal and helpful colleague to the prime minister, although he was of course forever aware of, and, within limits, working for, the interests of his own party. One imagines that he would have been a respectful if tough-minded rival in a different sort of election campaign, and that Churchill might very well have outshone and even outbid him. Instead, voters came to perceive Clement Attlee as Churchill's attractive antithesis: unflappable, unemotional, sensible, moderate, tolerant. They perceived his strengths. Unwittingly, Churchill had promoted a man who otherwise might have struggled to find the limelight.

THEN CHURCHILL COMMITTED A SECOND BLUNDER. AGAIN, HE COULD have played it very differently and much more to his benefit. He announced his intention to go to Potsdam following the campaign to meet Stalin and Harry Truman, who had succeeded President Franklin Roosevelt after the latter's death on April 12. There the Allied leaders would determine how to punish defeated Germany. Churchill wanted to present a united front to the foreigners, and so he issued an invitation to the leader of the Labour Party to join him. (Did it strike him as an odd invitation to make, given that he had just said Attlee would rule England with Gestapo methods if his party won the general election? Did the invitation suggest to voters that his initial charges had been merely rhetorical, and perhaps even insincere?) In any event, when the political scientist Harold Laski, a professor at the London School of Economics and longtime left-wing Labour Party apparatchik, learned of the invitation, he made what he may have thought was an innocuous statement: "Mr. Attlee can hardly . . . accept responsibility for agreements which . . . will have been concluded by Mr. Churchill as Prime Minister." Laski thought that the Labour Party leader should attend the Potsdam meeting as an observer only, for if Labour won the general election, it would naturally pursue a different foreign policy than Churchill would. The professor may, too, have thought that Attlee needed this kind of prodding, and that he had agreed too readily with Churchill's foreign policies, for he repeated the assertion several times in other public speeches.

Laski occupied the position of Labour Party chairman, a post given annually to the member of the National Executive Committee (NEC) with the most years of service who had never held it before. Churchill seized on the opening he thought Laski provided him. Who, he asked in a letter addressed to Attlee, but also delivered to the press for maximum publicity, determined Labour policy, the elected party leader, or the unelected party chairman, assisted by the unelected NEC? Laski had provided further evidence, the prime minister charged, of Labour's undemocratic basis and distrust of British-style freedom. A lengthy public correspondence ensued. Attlee insisted in a series of sharply worded yet pithy letters on Laski's limited role and influence; Churchill harped upon the professor's sinister aims and authority. Important Conservatives followed their leader. Oliver Lyttelton, whose duties as minister of production in the caretaker government Churchill had augmented by appointing president of the Board of Trade as well, referred to Laski and the rest of Labour's NEC as a "hidden and unelected Camarilla in the background." Oliver Stanley, secretary of state for the colonies, predicted that "at the Big Three Conference Truman would represent America, Stalin would represent Russia, and in the event of a Socialist Government being returned here, Attlee would represent Prof. Laski." Richard Law, a junior minister and son of a prime minister, charged that "the Socialists were proposing to do away with the control of Parliament and substitute for it the dictatorship of the Socialist Grand Council. That," Law added, "had a familiar and an ominous ring to it."

But so did some of the Conservative rhetoric about Laski. The prime minister seemed to be suggesting that a man whose name did not sound English was actually Labour's sinister puppet master. Beaverbrook went further. In a speech at Streatham he referred to the "secret protocols" of Laski's NEC, probably an unintentional evocation of the infamous Russian anti-Semitic fabrication "The Protocols of the Elders of Zion." He then "hereby declare[d] that Laski is aiming at the destruction of the Parliamentary system of Great Britain." Lord Croft, an undersecretary in the War Office, went beyond even this. He sneeringly termed Laski "that fine old English Labour man." Churchill, perhaps knowing that when Lord Croft's daughter married a German Jewish refugee Croft had said she was committing "social suicide," wrote to him: "Pray be careful, whatever the temptation, not to be drawn into any campaign that might be represented as anti-Semitism." No doubt the man who had led a crusade on behalf of all peoples against Nazi hypernationalism regretted having opened the door to such representations. But he had cause to regret the entire campaign directed against Harold Laski. There is no evidence that it resonated with voters. To the contrary, as one eminent figure has written, "the vast majority of the public did not understand what [Churchill] was on about." He would have done much better to have appeared magnanimous: offering the invitation to Attlee and letting it go at that, not least because Labour's leader had no intention of letting Laski or anyone else pull his strings. Probably Churchill would have done better to have never mentioned Laski at all.

There is a pathetic side to the episode as well. Laski was a distinguished scholar and a visible presence on the left wing of the Labour Party, but he suffered from delusions of grandeur, often claiming influence he did not have. He peppered important figures, both inside the Labour movement and outside it, with one letter after another, in handwriting so tiny that it was difficult to read. He peppered Winston Churchill, too, presuming on a slight connection that the latter had established at the outset of his parliamentary career with Laski's father, an influential figure in the Manchester Jewish community, which Churchill then was courting for votes.

Just before the Labour Party's annual conference in Blackpool, Laski had written to tell Churchill that he would be its acting chairman: "May I say that whatever remarks I may make in this official capacity are only relevant in a Pickwickian sense to a man for whom, party aside, I have an inherited affectionate respect?" If he was trying to play upon what he supposed to be a family connection, and thereby to head off in advance attacks that Churchill might aim at him in his new exalted position, it was a doomed effort, and a naïve one. A veteran of the unforgiving world of rough politics, Churchill would never permit an appeal of this nature to sway him.

Laski wrote to Churchill again at the outset of the general election campaign, and before the brouhaha over Attlee's role at Potsdam: "My colleagues who served with you in the recent Coalition have asked me to tell you . . . that whatever the political differences, the personal respect and affection remain unimpaired. I hope you will allow the Chairman of the Labour Party strongly to associate himself with this view." Churchill did not reply but sent a note to his private office: "I do not know on what official grounds Mr. Laski writes to me. I have no personal relations with him." This note surely would have mortified the professor, had he known of it. One is left with the impression that Laski hoped for, and may even have expected, a special dispensation: immunity from the hard knocks of politics, based upon a link with Churchill that existed only in his mind. Instead he became the Conservative bête noir of the campaign and brought the roof down on his own head.

Two parties fought for victory during the general election campaign of 1945—Conservative and Labour. The Liberals did not count. They put up 306 candidates, which gave them no chance at a majority in a Parliament of 640. With much fanfare they managed to enlist William Beveridge, who had declined to join the Labour Party. He proved a poor candidate and lost what had been considered a safe Liberal seat. Archie Sinclair, the Liberal air force service minister, lost his seat, too. In the end, voters returned only twelve Liberals to Parliament. Clem Davies, a chief organizer of the revolt against Chamberlain in 1940, would become leader of this postwar rump, a poor reward. As for the National Liberals, "that vermiform appendix," as one old Liberal called them because she judged them useless, eleven of forty-nine emerged victorious from the general election, but only because they faced no Conservative opponent. Churchill wrote to a Conservative who had stepped aside for one of them: "I thank you for your generous action. . . . This is a form of putting country before Party, for truly at this juncture the fortunes of the country do depend upon the shattering defeat of Socialism."

That was how Churchill hoped to frame the choice for electors. "As an old political campaigner, you will realize the advantage of having 'Socialists v. the rest' rather than 'Tories v. the rest,'" he wrote to an old friend and political ally. Conservatives hoped to appeal to liberal and progressive-minded voters by promising to implement the "Four Year Plan" that Churchill had adumbrated two years earlier, including national insurance, family allowances, education reform and a National Health Service. They hoped to appeal to the Conservative base by calling for an end to wartime controls. They thought they would appeal to everyone by demanding the triumphant return to office of Winston Churchill. They clung to his coat-tails and praised him to the skies. If not for him, Britain likely would have gone down to defeat in 1940, they trumpeted, expecting that he would be returned to power in 1945 for that reason alone.

For its part, Labour stated forthrightly in its Election Manifesto that it was "a Socialist Party and proud of it." It called for public ownership of the fuel and power industries, inland transport, and iron and steel production. Far from abolishing economic and price controls, Labour intended to maintain them, in order "to secure that first things shall come first in the transition from war to peace, and that every citizen . . . shall get fair play." As for Winston Churchill, the human Conservative trump card, Labour leaders knew better than to deny his greatness. But, as Bevin noted in a speech, the war had not been "a one-man business. We have contributed our share."

British voters faced a stark choice with regard to domestic policy in 1945. On foreign affairs the divide was not so clear. The leaders of both parties worried increasingly about Russia's plans for Eastern Europe, especially Poland. They both intended to maintain close links with America. They both hoped that some grouping of Commonwealth nations and colonies led by the United Kingdom would constitute a third power bloc economically and militarily, on a par or nearly so with the United States and the Soviet Union. Harold Laski was right to fear that Labour under Attlee would pursue a foreign policy much like Churchill's. In this regard the hopes of the left in 1945, including the Labour left, for a "socialist foreign policy" were doomed to disappointment.

As for their attitudes about the British Empire, former War Cabinet ministers differed by degrees only, with the exception of Churchill, who was a conspicuous outlier on this subject. The majority of them, reflecting majority opinion in the country as a whole, looked forward to more or less speedy independence for the remaining colonies, and then to a multiracial Commonwealth of Nations that would act as a unit in world affairs, in which Britain would be the first nation among equals. Churchill, however, opposed any reduction in the role or scope of the empire. He paid only lip service to the idea of independence for the colonies, which he deferred to an unmentioned future date. He opposed real independence even for the dominions, for as he told a gathering of dominion and Indian representatives on April 3, 1945, "independence and unity are the same thing if you think the same way." He affected to believe that the men sitting around the table with him that day all thought "the same way."

MEANWHILE, THE MINISTERS OF CHURCHILL'S ERSTWHILE GRAND Coalition had fanned out across the country, urging their competing programs and taking potshots at their former colleagues. Churchill had set the tone in his initial radio address. In its aftermath, Conservatives referred to "Gauleiter Laski." The *Daily Express* equated the Labour Party with the Nazi Party in Germany and the Fascist Party in Italy. From the other side, the left-wing *Tribune* reminded readers that "there are few Tory Ministers whose pre-war record is not tainted by pro-Nazi sympathies." *Tribune*, resurrected damning (indeed shocking) articles written by one of Churchill's sons-in-law, Duncan Sandys, for the German *Europäische Revue* in July and October 1936.

Political meetings were raucous; the heckling was fierce. Leo Amery, Churchill's secretary of state for India, spoke in Birmingham, where he had a stormy reception. Lord Beaverbrook spoke at Paddington in support of his friend Brendan Bracken. "There were boos, cat-calls, shouts and cheers," reported *The Times* the next morning. On June 18 he spoke to a raucous crowd at Battersea in support of two more Conservative candidates. "He warned the interrupters that they were doing incredible injustice to their own cause," reported the *Daily Express*. They began to chant: "Sit down. Sit down." Beaverbrook called the hecklers "hooligans." That hardly quieted them. He shouted above the din: "Idle and dissolute men come here to deny free speech. . . . Oh no. You will never silence the voices of free men." *The Times* reported that "at the end of the meeting, although he spoke for several minutes into a microphone, it was impossible to hear him." This kind of behavior occurred at most of the twelve meetings Beaverbrook addressed during the campaign.

Even Winston Churchill ran into it. On July 3 he addressed a crowd of 20,000 at Walthamstow Stadium, in outer northeast London. "There were many interruptions the moment he began," reported *The Times*. "Catcalls and boos were mixed with the greater rounds of applause and cheers from his supporters." But the old warhorse displayed a surer touch than Beaverbrook had. Whereas the Canadian had insulted his critics, Churchill chafed them good-naturedly. "In a free country everyone has a perfect right to cheer or boo as much as he likes. (Cheers and boos.) The winners cheer and the beaten boo." He played with his enormous audience: "I have come in the first place to say something to you which is not at all of a controversial character. So both the cheerers and booers can take a moment off. I want to congratulate London . . . upon her wonderful record in the war. Would you like to boo that?" The journalist recorded: "There was silence."

Later in the speech, he said: "In the year before the war we had built 350,000 houses. . . . Look out. Hold onto your chairs. This is one you will not like—two thirds of those houses were built by private enterprise. . . . Have a good boo about that; have a good boo—private enterprise." German bombers had destroyed those structures. Everyone knew it. But why had they not been rebuilt? At this point a section of the crowd began to chant: "We want Labour." Churchill gave it back to them: "That is exactly the cause. We want the labor." The reporter wrote: "This sally brought down the house and the loud laughter put everyone in a good humor again."

And so it continued. Churchill referred in his speech to "foolish faction fights about idiotic ideologies and philosophical dreams of absurd Utopias—worlds which will not be seen [until there is] . . . a great improvement of the human heart and improvement of human heads." This caused pandemonium. "I am sorry that one hurts. I cannot help it. . . . I repeat—improvement of human hearts and human heads before we can achieve the glorious Utopia that the Socialist woolgatherers place before us. Now where is the boo party?" They immediately made their presence known. He turned from them to look in the other direction: "Any help from this side?" Then came the cheers.

This does not seem to have been an exceptionally rowdy meeting for Churchill. A few days earlier, at Tooting Bec, in south London, Michael Gloor LePelley, a seventeen-year-old architectural student, tossed a firecracker in the prime minister's direction. He told the policeman who arrested him: "I do not know why I did it." He told the magistrate, who fined him the maximum of forty shillings: "My sole intention was to make a noise." Mr. LePelley senior wrote to Churchill: "As the father of the wretched boy . . . I wish to express my deepest regrets for what happened." Churchill took even this in stride: "All's well that ends well. I certainly hope his career will not be damaged and that he will be a real help to old England in the end." His good nature and tolerance on these occasions contrasted starkly with his reference to the Gestapo and the continuing attack upon Laski. He seemed, during the campaign, to swing between two poles: one charitable and good-humored, the other ungenerous and unbridled. But even when in the charitable mode he completely under-estimated the countrywide leftward swing.

Churchill embarked on June 25 upon a great tour of the country. He traveled by train, with his automobile hitched to it so that he could drive to his speaking engagements: Rugby, Leamington, Coventry, Birming-ham, on day one; Crewe, Manchester, Oldham, Huddersfield, Leeds on day two; seven more cities over the next two days, all the way to Scotland and back. He also stopped to speak, or at least to make an appearance, in many additional constituencies along the way, so that he averaged about ten engagements per day, an exhausting schedule, especially for a man well into the second year of his eighth decade. He spent nights on the train, but hardly for purposes of relaxation: "This is the only way in which the Prime Minister can keep in constant contact with Whitehall during his tour," one of his staff members explained.

Wherever he went, the crowds gathered in their thousands. It seemed almost like a royal progress. Churchill wrote to David Margesson, the for-mer Conservative Party chief whip who had served him as minister of war from 1940 to 1942, "I do not want any engagements between Glasgow and Edinburgh tomorrow, nor the people warned of the route. Otherwise they crowd out and stand along it for hours with flags, and it is impossible to go fast and one has to stop and take their kindly salutes." A Conservative candidate begged him to pass through his constituency during the tour, so that voters might "touch the hem of your garment." Churchill declined this honor, but the enthusiasm with which the people greeted him on the tour strengthened his conviction that he and his party would win when it came time for them to vote.

He simply didn't get it. "Just because we cheered the old bugger doesn't mean we're going to vote for him," one elector warned. In any event, the speaker could not cast his ballot for Churchill unless he lived in Wood-ford, Churchill's Essex constituency. Many Britons happily saluted the prime minister on tour while intending to vote for Labour. And meanwhile, in shrewd counterpoint, Attlee had embarked upon a national tour of his own. With his wife driving the family's modest Austin sedan, he traveled without fanfare or entourage, but wherever he went he spoke "to packed and enthusiastic meetings with large crowds listening to the Mike [*sic*] outside." There is no mention of hecklers or disturbances. The contrast cannot have worked to his disadvantage.

CHURCHILL'S CHARGES AGAINST LASKI AND LABOUR BAFFLED AND enraged that party's leaders. As Greenwood put it, "Mr. Churchill does not believe what he has said over the air on these matters. . . . [H]e was prompted to it by evil political advisers who know how to trade on fear, the meanest of all political weapons." Greenwood had Beaverbrook and Bracken in mind. So did everyone else. Attlee had said it in his first radio broadcast: The voice on the radio was Churchill's, but the mind behind the voice belonged to Beaverbrook.

These suspicions had a real basis. Although neither Beaverbrook nor Bracken had direct input into the prime minister's first radio broadcast, they did influence Churchill's other broadcasts and the Conservative campaign more generally. A single example of Bracken's cynical approach may suffice. Churchill asked him to comment on a draft speech that Sir John Anderson intended to deliver over the BBC. Bracken read it and wrote back: "While I agree with the Chancellor that it is necessary to maintain some control of investment during the reconstruction period, I see no reason why he should go out of his way to stress this necessity. In your broadcast you made an attack on controls which delighted most of our long-suffering public. . . . I hope you will persuade him not to refer to them." In other words, Bracken thought the chancellor should purposely mislead his listeners. As for Beaverbrook, his newspapers harped gleefully and incessantly on the supposed threat to democracy posed by Professor Laski. So did Beaverbrook in his speeches. He probably advised Churchill to do the same, for the prime minister incorporated some of Beaverbrook's language about Laski into his radio broadcasts and public letters to Attlee.

Nor was Laski the only Labour figure to draw the prime minister's ire. He seemed to hold special animus for Morrison, and not merely because he believed his former home secretary had pushed Labour to break up the Coalition. During the general election campaign, Morrison charged, accurately, that near the end of the war, when the V-2 rockets began raining down on London, Churchill had prohibited public warnings about them. Morrison made the charge in Lewisham, the constituency he hoped to represent in the next Parliament, a constituency that had been devastated by the V-2s. Churchill deemed this a cheap attack. He had had good reasons for prohibiting the warnings: they sometimes caused panic; they often came too late; they revealed how little Britain could do to stop the rockets. He went to Lewisham to speak for Morrison's opponent. "Of all the colleagues I have lost," he told his audience, Morrison was "the one I am least sorry to see the last of." His former home secretary riposted that Churchill's "spiteful and petty references to me are unworthy of the leader of a political party, let alone a Prime Minister."

Churchill felt ill will for Stafford Cripps, too. Before the war Cripps had made extreme statements. Once he had advised workers simply to stop making armaments. During the 1945 campaign Conservatives jumped on this. Cripps had just written to the members of his local Labour Party: "We must see to it that our standard of behavior sets an example of honesty and decency to everyone." But he incorrectly told his critics that the prewar statement merely had been part of an effort to pressure Chamberlain to leave office. Whatever their differences, Churchill had respected Cripps, whom he had tried to bring into his caretaker government only a month previously. Now, however, he wrote to Eden: "Mr. Baldwin was Prime Minister at the time Sir Stafford performed this dire and righteous resolution. This demolishes the last vestige of a stool upon which he can stand and proves him a liar never at a loss for corroborative detail."

It was as though the campaign had let not just the prime minister but also certain other War Cabinet ministers off a restraining leash. Finally, Lord Beaverbrook could say publicly what he had been saying privately about Labour's leaders for years: "Mr. Attlee is no great monster," he informed an audience in West Fulham, London, but "has got all the makings of a good little martyr." "Bevin . . . is past retiring age. . . . [He] is too old to do a great deal more mischief." As for Morrison, Beaverbrook said, the Communists "went down to Hackney and chased him away. He ran over London Bridge as fast as he could go—anywhere—down Old Kent Road (Loud laughter). And he never stopped until he got to Lewisham. . . . Herbert Morrison became a long distance runner." Morrison had in fact left Hackney, a safe working-class seat, for Lewisham, a more middle-class and therefore riskier one, not because he feared the Communist candidate in his former district but to demonstrate Labour's broad electoral appeal. (And in the event he did so; he won the seat.)

Of course, now Labour finally could say publicly what it thought of Lord Beaverbrook. He was, according to Attlee, the individual "in public life who is most widely distrusted by decent men of all parties." "The

Minister of Chaos," Bevin termed him, "the madman of Fleet Street." Greenwood reminded electors that Beaverbrook had been an appeaser. While Churchill had been warning of the Nazi menace, "Lord Beaverbrook declared that Britain would not be involved in war."

"AVOID THE SIDE ISSUES AND PERSONALITIES WHICH ARE PUT FORWARD only to confuse your minds," Attlee exhorted voters in a published "Appeal to the People." Focus on "the fundamental issues which you have to decide."

Despite the mudslinging, both sides did manage to address crucial matters during the campaign. Even the chief mudslingers did. Beaverbrook delivered ringing, compelling endorsements of free enterprise and liberty on many occasions. Attlee, Bevin and Morrison often put a sober case for government planning. Churchill told how the Conservatives would oversee a massive and primarily privately funded home construction program. Cripps, having rejoined the Labour Party, toured the country on its behalf, providing clear expositions of socialism's ethical and Christian bases. The caretaker Cabinet's non-party members, Woolton, who was now Lord President, and Anderson, who was now chancellor of the exchequer, both campaigning for the return of Churchill and a National Government, delivered serious, temperate addresses over the BBC. Woolton, explaining complex arguments in simple language, could sound almost like Herbert Morrison:

> The thing that concerns most of us is just the day-to-day running of our lives. Have I a job to go to? Can I get a home together, get enough food, bring up my children so that they have a rather better chance than I had? These are the real problems of daily life, and that is the sort of thing I have been trying to work out for the country. If you give Mr. Churchill an independent majority by voting for the candidates who support this Government, you may rely upon it that an enlightened policy will be vigorously pursued on the home front.

Anderson, even with Bracken advising him about what to leave out of his radio broadcast, could only deliver a wooden speech. It "might have been appreciated by a mid-Victorian meeting of the Royal Economic Society," Bracken groaned. Still, given the general tone of the campaign, some voters might have welcomed the chancellor's carefully reasoned and moderately stated defense of free enterprise.

Under exceedingly difficult circumstances, Anthony Eden managed to offer a noteworthy example of moderation and grace. He had returned from San Francisco on May 17, about a week after Attlee, to take part in the general election. Ten days later he delivered a broadcast over the BBC concerned mainly with foreign policy. He did not mention Professor Laski. But he had suffered from stomach ailments most of his adult life, and now one laid him low. His doctor diagnosed a duodenal ulcer and prescribed a month's bed rest. His mother died on June 19, but he was too ill to attend the funeral. Not a mudslinger by temperament, he did not even have the opportunity to sling it during a campaign he watched from home with growing unease. It was, he told a friend, "the dirtiest and cheapest" he had ever known. He did make one more radio broadcast for Churchill, on June 27, rising from his sickbed and speaking into a hook-up from his country house while still wearing pajamas and dressing gown. In this polarized campaign he advocated the "middle way": "Do not imagine that the choice before you at this election lies between complete State Socialism, as expounded by the Socialist Party, and an anarchy of unrestricted private enterprise. Private enterprise and Government control can and should exist side by side." He eschewed generalizations and personal attacks, instead making only a single pledge to his listeners: "We will do everything in human power to get the maximum number of houses in the shortest possible time."

That same day, his secretary brought him a telegram from London. It is not clear whether he gave it to Eden before the broadcast or after. If Eden's biographers had known that Eden saw it beforehand, surely they would have said so, but they did not. *The Times* of July 11, however, reported that he read it before going on air. At any rate, this is what the telegram said: "From Air Marshall Park to Anthony Eden: Have received signal from Wing Commander of your son's squadron reporting that the aircraft in which your son was flying on Saturday 23rd June has failed to turn up at destination in Burma." Eden doted on his son, as his diary reveals. It is hard to imagine the self-control necessary to deliver a national broadcast immediately after receiving a message of this character.

Whenever during that day he received the telegram, Eden revealed remarkable self-control during the week that followed. His diary records his dawning realization of what must be the truth, kept partially at bay by an ever-thinning ray of hope based on the failure of search parties to spot any wreckage. Churchill wrote to express sympathy; so did Attlee.

But Eden made sure to keep the news secret from the public until after the poll on July 5. He could not abide the thought of people voting for him out of sympathy. He rose from his sickbed and returned to the Foreign Office. Polling day came and went. Eden went out to Potsdam for the three-power talks on Germany, carrying on stoically while awaiting the verdict of England's voters, which was due on July 26. All the while he waited, too, for the dreaded telegram that would confirm what he knew already in his heart. On July 23 it finally arrived. His son's airplane had been found. It had indeed crashed. There were no survivors.

CHURCHILL ENDED THE CAMPAIGN AS HE BEGAN IT. HE GAVE A FOURTH and final radio broadcast on June 30, excoriating "this hitherto almost unknown person, Professor Laski[,] . . . [and the] utterly unconstitutional and undemocratic body lying in the background. . . . It would decide the action a Socialist Government could take in particular questions. . . . It could require the submission of ministers to its will." He was practically quoting one of Beaverbrook's letters of advice to him. He wrote again to Attlee on July 3 to repeat these charges, sending the letter to the press as well. It appeared the next day, along with Attlee's rebuttal, a further reminder, as if anyone needed it, of how badly at times the campaign had gone off the rails. The day after both letters appeared, Britain's voters finally cast their ballots.

DURING THE INTERVAL BETWEEN POLLING DAY, JULY 5, AND COUNTING day, July 26, Churchill took a week-and-a-half-long holiday on the French Atlantic coast, just north of Spain, his first real break since 1940. "I am painting a lot," he wired Beaverbrook. Then he went to Potsdam to meet Truman and Stalin. Eden joined him. Attlee (*pace* Professor Laski) joined him, too. This was the conference made notable in part by Churchill's failure to protect Poland from Russia; by the extension of Poland's western border into Germany; and by Truman telling the British prime minister that Americans had successfully detonated an atomic bomb in a trial run in New Mexico, while mentioning to Stalin only that America had a big new weapon. (Stalin knew about it already from his own sources, however.) Churchill returned to London on July 25 to learn the results of the election the next day.

All this time, Beaverbrook and the Conservative Party chairman, Ralph Assheton, had been sending him telegrams with general-election forecasts. Based upon reports from Conservative election agents, Assheton predicted a Conservative majority of 100. A few days later, Beaverbrook got his hands on Labour's estimate, which predicted 302 seats for Labour, including four Communists, and about 50 Liberals. This would leave the Conservatives and their allies with a majority of 38. It seemed to Beaverbrook a worst-case scenario; to Attlee it seemed the opposite: after it was all over, he told Churchill's private secretary that "in his most optimistic dreams he had reckoned that there might, with luck, be a Conservative majority of some forty seats." Churchill, who before he left the country had cautiously predicted to the king that he would win a majority of between 10 and 80 seats, could see no reason for revising his estimate. If anything, he thought he had understated his chances.

He returned from Berlin to London on the night of July 25, still confident. He went to bed at 1:00 A.M., which was early for him. "Just before dawn I woke suddenly with a sharp stab of almost physical pain," he wrote in his memoirs. "A hitherto subconscious conviction that we were beaten broke forth and dominated my mind." He suppressed this evil thought, rolled over and slept again, not rising until 9 A.M. An hour later he was in his bath when an assistant came rushing in to tell him the general election's initial results: Labour had taken 10 seats from sitting Conservatives. Churchill registered surprise, if not shock.

He had arranged in advance for the Map Room to be fitted up so that election results could be flashed on a screen and tallied as they came in. Fresh from his bath, dressed in one of his siren suits, cigar in hand, perhaps with that sharp pain stabbing at him again, he made his way to the outfitted room and sank into a chair. He had invited Beaverbrook, Bracken and the former Conservative chief whip, Margesson, to join him; also his private secretary, one of his daughters, and his brother. Later in the day, his wife and a second daughter would appear. By then the verdict was apparent. In fact, wrote the private secretary, "after half an hour it was clear there was going to be a landslide to the left." Churchill had intended to toast every Conservative gain by offering brandy to his guests: "I think there were only three during the day," recalled one of his aides.

At 1:30 they broke off for lunch. Churchill and his family dined with Beaverbrook and Bracken in what his daughter Mary described as "Stygian gloom." They could hardly take in the scope of the catastrophe. "It may be a blessing in disguise," Clementine told her husband. "At the moment it seems quite an effective disguise," he answered. Then they returned to the Map Room.

One by one his friends and colleagues and relations went down to defeat over the course of that long day: 5 Conservative Cabinet ministers, including Amery and Bracken; 8 departmental ministers and 19 junior ministers; he of the sunny forecasts, Ralph Assheton, the Conservative Party chairman; his own son Randolph; his son-in-law Duncan Sandys; and Amery's son. Among the principals in Churchill's War Cabinets, the Labour men all survived, but the Liberal, Sinclair, lost; of the non-party men, Anderson survived, but Woolton did not stand; among Conservatives, Beaverbrook did not stand, and only Eden remained. Churchill carried his constituency, but the tide lapped even at his feet. As a gesture of respect, neither the Labour nor the Liberal parties had put up a candidate against him. Into this void had stepped Alexander Hancock, a farmer. Standing as an Independent, he advocated a fair deal for workingmen—a one-hour workday. He received more than 10,000 votes to Churchill's 27,688. Had Churchill faced a serious candidate, the results would have been closer, possibly even shocking.

The 1945 general election was one of twentieth-century Britain's landslide elections. Labour won 393 seats; it possessed an absolute majority of 146 over all the other parties, the first time it had ever had one. The Conservatives and their allies had entered the campaign with 585 seats; they exited with about 220 (had the Liberal Party not divided the anti-Conservative vote, they would have exited with even fewer). In 1945 a majority of British voters would not support the party of prewar appeasement and prewar unemployment; they did not want a prime minister who seemed to relish war but not planning for postwar reconstruction. They had learned during 1940–1945 to believe in government economic planning, but most Conservatives opposed it. Some of them may have thought that they could vote for Labour and that Churchill could still return as prime minister. At 7 p.m., Churchill faced up to it. He turned to one of his assistants and said, "Fetch me my carriage and I shall go to the Palace and hand in my seals of office." He meant his Humber automobile. He had become an anachronism.

He had reached the nadir of the arc. And yet what had just happened was a testament to him. "They are perfectly entitled to vote as they please," he said later that night, back at Downing Street but no longer in office. "This is a democracy. This is what we've been fighting for."

Meanwhile, a curious and revealing incident was taking place nearby at Transport House, the Labour Party's headquarters on Smith Square, just up the river from Parliament. Attlee, Bevin and Morrison, all of whom had contested London seats and who had learned early of their victories, gathered there with a few others in the afternoon, first listening to the radio as more results came in, then conferring about next steps in Bevin's room. Attlee had in his mind, if not in his hand, a letter Morrison had written him two days before: "Whatever the result of the election may be, the new Parliamentary [Labour] Party is bound to include many new members. They should, I think, have an opportunity of deciding as to the type of leadership they want. In these circumstances I have decided that, if I am elected to the new Parliament, I should accept nomination for the leadership of the Party."

Morrison had important allies. One was Harold Laski. Another was Ellen Wilkinson, the Labour MP for Jarrow, a future minister of education, who had worked with him at the Home Office, and with whom he may have been having an affair. Stafford Cripps appears to have been another. Important journalists and trade unionists supported him; so did his Lewisham election agent, Jim Raison, who was an effective political fixer. They all thought Attlee lacked vision and charisma. They believed the times demanded a more dynamic leader, and they judged that the Parliamentary Labour Party, especially its left wing, would plump for Morrison. Had it come to a vote, they might have been proved right. Or not: Attlee had just led the party through the war and the general election to victory. His reputation had never been higher.

Morrison justified his bid for the leadership with a misinterpretation of the party constitution, however. Nowhere did it specifically state that the Labour Party must call a special leadership election before attempting to form a government. Moreover, he did not prepare his bid carefully. As the formidable Raison would later recall: "In the three weeks between the actual vote and the counting of the poll Herbert did nothing, perhaps because he wasn't sure that [a majority of Labour candidates] were in fact going to win."

But now they had won, and the bid had been launched. Shortly before 7 p.m., Churchill sent a message to Attlee, who was still closeted with Bevin and Morrison, saying that he was about to go to the palace to resign, and that he would advise the king to ask him to try to form a new government. Immediately Morrison argued that Attlee should not go to see the king if he was summoned until the PLP had either reaffirmed his leadership or elected someone else, such as himself. Bevin flew into a rage. As the Welsh MP, Jim Griffiths, who saw it, remembered it, "he went blue in the face." Bevin thought Morrison had just confirmed every negative assessment he had made of him over the past twenty years. Attlee, concise as always, said something like: "If the King asks you to form a government you say 'Yes' or 'No,' not 'I'll let you know later.'" Morrison continued to argue. Then the telephone rang. Cripps wished to speak with Morrison. As soon as Morrison left the room, Bevin whispered to Attlee: "Bugger off to the Palace." But Attlee had already made up his mind. Morrison returned to say that Cripps favored a leadership election, too. Neither Attlee nor Bevin would discuss the matter further.

A little later, Attlee left Transport House with the question seemingly still up in the air. It was not. Attlee's wife drove him to Buckingham Palace in their little Austin, parked it and waited while her husband went in to speak with the king. George VI asked him to form a new government. Attlee accepted the commission. Morrison did not know.

They all met again at a great Labour Party celebration later that night at Central Hall. It was packed, hot, jubilant, noisy. Morrison appeared, beaming. His allies were still canvassing for him at the celebration. "We can't have Attlee, he's no good, we need Herbert," Ellen Wilkinson said to one Labour MP. She cornered another and "they conversed through the mirror in the Ladies Room." Morrison took a couple of friends aside: "There is a chance I shall be offered the premiership. I am not sure I am big enough to do it. What do you think?" Then Attlee mounted the platform to speak. The boisterous room hushed. The little man announced that he had just returned from Buckingham Palace, where he had accepted the king's commission to form a government. The room erupted into cheers. Morrison and his election agent looked at each other, and then Morrison turned away. Attlee had defeated him again.

THE NEXT DAY, LABOUR'S LEADER BEGAN THE SAME PROCESS THAT Churchill had undertaken almost five years earlier: conferring with friends and allies, drawing up lists, balancing egos and talents, calling able men into his office, fulfilling the dreams of some, disappointing others. He was putting together the third Labour government in British history. The circumstances were different from 1940, but still fraught. Germany had ruined most of continental Europe; she had nearly ruined Britain.

The tasks of reconstruction would be monumental, and the treasury was empty. The country remained at war with Japan. Attlee's job was to fashion a government that could deal with all this while laying down the bases of a socialist society.

The prospect was daunting, but a new world beckoned. The most extraordinary prime minister of the most extraordinary British government of the twentieth century was about to enter the history books.

Coda

TWENTIETH-CENTURY BRITAIN HAD EXTENSIVE EXPERIENCE OF multiparty government before May 1940 when Winston Churchill built his Grand Coalition. Liberal prime minister H. H. Asquith brought Conservatives into his government in 1915 to prosecute World War I more efficiently and to maintain national unity. His Liberal successor, David Lloyd George, maintained and enlarged the Asquith coalition in 1916, bringing in the leader of the Labour Party. At the very beginning of 1919, after the "Khaki Election," and with the war just ended, he constructed another coalition government that lasted three more years. In 1931, Ramsay MacDonald put together a "National Government" to deal with the Great Depression. Stanley Baldwin, who followed MacDonald as prime minister in 1935, and then Neville Chamberlain, who followed Baldwin in 1937, claimed to have maintained the government's "national" character, although in fact it had become Conservative in everything but name. Still, when Churchill wound up his short-lived caretaker government to fight the general election of 1945, Britain had been served by some form of multiparty government for twenty-one out of the past thirty years.

Since World War II, British prime ministers have rarely constructed coalition governments. Labour governments have depended occasionally upon Liberal votes in the House of Commons, and Conservative governments upon MPs from Northern Ireland, but David Cameron's Conservative–Liberal Democrat combination, established in 2010, is the first genuine coalition government since Churchill's.

Britain's experience suggests that there are two sorts of coalition governments. A prime minister may organize one for arithmetical reasons when his or her own party does not command an absolute majority in the House of Commons, as David Cameron did. Or the leader may form one in order to deal with a national emergency, as Asquith, Lloyd George, MacDonald and Churchill did. In Churchill's case, the emergency could not have been graver. Britain faced imminent invasion and defeat at the hands of Adolf Hitler. The dry, detached Chamberlain had been unable to inspire the country or to persuade the leaders of the Liberal and Labour Parties to join him. They did not trust or respect or like him. Passionate Winston Churchill won them over, and then won over his countrymen.

But trust, respect and affection, no matter how unstinting, are not enough by themselves. Coalition governments, if they are to succeed, depend upon ministers of different parties sharing a common set of broad assumptions: that politics is not a zero-sum game; that the winner of an argument cannot expect to take all, or the loser to forfeit everything. One party to a coalition might win an argument on a certain issue, but it must then be willing to accept the other party's position on a different issue. No party to a coalition can insist upon winning all the time. Thus coalitions depend upon politicians' willingness to compromise. They depend upon this more than single-party governments do, since they will fall if compromise does not take place, whereas single-party governments generally fall only when they lose majority support.

Dictators may compromise on occasion, but often they do not have to. Democracies depend upon the willingness of politicians to compromise sometimes: if a democratically elected government sticks to an unpopular policy, voters will punish it for having failed to compromise. Coalitions depend upon compromise always—or at any rate upon permanent give and take. Refusal by any party to a coalition to bargain and deal will doom the coalition. Churchill's War Cabinet ministers edged toward such a refusal on two occasions. The first was in June 1940, when Halifax hinted that he might resign if Churchill did not approach Mussolini to intercede with Hitler. Churchill held fast, however, and Halifax backed down. The second was in February 1942, when Attlee indirectly threatened that his party would withdraw from the coalition in order to force a general election, at which Labour would demand speedy implementation of the Beveridge plan. Attlee was bluffing—he feared Labour would lose such an election. In any event, Churchill eventually compromised, agreeing to make some decisions on implementing Beveridge's suggestions even while the war continued. The fact that there were only two such threats during five years of unremitting tension is remarkable. The ultimate success of Winston Churchill's Grand Coalition, a government that spanned the political spectrum, testifies to its ministers' willingness to give a little to get a little. Attlee said in Stoke, early in 1941: "Democracy works in this country because we intend that it shall work. We have the habit first of all of tolerance, and secondly of submitting to the will of the majority, and thirdly of practicality."

Ministers in coalition governments feel more compelled to compromise than single-party governments do, especially when national survival is at stake. Churchill, who understood better than most what the stakes were in 1940, absolutely insisted upon compromise. He hushed his party members when they complained about Labour; he exhorted Labour ministers to set aside party differences when they complained about Conservatives. For five years he successfully juggled a team of extraordinarily capable, ambitious and ideologically disparate men. He did not do it perfectly. Master juggler though he was, he could not always keep them all spinning in the air at once. Some of his War Cabinet ministers fell to earth with a bump. But, for the most part, they, too, understood their country's dangerous situation and the need for compromise, the need for maintaining the Grand Coalition. Despite this general understanding, could only Churchill have successfully juggled this group? The answer must be yes. It is impossible to imagine the puritanical Stafford Cripps or the unscrupulous Beaverbrook keeping all the balls spinning for long, and no other War Cabinet minister seriously considered trying.

Even with Churchill in charge, the War Cabinet ministers sniped and snarled at one another continually. They intrigued against one another. Two intrigued against the prime minister himself. This should not surprise us; it is more astonishing that such incongruent men managed to work together at all than that they sometimes failed to do so. After all, the ideological chasm dividing, say, the orthodox Conservative Kingsley Wood from the radical socialist Stafford Cripps in 1942 stretched far wider than the seemingly unbridgeable one that separates conservative Republicans from liberal Democrats in the United States today.

Attlee spoke an essential truth at Stoke, then, when he claimed that ministers were tolerant, practical and committed to majority rule, but he did not speak the entire truth. They conspired against one another, too. Yet, over time, the gloss he applied to the truth came to hide the rougher, less edifying reality. The protagonists of Churchill's War Cabinet forgot

about the backbiting and competition in which they had engaged, emphasizing instead how seamless their cooperation had been. They burnished
the memories of those earlier days, as old men often do who regret the
passing of youth, or relative youth. They liked to say that there once had
been giants, among whom they had numbered. This book has shown those
giants as they really were, harnessed together to a common purpose, but
often pulling in opposite directions. It has shown Churchill's War Cabinet
ministers, and the prime minister himself, members of Britain's grandest
Coalition, with warts and all.

PRIME MINISTER CLEMENT ATTLEE, FOREIGN SECRETARY ERNEST BEVIN,
Lord President and Deputy Prime Minister Herbert Morrison, President
of the Board of Trade Stafford Cripps, and Chancellor of the Exchequer
Hugh Dalton formed the core of the Labour government that took power
in July 1945, replacing the caretaker regime that Churchill had established after the dissolution of his more broad-based Grand Coalition.
Greenwood was out. He had ceased to count sometime after 1940 and
never mounted a comeback, although he continued to serve on various
committees and as party treasurer. The "Big Five" dominated for the next
half-decade.

They faced, when they came into power, a ruined Europe; a rampant
USA; a Soviet Army of more than 11 million; a restive British Empire; and
exhaustion and empty coffers at home. They nevertheless established, over
the next six years, the generous welfare state outlined in the Labour Party's Election Manifesto of 1945. They set up the National Health Service.
They carried out the program of nationalization that Labour had promised, first of the coal mines, then the railways and the Bank of England,
and then the others. They launched, not altogether happily, the process
of decolonization. Bevin, at the Foreign Office, played a major role in coordinating the European response to the Marshall Plan, and also in the
formation of the North Atlantic Treaty Organization (NATO). Many Labour supporters have regarded the Labour governments of this period as
their touchstones—especially the third Labour government (1945–1950),
but also the fourth, elected with a much reduced majority in 1950 and
terminated prematurely a year later, when Attlee ill-advisedly sought to
strengthen it by calling another general election. Certainly these two Labour governments represent the high-water mark of twentieth-century
British socialism.

Rivalry and conflict among the Labour leaders did not cease in 1945, however. It intensified, in fact, because there were no longer any Conservatives, Liberals or independents in government for the Big Five to rub up against. For obvious reasons, Attlee no longer trusted Morrison. Bevin had never trusted Morrison. Morrison, for his part, continued to hanker after the leadership of the Labour Party and the premiership of the country. In 1947, matters came to a head when Cripps, Dalton and Morrison all agreed that Attlee had to go. But Cripps favored Bevin for the top spot, and Bevin did not want it—he remained loyal to "the little man." Sharp and decisive as ever, Attlee promoted Cripps, demoted Morrison, and put an end to the conspiracy.

By 1950, Labour's Big Five had been working flat out for a decade, and the pace had taken a physical toll. Bevin ate, drank and weighed too much. He smoked too much as well. He suffered from angina. He caught pneumonia. He could no longer travel. Toward the end, whenever he attended Cabinet meetings he would deliver his reports and then doze off. Finally, Attlee decided he must tell his closest and most powerful colleague to resign. He did it on March 9, 1951, over the telephone, while Bevin and the rest of the Foreign Office staff were celebrating Bevin's seventieth birthday. When the big man got home that afternoon, he told his wife: "I've got the sack." It broke his heart. When Attlee tried to soften the blow by making him Lord Privy Seal, Bevin said disconsolately, "But I am neither a lord, nor a privy, nor a seal." He died on April 4, a few months before Labour lost in the poorly timed general election of October 1951.

As for "Austerity Cripps," as the public called the vegetarian who lived on carrot juice and nuts and berries, he seemed positively to enjoy coping with the challenge of postwar shortages. While president of the Board of Trade, he took a leading role in the process that produced an independent India, trying hard, but failing, to keep Muslims and Hindus united. On the domestic front he became for a time, in the words of his best biographer, Britain's "economic supremo," a democratic socialist under whose aegis were implemented a full range of Keynesian prescriptions. In his personal life and appearance he was the opposite of Ernest Bevin, but that did not save him. He suffered from a spinal infection, and then doctors discovered stomach tumors. He resigned as chancellor on October 20, 1950, a few months before Bevin was dismissed, and lasted a little longer than Bevin, dying of cancer of the bone marrow early in 1952, three days before his sixty-third birthday.

In comparison with Bevin and Cripps, Attlee and Morrison enjoyed good health as they aged. Despite conflicting ambitions, the two men worked well together, orchestrating and coordinating Labour's domestic program. Attlee relied upon Morrison's political skills for dealing with both the party and Parliament, and Morrison did not disappoint. But when Bevin stepped down as foreign minister, Attlee chose Morrison to replace him. This arrangement did not work. Morrison knew a great deal about the domestic scene and politics, but relatively little about foreign affairs. In any event, he held the post only for a short period of time, from March 1951 when Bevin left office until Labour lost the general election in October.

Although Attlee had designated Morrison his deputy prime minister in 1945, he did not want him as a successor. When Labour left office he held onto leadership of the party to keep Morrison from getting it. The "cocky Cockney" had to wait, clinging grimly to the second position, his eye still fixed on the spot above. But Attlee would not let go until 1955, when Labour lost to the Tories yet again. By then, as he knew, the party was ready to turn to a new generation for leadership. But Morrison, who was now sixty-seven years old, still staked his claim in the PLP election that followed. He finished at the bottom of the poll, behind Aneurin Bevan, age fifty-eight, who came in second, and Hugh Gaitskell, age forty-eight, who won. It was a humiliating end to Herbert Morrison's twenty-year quest for headship of the Labour Party and a chance at leadership of the country.

Attlee entered the House of Lords as Earl Attlee. His reputation remained high; he would act as Labour's *eminence gris* until he died in 1967 at the age of eighty-four. Morrison, too, entered the Lords, as a life peer in 1959. He stayed more politically active than Attlee, intervening in debates in the upper house and serving for a time as president of the British Board of Film Censors, but he was never again at the center of events. He was seventy-seven years old when he passed away in 1965.

THE LIBERAL ARCHIE SINCLAIR LOST HIS SEAT IN THE GENERAL ELECTION of 1945. He came in at the bottom of the poll in a remarkable three-way contest that saw one of the few Conservative gains of the year—and a margin of only sixty-one votes separating the top candidate from the bottom. Sinclair lost once more in 1950, by a slightly wider margin, and never stood for Parliament again. He accepted a peerage in 1952 and entered the House of Lords, but he, too, suffered from poor health. Although he would speak occasionally in the Upper Chamber, his political career essentially had ended.

Sir John Anderson, who stood in 1945 as a National candidate, not a Conservative one, kept his parliamentary seat. He sat on the Opposition front bench with Churchill during Labour's years in power, but did not join the Conservative government that took office in 1951. Instead, "Pomposo" became chairman of the Port of London authority and of the Covent Garden Opera Trust as well as the director of several companies. He, too, accepted a peerage. He never again played a significant political role.

By way of contrast, Lord Woolton dropped his non-party status and rededicated himself to politics. As the results of the 1945 general election poured in, he wrote to Churchill: "I am ashamed of the public." It is said that he joined the Conservative Party the very next day. At any rate, on July 1, 1946, he became Conservative Party chairman, tasked with the general modernization, reorganization and revitalization of the party's apparatus. He enjoyed remarkable success, overhauling and improving its machinery and finances at both local and national levels. He had much to do with preparing it for the general elections of 1950 and 1951, when first it recovered much lost ground and then beat Labour by a whisker and returned to power. He never stood for Parliament, but he did join the government in 1951 as Lord President of the Council and coordinating minister of food and agriculture. An exponent of the "middle way," he accepted the welfare state but never socialism, and therefore advocated privatizing the industries that Labour had taken into public ownership. He opposed the BBC's television monopoly. Meanwhile, the man who had considered breaking away from Churchill to found and lead a centrist party rose, step by step, on Churchill's recommendation, from marquis to viscount to earl. In the same year that he received that final honor, 1955, he stepped down as Conservative Party chairman and away from politics at last. It had been a good run for the son of a lower-middle-class saddler from Salford.

THE CONSERVATIVE LORD HALIFAX NEVER RESUMED HIS PLACE IN THE political world. In 1946, Attlee recalled him from Washington and replaced him with Clark Kerr, the man who previously had replaced Stafford Cripps as ambassador to Russia. Churchill invited Halifax to sit on the Opposition front bench, but he declined. He spent his remaining years collecting honors, devoting himself to good works, traveling, enjoying his Yorkshire estates, and speaking occasionally in the House of Lords. He seems never to have engaged in the kind of critical exercise that might have led him to rethink the position he had taken in June 1940 about approaching Mussolini to intervene with Hitler.

Halifax's protégé, R. A. Butler, however, continued to rise. He had advised, almost alone among the Conservative hierarchy, against the June date for the 1945 general election. The party had good reason to regret ignoring him. Henceforth it paid more attention, but perhaps not enough to suit him. Butler rose to become chancellor of the exchequer in 1951; he served as home secretary in the governments of 1955 and 1959, but he never gained the top position. He has been described as "one of the best Prime Ministers we never had" among Britain's "Prime Ministers Who Never Were."

As for Anthony Eden, even during the war he had been the prince in waiting; now, with the war finished, almost everyone, except Winston Churchill, thought his wait must soon come to an end. He kept his parliamentary seat comfortably in 1945 despite the general Conservative debacle. Then, however, instead of grasping the laurel of victory and the reins of the party, he found himself sitting on the Opposition front bench, once more in the shadow of Winston Churchill. For a brief period he considered leaving England altogether; he thought he might be chosen the first secretary general of the United Nations, but the Soviets vetoed this prospect. When the Conservatives returned to office in 1951, Eden regained his position as foreign secretary. Churchill, now age seventy-seven, had resumed the premiership.

Eden's marriage, long unhappy, did not survive the death of his son in the Far East. He faced the early postwar years sorrowful and alone. In August 1952, however, he wed Clarissa, daughter of Churchill's brother, Jack. Two years later, on November 30, 1954, the prime minister turned eighty. Still, he would not hand over the torch, even though now it would be kept within the family. Eden chafed. Indeed, the Conservative Cabinet had begun to chafe, too. The old man thought he could still play a decisive world role, mediating between the Americans and the Russians. He stepped down, with great reluctance, only in April 1955, and Eden stepped up with a sense of finally being able to breathe. Then, exhibiting some bravery, the new prime minister called a general election. If he won it, the victory would provide him with a mandate.

He did win it, but soon plunged into disaster: the ill-conceived and ill-fated collusion with France and Israel aimed at forcing Egyptian president Abdel Nasser to let go of the recently nationalized Suez Canal. It is possible that Eden's poor health played a role in this debacle: in 1953, a surgeon did permanent damage to his bile duct while working on his gall bladder. As a result Eden suffered from recurrent and painful abdominal infections. Doctors prescribed a cocktail of powerful drugs that are now known to impair judgment. Eden came down with another infection in November 1956, just as the operation in Suez was taking place. Its failure and his breakdown coincided. On November 21, he and his wife left England for Jamaica, where he would recuperate at "Goldeneye," the holiday villa belonging to Ian Fleming, author of the James Bond novels. Butler would "mind the baby" in his absence. But Eden never returned to power. With his health and reputation shattered, he resigned as prime minister less than two months later. Harold Macmillan, who had been steadily climbing the Conservative ladder, rising from air minister for Churchill's caretaker government to housing minister and then defense minister for Eden, edged Butler out of the way to take Eden's place.

Anthony Eden had waited for the premiership for close to fifteen years; he held it for a year and a half. He would live another two decades, collecting many honors, writing his memoirs and entering the House of Lords as the first Earl of Avon, but his time in the spotlight had ended. He died on January 14, 1977, at the age of seventy-nine.

MANY CONSERVATIVES SOUGHT A SCAPEGOAT FOR THEIR LOSS IN 1945. They did not have far to look. "Expel Lord Beaverbrook," cried one at a meeting meant to discuss reasons and remedies for the party's plight. The room, which was crowded with Conservative candidates, most of whom had failed at the polls, erupted with cheers and applause. Beaverbrook soon obtained a verbatim transcript of what had been said at this meeting, but he took it in stride. Aside from the period in 1942 when he had thought he might become prime minister, he never relished a career in politics. He had never been a good party man, and he knew that good party men—of all parties—hated him. He did like to be near the center of power, but he could not be now that Churchill was no longer prime minister. And when Churchill did become prime minister again in 1951, Beaverbrook kept his distance, because he disagreed with Churchill's policies. He believed, as he always had, in "imperial preference," which meant Britain and the colonies and dominions practicing free trade among themselves while putting up tariffs to keep out everybody else's goods. He wanted his country to keep away from Europe and to hold the Americans at arm's length. He thought, as A. J. P. Taylor wrote, that the Cold War was a false alarm, and that Russia would not attack the West. Churchill accepted none of this, and Beaverbrook would not quarrel publicly with him. But for a short period the two men rarely saw each other.

Always restless, after the war Beaverbrook shuttled continually during cold months between properties he owned in the Bahamas, Jamaica and the French Riviera. He spent spring and summer in England, either at Cherkley or in London. He had turned sixty-six in 1945, but age never slowed him down; he remained as dynamic and productive as ever. Even when traveling he kept a close eye and tight rein on the editors and journalists of his newspapers, although claiming that they had absolute freedom. A generous philanthropist, he gave so much money to the University of New Brunswick that its faculty and administration elected him as chancellor, a ceremonial post that he nevertheless took seriously.

Beaverbrook, too, mulled the past. In addition to managing his newspapers, he wrote a number of books, mainly biographies and histories, the latter about the days of H. H. Asquith and David Lloyd George. Even his many enemies admitted that they were first rate. He wanted to write about Churchill during World War II, but not until his friend had died, for he meant not only to sing his praises but also, as he once wrote, to point out his failings and—particularly relevant here—"to emphasize the drama of Churchill's precarious hold on power."

The two old friends found each other again once Churchill had stepped away permanently from No. 10 Downing Street. Thereafter, the former prime minister dined frequently at Cherkley, and he often visited Beaverbrook's villa on the coast of France. During the war Beaverbrook had tried his friend's patience countless times. He knew how deep his debt was to the older man. In 1958, he wrote to him of 1940: "I acknowledge that it was the most glittering, glorious and glamorous era of my whole life. I packed more into twelve months of danger and escape than into just on eighty years of a not unexciting existence."

Beaverbrook kept up an astonishingly hectic schedule until the very end of his life. On May 25, 1964, at his eighty-fifth birthday party, celebrated at the Dorchester Hotel in London, he presided over a great dinner with six hundred guests. He "ate heartily and outshone all the others in gaiety," reported A. J. P. Taylor, who was there. In a witty speech, Beaver-brook informed them all that he was looking forward to further adventures. His body was breaking down, but his mind and spirit remained as fresh and active as ever. He died two weeks later.

DID CHURCHILL EVEN KNOW? HIS LAST TWO YEARS WERE MUCH WORSE than his friend's. He suffered a series of strokes, sank into depression and torpor, took no interest in his surroundings and rarely spoke.

When Labour won in 1945, Churchill could have gracefully relinquished his position as leader of the Conservative Party. He did no such thing. For six years he presided over the Opposition front bench, and then in 1951 he returned to No. 10 with a majority of just 17 members. He was seventy-seven years old. All the biographers agree: he had seen his best days. If anyone deserved time for resting on laurels it was he. Instead, a shadow of his former self, he attempted to govern a fractious party and nation. He called upon most of the Conservatives who had served him during the war, and some of the generals, to return to service. Almost all of them swallowed their doubts and did so.

He loved the paraphernalia and pomp of office, but not the detail work. He could be charming and witty as ever, and on occasion as brilliant; but, although he continued writing his own speeches until the very end of his career, he no longer read documents or dispatched memos demanding "Action This Day." He ran his Cabinet meetings even less efficiently than during the war, which is saying a lot; eventually he began dispensing with them altogether. Domestic affairs always had bored him. He instructed the relevant ministers to keep things quiet on the home front—for example, by maintaining high wages in the nationalized industries, even if the wages led to inflation. Despite his flirtation with Friedrich Hayek's outlook during the general election of 1945, he made no attempt to roll back the welfare state Labour had created, setting a precedent for postwar Conservative prime ministers that would last, by and large, until Margaret Thatcher came to power in 1979.

As always, he focused on foreign affairs. He wanted to assert Britain's greatness again. He believed it would be founded upon an unshakable Anglo-American alliance. He did not know that President Eisenhower, who was outwardly affable, but inwardly cold, secretly deemed him a sentimental old man, and his country a second-rate power. Above all, he wanted to save the world from an atomic holocaust by brokering a deal between Russia and the United States. His mind reverted to the great meetings with Stalin and FDR. He would re-create them with the new leaders of Russia and America. He would be, once again, the indispensable man.

But he could not be such a figure: Britain had neither the leverage nor the strength for it, whoever led her and whatever his age. And then, anyway, on June 23, 1953, he suffered a severe stroke (he had suffered a mild one four years earlier). This time he thought he was done for; testimony to his will to live and govern, he recovered fully over a four-month period. He would hang onto power for another two years. Sometimes he felt really well; he could dominate the House, and he believed the world needed him. He dreamed of international summitry. But meanwhile there was Eden, waiting, with ever-increasing impatience, for the crown; the rest of the Cabinet, convinced by now that the old man really should give it up, was waiting, too. Churchill rather cruelly strung Eden along, writing him complementary letters that always wound up postponing the date of his departure.

He had three reasons for hanging on. First, he really did believe the world needed him to keep the peace between America and Russia. But Eisenhower had no intention of indulging Churchill's desire for a summit meeting, something Churchill only reluctantly and belatedly recognized. Second, as Churchill told his doctor in 1954, "I think I shall die quickly once I retire. There would be no purpose in living when there is nothing to do." Finally, he had convinced himself that the heir apparent did not deserve to inherit: "I don't believe Anthony can do it," he told his private secretary on the evening of April 4, 1955. But by then it was impossible to steer the premiership to anyone else. He knew that he was slipping—everyone knew it. The very next day, he did finally let go of the reins of power.

He lived ten more years, his health declining a little with each of them. He refused a dukedom in order to keep his place in the House of Commons. He sat on the front bench and would enter the division lobbies, but he never addressed the House again. He did make an occasional public speech during these early years of his retirement. And he put the finishing touches to a work he had begun many years before, *History of the English Speaking Peoples*. He watched acidulously over Anthony Eden's premiership, which culminated in the debacle at Suez. He became increasingly frail, increasingly deaf, and increasingly withdrawn, and the warm sun of southern France and the Caribbean called to him. He enjoyed cruising aboard the yacht of the Greek magnate Aristotle Onassis. But his decline was inexorable. In June 1962 he fell and broke his hip. Such a mishap often signals the beginning of the end.

His old friend Beaverbrook did the best he could for him. He reserved a bedroom at Cherkley for his use. The adjoining bathroom contained a shaving mug engraved with Churchill's initials. The former prime minister came to dinner in a wheelchair one night after he had broken his hip. The other guests were Beaverbrook's nephew, Jonathan Aitken, and the chief foreign correspondent and chief leader writer of the *Daily Express*. Churchill raised a toast to them with his first glass of champagne: "To love, peace and health, and honest friends." Then he turned silent and seemed distracted. No one could rouse him, although they all tried. Finally the great man turned to Aitken and asked if he had been beaten at school. Aitken shook his head. "Pity," said Churchill, lapsing into silence again. Only when Aitken quoted a recent newspaper article saying that Churchill's greatness had lain in his oratory did he speak once more. "'Fraid it's ballsh. I was never an orator." But then, lucidly, self-deprecatingly, he explained why he had not been. The great orators never knew in advance what they would say: "Their phrases were dictated by some inner god." He himself had written out beforehand every speech he ever gave. He stopped talking and dozed off. It had been a rare interjection, and his interjections grew ever rarer. He died on January 24, 1965. The queen decreed a state funeral.

ON JULY 27, 1945, CHURCHILL HAD CONVENED A FINAL MEETING OF HIS caretaker government in the Cabinet Room at No. 10. Across the road, in the House of Commons, Attlee was busy drawing up lists of names for the Labour government. All was bustle and cheer and purposiveness there. At Downing Street the caretaker ministers, or rather, former ministers, sat stunned and silent. Many had lost their parliamentary seats. They still could not grasp the enormity of the Conservative defeat. Churchill somberly bid them each farewell. Afterward, Eden lingered for a few minutes to speak with him: "He was pretty wretched, poor old boy," observed the younger man. Then Eden, too, left the room. "I couldn't help reflecting, as I walked down the passage, on all that the experience of these war years in that Cabinet Room has meant to me," he wrote in his diary. "I cannot believe I can ever know anything like it again." None of them could, or would.

ACKNOWLEDGMENTS

I WOULD LIKE TO THANK A NUMBER OF PEOPLE AND INSTITUTIONS FOR helping me with this book in one way or another.

My home university, the Georgia Institute of Technology, has facilitated my research with travel grants and a reduced teaching load. In this regard Jackie Royster, dean of the Ivan Allen College of Liberal Arts at Georgia Tech, and Steve Usselman, chairman of the School of History, Technology and Society in the Ivan Allen College, have been wonderfully supportive. I thank them both heartily.

I would also like to thank the archivists at the Churchill Archives Centre, Churchill College, Cambridge University, and at the Bodleian Library, Oxford University, for their helpfulness in locating materials, as well as the staff at the National Archive at Kew. In fact, I encountered nothing but helpfulness wherever I went for my research, including the British Library, the Borthwick Institute at York University, the University of Birmingham, the London School of Economics, the House of Lords Records Office, and Trinity College, Cambridge University. So I extend my thanks to the archivists who helped me at all those places.

In addition I am grateful to the Borthwick Institute for permission to quote from the papers of Edward Frederick Lindley Wood, Earl Halifax; to the present Lord Woolton for permission to quote from the papers of his grandfather, the first Lord Woolton; and to Mr. Charles Simon for permission to quote from the papers of Viscount Simon.

Friends and colleagues who read either portions of the manuscript or drafts of the entire text include (in alphabetical order by last name) Chris Clark, John Drucker, Rob Harding, John Krige, David Clay Large, Jenny Smith and Peter Weiler. All offered encouragement and good advice. John Drucker offered this and more: food and drink on practically a regular basis. I wish to thank them all, and him particularly.

I would also like to express my thanks to my agents in New York and London, Christy Fletcher and Peter Robinson, both of whom have been wonderfully supportive on this project, as with all the others. Lara Heimert, at Basic Books in New York City, is an extraordinary editor (but I knew that already). Mike Harpley, at Oneworld Publishers in London, for whom this is my first book, has been a pleasure to work with.

As usual, the most profound thanks go to my wife, Margaret Hayman, who has never turned a deaf ear, and never will.

—*Jonathan Schneer*

NOTES

INTRODUCTION

xix who led them: See Doris Kearns Goodwin, *Team of Rivals: The Political Genius of Abraham Lincoln* (New York, 2005).

PROLOGUE

xxiii ". . . no adequate defense [for them]": Quoted in Martin Gilbert, *The Churchill War Papers*, vol. 1, *At the Admiralty* (New York, 1993), 1200.

CHAPTER 1

3 wonderful spring weather: There is much testimony to the beautiful spring. See, e.g., John Martin, "Five Years at No. 10 (1940–45)," unpublished diary, Martin Collection, Churchill College, Cambridge University, p. 1. Martin served as Churchill's principal private secretary during the war years.

4 twice as many votes as Labour: The numbers were: Conservative, 387; Labour, 154; Liberal Nationalist, 33; Liberal, 21; National Liberal, 8; Independent Labour, 4; Irish Nationalist, 2; National Independent, 2; National, 1; Communist, 1.

4 one non-party man: Chamberlain's War Cabinet in May 1940 consisted of himself, Churchill, Halifax, Sir Samuel Hoare (secretary of state for air), Sir Kingsley Wood (Lord Privy Seal), Sir John Simon (chancellor of the exchequer), Lord Hankey (minister without portfolio), and Oliver Stanley (minister of war). Simon belonged to the National Liberals, Hankey to no party. A second National Liberal, Leslie Hore-Belisha, had been a less enthusiastic appeaser; Chamberlain dropped him as minister of war in January 1940 and offered him the Board of Trade, but Hore-Belisha declined it and left the government.

5 **Czechoslovakia in 1938:** Oliver Stanley, the secretary of state for war, shared them—although without ever saying so publicly.

5 "**. . . Forgive me":** Gilbert, *Admiralty*, 1205–1206.

5 **elsewhere on the continent:** Ibid., 1207.

5 **British war production:** Martin Gilbert, *Winston S. Churchill*, vol.6, *Finest Hour, 1939–1941* (London, 1983), 289.

5 "**. . . shot at without result":** Winston Churchill, *The Story of the Malakand Field Force* (London, 1898), 107.

6 "**. . . against uncivilized tribes":** But the record is unclear. He may have meant only tear gas, and in any event no gas was employed then.

8 **could not do it:** Robert Blake, "How Churchill Became Prime Minister," in Robert Blake and William Roger Louis, eds., *Churchill: A Major New Assessment of His Life in Peace and War* (Oxford, 1993), 259.

8 "**. . . time comes we are ready":** Transcript of speech, undated, Attlee Papers, Bodleian Library, Oxford University, dep. 1, fol. 53.

8 "**. . . as I jolly well can":** *Daily Mail*, May 6, 1940.

8 **censure that weekend:** This is the title of Lynne Olson's *Troublesome Young Men* (New York, 2007). She is quoting a line in a 1928 letter from Harold Macmillan to Winston Churchill: "You have always been most kind to those of us who are ordinarily classed merely as troublesome young men."

8 **from both Houses:** Salisbury to James Stuart, May 31, 1941, Conservative Party Archives, Bodleian Library, Oxford University, Whip 1/4.

9 **with both of them:** Robert Boothby, "Draft Outline," paper on Davies's role in Chamberlain's fall, n.d., Clement Davies Papers, National Library of Wales, I/2/8.

9 **prime minister to lead it:** The four ministers without portfolio would have been Churchill, Lloyd George, Morrison and Eden. The best biography of Cripps is Peter Clarke, *The Cripps Version* (London, 2003).

10 "**. . . would [have] to be Halifax":** Stafford Cripps, diary entry, May 2, 1940, Stafford Cripps Papers, Bodleian Library, Oxford University, SC5/1.

10 **in a new administration:** Bernard Donoughue and G. W. Jones, *Herbert Morrison: Portrait of a Politician* (London, 1973), 275.

10 "**. . . expect it to be under Halifax":** The intimate was Brendan Bracken. Leo Amery, *My Political Life*, vol. 3, *The Unforgiving Years, 1929–1940* (London, 1955), 371. Many years later Attlee denied he said this to Bracken, but Bracken had reported it not only to Amery but also to Sir E. L. Spears, who likewise recorded it in his diary, which was later published as *Prelude to Dunkirk* (London, 1954), 131. See also A. J. P. Taylor, "They All Want to Be Heroes Now," *Sunday Express*, January 19, 1964.

10 "**. . . pass on to you":** The close aide was R. A. Butler. Butler to Halifax, May 9, 1940, Halifax Papers, York University, A4/410/16.

10 "**. . . down this time":** Quoted in Keith Feiling, *The Life of Neville Chamberlain* (London, 1970), 439.

10 "very bad and gloomy": David Dilkes, ed., *The Diaries of Sir Alexander Cadogan, 1938–45* (London, 1971), 277.

10 ". . . weather the storm": A. J. Sylvester to David Lloyd George, May 6, 1940, Lloyd George Papers, House of Lords Records Office, LG/G/24/1, Sylvester Daily Minutes.

11 were cowards: Margesson to Chamberlain, June 5, 1940, Chamberlain Papers, University of Birmingham, NC8/35/47.

11 Davies of the Vigilantes: We do not know what time this meeting occurred.

11 ". . . a good chance . . . ": Gilbert, *Admiralty*, 1221.

11 ". . . head of affairs": Quoted in Gilbert, *Finest Hour*, 290. The letter writer was Lord Lloyd. He blamed not only Labour but also the "subservience of the Commons majority."

12 ". . . reap the whirlwind": Quoted in Olson, *Troublesome Young Men*, 290.The rebel was Robert Boothby. His two guests in the tearoom were his lover, Dorothy Macmillan, who was the wife of Harold Macmillan, an equally committed rebel, and Baffy Dugdale, Arthur Balfour's niece and a leading English Zionist.

12 news to Lord Salisbury: Ben Pimlott, *Hugh Dalton: A Life* (London, 1985), 273.

12 alternative Cabinets: Nigel Nicolson, ed., *The Diaries of Harold Nicolson: The War Years, 1939–1945* (New York, 1967), May 7, 1940, 77.

13 ". . . talking nonsense": John Simon, diary entry, May 9, 1940, John Simon Papers, Oxford University, Simon 12.

13 ". . . gesture of irritation": Nicolson, ed., *Diaries*, May 7, 1940, 76.

14 ". . . in Berlin": Commander Sir Archibald Southby, Epsom.

14 ". . . get away with it": John Colville, *The Fringes of Power* (Boston, 1985), May 7, 1940, 117.

15 ". . . I meant trouble": Amery, *My Political Life*, 3:360.

17 judged Harold Macmillan: Harold Macmillan, *The Blast of War* (London, 1968), 56.

17 fifty years: Amery, *My Political Life*, 3:365.

17 his history of the war: Winston Churchill, *The Second World War*, vol. 1, *The Gathering Storm* (Boston, 1948), 659.

17 "the best PM in sight": Dilkes, ed., *Cadogan*, May 8, 1940, 277.

18 ". . . support from the Conservatives": Typescript, Attlee Papers, Churchill College, Cambridge University, ATL 1/16.

18 Dalton did not: Quoted in Olson, *Troublesome Young Men*, 296.

18 Salisbury warned them: Nicolson, ed., *Diaries*, May 8, 1940, 78.

18 committee disagreed: David Freeman, "Who Really Put Churchill in Office?" abstract of Larry L. Witherell, "Lord Salisbury's Watching Committee and the Fall of Neville Chamberlain, May 1940," *English Historical Review*, November 2001, Churchill Centre, www.winstonchurchill.org/support/the-churchill-centre

/publications/finest-hour/issues-109-to-144/no-114/651-witherell-larry-l-qlord
-salisburys-watching-committee-and-the-fall-of-neville-chamberlain-may-1940q.

19 "had even brigade training": Quoted in Herbert Morrison, *Hansard,*
"Conduct of War," May 8, 1940, vol. 360.

20 answered the call: Ibid., Boothby, "Draft Outline."

20 ". . . bells of Criccieth": "Lloyd George After 50 Years," *Christian Science
Monitor,* April 16, 1940.

21 "absolutely devastating": Quoted in William Manchester, *The Last Lion:
William Spencer Churchill, Alone, 1932–1940* (Boston, 1988), 659.

21 leadership and fire: Cripps, diary entry, May 8, 1940, Cripps Papers,
SC5/1.

21 ". . . stick to the ship": Manchester, *Alone,* 659.

22 ". . . had ever taken part": Amery, *My Political Life,* 3:368.

22 Labour's Hugh Dalton: Olson, *Troublesome Young Men,* 302.

22 grant him an audience: Quinton Hogg explained this to his father, Doug-
las Hogg, Lord Hailsham, who then wrote a letter explaining his son's conduct to
the Prime Minister; Hailsham to Chamberlain, May 10, 1940, Chamberlain Collection, NC7/11/33/73.

23 a Chamberlain loyalist: Henry Channon, diary entry, May 8, 1940,
quoted in Gilbert, *Admiralty,* 1252.

23 ". . . pleasant moment": Amery, *My Political Life,* 3:368.

23 "Rule Britannia": Josiah Wedgewood, *Memoirs of a Fighting Life* (London, 1941), 244.

23 ". . . surging around him": Robert Boothby, *I Fight to Live* (London, 1947),
218.

24 cloudless once again: Antony Beevor, *The Second World War* (Boston,
2012).

Chapter 2

25 preferred Halifax: As Hugh Dalton reported to Butler (and Butler to Halifax, May 9, 1940), Halifax Papers, A4.410.16.

25 not serve under either: Quoted in Olson, *Troublesome Young Men,* 309.

25 become prime minister: As reported by Brendan Bracken to Beaverbrook. See A. J. P. Taylor, *Beaverbrook* (New York, 1972), 409.

25 "would soonest serve under": Amery, *My Political Life,* 3:370.

25 at least to discuss: Attlee to Lawrence Thompson, July 19, 1965, Herbert
Morrison Papers, London School of Economics, Morrison 8/2.

26 before the debate began: John Simon, diary entry, May 8, 1940, Simon
Papers, Simon 11.

26 after it had finished: Maurice Hankey to Chamberlain, May 9, 1940,
Hankey Papers, Churchill College, Cambridge University, 4/32.

27 ". . . **majority deserts us**": Churchill, *Gathering Storm*, 661.

27 **had been in vain:** Ibid.

27 ". . . **were fairly satisfied**": Colville, *Fringes of Power*, May 8, 1940, 119–120.

27 **Paris and Berlin:** Dilkes, ed., *Cadogan*, May 9, 1940, 277.

27 **the prime minister flat:** See, among many, Amery, *My Political Life*, 3:370–372; Blake, "How Churchill Became Prime Minister," 257–273.

28 **replace Chamberlain as prime minister:** Nicolson, ed., *Diaries*, May 9, 1940, 80.

28 **under Halifax, if necessary:** Cripps, diary entry, May 9, 1940, Cripps Papers, SC5/1.

28 ". . . **must be formed**": Eden, diary entry, May 9, 1940, Lord Avon Papers, Birmingham University, 20/1/13–20A.

28 **both had survived them:** Beaverbrook to Chamberlain, May 8, 1940, Chamberlain Papers, NC7/11/33/22.

28 **spot for himself:** Taylor, *Beaverbrook*, 409.

28 **Amery should become prime minister:** Amery, *My Political Life*, 3:370. He told it to Leslie Hore-Belisha, formerly Chamberlain's minister of war.

29 **a prime minister who could:** Churchill, *Gathering Storm*, 555.

29 **post-debate pessimism:** Ibid.

29 **wanted him to take it:** Halifax, diary entry, May 9, 1940, Halifax Papers, A7.8.3–12 facs.

29 ". . . **servants and butlers**": D. J. Dutton, "Lord Halifax," *Oxford Dictionary of National Biography*.

30 ". . . **accept the Premiership**": Colville, *Fringes of Power*, May 10, 1940, 122.

30 **honorary Prime Minister:** R. A. Butler, *The Art of the Possible* (London, 1971), 94.

31 ". . . **next thousand years**": Quoted in Beevor, *Second World War*, 80.

31 **undersecretary Alexander Cadogan:** Dilkes, ed., *Cadogan*, May 9, 1940, 280.

31 ". . . **to one who couldn't**": Robert Boothby to Churchill, May 9, 1940, Churchill Papers, Churchill College, Cambridge University, Chartwell Trust, CHAR 2.

31 **reached similar conclusions:** Olson, *Troublesome Young Men*, 308.

32 ". . . **make plain his willingness**": Eden, diary entry, May 9, 1940, Avon Papers.

32 ". . . **don't say anything**": Anthony Eden, *The Reckoning: The Memoirs of Anthony Eden, Earl of Avon* (London, 1965), 96–97. There is a one-page memo in the Beaverbrook Papers at the House of Lords Record Office, BBK D/489, "Kingsley Wood Question and Answer," in which Wood is quoted as saying that Chamberlain knew from the outset of the war that he would have to step down and that he always favored Churchill as his successor. However, this statement contradicts all other evidence. With regard to keeping silent, apparently Churchill's PPS, Bracken,

had offered the same advice as Wood before lunch, when Beaverbrook visited. See Taylor, *Beaverbrook*, 409.

32 decisive battle of the war: Clement Davies Papers, I/2/8.

34 MP remembered: Interview with James Griffiths, January 12, 1968, Herbert Morrison Papers.

34 ". . . with a tough tongue": Ibid., Interview with Kingsley Martin.

34 ". . . sharp, concise": Ibid., Interview with Miss F. Jones.

34 strategic government committees: See, most recently, Robert Crowcroft, *Attlee's War: World War II and the Making of a Labour Leader* (London, 2011).

34 Downing Street that afternoon: Lord Camrose, "Notes of a Conversation with Mr. Neville Chamberlain," quoted in Gilbert, *Admiralty*, 1261.

35 "quite sincere": Quoted by Kenneth Harris, *Attlee* (London, 1982), 174.

35 ". . . orating, Winston": Quoted in Manchester, *Alone*, 668.

35 ". . . have you either": Harris, *Attlee*.

35 ". . . not be Prime Minister?": Colville, *Fringes of Power*, May 11, 1940, 123.

35 ". . . of Armistice Day": Churchill, *Gathering Storm*, 663.

36 ". . . less honorary Prime Minister": Halifax, diary entry, May 10, 1940, Halifax Papers, A.7.8.3–12.

36 run the British Army: Eden, diary entry, May 9, 1940, Avon Papers.

37 conversation many years later: Quoted in Gilbert, *Finest Hour*, 306.

37 intention be known: Amery, *My Political Life*, 3:373.

37 ". . . seemed for some time": Eden, diary entry, May 10, 1940, Avon Papers.

38 11:30 Cabinet: John Simon, quoted by Eden, *Reckoning*, 97–98.

38 ". . . course of the day": Nicolson, ed., *Diaries*, May 10, 1940, 82.

38 ". . . situation was calmer": Halifax, diary entry, May 10, 1940, Halifax Papers.

38 ". . . government position": Eden, diary entry, May 10, 1940, Avon Papers.

39 ". . . energies to this end": Harris, *Attlee*, 175.

39 ". . . himself to resignation": "Prime Minister's Consultations" and "From Our Political Correspondent," *Yorkshire Post*, May 10, 1940.

40 one of Chamberlain's secretaries: Ms recollection, Attlee Papers, Cambridge, ATLE 1/16.

40 ". . . to do so that evening": War Cabinet Minutes, Cabinet Papers, 65/7, May 10, 1940.

40 where there was oil: Halifax, diary entry, May 10, 1940, Halifax Papers.

40 "the obvious man": J. W. Wheeler Bennett, *King George VI: His Life and Reign* (London, 1958), 444.

40 ". . . man to send for": Gilbert, *Admiralty*, 1281.

41 ". . . and for this trial": Winston Churchill, *The Second World War*, vol. 2, *Their Finest Hour* (Boston, 1949), 667.

41 ". . . Labour and Liberal Parties": Ibid., 665.

41 **"full of fire and determination":** Wheeler-Bennett, *George VI*, 443–444.

43 **". . . there is no survival":** *Hansard*, May 13, 1940.

CHAPTER 3

47 **". . . invasion of the Low Countries":** Nancy Dugdale, wife of Thomas Dugdale, MP, quoted in Andrew Roberts, *Eminent Churchillians* (London, 1994), 146.

47 **". . . Party & in the country":** Sir Patrick Spens to Chamberlain, September 5, 1940, Chamberlain Papers, NC7/11/33/162.

48 **the former prime minister:** Colville, *Fringes of Power*, May 10, 1940, 122. Those present in addition to Butler were John Colville, Chamberlain's private secretary; Alexander Cadogan, a permanent undersecretary at the Foreign Office; and Butler's PPS, Sir Henry "Chips" Channon, MP for Southend.

48 **for more than a year:** As Andrew Roberts has shown in *Eminent Churchillians*, "The Tories Versus Churchill," 137–210.

48 **"to hold":** Maurice Hankey to Samuel Hoare, May 12, 1940, Hankey Papers, 4/32.

48 **complained the day after that:** Halifax, diary entries, May 11–13, 1940, Halifax Papers.

48 **". . . know they can't be":** Chamberlain to Mary Crownshield Endicott, May 11, 1940, Chamberlain Papers, NC1/20/1/198.

48 **"was clearly hating it all":** Eden, diary entry, May 12, 1940, Avon Papers.

48 **". . . wanted again later":** Chamberlain, reporting on his conversation with Kingsley Wood to Mary Crownshield Endicott, October 1, 1940, Chamberlain Papers, NC1/20/1/202.

49 **stood for it:** Stafford Cripps, manuscript of an article, probably written for the *Tribune*, Cripps Papers, SC35/3.

49 **". . . Government was formed":** Sir Richard Acland to David Lloyd George, May 17, 1940, Lloyd George Papers, LG G/1.

49 **". . . a very bad one":** Cripps, diary entry, May 13, 1940, Cripps Papers, SC5/1.

49 **". . . throw it at others":** Quoted in Taylor, *Beaverbrook*, 327.

49 **magnate into the Cabinet:** Halifax, diary entry, May 15, 1940, Halifax Papers.

49 **after his appointment:** Halifax, diary entry, May 12, 1940, Halifax Papers.

50 **". . . contribute much else":** Chamberlain Papers, NC7/9/82.

50 **". . . this arrangement":** Churchill, *Finest Hour*, 9.

50 **". . . drinking again":** Interview with Philip Noel-Baker, Herbert Morrison Papers, 6/1.

50 **". . . slow and unimperative":** Ben Pimlott, ed., *The Second World War Diary of Hugh Dalton: 1940–45* (London, 1986), diary entry, June 18, 1940, 42.

50 **". . . represent the party":** Quoted in Donoughue and Jones, *Morrison*, 274.

50 reasons, for many years: In 1931 Morrison had wanted to join the National Government led by the Judas Iscariot of the Labour Party, Ramsay MacDonald, whom Bevin despised; he opposed trade-union participation on boards of nationalized or municipalized industries, which Bevin strongly favored; he was a party man, whereas Bevin was a trade-union man.

50 snapped in reply: See, for example, "Not While I'm Alive, He Ain't," part 1, presented by Brian Walden, BBC News, *The Westminster Hour*, March 31, 2002, transcript, http://news.bbc.co.uk/2/hi/programmes/the_westminster_hour /1899102.stm. This is a well-known quotation, however, and can be found elsewhere.

51 his immediate left: Dilkes, ed., *Cadogan*, May 13, 1940, 282, with a seating diagram.

52 ". . . would go to France": Ibid., May 16, 1940, 284.

53 ". . . German Government": Halifax to Brocket, March 12, 1940, Papers of Foreign Secretaries, National Archive, UK, FO 800/326. See also the *Telegraph*, August 30, 2008.

53 Saturday, May 25: Quoted in Ian Kershaw, *Fateful Choices: Ten Decisions That Changed the World, 1940–1941* (London, 2007), 32. The other great secondary source for these discussions is John Lukacs, *Five Days in London, May 1940* (New Haven, CT, 1999).

54 ". . . our own Empire": National Archive, UK, Confidential Annex, May 26, 1940, 3.

54 ". . . could never accept": Ibid.

54 ". . . had her way": Ibid.

55 ". . . tamely were finished": Ibid., May 28, 1940, 4 P.M. meeting, 4.

55 ". . . Nazi tyranny": Ibid., May 27, 1940, 4:30 P.M. meeting, 5.

55 ". . . think and reason": Halifax, diary entry, May 27, 1940, Halifax Papers.

56 ". . . to run out": National Archive, UK, Confidential Annex, May 28, 1940, 4 P.M. meeting, 3.

56 ". . . ultimate capitulation": Ibid., 4.

57 ". . . become a slave state": Pimlott, ed., *Diary of Hugh Dalton*, May 28, 1940, 27–29.

57 ". . . blood upon the ground": Ibid.

57 ". . . me on the back": Churchill, *Finest Hour*, 100.

58 ". . . useful purpose": National Archive, UK, Confidential Annex, May 27, 1940, 4:30 P.M. meeting, 2.

58 ". . . affect our independence": Ibid., May 28, 1940, 4 P.M. meeting, 3.

Chapter 4

61 will become apparent: It could be said that Churchill as minister of defense had departmental responsibilities, but as the responsibility was to prosecute the war, this doesn't count.

62 **"a spoilt child":** Alex Danchev and Daniel Todman, eds., *War Diaries, 1939–1945: Field Marshal Lord Alanbrooke* (Los Angeles, 2001), September 8, 1942, 319, and August 19, 1944, 444.

63 **across from St. James's Park:** On two occasions the War Cabinet met at Dollis Hill in northwest London under the Post Office Research Station. But that was much less centrally located and much less convenient.

63 **". . . I'll direct the war":** Richard Holmes, *Churchill's Bunker: The Secret Headquarters in Wartime London* (New Haven, CT, 2009), 2.

65 **". . . about 34,000 'Allies'":** Dilkes, ed., *Cadogan*, May 26–June 1, 1940, 290–293.

66 **morale on the home front:** Max Hastings, *Winston's War: Churchill 1940–1945* (New York, 2011), 40–44; Paul Addison, *The Road to 1945* (London, 1982), 107–109.

66 **conquests thus far:** Hastings, *Winston's War*, 40–44; John Lukacs, *The Duel* (New Haven, CT, 1990), 106–130.

66 **". . . their finest hour":** Again, some scholars suggest an alternative view: the German Army would take months to digest its victories on the continent, so an attempted invasion was not imminent; British armed forces were better situated and better equipped to defend the island than to wage war anywhere else. See, e.g., Hastings, *Winston's War*, 65.

67 **". . . be done today":** "F. A. L." to Prime Minister, June 30, 1940, National Archive, UK, CAB 120/442.

67 **". . . year to complete":** Ibid., "The Employment of Volunteer Labour for Making Fields and Open Spaces Unfit for Aircraft Landings," unsigned note. Illegible to General Ismay, July 26, 1940.

67 **". . . for firing":** Churchill to Eden, July 3, 1940, Churchill Papers, CHAR 20/2A.

67 **uniforms to confuse them:** Ismay to Major General F. G. Beaumont-Nesbitt, July 3, 1940, National Archive, UK, CAB 120/445.

67 **". . . lunatics and wild animals?":** Duncan Sandys to Findlater Stewart, August 8, 1940, National Archive, UK, CAB 120/468.

67 **". . . question of wild animals":** Ibid., Rootham to Sandys, August 26, 1940.

68 **". . . week's food":** Maurice Petherick to Churchill, July 3, 1940, Churchill Papers, PREM 4/37/8.

68 **advised the prime minister:** Alexander Murray, Master of Elibank, to Churchill, June 23, 1940, Churchill Papers, PREM 4/37/5A.

68 **". . . work of defense":** Leo Amery, untitled paper, June 16, 1940, Amery Papers, Churchill College, Cambridge University, 2/1/31, file 1.

68 **landing on the east coast:** Josiah Wedgewood to Churchill, May 21, 1940, Churchill Papers, CHAR 20/8.

68 on the southwest coast: Tom Horabin to Churchill, July 1940, National Archive, UK, CAB20/438.

68 ". . . destruction of the fleet": "Bobbety" [Lord Cranborne] to Churchill, June 28, 1940, Churchill Papers, PREM 4/37/5A.

68 ". . . the salt sea": Churchill to Wedgwood, July 5, 1940, Churchill Papers, CHAR 20/8.

68 ". . . burn and forget": Walter Eliot to Churchill, June 25, 1940, and Churchill to Eliot, June 28, 1940, Churchill Papers, CHAR 20/1.

69 ". . . under the Minister of Labor, Ernest Bevin": Clement Attlee, "Broadcast of the Lord Privy Seal," Attlee Papers, Oxford, dep. 1.

70 without becoming a member of Parliament: Interview with Mrs. D. Robinson, private secretary to Labour Party Secretary J. S. Middleton, March 11, 1968, Herbert Morrison Papers, Interviews.

70 ". . . who saved them": Quoted in Peter Weiler, *Ernest Bevin* (Manchester, UK, 1993), 103.

70 ". . . community as a whole": Speech at the Rotary Club Luncheon by the Rt. Hon. Ernest Bevin, MP, November 20, 1940, Churchill Papers, PREM 4/83/A.

71 ". . . rest of the departments": Weiler, *Bevin*, 104.

71 ". . . under war conditions": "Report of Speech by the Right Hon. Ernest Bevin at Theatre Royal, Norwich," February 4, 1945, Ernest Bevin Papers, Churchill College, Cambridge University, 4/7.

72 plowed forward: Bevin's successes and those of his colleagues contradict the argument, advanced by a few historians, that Britain's wartime economy proved significantly less productive and efficient than Germany's. See Correlli Barnett, *The Audit of War* (London, 1986), which argues for British incompetence, and David Edgerton, *Britain's War Machine* (London, 2011), which argues persuasively against this view.

73 ". . . not appreciate him": George R. I. [Rex Imperator] to Churchill, May 10, 1940, Churchill Papers, CHAR 20/11.

73 ". . . almost nonexistent": Quoted in Kenneth Young, *Churchill and Beaverbrook* (New York, 1966), 29.

73 ". . . part of their relationship": Quoted in Anne Chisolm and Michael Davie, *Beaverbrook: A Life* (London, 1992), 446.

74 stayed for dinner: Taylor, *Beaverbrook*, 410.

74 ". . . always buoyant": Churchill, *Finest Hour*, 178.

74 ". . . get along home": Chisolm and Davie, *Beaverbrook*, 378.

74 loved him: Taylor, *Beaverbrook*, 424.

75 ". . . listen to them talking": W. P. Crozier, *Off the Record: Political Interviews, 1933–1944*, edited by A. J. P. Taylor (London, 1973), interview with Lord Beaverbrook, August 24, 1940, 197. This book consists of the interviews W. P. Crozier, editor of the *Manchester Guardian*, conducted with leading British political figures—but which he did not publish at the time.

75 Battle of Britain: Tom Driberg, *Beaverbrook: A Study in Power and Frustration* (London, 1956), 256.

75 "... shortage of aircraft": Quoted in Taylor, *Beaverbrook*, 418.

76 rate of production: Chisolm and Davie, *Beaverbrook*, 259.

76 "... call from Lord Beaverbrook": Quoted in Taylor, *Beaverbrook*, 423.

76 it quadrupled: Chisolm and Davie, *Beaverbrook*, 395.

76 twice that of Germany's: Roy Jenkins, *Churchill* (London, 2002), 633. This would seem to represent yet another nail in the coffin of the argument about British inefficiency during the war.

76 all-time low: Taylor, *Beaverbrook*, 417–421.

77 "... ability and force of character": Ibid., 456.

77 fellow Cabinet minister: Ibid., 425.

77 "... himself, Beaverbrook and Ernest Bevin": Unknown to Violet Bonham Carter, June 15, 1964, Violet Bonham Carter Papers, New Bodleian Library, Oxford University, Box 203, 103.

77 entire country: Hastings, *Winston's War*, 64. At Dunkirk, Britain had lost 700 tanks, 2,500 guns (1,200 field and bigger guns; 1,300 antiaircraft and antitank guns), and 120,000 vehicles. See George Thomas, *Vote of Censure* (New York, 1968), 48.

77 "... one district to another": Crozier, *Off the Record*, interview with Anthony Eden, July 27, 1940, 184.

78 pull things together: Halifax, diary entry, September 28, 1940, Halifax Papers.

78 last-ditch defense: Alanbrooke would successfully extract them later, a second, uncelebrated Dunkirk.

78 "... by night and by day": Eden to Churchill, June 25, 1940, Avon Papers, AP20/8/24.

78 "the attempt was coming": Crozier, *Off the Record*, interview with Eden.

78 "commence ... Monday, July 1: "Extract from Conclusions of War Cabinet Meeting," Tuesday, June 25, 1940, National Archive, UK, CAB 120/439.

78 who took them in: Ibid., "Evacuation of Civil Population," n.d.

78 "... turn the Germans out": Ibid., "If the Invader Comes," n.d.

79 "... orders of the enemy": Burgis Papers, Churchill College, Cambridge University, BRGS 2/1, July 26, 1940.

79 "on or about July 8": Zaleski to Halifax, June 29, 1940, National Archive, UK, CAB 120/438.

79 "... enemy to move": "Summarized Notes of Meeting Held by Prime Minister in Upper War Room at 1700, Sunday, 30th June 1940," National Archive, UK, CAB 120/443.

79 marshaling yards: War Cabinet Minutes, National Archive, UK, Confidential Annex, July 3, 1940.

79 "... **cut from the sea**": "General Ismay. Following for C.O.S. Committee," National Archive, UK, CAB 120/438.

79 Turks had warned Halifax: Dilkes, ed., *Cadogan*, July 1, 1940, 308.

79 "... **patrolling forces**": "Invasion. Minute by the Prime Minister," to C.-in-C., Home Forces, C.I.G.S., General Ismay," July 10, 1940, Churchill Papers, CHAR 23/4.

79 "... **Straits of Dover**": National Archive, UK, Confidential Annex, July 9, 1940.

79 reinforcement by sea: Churchill to First Lord, First Sea Lord, V.C.N.S., July 25, 1940, National Archive, UK, CAB 120/443.

79 "... **small coastal raids**": "Memorandum on the General Policy for the Development of Offensive Operations," National Archive, UK, CAB 118/35.

81 "... **set Europe ablaze**": Pimlott, ed., *Diary of Hugh Dalton*, July 22, 1940, 62.

81 "... **subsequently ignited**": National Archive, UK, Confidential Annex, August 5, 1940.

81 "... **means of victory**": Burgis Papers, 2/2, August 16, 1940.

81 "... **hankering after them**": Dilkes, ed., *Cadogan*, July 2, 1940, 309.

81 "... **the same object**": A. J. Sylvester to Lloyd George, July 2, 1940, Lloyd George Papers.

81 "... **reasonable conditions**": Ian Gilmour, "Richard Austen Butler," *Oxford Dictionary of National Biography*.

81 small peace party in the House of Commons: R. J. Davies to Butler, August 1, 1940, Butler Papers, Trinity College, Cambridge University, RAB E3.

82 "... **without giving anything away**": Ibid.

82 chastisement would suffice: Churchill to Halifax, June 25, 1940, Churchill Collection, PREM 4/100/8.

CHAPTER 5

83 positively pro-German: This was part of the litany reported to David Lloyd George by his principal private secretary, A. J. Sylvester, on July 2, 1940. See A. J. Sylvester Report, July 2, 1940, Lloyd George Papers.

84 two destroyers: For this dark episode, see, among many, Churchill, *Finest Hour*, 232.

84 "... **Operation against England**": Beevor, *Second World War*, 126.

84 rather endearingly: Quoted in Jonathan Schneer, *The Thames: England's River* (London, 2005), 200.

84 "... **he's crying**": Quoted in Martin Gilbert, *The Churchill War Papers*, vol. 2, *Never Surrender* (New York, 1995), 789.

85 "... **water, electricity**": Burgis Papers, 2/2, September 9, 1940. I have "translated" his shorthand where I am able to understand it and have corrected his punctuation.

86   ... **"civil population & Egypt"**: Ibid., 2/2, September 11, 1940.

86   **"Winston's judgment"**: Eden, diary entry, August 7, 1940, Avon Papers.

86   **". . . Cooper [minister of information]"**: Colville, *Fringes of Power*, August 11, 1940, 220.

86   **Attlee as well**: Eden, diary entry, August 19, 1940, Avon Papers.

86   **himself, Beaverbrook and Eden**: Ibid., August 21, 1940.

86   **". . . appeared to be tired"**: Ibid., September 6, 1940.

86   **". . . felt so lonely"**: Ibid., August 21, 1940.

86   **". . . dread in my heart"**: Ibid., December 18, 1940.

86   **Chamberlain's health**: A. J. Sylvester Report, June 3, 1940, Lloyd George Papers.

86   **". . . operation to his inside"**: Halifax to Hoare, July 30, 1940, Papers of Foreign Secretaries, National Archive, UK, FO 800/323.

87   **". . . out in politics"**: Crozier, *Off the Record*, interview with Beaverbrook, August 24, 1940, 198.

87   **". . . have a set-back"**: Churchill to Chamberlain, August 31, 1940, Chamberlain Papers, NC7/9/94.

87   **". . . attending to anything else"**: Chamberlain to Halifax, September 23, 1940, Halifax Papers, A4.410.17.

87   **ascendency to be permanent**: Quoted in Feiling, *Chamberlain*, 450.

87   **". . . These are great days"**: Churchill to Chamberlain, September 24, 1940, Chamberlain Papers, NC7/9/98.

87   **". . . ought to have done"**: Chamberlain to Simon, October 6, 1940, Simon Papers, MS Simon 87/5.

88   **about the changes**: Churchill to Halifax, September 29, 1940, Churchill Papers, CHAR 2/395.

88   **". . . argument had any force"**: "Party Meeting at the Caxton Hall, . . . " Conservative Party Archive, Whip 2/5.

89   **". . . marked him out"**: Colville, *Fringes of Power*, December 12, 1940, 309.

89   **"Winston [went] bust"**: A. J. P. Taylor, ed., *Lloyd George: Twelve Essays* (New York, 1971).

89   **". . . lesser alternatives"**: Churchill to Halifax, December 18, 1940, Halifax Papers, A4.410.19.

89   **". . . odious thought"**: Ibid., December 19, 1940.

90   **". . . discreet and adequate"**: Ibid., Halifax to Churchill, December 20, 1940.

90   **". . . restraining W.C."**: Eden, diary entry, December 18, 1940, Avon Papers.

90   **". . . our Ambassador to the United States"**: Halifax, diary entry, December 20, 1940, Halifax Papers.

90   **". . . opinion than I should"**: Ibid.

90   **". . . relieved at your decision"**: Churchill to Eden, September 10, 1941, and Eden's penciled reply on same page, September 11, 1941, National Archive, UK, PREM 4/100/8.

91 "... **half beautiful woman**": These quotations can be found on the Wikipedia entry for "Anthony Eden Hat," accessed June 17, 2014.

92 **streak of principle:** See David Dutton, *Anthony Eden: A Life and Reputation* (London, 1997); Robert Rhodes James, *Anthony Eden: A Biography* (London, 1986); D. R. Thorpe, *Eden: The Life and Times of Anthony Eden, First Earl of Avon, 1897–1977* (London, 2011).

CHAPTER 6

95 "**astonishingly unassailable**": Walter Monckton to Cripps, January 20, 1941, Stafford Cripps Papers, SC5/2.

95 **loved champagne:** Amery to Hoare, February 14, 1941, Amery Papers, 2/1/32.

96 **pages noiselessly:** Mary T. G. Thompson, "Secretary to Churchill," in Charles Eade, ed., *Churchill, by His Contemporaries* (London, 1955), 235–239.

96 "... **produce his socks!**": Eden, diary entry, April 24, 1942, Avon Papers.

97 **fearless sense of style:** Material on Churchill's routine are taken from Martin Gilbert, *Winston Churchill's War Leadership* (New York, 2004), 9–18, and John Keegan, *Winston Churchill* (London, 2007), 130–132.

98 "... **check waistcoats**": "Luncheon with Mr. Churchill ... Between October 1939 and March 1954," Charles Eade Papers, Churchill College, Cambridge University, 2/2.

98 "... **lighting my fire**": Eden, diary entry, October 10, 1941, Avon Papers.

98 "... **shpeak to me in the morning**": R. A. "Rab" Butler, diary entry, "A Visit to Chequers," March 11, 1943, Butler Papers, RAB G15.

99 "... **little lime juice**": Churchill to Woolton, July 14, 1940, Churchill Papers, CHAR 20/2A.

99 "... **another sardine**": Eden, diary entry, September 11, 1941, Avon Papers.

99 "... **dictatorial publicity**": Churchill to Woolton, February 25, 1941, Woolton Papers, Bodleian Library, Oxford, Ms Woolton 3.

99 "... **great difficulty**": Ibid., Woolton to Churchill, February 26, 1941.

99 **wholesale arrests:** Ibid., Churchill to Woolton, March 2, 1941.

99 **in their troubles:** See, for example, Churchill to Alexander, June 2, 1941, Alexander Papers, Churchill College, Cambridge University, 5/6; Churchill to Morrison, May 29, 1942, Morrison Papers, 8/2; Churchill to Bevin, September 24 (?), 1942, Bevin Papers, Bevin 3/1; Churchill to Duff Cooper, June 12, 1940, Churchill Papers, PREM 4/83/1A.

100 **mollify the 1922 Committee:** The file of papers dealing with this incident includes Churchill to Bevin, May 4, 1941, in which the Prime Minister asks his Minister of Labor, almost plaintively, "What am I to say [to the 1922 Committee]?": Churchill Papers, PREM 4/83/1A.

101 "... **view of Cabinet against**": War Cabinet Minutes, June 15, 1942, National Archive, UK, CAB 195/1.

101 **wildest schemes:** D. R. Thorpe, "Anthony Eden," *Oxford Dictionary of National Biography.*

102 **cabled it to Britain's leader:** Jenkins, *Churchill,* 666.

103 "... **President might say**": War Cabinet Minutes, Burgis Papers, Burgis 2/5, August 25, 1941. Halifax retained the right to participate in War Cabinet meetings whenever he returned to Britain. Mackenzie King was the Canadian Liberal prime minister.

103 "... **any foreign wars**": Roosevelt said this while campaigning in Boston, October 30, 1940.

103 "... **good sense**": See The Churchill Centre's website at winstonchurchill .org, speeches, 1941.

104 "**most useful**": Eden, diary entry, December 3, 1941, Avon Papers.

104 "... **leave these shores**": Eden, diary entry, December 4, 1941, Avon Papers.

104 "... **and 300 aircraft**": Danchev and Todman, eds., *Alanbrooke,* December 4, 1941, 207.

105 "... **accept last night!**": Ibid., and December 5, 1941, 208.

105 "... **been gained**": Eden, *Reckoning,* 329.

105 "... **instead of 1649**": Morrison to Simon, March 27, 1942, Simon Papers, MS Simon 89.

106 "... **know any better**": Woolton, diary entry, October 24, 1942, Woolton Papers, MS Woolton 2.

106 **use the quote:** Interview with Anthony Eden, September 25, 1968, Morrison Papers, LSE, Morrison 6/1.

106 "... **colleagues and himself**": "Conservative Private Members (1922) Committee, Minutes of a Meeting Held in Room 14 at 12:30 on 22nd Jany," Conservative Party Archive, 1922/4.

106 **conscription of labor:** Sylvester to Lloyd George, January 10, 1941, Lloyd George Papers, LG/G/24/1.

106 "... **release on that account**": Beaverbrook to Churchill, January 3, 1941, Churchill Papers, CHAR 20/20.

106 "... **than anybody else**": "Max" to Alexander, undated note, Alexander Papers, AVAR 5/5.

106 "... **where he wants him**": Sylvester to Lloyd George, January 10, 1941, Lloyd George Papers, LG/G/24/1.

107 "... **affectionate devotion**": "Max" to Alexander, undated note, Alexander Papers, AVAR 5/6.

107 "... **Ministerial service**": Beaverbrook to Morrison, December 3, 1941, Morrison Papers, Morrison 8/2.

107 "... **speech you ever made**": Beaverbrook to Morrison, November 28, 1941, Beaverbrook Papers, BBK C/218b.

107 ". . . you as Prime Minister": Ibid., Beaverbrook to Morrison, November 23, 1942.

107 ". . . determine to build it": Beaverbrook to Bevin, November 22, 1941, Bevin Papers, Bevin 3/1.

107 ". . . platform of the Government itself": Ibid., Bevin to Beaverbrook, November 24, 1941.

107 Beaverbrook Papers, however: Beaverbrook to Attlee, December 26, 1943, Beaverbrook Papers, BBK/C/16.

108 ". . . Beware of flattery": Quoted by Taylor in *Beaverbrook*, 446.

108 Deidesheimer Hofstuck 1937: Churchill to Beaverbrook, June 10, 1941, Churchill Papers, CHAR 2/95.

108 ". . . exhilarating gift": Gilbert, *Finest Hour*, 1102, fn 5.

108 ". . . he will alter it": Sylvester to Lloyd George, January 8, 1941, Lloyd George Papers, LG/G/24/1.

108 "'. . . the great one'": Ibid., Sylvester to Lloyd George, March 6, 1941.

108 Production grumbled: Leslie Hore-Belisha, diary entry, March 16, 1942, Hore-Belisha Papers, Churchill College, Cambridge University, HOBE 1/9. Hore-Belisha was recording a conversation with Sir William Rootes.

108 friend, Lord Trenchard: Nicolson, ed., *Nicolson*, June 17, 1941, 172.

108 ". . . moods irritating": Eden, diary entry, July 9, 1941, Avon Papers.

108 ". . . pieces himself": Eden, diary entry, March 7, 1942, Avon Papers.

108 May 1, 1941, War Cabinet meeting: Dilkes, ed., *Cadogan*, May 1, 1941, 375.

108 ". . . weakness to recede": Ibid., May 26, 1941, 381.

109 ". . . irascibility & rudeness . . .": Quoted in Gilbert, *Finest Hour*, 587–588.

109 ". . . about this attitude": Sylvester to Lloyd George, March 6, 1941, Lloyd George Papers, LG/G/24/1.

109 ". . . we can avoid it": Alexander to Churchill, July 29, 1940, Alexander Papers, AVAR 5/4.

109 ". . . brutally with him": Woolton, diary entry, March 25, 1943, Woolton Papers, Ms. Woolton 3.

109 ". . . stand up to him": Crozier, *Off the Record*, interview with Herbert Morrison, May 28, 1942, 324.

109 "harangue": Hankey, diary entry, April 28, 1941, Hankey Papers, HNKY 1/7.

109 "time by the War Cabinet": Ibid., Hankey, diary entry, May 1, 1941.

110 ". . . aspects of military situation": Eden, diary entry, April 14, 1941, Avon Papers.

110 ". . . unnecessarily long Cabinets": Attlee to Churchill, January 19, 1945, Churchill Papers, CHUR 2/4.

111 ". . . than to the Germans": A. J. P. Taylor, *The Second World War* (London, 1975), 106.

111 "... **that were lacking**": *The Times*, November 5, 1941.

112 "... **that is a mistake**": Unidentified news clipping, November 17, 1941, Churchill Papers, CHAR 20/29A.

112 "... **teach him to spell**": Churchill to Sinclair, November 22, 1941, Churchill Papers, CHAR20/29A.

112 "... **actions and decisions**": Woolton, diary entry, December 6, 1941, Woolton Papers, Ms Woolton 2. The Conservative MP was Alan Lennox-Boyd, the Cabinet minister Woolton.

112 "... **anti-Churchill**": *The Star*, December 16, 1942, quoted in Kevin Jefferys, ed., *Labour and the Wartime Coalition: From the Diary of James Chuter Ede, 1941–1945* (London, 1987), December 16, 1942, 32.

112 "... **manager of the war effort**": *Daily Mirror*, November 14, 1941.

112 "... **would not improve**": *The Times*, June 10, 1941, Churchill Papers, CHAR 20/62.

112 "... **pend both in the War Cabinet and the Administration**": "Opposition Grows in House and Country; Churchill Contemplates Big Cabinet Shake-Up," *Cavalcade*, November 1, 1941, Cripps Papers, SC24/4.

113 "... **something serious**": Bower to Amery, January 1, 1942, Amery Papers, AMEL 2/1/34.

CHAPTER 7

116 **electrical trades**: See Hugh Armstrong Clegg, *A History of British Trade Unions Since 1889*, vol. 2 (Oxford, 1994).

116 **"parrot food"**: Kevin Jefferys, ed., *Ede*, November 22, 1942, 110.

117 "... **vices I admire**": Quoted in Clarke, *Cripps Version*, 355. I take Cripps's biographical details from this study.

117 "... **2,000 years ago?**": "The Challenge of Christianity," Cripps Papers, Cripps 14.

117 **poor and oppressed**: Addison, *Road*, 205.

117 "... **goes God**": Quoted in Clarke, *Cripps Version*, xiv.

118 **generosity and rectitude**: This did not prevent the authorities from opening a file on him and noting when he spoke to others on the far left, particularly Communists whose telephones they tapped. The file has been weeded, but the remnants may be read today at the National Archive in Kew, London. See National Archive, KV2/668.

119 "... **pity to move him**": Quoted in Clarke, *Cripps Version*, 310.

119 **getting rid of Chamberlain**: Ibid., 78.

119 **bringing down Chamberlain**: See Chapter 1.

120 "... **Utopia in one bound**": Quoted in the *Oxford Dictionary of National Biography* entry on Stafford Cripps, by Peter Clarke and Richard Toye.

120 "... **dares to talk**": Cripps to Monckton, February 2, 1941, Monckton Papers, New Bodleian Library, Oxford, Dep. Monckton Trustees 3.

121 "... **soothe him**": Butler to Cadogan, January 21, 1941, Butler Papers, RAB E3/3/164.

121 "... **relations with Moscow**": "Cripps, R. Stafford," report on October 29, 1940, National Archive, UK, KV2/668.

122 "... **facts of everyday life**": Cripps, "Confidential," December 3, 1940, Cripps Papers, SC 5/2/34.

122 "... **rule our own lives**": "Confidential," December 3, 1940, Cripps Papers, SC5/2.

122 "... **Russian people**": Quoted in Jenkins, *Churchill*, 660.

122 **Cripps's diplomatic career**: Clarke and Toye, *Oxford Dictionary of National Biography*, on Cripps.

123 "... **join the Government**": Cripps, diary entry, September 29, 1941, Cripps Papers, SC36/2.

123 "... **keen to win the war**": Ibid., September 29, 1941.

123 "... **person possible**": Ibid., October 1, 1941.

123 "... **Labour questions**": Ibid., September 29, 1941.

123 "... **should be produced**": Pimlott, ed., *Diary of Hugh Dalton*, January 29, 1942, 357.

123 "... **sake of a diplomatic career**": Cripps to Eden, September 14, 1941, Cripps Papers, SC35/2.

123 "... **on October 15**": Ibid., Cripps to Eden, October 1, 1941.

123 "... **position out here**": Ibid., Stafford Cripps to Isobel Cripps, November 5, 1941.

124 "... **wide sections of the public**": Quoted in Addison, *Road*, 134.

124 "... **somewhere to go!**": *Reynolds News*, July 20, 1941, Cripps Papers, SC36/2. This file contains typewritten copies of newspaper clippings.

124 "... **controversies of the war years**": Ibid., *News Chronicle*, January 3, 1942.

124 "... **talk of him as the next P.M.**": Ibid., *Reynolds News*, February 1, 1942.

124 "... **reflexively pro-Russian**": Jenny Lee to Isobel Cripps, August 15, 1941, Cripps Papers, SC34/4.

125 "... **Embassy to someone else? ...**": Monckton to Cripps, January 20, 1941, Cripps Papers, SC5/2.

125 "... **personnel and policies**": Ibid.

125 "... **fist into his face**": Eden, diary entry, November 14, 1941, Avon Papers.

125 "... **critical friend**": Clarke, *Cripps Version*, 259.

127 **present in the chamber**: Labour Press Service, February 4, 1942.

127 "**misfortunes still to come**": Sylvester to Lloyd George, January 30, 1942, Lloyd George Papers, LG/G/24/1.

127 "... **and say nothing**": Butler to Laithwaite, January 31, 1942, Butler Papers, RAB 914.

127 ". . . **display of applause**": Sylvester to Lloyd George, January 26, 1942, Lloyd George Papers, LG/G/24/1.

127 **including even Beaverbrook:** Beaverbrook Papers, BBK D/448. This file contains a memo written by Beaverbrook about the circumstances of his resignation from the government during the period, and includes references to his meetings with Cripps, who was soliciting advice about joining it.

128 ". . . **helpful critic**": See his letter to the prime minister. I am quoting from a copy in Beaverbrook's papers, BBK D/448.

128 ". . . **friendly advice**": Churchill to Cripps, January 31, 1942, Cripps Papers, SC 35/1.

128 ". . . **Nazi invaders**": Pamphlet repeating the broadcast entitled "Are We Going All Out?" Cripps Papers, SC 14.

129 ". . . **Cripps is the man!**": Sylvester to Lloyd George, February 9, 1942, Lloyd George Papers, LG/G/24/1.

130 ". . . **high places**": Ibid., Sylvester to Lloyd George, February 13, 1942.

130 ". . . **to break it**": Woolton, diary entry, February 13, 1942, Woolton Papers, Woolton 2.

130 ". . . **braver soldiers**": Hastings, *Winston's War*, 203.

130 "**heading for a downfall**": Woolton, diary entry, February 15, 1942, Woolton Papers, Woolton 2.

130 **private meeting of Labour MPs:** Sylvester to Lloyd George, February 19, 1942, Lloyd George Papers, LG/G/24/1.

131 ". . . **should be in the War Cabinet**": 1922 Committee Minutes, 1922/4, Conservative Party Archive. The meeting took place on February 18, but the minutes were not recorded until March 4, 1942.

131 **prominently Eden's and Beaverbrook's:** Sylvester to Lloyd George, February 12, 1942, Lloyd George Papers, LG/G/24/1. Cripps saw Bevin five times during February 15–18. Clarke, *Cripps Version*, 265.

131 "**Parliament is given over to intrigue**": Jefferys, ed., *Ede*, February 18, 1942, 51.

131 **if only to contain him:** Eden, diary entry, February 16, 1942, Avon Papers.

131 **bringing in Cripps:** Beaverbrook to Churchill, February 17, 1942, Churchill Papers, CHAR 20/52.

132 ". . . **Pope during the war**": Dilkes, ed., *Cadogan*, February 17, 1942, 435— but this is a note by Dilkes.

134 "**with great approval**": Hore-Belisha, diary entry, February 18, 1942, Hore-Belisha Papers, HOBE 1/9.

134 **10:30 that night:** Brendan Bracken and the Conservative Party chief whip also attended this meeting. Eden, diary entry, February 18, 1942, Avon Papers.

135 "**I never did**": Beaverbrook's account of his role in the reconstruction, Beaverbrook Papers, BBK D/448, 18.

CHAPTER 8

137 ". . . **regeneration of the war effort**": *Labour Discussion Notes*, March 1942, SC 24/4.

137 been dropped: George Thomson, *Vote of Censure* (New York, 1968), 128.

137 ". . . **indolent manufacturer**": Beverly Baxter to Beaverbrook, February 25, 1942, Beaverbrook Papers, HIST/184/C/28.

138 ". . . **out of his eyes**": Ibid.

138 ". . . **flooded with tears**": Sylvester to Lloyd George, March 9, 1942, Lloyd George Papers, G/24.

138 ". . . **why that has been done**": Halifax, diary entry, February 20, 1942, Halifax Papers, A7.8.10.

138 significant aspect: *News Chronicle*, February 26, 1942.

139 ". . . **unnecessary expenditure**": *Hansard*, February 25, 1942.

139 ". . . **man if he met one**": Woolton, diary entry, September 8, 1942, Woolton Papers. Woolton recalls her saying this "just before he came into the Government."

139 ". . . **popular for very long**": Sinclair to Lloyd George, February 26 and 27, 1942, Lloyd George Papers, LG/G/24.

140 right not to participate: Clarke and Toye, *Oxford Dictionary of National Biography*, entry on Stafford Cripps.

140 modified in this instance: Quoted in Pimlott, ed., *Diary of Hugh Dalton*, March 5, 1942, 390.

140 ". . . **WC in the background**": Leslie Hore-Belisha, diary entry, February 25, 1942, Hore-Belisha Papers, HOBE 1/9.

140 ". . . **certainly replace Winston**": Quoted in Clarke, *Cripps Version*, 289.

141 ". . . **premiership is his goal**": Woolton, diary entry, March 3, 1942, Woolton Papers.

141 ". . . **private houses**": Hankey to Hoare, March 12, 1942, Hankey Papers, 4/34.

141 ". . . **is very low**": Sylvester to Lloyd George, March 19, 1942, Lloyd George Papers, G/25.

141 ". . . **disasters as I have**": Quoted in Martin Gilbert, *Winston S. Churchill*, vol. 7, *Road to Victory, 1941–1945* (London, 1986), 80–81.

142 Franklin D. Roosevelt: *Hansard*, July 2, 1942.

142 also on the home front: See, among many, Jenkins, *Churchill*, 693–695.

142 only nineteen names: Sylvester to Lloyd George, June 26, 1942, Lloyd George Papers, G/25.

142 no longer had confidence in Churchill's leadership: Ibid., Sylvester to Lloyd George, June 26, 1942.

143 anxieties and vote to support the government: Ibid., Sylvester to Lloyd George, July 1, 1942.

143 **"mishand[ling] the thing"**: Ibid., Sylvester to Lloyd George, June 25–26, 1942.

144 **". . . understand the home front"**: Butler, diary entry, "July 1942," Butler Papers, RAB G14/59. We do not know what Lyttelton and Eden made of Cripps's plan. But Eden wrote in his diary two months before the dinner described by Butler that when Cripps returned from India, "he and I and Oliver will have to have a heart to heart and then tackle Winston." But Eden was thinking not of supplanting Churchill, but of persuading him to share general direction of the war.

144 **"did it badly"**: Eden, *Reckoning*, 385.

144 **". . . personalities and practices"**: Ibid.

144 **almost always critically**: "Central Direction of the War," *Hansard*, July 1, 1942.

144 **Cheshire cat**: But Nicolson describes only a "flickering smile." Nicolson, ed., *Nicolson*, July 2, 1942, 231.

146 **abstained nevertheless**: Sylvester to Lloyd George, July 3, 1942, Lloyd George Papers, G/25.

147 **"I don't want to be Prime Minister"**: Woolton, diary entry, July 13, 1942, Woolton Papers.

147 **old friend and ally**: Cripps to Churchill, July 2, 1942, Churchill Papers, CHAR 20, 56/B.

148 **earlier recommendations**: Ibid., Cripps to Churchill, July 30, 1942.

148 **almost everything Cripps had proposed**: Ibid., Churchill to Cripps, September 2, 1942.

148 **". . . indefinite time"**: Theresa Cripps, diary entry, September 3, 1942, Cripps Papers, SC35/3, A3/1.

148 **diminished his influence**: Cripps to Churchill, September 21, 1942, Churchill Papers, CHAR 20, 56/B.

148 **". . . attention to their duties"**: *Hansard*, September 7, 1942.

149 **". . . onus is on the House"**: Ibid., September 8, 1942.

149 **". . . spoiled the effect"**: Harvey Watt to Churchill, September 12, 1942, Harvey Watt Papers, Churchill College, Cambridge University, HARV 2/1.

149 **". . . rest unanswered"**: James Stuart to Churchill, September 9, 1942, Churchill Papers, PREM 4/60/4.

149 **also reported to Churchill**: Watt to Churchill, September 12, 1942, Watt Papers, HARV 2/1.

149 **". . . engagements etc."**: National Archive, CAB 195/1, September 9, 1942.

150 **". . . less than it was"**: Jefferys, ed., *Ede*, September 20, 1942, 97.

150 **". . . vegetarian diet"**: Eade, "Luncheon with Mr. Churchill . . . " September 30, 1942, Eade Papers, 2/2.

150 **". . . ignore him"**: Jenny Lee to Gordon King, September 17, 1942, Churchill Papers, CHAR 20/58.

150 ". . . **reliance upon my help**": Cripps to Churchill, September 21, 1942, Churchill Papers, CHAR 20/56/B.

150 ". . . **seven months ago**": Churchill to Cripps, September 22, 1942, Churchill Papers, CHAR 20/54/B.

151 "**without agreement**": Eden, diary entry, October 1, 1942, Avon Papers.

152 ". . . **no PM could accept it**": Eden, diary entry, October 2, 1942, Avon Papers.

152 **political naïveté**: Clarke, *Cripps Version*, 366.

152 **opinion of Cripps's action**: "Tenth Report on Sir Stafford Cripps: Cripps Leaves the War Cabinet," Cripps Papers, SC36/1.

CHAPTER 9

156 ". . . **influence today**": Beaverbrook to Churchill, n.d., Churchill Papers, CHAR 20/24.

156 ". . . **all be yours**": Beaverbrook to Churchill, November 30, 1941, Churchill Papers, CHAR 2/416.

156 ". . . **resistance in the free world**": Beaverbrook to Churchill, February 26, 1942, Churchill Papers, CHAR 20/52.

156 ". . . **guardian of mankind**": Beaverbrook to Churchill, n.d., Churchill Papers, CHAR 20/24.

156 ". . . **touch of sadism**": Chisolm and Davie, *Beaverbrook*, 394.

156 ". . . **headmaster of his school**": John Moore-Brabazon, *The Brabazon Story* (London, 1956), 201.

156 ". . . **That's me**": Beaverbrook to Churchill, October 25, 1941, Churchill Papers, CHAR 20/20.

157 ". . . **passion to pull strings**": A. G. Gardiner, the great Liberal editor, quoted in Chisolm and Davie, *Beaverbrook*, 438.

157 ". . . **ninety-eight percent crook**": Sylvester to Lloyd George, October 24, 1941, Lloyd George Papers, LG/G/24/1.

157 ". . . **cat that walks alone**": Beaverbrook to Churchill, January 3, 1941, Churchill Papers, CHAR 20/20.

157 ". . . **'urgency and speed'**": Beaverbrook to Churchill, March 17, 1942, Churchill Papers, CHAR 20/55.

158 ". . . **have got to go on**": Churchill to Beaverbrook, n.d., Churchill Papers, CHAR 20/20.

158 ". . . **will look much better**": Churchill to Beaverbrook, December 15, 1940, Churchill Papers, CHAR 20/4A.

158 ". . . **counsel and comfort**": Churchill to Beaverbrook, n.d., Churchill Papers, CHAR 20/20.

158 ". . . **to accept [it]**": Churchill to Beaverbrook, January 12, 1942, Churchill Papers, CHAR 20/52.

158 "... **regarded as desertion**": Churchill to Beaverbrook, n.d., Churchill Papers, CHAR 20/20.

158 "... **have given you**": Ibid., Churchill to Beaverbrook, n.d.

158 "... **allow it if there were**": Ibid., Churchill to Beaverbrook, October 30, 1941.

158 "... **upon which we stand**": Ibid., Churchill to Beaverbrook, n.d.

158 "... **luncheon, if you like**": Ibid., Churchill to Beaverbrook, October 26, 1941.

158 "... **done miracles**": Crozier, *Off the Record*, interview with Winston Churchill, July 26, 1940.

158 **smash Churchill's government**: Sylvester to Lloyd George, July 8, 1940, Lloyd George Papers, LG/G/24/1.

159 "... **propaganda for himself**": Eden, diary entry: May 15, 1941, Avon Papers. The rival was Lord Camrose.

159 "... **you know all about him**": Crozier, *Off the Record*, interview with Lord Beaverbrook, May 21, 1941, 218.

159 "... **was in despair**": Halifax, diary entry, October 14, 1940, Halifax Papers, A.7.8.3.12, FACS.

159 **powerful movement**: Taylor, *Beaverbrook*, 530–531; Driberg, *Beaverbrook*, 280–283; Chisolm and Davie, *Beaverbrook*, 435–442.

161 "... **gifts on the tree**": Quoted in Chisolm and Davie, *Beaverbrook*, 412.

161 "... **Madame Maisky**": Ibid., 416.

161 "**Now we shall win the war**": Quoted in Taylor, *Beaverbrook*, 487.

161 "... **faithful friend now**": Martin Gilbert, *The Churchill War Papers*, vol. 3, *The Ever-Widening War* (New York, 2001), Beaverbrook to Churchill, October 2, 1941.

161 "... **done it but you**": Churchill to Beaverbrook October 3, 1941, Churchill Papers, CHAR 20/43.

162 "... **top of the world**": Chisolm and Davie, *Beaverbrook*, 419.

162 "... **succeed Spencer**": Sylvester to Lloyd George, October 29, 1941, Lloyd George Papers, LG/G/24/1.

162 "... **all Beaverbrook**": Ibid., Sylvester to Lloyd George, October 24, 1941.

163 "... *lead* **the Labour Party**": Ibid., Sylvester to Lloyd George, October 31, 1941.

163 "... **strike before it is too late**": Quoted in Chisolm and Davie, *Beaverbrook*, 421.

163 "... **Chiefs of Staff didn't**": Ibid., 422.

163 "... **wants the top job**": Ibid.

164 "... **coming Prime Minister of Britain**": See Taylor, *Beaverbrook*, 530–535; Chisolm and Davie, *Beaverbrook*, 435–443; Driberg, *Beaverbrook*, 283.

164 "... '**Hidden Hand**'": Bonham Carter to Driberg, June 16, 1964, Violet Bonham Carter Papers, Box 169.

164 ". . . **witnesses to prove it**": Ibid., Driberg to Bonham Carter, June 18, 1964.

164 "**at once tackled him**": Oliver Harvey, diary entry, October 21, 1941, quoted in Gilbert, *Ever-Widening War*, 1362.

165 ". . . **no right to Gibraltar**": Leslie Hore-Belisha, diary entry, March 15, 1942, Hore-Belisha Papers, HOBE 1/9.

165 ". . . **policy over and over again**": Beaverbrook to Eden, March 3, 1942, Beaverbrook Papers, BBK D/427.

165 **production targets**: Thomson, *Vote of Censure*, 57.

166 ". . . **weaken his authority**": Beaverbrook to Eden, March 3, 1942, Beaverbrook Papers, BBK D/427.

167 ". . . **creation of an opposition**": Hore-Belisha, diary entry, March 17, 1942, Hore-Belisha Papers, HOBE 1/9. Yet even here Beaverbrook expressed ambivalence, telling his luncheon guest that "he felt bound" to Churchill, who had not dismissed him from the government, but rather had regretfully accepted his resignation and charged him with a new task, the second trip to America to coordinate "pooling resources."

167 ". . . **anti-Churchill party?**": Quoted in Chisolm and Davie, *Beaverbrook*, 439.

167 ". . . **join as Prime Minister**": Halifax, diary entry, October 10, 1943, "Secret Diary."

167 ". . . **advocate his Russian views**": Eden, diary entry, February 28, 1942, Avon Papers.

167 **mounted across the English Channel**: Beaverbrook to Churchill, March 17, 1942, Churchill Papers, CHAR 20/55.

167 ". . . **Premiership or nothing now**": Thomson, *Vote of Censure*, 135; Taylor, *Beaverbrook*, 517.

167 ". . . **no friendship at the top**": See, for example, "There Is No Friendship at the Top," July 17, 2007, Lord George Society, http://lloydgeorgesociety.org.uk/en /article/2007/130326/there-is-no-friendship-at-the-top.

168 "**tranquility**": Beaverbrook Papers, BBK D/448. This is Beaverbrook's nineteen-page account of the events surrounding his resignation. It is dated February 28, 1942.

168 ". . . **needing rest**": Reuter's Report, Churchill Papers, CHAR 20/55.

168 **amounted to demotion**: Chisolm and Davie, *Beaverbrook*, 430.

168 ". . . **remain great**": *Daily Express*, March 31, 1942.

168 ". . . **dynamic, opportunist**": Halifax, diary entry, March 25, 1942, Halifax Papers.

169 ". . . **believe I could do it**": Ibid.

169 ". . . **Marlborough**": Quoted in Chisolm and Davie, *Beaverbrook*, 431.

169 ". . . **think he will**": Quoted in Taylor, *Beaverbrook*, 527.

170 ". . . **wishful thinking**": Halifax, diary entry, April 21, 1942, Halifax Papers.

171 "... **betrayed Russia to her German enemy":** Lord Beaverbrook, "A Second Front in Europe to Aid Russia," speech delivered before the Bureau of Advertising of the American Newspaper Publishers Association, April 23, 1942, www.ibiblio.org/pha/policy/1942/1942–04–23b.html.

171 "... **negotiated peace":** Quoted in Thomson, *Vote of Censure*, 156.

171 "... **Send for Beaverbrook":** Driberg to Bonham Carter, June 18, 1964, Violet Bonham Carter Papers, Box 169.

171 **complained about it to him:** Thomson, *Vote of Censure*, 169.

172 **conspiring against the government?:** Alan Bullock, *The Life and Times of Ernest Bevin*, vol. 2, Minister of Labour, 1940–1945 (London, 1967), 177.

172 **and to speculate:** Thomson, *Vote of Censure*, 177.

172 "... **willing to serve you":** Ibid., 135.

172 **insist on waiting:** For the classic rebuttal, however, see John Grigg, *1943: The Victory That Never Was* (London, 1999).

172 **East London:** Beaverbrook Papers, BBK/D/454.

173 **may be seen online:** For example, a clip of the speech is available from ITN Source at www.itnsource.com/en/shotlist/BHC_RTV/1942/06/25/BGU40823 0002/?s=beaverbrook%20speech.

173 **another account:** Taylor, *Beaverbrook*, 536.

173 "... **launch that movement now":** Beaverbrook, typescript of speech in Birmingham, June 21, 1942, Beaverbrook Papers, BBK/C/56.

174 "... **100 to 1 against":** Quoted in ibid., 536.

174 **spoke for it at the House of Lords:** On February 23, 1943.

174 "... **unassailable":** Quoted in Taylor, *Beaverbrook*, 537.

175 "... **beyond the possibilities":** "Conduct of the War," July 1, 1942, *Hansard*, vol. 123, http://hansard.millbanksystems.com/lords/1942/jul/01/conduct-of -the-war.

176 "... **against Max Beaverbrook":** Halifax, diary entry, July 15, 1942, "Secret Diary," Halifax Papers.

176 "... **opinion in the House":** James Stuart to Churchill, July 15, 1942, Churchill Papers, CHAR 20/52.

176 "... **lonely man":** Sylvester to Churchill, July 13, 1942, Lloyd George Papers, LG/G/25.

177 "... **meal together soon":** Churchill to Cripps, October 1, 1943, Churchill Papers, CHAR 20/94B.

CHAPTER 10

180 **"Pomposo":** Bracken to Beaverbrook, March 27, 1945, Beaverbrook Papers, BBK/D/128.

180 "... **zero in Cabinet":** Eden, diary entry, February 18, 1942, Avon Papers.

181 ". . . staff of five or six": "Study of Post-War Problems," December 30, 1940, Churchill Papers, CHAR 23/4.

181 ". . . reluctantly add myself": Churchill to Greenwood, February 4, 1941, Churchill Papers, CHAR 20/21A.

181 ". . . painful interview with Lloyd George": Thomas Legge and Marie-Louise Legg, entry on William Allen Jowitt, *Oxford Dictionary of National Biography*.

181 ". . . some convictions": Ibid.

181 far-reaching reform: Churchill also had a second committee, chaired by a former judge and member of the House of Lords, Augustus Uthwatt, looking into how to avoid postwar speculation in land, and a third committee under Lord Justice Scott investigating postwar land utilization in rural areas. Nothing in their past suggested that either man would favor radical measures. The prime minister may have thought, then, that by now he had the dreamers in both parties under control, either self-censoring in order to maintain the Grand Coalition, or politically diverted, or absorbed with mind-numbing committee work. Such confidence, if he felt it, was misplaced, however.

181 ". . . suspect very little": Woolton, quoted in Stephen Brooke, *Labour's War* (Oxford, 1992), 169.

182 ". . . equal chance": Home Intelligence Division, UK, "Public Feeling on Post-War Reconstruction," November 1942, National Archive, UK, CAB 118/73.

182 as an ethical ideal: Jose Harris, entry on William Beveridge, *Oxford Dictionary of National Biography*.

183 prospective report: James Stuart to Churchill, May 12, 1942, Churchill Papers, CHAR 20/60.

183 90 percent of Conservative backbenchers supported them: Kevin Jefferys, *The Churchill Coalition and Wartime Politics, 1940–1945* (Manchester, UK, 1991), 119.

183 ". . . nervous of Sir William Beveridge's views": R. A. Butler, memo, August 27, 1942, Conservative Party Archive, RAB 2/6–10.

183 ". . . not in uniformity": Butler to C. Allport, August 21, 1942, Butler Papers, RAB G14/68.

183 ". . . windbag and a dreamer": Quoted in Jefferys, ed., *Ede*, February 16, 1943, 119.

183 ". . . economically impossible": Churchill to Chancellor of the Exchequer, etc., December 17, 1942, National Archive, UK, CAB 123/43.

183 more than it could pay for: Ibid., Wood to Churchill, December 17, 1942.

183 easy to shoot down: R. A. Butler, memo, August 28, 1942, Conservative Party Archive, RAB2/6–10.

184 ". . . cupboard was": E. E. Bridges to Anderson, October 29, 1942, National Archive, UK, CAB 123/43.

184 "half way to Moscow": War Cabinet Minutes, November 16, 1942, National Archive, UK, CAB 195/2.

185 ". . . welcome it in principle?": War Cabinet Minutes, November 26, 1942, National Archive, UK, CAB 195/2.

185 ". . . reasonably possible": Quoted in Gilbert, *Road to Victory*, 337.

186 ". . . Administrative difficulties": War Cabinet Minutes, February 12, 1943, National Archive, UK, CAB 195/2.

186 ". . . Utopia and Eldorado": "Promises about Postwar Conditions, Note by the Prime Minister," February 15, 1943, Churchill Papers, CHAR 23/11.

187 ". . . reject a scheme": Ibid.

187 cogently argued response to Churchill's memo: Attlee to Churchill, February 15, 1943, Attlee Papers, Cambridge, ATLE 2/2.

188 ". . . shelve the whole matter": Jefferys, ed., *Ede*, February 16, 1943, 119.

188 acute political crisis: Ibid., February 17, 1943, 121.

191 ". . . own delight": Pimlott, ed., *Diary of Hugh Dalton*, February 18, 1943, 555–556.

191 ". . . bring down the Government": Nicolson, ed., *Nicolson*, February 18, 1943, 282.

192 ". . . Labour side in the House of Commons": *Manchester Evening News*, September 7, 1940.

192 ". . . big progressive outcome": *Hansard*, February 18, 1943.

CHAPTER 11

196 wouldn't have him: They were right about this. See his best biographers, Donoughue and Jones, *Morrison*, 159–179.

197 ". . . civilized dormitories": Ibid., 289.

197 people cheered: Ibid., 296.

197 but never responded: Ibid., 314.

197 ". . . put his case well": Interview with Anthony Eden, September 25, 1968, Morrison Papers, 6/1.

198 ". . . together as a family": Herbert Morrison, "Social Security and National Welfare, A Program for the Future," Swindon, December 20, 1942, in Morrison, *Prospects and Policies* (New York, 1944), 2–9.

198 ". . . and sectionalism": Ibid., and "Post-War Trade, Home and Export, Nottingham, February 13, 1943, in the same work, 10–18.

199 ". . . great need of it": Winston Churchill, *The Second World War*, vol. 4, *The Hinge of Fate* (New York, 1985), 651–652.

199 ". . . main attention to the war": Churchill to Beveridge, February 16, 1943, Churchill Papers, CHAR 20 93/A.

199 verbal report about the debate from his PPS: "Report by Parliamentary Private Secretary," February 19, 1943, Watt Papers, HARV 3/1.

199 had done the same: All Conservative and Liberal National MPs had supported the motion welcoming the report, but, apart from ministers and whips, only two Labour members and only three Liberals. Greenwood had voted against his own motion. In all, including tellers, 338 members had voted aye, and 121 had voted nay. James Stuart to Churchill, February 19, 1943, National Archive, UK, PREM 4/65/1.

200 reciting portions of it: Gilbert, *Road to Victory*, 354.

200 "... **resolved not to**": For this speech, see Winston Churchill, "A Four Year Plan for England," Post-War Councils on World Problems, Broadcast from London over BBC, March 21, 1943, www.ibiblio.org/pha/policy/1943/1943-03-21a.html.

200 "... **British listeners**": *Report of the Forty-Third Annual Conference of the Labour Party* (London, 1944), 113.

201 "... **in step**": Churchill, "Four Year Plan."

201 "... **ardent discussion of postwar problems**": National Archive, UK, CAB 195/2, April 15, 1943.

202 "... **more and more State control**": Waldron Smithers to Churchill, June 8, 1944, Churchill Papers, CHAR 20/146B.

202 "... **not only trade but liberty**": Brendan Evans and Andrew Taylor, *From Salisbury to Major* (Manchester, UK, 1996), 67.

202 than Kingsley Wood had: Report by Parliamentary Secretary, Watt Papers, HARV 3/1, February 26, 1943.

202 had adumbrated: Ibid., March 12, 1943.

202 Tory Reform Group (TRG): Ibid., March 19, 1943.

202 "... **see maintained**": *The Times*, March 18, 1943.

202 "... **policy after the war**": Eden, Mansion House, May 29, 1941, Avon Papers, 12/2/27–31K, Speeches, 5.

202 "... **disaster upon ourselves**": Eden, Leamington, September 26, 1942, Avon Papers, Speeches, 19.

203 "... **instead of the shareholder**": Beaverbrook, "Post War," Beaverbrook Papers, BBK/D449.

203 "... **five hundred will do?**": Ibid., Erskine Hill to Beaverbrook, December 24, 1942.

203 "... **provide the way**": Ibid., Hill to Beaverbrook, March 1, 1943.

203 "... **standard for the rest?**": Woolton, Constitutional Club, March 6, 1943, Woolton Papers, Ms Woolton 13.

204 "... **setting the stage admirably**": Hooper to Woolton, June 6, 1943, ibid.

204 "... **of use to you**": Hooper to Woolton, December 17, 1943, Woolton Papers, Ms Woolton 15.

204 obsequious letter to the prime minister: Ibid., Woolton to Churchill, February 7, 1944.

204 "... **way of support**": Ibid., Woolton, "Conversation with E. Hill abt Future of Conservative Party," November 13, 1943.

204 "... **but intrigue**": Gordon F. Millar, *Oxford Dictionary of National Biography*, entry on Sir Alexander Galloway Erskine-Hill.

205 "... **down the drain**": Morrison, "The Future of the Labour Party and the Problem of Monopoly Control," in *Prospects and Policies*, 28–38.

206 "... **ought to be**": Morrison, "Postwar Economic Questions," in ibid., 39–47.

206 "... **needed after the war**": Morrison, "The Postwar Future of the Emergency Wartime Controls of Industry," in ibid., 48–55.

206 "... **operation or control**": Morrison, "A Restatement of Some Socialist Principles Applied to Postwar Questions of Industrial Organization," in ibid., 56–75.

207 "... **postwar destiny**": Donoughue and Jones, *Morrison*, 329.

207 **treated shabbily:** Pimlott, ed., *Diary of Hugh Dalton*, June 15, 1943, 607.

207 "... **who will control industry**": Quoted in Donoughue and Jones, *Morrison*, 329.

208 "... **petered out**": Lord Moran, *Churchill: Taken from the Diaries of Lord Moran* (Boston, 1966), 100.

208 "... **good humor**": Crozier, *Off the Record*, interview with Herbert Morrison, October 22, 1943, 384.

209 "... **join the National League for Freedom?**": *Hansard*, October 12, 1943.

209 "... **angered by them**": Pimlott, ed., *Diary of Hugh Dalton*, November 2, 1943, 663.

210 "... **implementation where necessary**": War Cabinet, "The Need for Decisions," June 26, 1943, National Archive, UK, CAB 118/33.

210 **postponing them:** Ibid., Wood to Churchill, July 1, 1943.

210 "... **early discussion**": Ibid., Attlee to Churchill, July 13, 1943.

210 "... **very much longer**": Ibid., Morrison to Attlee, August 30, 1943.

210 "... **will be no loss**": Eden, diary entry, September 21, 1943, Avon Papers.

210 **proposals and much more:** For more on the Common Wealth movement, see Addison, *Road*, 159–160, 225–226, 249–250.

211 "... **controversial or not**": Winston Churchill, *The Second World War*, vol. 5, *Closing the Ring* (Boston, 1951), 170.

211 "... **meet these two points**": War Cabinet Conclusions, October 21, 1943, National Archives, UK.

211 "... **taken in good time**": Crozier, *Off the Record*, interview with Herbert Morrison, October 23, 1943, 384.

212 "... **new expenditure**": Pimlott, ed., *Diary of Hugh Dalton*, May 19, 1944, 748.

212 "... **dominating force**": Churchill to Attlee, January 20, 1945, Churchill Papers, CHUR 2/4.

CHAPTER 12

217 "... **highly strung condition**": Danchev and Todman, eds., *Alanbrooke*, June 5, 1944, 554.

217 **only military matters:** Ibid., May 27, 1944, 551.

217 rages during these weeks: Dilkes, ed., *Cadogan*, June 1, 1944, and June 5, 1944, 633–634.

217 ". . . may have been killed?": William Manchester and Paul Reid, *The Last Lion: Winston Spencer Churchill, Defender of the Realm, 1940–1965* (Boston, 2012), 838.

218 ". . . Seine estuary": Nicolson, ed., *Nicolson*, June 6, 1944, 375.

218 "white as a sheet": Ibid.

218 ". . . according to plan": Winston Churchill, *The Second World War*, vol. 6, *Triumph and Tragedy* (Boston, 1953), 5–6.

218 ". . . silent coast": Ibid., 13.

219 ". . . arms outstretched": Eden, *Reckoning*, 526.

219 "Cheap at the price": Ibid.

220 been defeated: Eden, diary entry, September 30, 1940, Avon Papers.

220 case of his death: Quoted in Thorpe, *Eden*, 272.

220 ". . . denied me": Churchill, *Triumph and Tragedy*, 590.

220 ". . . deterioration": Eden, diary entry, July 6, 1944, Avon Papers.

220 many other diarists: e.g., Colville, *Fringes of Power*, April 23, 1945, 591–592.

221 ". . . likely to have": Churchill to Smuts, December 3, 1944, Churchill Papers, CHAR 20/176.

221 ". . . I am a Tory": *The Times*, June 27, 1945.

221 ". . . willing to serve": *The Times*, March 22, 1943.

222 ". . . continuing after the war": Butler memo to self, September 17, 1943, Conservative Party Archive, RAB 2/6–10.

222 Attlee, who had agreed with it: Pimlott, ed., *Diary of Hugh Dalton*, September 14, 1943.

222 indicated to Eden: Stephen Brooke, *Labour's War* (Oxford, 1992), 304.

222 ". . . the 'black coats'": Ibid., 309.

222 ". . . two alternative programs": Ibid., 305. This appears to be a decisive argument against historians who have emphasized political consensus in wartime Britain. The first and best exponent of this argument is Addison, *Road*.

**223 ". . . discredit you": ". . . Week Ending April 14, 1945," Watt Papers, 5/1.

223 ". . . in favor of an early election": Ibid.

223 ". . . postponing until the autumn": Ralph Assheton to Churchill, May 15, 1945, Churchill Papers, CHAR 2/549.

223 "Demand election at earliest": Ibid., "W" to Churchill, n.d., but it must have been May 11, 1945.

223 ". . . prefer an October election": Ibid., Butler to Churchill, n.d., but it must have been May 11, 1945.

224 ". . . God save the King": Quoted in Gilbert, *Road to Victory*, 1344.

224 ". . . waved their Order Papers": Harold Nicolson to Nigel Nicolson, May 8, 1945, quoted in Nicolson, ed., *Nicolson*, 457.

224 "... **roared again**": Camrose Papers, quoted in Gilbert, *Road to Victory*, 1347.

225 "... **must be faced by him**": Morrison to Attlee, May 11, 1945, Bevin Papers, 3/3.

225 "... **three or four days**": Churchill to Eden, May 11, 1945, Churchill Papers, CHAR 2/550.

226 **accepted it immediately:** Ibid., Churchill to Attlee, May 18, 1945.

226 "... **best to keep us together**": Churchill, *Triumph and Tragedy*, 593.

226 **election sometime in the autumn:** Evans to Beaverbrook, May 30, 1945, Beaverbrook Papers, BBK/D/475. This is a confidential memo reporting on Bevin's view of the discussions with Churchill.

227 "... **on principle and policy**": Attlee to Churchill, May 21, 1945, Churchill Papers, CHAR 2/550.

227 **forcing the issue:** Interview with Alex Black, Morrison Papers, 6/1.

227 "... **no longer exist**": Churchill to Attlee, May 22, 1945, Churchill Papers, CHAR 2/550.

227 "... **who'd asked me**": Eden, *Reckoning*, 622.

228 "... **so much together**": Churchill, *Triumph and Tragedy*, 596.

228 **gathered around it:** Pimlott, ed., *Diary of Hugh Dalton*, May 28, 1945, 865.

229 "... **this election and afterwards**": Colville, *Fringes of Power*, May 27, 1945, 604.

229 "... **activity until after the election is over**": Beaverbrook to Stuart, September 27, 1944, Beaverbrook Papers, BBK/D/145.

CHAPTER 13

231 "... **very, very partisan**": Jenkins, *Churchill*, 790.

231 **a large audience:** Colville, *Fringes of Power*, June 1, 1945, 606.

232 "... **form of *Gestapo***": *The Times*, June 5, 1945.

232 "... **strategic blunder**": Quoted in Harris, *Attlee*, 256.

232 "... **modest about**": See, for example, Winston Churchill Quotes, ThinkExist.com, http://en.thinkexist.com/quotation/mr-attlee_is_a_very_modest_man-indeed_he_has_a/150133.html.

233 "... **mind was that of Lord Beaverbrook**": Election Speech, June 5, 1945, Attlee Papers, Oxford, dep. 17.

233 **to join him:** Oddly, given the dreadful intentions he had ascribed to Labour's leader, he wrote to him solicitously: "It ... might be of some convenience to you that you should have a Government servant ... to look after your luggage and deal with your personal requirements," and recommended a Downing Street employee: "He is thoroughly trustworthy and is a very good valet." Churchill to Attlee, July 11, 1945, Churchill Papers, CHAR 194/B.

234 ". . . **Mr. Churchill as Prime Minister**": *The Times*, June 15, 1945.

234 **unelected NEC?:** Delegates to Labour Party annual conferences elected the members of the NEC. But there was no general popular election for them.

234 ". . . **Camarilla in the background**": *The Times*, June 27, 1945.

234 ". . . **represent Prof. Laski**": *Sunday Times*, June 17, 1945.

234 ". . . **ominous ring to it**": Ibid.

235 ". . . **system of Great Britain**": *The Times*, June 21, 1945.

235 "**social suicide**": Andrew S. Thompson, entry on Henry Page Croft, *Oxford Dictionary of National Biography*.

235 ". . . **represented as anti-Semitism**": Churchill to Henry Page Croft, June 20, 1945, Henry Page Croft Papers, Churchill College, Cambridge University, CRFT1/2.

235 ". . . **what [Churchill] was on about**": Jenkins, *Churchill*, 794.

235 **influence he did not have:** Kingsley Martin, *Harold Laski: A Biographical Memoir* (London, 1953).

235 ". . . **affectionate respect?**": Laski to Churchill, April 21, 1945, Churchill Papers, CHAR 20/198/A.

236 ". . . **with this view**": Laski to Churchill, June 3, 1945, ibid.

236 ". . . **relations with him**": Ibid., Churchill, on Private Office stationery, June 17, 1945.

236 "**that vermiform appendix**": Bonham Carter to Churchill, June 1, 1945, Violet Bonham Carter Papers, MS 164.

236 ". . . **defeat of Socialism**": Churchill to Major Stucley, n.d., Churchill Papers, CHAR 2/546/A.

236 ". . . **'Tories v. the rest'**": Churchill to Croft, March 17, 1945, Croft Papers, CRFT1/2.

237 ". . . **shall get fair play**": Labour Party Election Manifesto, 1945, "Let Us Face the Future."

237 ". . . **contributed our share**": Beven, Speech, April 7, 1945, Bevin Papers, Bevin 4/8.

238 ". . . **think the same way**": War Cabinet Minutes, April 3, 1945, Burgis Papers, Churchill College, Cambridge University.

238 "**Gauleiter Laski**": *Daily Express*, June 19, 1945. Harold Macmillan appears to have been the first to use this objectionable phrase.

238 **Fascist Party in Italy:** William Barkley in the *Daily Express*, June 6, 1945: "You cannot have the old House of Commons, vigilant of the individual welfare once you have a socialist conception of Britain. You did not have it in Germany or in Italy. . . . [T]he Socialist idea which was spawned there is now annihilated by the force of our arms.

238 *Europäische Revue*: *Tribune*, June 22, 1945.

238 **stormy reception:** *The Times*, June 23, 1945.

238 ". . . **shouts and cheers**": *The Times*, June 24, 1945.

238 ". . . **free men**": William Barkley, typescript of piece that would have appeared in the *Daily Express* the next day, in Beaverbrook Papers, BBK F/165.

239 ". . . **help from this side?**": *The Times*, July 4, 1945.

239 ". . . **make a noise**": *The Times*, July 5, 1945.

239 ". . . **regrets for what happened**": LePelley to Churchill, July 5, 1945, Churchill Papers, CHAR 2/553/B.

239 ". . . **old England in the end**": Ibid., Churchill to LePelley, July 7, 1945.

240 ". . . **Whitehall during his tour**: Memo issued by 10 Downing Street, n.d., Churchill Papers, CHAR 2/553/A.

240 ". . . **kindly salutes**": Ibid., Churchill to Margesson, June 27, 1945.

240 ". . . **your garment**": John Ramsden, *The Age of Churchill and Eden, 1940–1957* (London, 1995), 84.

240 ". . . **doesn't mean we're going to vote for him**": Ibid.

240 ". . . **Mike [*sic*] outside**": Clem Attlee to Tom Attlee, July 3, 1945, Attlee Papers, Oxford, MS Eng., C 4793.

241 ". . . **political weapons**": Arthur Greenwood, *The Times*, June 20, 1945.

241 ". . . **refer to them**": Bracken to Churchill, June 6, 1945, Churchill Papers, CHAR 2/548/A.

241 **Beaverbrook in his speeches**: Beaverbrook to Churchill, n.d., but June 27, 1945, from internal evidence, Churchill Papers, CHAR 2/552.

241 **public letters to Attlee**: See, for example, Churchill to Attlee, July 3, 1945, "not final," Churchill Papers, CHAR 20/194/B (but the final draft also follows Beaverbrook's points, although not his precise wording).

242 ". . . **see the last of**": *Daily Express*, July 5, 1945.

242 ". . . **let alone a Prime Minister**": *The Times*, July 5, 1945.

242 ". . . **decency to everyone**": Cripps to "Members of the General Council and the Executive Committee," May 28, 1945, Cripps Papers, SC12/2.

242 ". . . **corroborative detail**": Churchill to Eden, June 14, 1945, Churchill Papers, CHAR 20, 194/B.

242 ". . . **long distance runner**": Transcript of Beaverbrook speech, July 3, 1945, Beaverbrook Papers, BBK/F/65.

242 ". . . **decent men of all parties**": *The Times*, June 21, 1945.

243 ". . . **madman of Fleet Street**": *The Times*, June 16, 1945.

243 ". . . **involved in war**": *The Times*, June 23, 1945.

243 ". . . **have to decide**": *The Times*, June 25, 1945.

243 ". . . **pursued on the home front**": *The Times*, n.d. This is a clipping from the newspaper held in Churchill Papers, CHAR 2/558, with hundreds of other clippings.

243 ". . . **Royal Economic Society**": Bracken to Churchill, June 6, 1945, Churchill Papers, CHAR 2/548/A.

243 **defense of free enterprise**: *Daily Telegraph*, June 8, 1945.

244 **not mention Professor Laski**: A. E. Broadcast, May 27, 1945, Churchill Papers, CHAR 2/548/A.

244 "**the dirtiest and cheapest**": James, *Eden*, 304.

244 "**. . . shortest possible time**": *Royal Leamington Spa Courier and Warwickshire Standard*, June 29, 1945.

244 "**. . . destination in Burma**": Air Marshal Park to Eden, June 27, 1945, Churchill Papers, CHAR 20/197/A.

245 "**. . . Ministers to its will**": *The Times*, July 1, 1945.

245 "**I am painting a lot**": Churchill to Beaverbrook, July 11, 1945, Churchill Papers, CHAR 2/548/B.

246 **majority of 100**: Ibid., Assheton to Churchill, July 10, 1945.

246 **majority of 38**: Ibid., Beaverbrook to Churchill, July 15, 1945.

246 "**. . . some forty seats**": Colville, *Fringes of Power*, 611.

246 **understated his chances**: William Manchester and Paul Reid, *The Last Lion: Winston Spencer Churchill, Defender of the Realm, 1940–1965* (Boston, 2012), 943.

246 "**. . . dominated my mind**": Churchill, *Triumph and Tragedy*, 675.

246 **if not shock**: Martin Gilbert, *Winston S. Churchill*, vol. 8, *Never Despair, 1945–1965* (Boston, 1988), 106.

246 "**. . . landslide to the left**": Ibid., 107.

246 **only three during the day**: Ibid.

247 "**. . . effective disguise**": Manchester and Reid, *Defender*, 950.

247 **possibly even shocking**: Many years later, the socialist stalwart Fenner Brockway, who was still a member of the Independent Labour Party (ILP) in 1945, told me that he had wanted to stand against Churchill in the general election, but that the ILP leader, James Maxton, had vetoed this. Brockway thought he would have won.

247 "**. . . seals of office**": Gilbert, *Never Despair*, 109.

247 "**. . . been fighting for**": Ibid., 111.

248 "**. . . leadership of the Party**": Morrison to Attlee, July 24, 1945, Attlee Papers, Oxford, dep. 18.

248 **political fixer**: Second interview with Jim and Mabel Raison, n.d., Morrison Papers.

248 "**. . . going to win**": Ibid.

249 "**. . . blue in the face**": Interview with James Griffiths, MP, January 12, 1968, Morrison Papers.

249 "**'. . . let you know later'**": Quoted in Harris, *Attlee*, 263.

249 "**. . . we need Herbert**": Interview with Dame Leah Manning, August 8, 1968, Morrison Papers.

249 "**. . . Ladies Room**": Interview with Lady Summerskill, September 24, 1968, Morrison Papers.

249 "**. . . What do you think?**": Quoted in Donoughue and Jones, *Morrison*, 341–342. See also Interview with R. H. Boon, February 27, 1967, Morrison Papers.

249 **Morrison turned away**: Second interview with Jim and Mabel Raison, n.d., Morrison Papers.

Coda

253 "... **thirdly of practicality**": Attlee, unidentified speech, n.d., Attlee Papers, Oxford, dep. 2. Internal evidence shows the speech to have been delivered at Stoke early in 1941.

255 "... **got the sack**": Alan Bullock, *The Life and Times of Ernest Bevin*, vol. 3, *Foreign Secretary, 1945–1951* (New York, 1983), 833.

257 "... **ashamed of the public**": Woolton to Churchill, July 26, 1945, CHAR 2/560.

258 "... **Who Never Were**": See Francis Beckett, ed., *The Prime Ministers Who Never Were* (London, 2011).

259 **cheers and applause**: "Summary of Conservative Candidates Conference ..." October 5, 1945, Beaverbrook Papers, BBK D/479.

260 "... **hold on power**": Taylor, *Beaverbrook*, 657.

260 "... **unexciting existence**": Ibid., 620.

261 "... **others in gaiety**": Ibid., 668.

262 "... **nothing to do**": Quoted in Jenkins, *Churchill*, 887.

263 **Churchill's initials**: Cherkley Court website, www.cherkleycourt.com.

263 **dozed off**: Ibid.

263 "... **anything like it again**": Eden, diary entry, July 27, 1945, Avon Papers.

BIBLIOGRAPHY

Unpublished Sources

CAMBRIDGE UNIVERSITY
Churchill College:
A. V. Alexander Papers
Leo Amery Papers
Clement Attlee Papers
Ernest Bevin Papers
Brendan Bracken Papers
Lawrence Burgis Papers
Alexander Cadogan Papers
Churchill Papers
Lord Croft Papers
Charles Eade Papers
Maurice Hankey Papers
Hore-Belisha Papers
David Margesson Papers
John Martin Papers
Duncan Sandys Papers
Harvey Watt Papers

Trinity College:
R. A. Butler Papers

OXFORD UNIVERSITY
New Bodleian Library:
Violet Bonham Carter Papers

Stafford Cripps Papers
Geoffrey Dawson Papers
Arthur Greenwood Papers
Walter Monckton Papers
Sir John Simon Papers
Lord Woolton Papers

Bodleian Library:
Clement Attlee Papers
Conservative Party Archive

LONDON SCHOOL OF ECONOMICS AND POLITICAL SCIENCE
Hugh Dalton Papers
Herbert Morrison Papers

HOUSE OF LORDS RECORD OFFICE
Lord Beaverbrook Papers
David Lloyd George Papers

NATIONAL ARCHIVE, UK
CAB 66
CAB 118
CAB 120
CAB 123
CAB 127
KV 2/668
FO 800 (Papers of Foreign Secretaries)
Anthony Eden
Lord Halifax

UNIVERSITY OF BIRMINGHAM LIBRARY
Avon (Anthony Eden) Papers
Neville Chamberlain Papers

UNIVERSITY OF YORK (BORTHWICK INSTITUTE)
Lord Halifax Papers

BRITISH LIBRARY
Lord Cecil Papers

NATIONAL LIBRARY OF WALES
Clement Davies Papers

Published Sources

BOOKS

Addison, Paul. *The Road to 1945*. London, 1982.

———. *Churchill on the Home Front, 1900–1955*. London, 1992.

Amery, L. S. *My Political Life*, vol. 3, *The Unforgiving Years, 1929–1940*. London, 1955.

Attlee, Clement. *As It Happened*. New York, 1954.

Ball, Stuart. *The Conservative Party and British Politics, 1902–51*. New York, 1995.

———, ed. *Parliament and Politics in the Age of Churchill and Attlee: The Headlam Diaries, 1935–1951*. Cambridge, UK, 1999.

Barker, Elizabeth. *Churchill and Eden at War*. New York, 1978.

Barnett, Correlli. *The Audit of War*. London, 1986.

Beckett, Francis, ed. *The Prime Ministers Who Never Were*. London, 2011.

Beevor, Antony. *The Second World War*. Boston, 2012.

Blake, Robert, and William Roger Louis, eds. *Churchill: A Major New Assessment of His Life in Peace and War*. Oxford, 1993.

Boothby, Robert. *I Fight to Live*. London, 1947.

Brooke, Stephen. *Labour's War*. Oxford, 1992.

Bullock, Alan. *The Life and Times of Ernest Bevin*, vol. 2, *Minister of Labour, 1940–1945*. London, 1967.

———. *The Life and Times of Ernest Bevin*, vol. 3, *Foreign Secretary, 1945–1951*. New York, 1983.

Butler, R. A. *The Art of the Possible*. London, 1971.

Calder, Angus. *The People's War*. London, 1982.

Cannadine, David, ed. *Blood, Toil, Tears and Sweat: The Speeches of Winston Churchill*. London, 1990.

Carter, Violet Bonham. *Winston Churchill as I Knew Him*. London, 1965.

Catherwood, Christopher. *His Finest Hour*. Devon, UK, 2010.

Chisolm, Anne, and Michael Davie. *Beaverbrook: A Life*. London, 1992.

Churchill, Winston. *The Second World War*, vol. 1, *The Gathering Storm*. Boston, 1948.

———. *The Second World War*, vol. 2, *Their Finest Hour*. Boston, 1949.

———. *The Second World War*, vol. 3, *The Grand Alliance*. Boston, 1950.

———. *The Second World War*, vol. 4, *The Hinge of Fate*. Boston, 1950.

———. *The Second World War*, vol. 5, *Closing the Ring*. Boston, 1951.

———. *The Second World War*, vol. 6, *Triumph and Tragedy*. Boston, 1953.

Clarke, Peter. *My Life of Strife*. London, 1948.

———. *The Cripps Version*. London, 2002.

———. *The Last Thousand Days of the British Empire*. London, 2008.

Clegg, Hugh Armstrong. *A History of British Trade Unions Since 1889*, vol. 2. Oxford, 1994.

Cockett, Richard, ed. *My Dear Max*. London, 1990.

Colville, John. *The Fringes of Power*. Boston, 1985.

Cowling, Maurice. *The Impact of Hitler*. Cambridge, UK, 1975.

Crowcroft, Robert. *Attlee's War: World War II and the Making of a Labour Leader.* London, 2011.

Crozier, W. P. *Off the Record: Political Interviews, 1933–1943.* Edited by A. J. P. Taylor. London, 1973.

Danchev, Alex, and Daniel Todman, eds. *War Diaries, 1939–1945: Field Marshal Lord Alanbrooke.* Los Angeles, 2001.

Dilkes, David, ed. *The Diaries of Sir Alexander Cadogan, 1938–1945.* London, 1971.

Donoughue, Bernard, and George Jones. *Herbert Morrison: Portrait of a Politician.* London, 1973.

Driberg, Tom. *Beaverbrook: A Study in Power and Frustration.* London, 1956.

Dutton, David. *Anthony Eden: A Life and Reputation.* London, 1997.

Eade, Charles, ed. *Churchill, by His Contemporaries.* London, 1955.

Eden, Anthony. *The Reckoning: The Memoirs of Anthony Eden, Earl of Avon.* Boston, 1965.

Edgerton, David. *Britain's War Machine.* London, 2011.

Evans, Brendan, and Andrew Taylor. *From Salisbury to Major.* Manchester, UK, 1996.

Feiling, Keith. *The Life of Neville Chamberlain.* London, 1970.

Gilbert, Martin. *Winston S. Churchill,* vol. 6, *Finest Hour, 1939–1941.* London, 1983.

———. *Winston S. Churchill,* vol. 7, *Road to Victory: 1941–1945.* London, 1986.

———. *Winston S. Churchill,* vol. 8, *Never Despair, 1945–1965.* Boston, 1988.

———. *Churchill: A Life.* New York, 1992.

———. *The Churchill War Papers,* vol. 1, *At the Admiralty.* New York, 1993.

———. *The Churchill War Papers,* vol. 2, *Never Surrender.* New York, 1995.

———. *The Churchill War Papers,* vol. 3, *The Ever-Widening War.* New York, 2001.

———. *Winston Churchill's War Leadership.* New York, 2004.

Goodwin, Doris Kearns. *Team of Rivals: The Political Genius of Abraham Lincoln.* New York, 2005.

Grigg, John. *1943: The Victory That Never Was.* London, 1999.

Halifax (Lord Halifax). *Fullness of Days.* London, 1957.

Harris, Jose. *William Beveridge: A Biography.* Oxford, 1997.

Harris, Kenneth. *Attlee.* London, 1982.

Hastings, Max. *Winston's War: Churchill 1940–1945.* New York, 2011.

Hogg, Quinton. *The Left Was Never Right.* London, 1945.

Holmes, Richard. *Churchill's Bunker: The Secret Headquarters in Wartime London.* New Haven, CT, 2010.

Hunter, Ian, ed. *Winston and Archie.* London, 1988.

James, Robert Rhodes. *Anthony Eden: A Biography.* London, 1986.

Jefferys, Kevin. *The Churchill Coalition and Wartime Politics, 1940–1945.* Manchester, UK, 1991.

———, ed. *Labour and the Wartime Coalition: From the Diary of James Chuter Ede, 1941–45.* London, 1987.

Jenkins, Roy. *Churchill: A Biography.* London, 2001.

Johnson, Paul. *Churchill.* London, 2009.

Keegan, John. *Winston Churchill.* London, 2007.

Kershaw, Ian. *Fateful Choices: Ten Decisions That Changed the World, 1940–1941*. London, 2007.

Kramnick, Isaac, and Barry Sheerman. *Harold Laski: A Life on the Left*. London, 1993.

Lavery, Brian. *Churchill Goes to War*. Annapolis, MD, 2007.

Lee, J. M. *The Churchill Coalition, 1940–1945*. Hamden, CT, 1980.

Louis, Roger, ed. *Yet More Adventures with Britannia*. New York, 2005.

Lukacs, John. *The Duel*. New Haven, CT, 1990.

———. *Five Days in London, May 1940*. New Haven, CT, 2001.

———. *Churchill: Visionary, Statesman, Historian*. New Haven, CT, 2002.

———. *Blood, Toil, Tears and Sweat*. New York, 2008.

Macmillan, Harold. *The Blast of War*. London, 1968.

Manchester, William. *The Last Lion: Winston Spencer Churchill, Alone, 1932–1940*. Boston, 1988.

Manchester, William, and Paul Reid. *The Last Lion: Winston Spencer Churchill, Defender of the Realm, 1940–1965*. Boston, 2012.

Martin, Kingsley. *Harold Laski: A Biographical Memoir*. London, 1953.

Moore-Brabazon, John. *The Brabazon Story*. London, 1956.

Moran (Lord Moran). *Churchill: Taken from the Diaries of Lord Moran*. Boston, 1966.

Morrison, Herbert. *Prospects and Policies*. New York, 1944.

Mukerjee, Madhusree. *Churchill's Secret War*. New York, 2010.

Nicolson, Nigel, ed. *The Diaries and Letters of Harold Nicolson: The War Years, 1939–1945*. New York, 1967.

Olson, Lynn. *Troublesome Young Men*. New York, 2007.

Parker, R. A. C. *Chamberlain and Appeasement*. New York, 1993.

Pimlott, Ben. *Hugh Dalton: A Life*. London, 1985.

———, ed. *The Second World War Diary of Hugh Dalton, 1940–45*. London, 1986.

Ramsden, John. *The Age of Churchill and Eden, 1940–1957*. London, 1995.

Reynolds, David. *In Command of History*. London, 2010.

Robbins, Keith. *Churchill*. London, 1992.

Roberts, Andrew. *Eminent Churchillians*. London, 1997.

———. *"The Holy Fox": The Life of Lord Halifax*. London, 1997.

———. *Masters and Commanders*. London, 2009.

Roberts, Brian. *Randolph*. London, 1984.

Shinwell, Emmanuel. *Lead with the Left*. Littlehampton, UK, 1981.

Soames, Mary, ed. *Winston and Clementine*. London, 1999.

Strauss, Patricia. *Cripps: Advocate Extraordinary*. London, 1942.

Taylor, A. J. P., ed. *Lloyd George: Twelve Essays*. New York, 1971.

———. *Beaverbrook*. New York, 1972.

———. *The Second World War*. London, 1975.

Thomson, George. *Vote of Censure*. New York, 1968.

Thorpe, D. R. *Eden: The Life and Times of Anthony Eden, First Earl of Avon, 1897–1977*. New York, 2011.

Wedgewood, Josiah. *Memoirs of a Fighting Life*. London, 1941.

Weiler, Peter. *Ernest Bevin*. Manchester, UK, 1993.

Wheeler-Bennett, John. *King George VI: His Life and Reign*. London, 1958.

———. *John Anderson, Viscount Waverley*. London, 1962.

———, ed. *Action This Day*. London, 1969.

Wilson, S. S. *The Cabinet Office to 1945*. London, 1975.

Young, Kenneth. *Churchill and Beaverbrook*. New York, 1966.

ONLINE SOURCES (CONSULTED SYSTEMATICALLY)

Hansard

Oxford Dictionary of National Biography

National Archive, UK, CAB 65 (War Cabinet Conclusions, "Confidential Annex," 1939–1945)

National Archive, UK, CAB 195 (War Cabinet Minutes, 1939–1945)

INDEX